Shaping Minnesota's Identity

The *Sebeka Centennial Mural* (2001) depicts the history
of the town of Sebeka, Minnesota.

1880s The Ojibwe-Anishinaabe, the first inhabitants of the area, harvested and
processed wild rice grown on lakes and rivers.

1900s Lumberjacks felled and branded white pine logs, then floated them to sawmills downriver, often via the Red Eye River.

Shaping Minnesota's Identity

150 Years of State History

by Steven J. Keillor

ISBN 13: 978-1-880654-37-8 (hc.)
ISBN 13: 978-1-880654-36-1 (pbk.)
Library of Congress Control No. 2007 2007939720.

Cover image: Elsa Jemne, color study for her mural, *Development of the Land* (1938), in the Ladysmith, Wisconsin, post office. The mural was later painted over. Courtesy of the National Museum of American Art, Smithsonian Institution. Other murals by Elsa Jemne are in the Ely and Hutchinson post offices and the Minneapolis Armory.

Images of the *Sebeka Centennial Mural* are contained in the initial and final color pages. Photographs by Rebecca Komppa. Courtesy of Marilyn Lindstrom.

Sebeka Centennial Mural Team Core Participants:
Mural director Marilyn Lindstrom, Sebeka High School Art Students from 1997 through 2001, Katrine Keranen, Dave Kerkvliet, Reynold Martini, Elsie Martini, Joyce Palmer, Pam Robinson, Mindy Malenius, Katie Nelson, Debbee Carlson, Marvin Salo, Robert DesJarlait, Betty Lake, Marianne Kilbourne, Myrna Kempf, Don Isaacson, Debbie Carlson, Rebecca Komppa, Sheli Daniels, Vanessa Tormanen, Amy Shellenberger, Kelli Shellenberger, and Chris Stout.

Published by Pogo Press
An Imprint of Finney Company
8075 215th Street West
Lakeville, Minnesota 55044
www.finneyco.com
www.pogopress.com

Printed in the United States of America
1 3 5 7 9 10 8 6 4 2

To My Grandson, Owen Keillor

About the Author

A lifelong resident of the state, Steven J. Keillor earned his Ph.D. in History at the University of Minnesota. He is an author and teaches Minnesota history at Bethel University in St. Paul. Keillor has three children and two grandchildren, and he resides with his wife Margaret in Askov, Minnesota.

Other Books by Steven J. Keillor:

Hjalmar Petersen of Minnesota: The Politics of Provincial Independence
(St. Paul, MN: Minnesota Historical Society Press, 1987)

With Millard F. Gieske. *Norwegian Yankee: Knute Nelson and the Failure of American Politics, 1860–1923*
(Northfield, MN: Norwegian-American Historical Association, 1995)

This Rebellious House: American History and the Truth of Christianity
(Downers Grove, IL: InterVarsity Press, 1996)

Cooperative Commonwealth: Co-Ops in Rural Minnesota, 1859–1939
(St. Paul, MN: Minnesota Historical Society Press, 2000)

With James A. Wright. *No More Gallant a Deed: A Civil War Memoir of the First Minnesota Volunteers*
(St. Paul, MN: Minnesota Historical Society Press, 2001)

Grand Excursion: Antebellum America Discovers the Mississippi
(Afton, MN: Afton Historical Society Press, 2004)

God's Judgments: Interpreting History and the Christian Faith
(Downers Grove, IL: IVP Academic, 2007)

Prisoners of Hope: Sundry Sunday Essays
(Vancouver, BC: Regent College Publishing, 2007)

Table of Contents

Introduction

This book is an interpretation of Minnesota history in the form of a narrative or story. It does not pretend to be comprehensive—to list all the persons, places, and events that "should" be included in a history of Minnesota. It includes what is important for the interpretation and the story. The reader will notice that the standard topics of prehistoric peoples, the French and British fur trade, and the period of Dakota and Ojibwe control of the land are omitted. I argue that these topics are better discussed in histories of prehistoric North America, the fur trade, and American Indians. The peoples and events involved extend far beyond the borders of this state, so a broader perspective is needed than that of Minnesota history. The sesquicentennial of Minnesota's statehood is a good opportunity to narrate the history of the *state*.

The history of an American *state* has a plot: does the state succeed or fail in forming a society and governing it, in doing what the American Founders intended that a state should do? This plot line of failure or success drives the story forward and gives us the basic question that the interpretation must answer. It helps us to decide which persons, places, and events should be included—those that are vital for the interpretation. But the interpretation is not a complicated academic matter. It is simply an assessment of how the state succeeded or failed at its tasks, and why.

This is also not an academic attempt in that I am not a political scientist or lawyer or economist dividing one part of Minnesota's experience from the other parts. There is no separation of church and state, of business and state, of sports and state in this story. Every part of the story affects every other part. I have tried to tell the story of ordinary Minnesotans, using their reminiscences and letters. Also, to look at social, cultural, religious, and economic matters *at the same time* as the political and governmental, I often tell the personal story of individual governors as symbols of both aspects of this history.

As we get closer to the present, the list of persons, places, and events that "should" be included becomes ever longer. The book becomes more selective and less comprehensive as it nears the present.

My thanks go to Molly and John Harris of Pogo Press for their confidence and assistance in this project. Special thanks to my wife Margaret, for this book is the culmination of years of her sacrificing me to Minnesota's history. Debbie Miller and Patrick Coleman of the Minnesota Historical Society staff have made helpful suggestions. Thanks to Professors Kevin Cragg, G. W. Carlson, and Diana Magnuson of Bethel University, and to my Minnesota history classes there over the years. My selection of material for this book has been shaped by my students' interests. Responsibility for this interpretive narrative rests with me alone. The historian has personal opinions and past involvements, but he or she must try to be like a good referee—fair, unbiased, observant, non-partisan, and complete. I have tried to be that. Readers may think I have seen only the retaliation, missed the play altogether, misunderstood what I did see, forgotten what the rules are, or applied the wrong rule. The reader must be the referee judging my performance.

Prologue
Statehood Comes by Steamboat

The news that Congress had passed and the President had signed an act granting statehood to Minnesota arrived in Winona on Wednesday evening, May 12, 1858, on board the steamboat *Milwaukee*, which left La Crosse, Wisconsin, that day bound for St. Paul. Railroad tracks and the accompanying telegraph reached only as far west as La Crosse, where the telegram announcing Minnesota's admission was received earlier on Wednesday. When the *Milwaukee* docked, "the enthusiasm of our citizens rose to the culminating point," reported the *Winona Times*. "Finn's artillery was immediately ordered out, and ONE HUNDRED GUNS fired in honor of the event; while the Band performed all the stirring National 'melodies of many lands,' besides our own."[1]

That was the Democratic version of events. The *Winona Republican* wrote, "The crowd who had assembled to hear the news quietly dispersed, [but] several anvils charged with powder were soon after fired off; three glasses of beer drank, (this is a *fact*)"—the *Republican* hinted it was Democrats who lifted glasses and anvils.[2]

Winona was the only steamboat landing where the 32nd state's admission aroused any popular demonstration to speak of—if the Democratic *Times* was correct in speaking of one in Winona. In Red Wing, the Swedish-language *Minnesota Posten* related that the news "caused little or no joy or sorrow; here in our own good city we didn't hear a single hurrah!" Away from the river, in Rochester, "[t]here was no particular excitement." The delay a major cause . Five months earlier, a copy of Minnesota's new constitution was delivered to Congress as Minnesota's required offering to the admission process. It had turned in its dance card only to cool its heels, with no one inviting it in. For five months, Democrats and Republicans had bickered—not over Minnesota but over Kansas. Minnesota's status as a new state without slavery was assumed by all due to its northern location. Whether Kansas would enter the Union as a slave or a free state deeply divided Congress. Southerners refused to admit

Minnesota first, lest its new senators vote against a pro-slavery Kansas. Many Northerners and all Republicans opposed the admission of Kansas as a slave state. Not until the two sides temporarily compromised on Kansas did Congress pull the Minnesota measure out of limbo and welcome the newcomer.[3]

Slavery was not at issue in Minnesota's new identity as a state, Democrats and Republicans agreed. They agreed that a new state had the sovereign power to establish its identity and character, within the framework the national government laid down. The *Winona Republican* described the momentous issues at stake as Minnesota became "an independent member" in the Union equal to older states. Gone was her dependent status, "that series of beggings and petitionings for Federal support." Yet with independence came "heavy responsibilities," including the need to win a good credit rating. Minnesota had to "establish a character for ability, honesty, and integrity." Temptations to disreputable behavior would arise— the *Republican* hinted they would come from Democrats. Giving in to them would sully Minnesota's reputation. Statehood was the starting gun in a contest between "Error, Ignorance, or Fanaticism" and the desirable qualities of "Education, Science, General Intelligence, Virtue, Liberty."[4]

The state's first governor, Democrat Henry Hastings Sibley, had been elected before statehood. Now he could be sworn into office. In his inaugural address on June 3, 1858, he also welcomed the freedom "from the trammels of Territorial vassalage" and the state's deliverance "from the anarchy" of "armed men banded together" that had "afflicted" Kansas. Naturally, he welcomed his deliverance from his odd status as a state governor without a state. He held out high hopes for the state, due to its natural resources and enterprising people but also as the site of a transcontinental railroad. Minnesota would become "one of the most powerful of the Northwestern States." He did not specify what sort of society it would become—perhaps implying that the state government should not deliberately shape the society or the character of its citizens. Democrats believed in local control and personal freedom of individuals.[5]

Minnesota and Its Capital City Are Introduced to the Nation: June 1854

Another reason for the lack of excitement was that a telegram traveling on board a steamboat lacked drama. Minnesota's introduction to the older states came dramatically in early June 1854, when hundreds of the nation's business and political leaders, writers, journalists, and cultural elite boarded five steamboats, stopped at the same towns where the telegram 'stopped,' and celebrated Minnesota's future with a ball, reception, and speeches at its capitol in St. Paul. On the Grand Excursion were forty-three newspaper correspondents or editors, including the well-known Charles Dana of the *New York Tribune*, and their detailed reports appeared in papers throughout the Midwest and East. Never before and rarely since has Minnesota received such intense journalistic coverage, which Easterners read eagerly because it was for many their first news of that area. During Thursday, June 8, these visitors saw the usual tourist sites that highlighted Minnesota's nature and history—the Falls of St. Anthony, Minnehaha Falls, Fort Snelling, etc.—but it was the formal evening events that foretold the future of this state-in-the-making. Since Minnesota was like a debutante being introduced to the nation, it was only fitting that formal dancing should introduce individual Minnesotans —and Minnesotans' collective social graces—to the Easterners.

More exactly and importantly, perhaps, it was St. Paul's 'coming-out' as a capital city, and much of the praise was for how unexpectedly beautiful it looked. Nothing in the U.S. constitutional and legal system required a capital to aspire to high standards—apart from providing a site for executive, judicial, and legislative branches to meet and function. Informally, however, the past accomplishments of political capitals like Boston and Philadelphia and cultural capitals like New York City had raised the bar. And more distant European capitals like London and Paris contributed to the social, intellectual, financial, and cultural connotations of the word 'capital.' Expecting the visitors on June 9, St. Paul was taken by surprise on June 8 but recovered in time to offer a ball complete with musicians and delicacies befitting a capital city: "200 pounds of assorted cakes, 950 sandwiches, thirty cooked hams, various cooked chickens, coffee, milk, almonds, and twenty-one pounds of fancy candies."[6] St. Paul's leaders scrambled, and their reward was the visiting editors' praise that helped build some protection for the city's status as a capital, which was still precarious in the early 1850s. Most other territories that became states moved their capitals at least three times as their areas of settlement shifted.[7]

A state was a political creature, so it was only fitting to envisage its future inside a governmental building, a two-story brick edifice with an impressive 42-foot-wide front portico supported by four columns. Inside, under the dome, were the chambers of the House of Representatives and of the Council; the speeches were given in the latter. Sibley introduced the territory's governor,

Willis A. Gorman, who welcomed the very distinguished visitors "who had come so vast a distance to behold the infancy of the future State of Minnesota." Ex-President Millard Fillmore, the most important visitor, speculated that St. Paul might become "a central point" on a transcontinental railroad. Fillmore "had expected to find only a wilderness, but arrived where churches and school houses, and thriving communities existed." George Bancroft gave the key closing talk. He "concluded by bidding Minnesota be the North Star of the Union, shining forever in unquenchable luster," a remark that drew "a general burst of applause throughout the crowded room." This was high praise and a flattering prophecy from the nation's greatest historian—far more exciting than a telegram announcing a long-delayed act of Congress. The North Star guided travelers and, in Bancroft's figurative terms, the nation itself.[8] That Minnesota might guide the nation was flattery, but the state would play some role in the nation's affairs.

In the 1850s, Americans did not separate politics and government from culture, education, religion, and the economy. There was no real 'wall of separation between church and state,' even if no single denomination could control the government. This Grand Excursion of June 1854 with its mixture of cultural and religious and business leaders showed that American society functioned as one whole, not as separate spheres. Likewise, the corner of American society that Minnesotans were constructing would combine business, religion, education, and other aspects of life into one state society.

The less flattering reality was that excursionists and many Minnesotans saw New England as the North Star pointing out the new state's future course. The new state would be a beacon only as it reflected New England's light. Famous author Catharine Sedgwick, who came on the Grand Excursion, expressed this in her article on the trip. She had the religious perspective of a New England Unitarian who foresaw "the multitudes . . . enter[ing] in and possess[ing] this land of promise prepared for them by the universal Father." Prepared for them by New Englanders too, for "[f]irst must come our eastern people, with their dauntless enterprise, their infinite ingenuity, their inventive genius, their Puritan armor, the Bible and the school-book." Then would come those "crushed under the iron hoof of despotisms"—perhaps European immigrants, perhaps blacks freed from Southern slavery—Sedgwick did not specify who. She was especially delighted to meet Harriet Bishop, a Vermonter who came to St. Paul in 1849 as a missionary-schoolteacher. The Bible and the schoolbook would create a new New England in this western wilderness.[9]

Catharine Sedgwick on the Grand Excursion

"When our steamers were lying at St. Paul's, we were visited by a young lady who was sent there as a teacher . . . five years ago . . . and now, in the midst of that busy hive of a population of 5,000 (it may be 6,000 now—I speak of three weeks since!), she has a large boarding-school! Such a fact urges promptness, constancy, and heroism in the cause of Western education. . . . Not in the school-house only, but from the pulpit, in the administration of the laws, in the field, by the way, and, above all, in the homes, where the foundations of moral and religious education must be laid."[10]

Americans had a sense that their westward movement followed lines of latitude. At 45 degrees north latitude, St. Paul was almost exactly as far north as Bangor, Maine. Extended eastward, Minnesota's southern border line passed through central Vermont and New Hampshire. Old Stock Americans whose families had been in America for generations tended to follow these latitudes as they moved west; New Englanders went into upstate New York, Ohio's Western Reserve, the northern plains of Indiana and Illinois, and then into southern Wisconsin. By the end of the 1850s, Minnesota had a larger percentage of its total Old Stock population coming from New England (36.8 percent) than any other Midwestern state. And, many of its people from New York state (42.2 percent) were Yankee sons and daughters only "one step removed" from New England. Thus, nearly 80 percent of Old Stock settlers came from New England backgrounds. They brought the combined religious, educational, cultural, and political traits of the Yankee: the centrality of the village church on the green, the necessity of public education, the founding of colleges, and a strong reform emphasis on anti-slavery, anti-liquor, and anti-illiteracy.[11]

A State Has Some (But Not Complete) Freedom to Shape Its Own Society

Yankee migrants could not expect to exercise the same independence shown by their seventeenth-century Puritan ancestors who shaped new colonies and new societies to fit their Puritan religious blueprint. A vast ocean separated them from their English rulers, who were distracted by civil war and hampered by slow seaborne connections. Minnesota's Yankees had limited power to shape a new society because the federal Constitution limited states. The federal government designed the land-survey system, set up land offices that sold frontier lands it owned, established the Territory of Minnesota according to rules outlined in the Northwest Ordinance of 1787 and other statutes, appointed Minnesota's earliest government officials, retained the right to veto laws the Territory's legislature passed, and reserved to itself the right to decide whether or not Minnesota would be admitted as a state and, if so, within what boundaries.

A new state was not a nearly-independent colony like 1640s Massachusetts, but neither was it a mere administrative subdivision for the convenience of bureaucrats in Washington. The original thirteen states retained a degree of independence to regulate their internal affairs, even under the federal Constitution, and they bequeathed this to the new states. Historical geographer D. W. Meinig explains the status of states: "these new western states would not develop as discrete cultures" utterly distinct from each other, as colonial Massachusetts and South Carolina had been, but neither would they "be no more than arbitrary territorial segments of 'American' culture. Each new state would perforce develop its own social character . . . Each new state would have its special interests and in support of these would look to some members of the union more than to others."[12] When Minnesotans prepared their frontier society for statehood and relished Bancroft's flattering prophecies, they knew they were forming the "social character" of a new state. Would it acquire "a character for ability, honesty, and integrity" or a reputation for "Error, Ignorance, or Fanaticism"? Which abilities or errors would it be known for?

The *Winona Republican* worried about future uncertainties from Minnesotans' perspective. The older, Eastern states also wondered what sort of newcomer they were admitting as an equal into their midst. James Madison expressed these concerns seventy years earlier: "Will the settlements which are beginning to take place on the branches of the Mississippi, be so many distinct Societies, or only an expansion of the same Society? So many new bodies or merely the growth of the old one? Will they consist of a hostile or a foreign people, or will they not be a bone of our bones, and flesh of our flesh?" This was not merely an abstract political question. It touched on intimate matters of friendships, business connections, social trust, and membership in common organizations. Madison thought these new societies would be "bone of our bones," with the bond "strengthened by the ties of friendship, of marriage" and blood relations.[13]

As the Eastern editors on the Grand Excursion assessed Minnesota, they too worried that it might become a wild frontier society of barbarians—and they wrote or spoke some satires on the wild West. Standing by the St. Paul levee, a Cincinnati editor pretended to be St. Paul's mayor welcoming visitors to "the horse-pie-talities" of a capital city that was awash in liquor, misspellings, and real estate speculations.

St. Paul's "Mayor" Welcomes You

"Feller Citizuns. I am glad to see you here in the Great Northwest—in this part of a great kendtry which is bounded on the East by the Atlantic, on the West by the Pacific, and is split in two by the Big Ditch of the Mississippi. . . . Feller Citizuns, I reckon you're mighty dry by this time; and if you'll come over to the grocery [saloon] across the square, we will all take a drink to our better acquaintance."[14]

Such fears of a failed state in the West were expressed in humorous terms, but they were the opposite side of the flattery Bancroft uttered. Only the future would reveal which side was correct.

For Massachusetts, settlement and self-government occurred at the same time. The Puritans left England armed with a corporate charter giving them rights of self-government. In the case of Minnesota, a lengthy period of settlement under federal control and a shorter period as a partially self-governing territory preceded the grant of self-government in the form of statehood. That was a key difference. The primary rule that governed the pre-statehood period was the Northwest Ordinance of 1787.[15] Crucial in forming the new society was that period, when the frontier and the territory was governed according to that ordinance.

1. "When the *Milwaukee* docked," *Winona Times*, 15 May 1858, 2.
2. "'The crowd'," *Winona Republican*, 19 May 1858, 3.
3. "In Red Wing," this paragraph is based on Bertha L. Heilbron, "Minnesota Statehood Editorials," *Minnesota History*, June 1933, 173-90; and William Watts Folwell, *A History of Minnesota*, Vol. II, rev. ed. (St. Paul: Minnesota Historical Society, 1961), 9-17.

4. "described the momentous issues," *Winona Republican*, 19 May 1858, 2.

5. "state's first governor," Sibley's Inaugural, in *Lake City Tribune*, 12 June 1858, 1; Rhoda R. Gilman, *Henry Hastings Sibley: Divided Heart* (St. Paul: Minnesota Historical Society Press, 2004), 156-57.

6. "recovered in time," Steven J. Keillor, *Grand Excursion: Antebellum America Discovers the Mississippi* (Afton, Minn.: Afton Historical Society Press, 2004), 170-72, 188.

7. "at least three times," D. W. Meinig, *Continental America, 1800–1867* (New Haven, Conn.: Yale University Press, 1993), 441.

8. "Inside, under the dome," Keillor, *Grand Excursion*, 17, 180,186-89; *Minnesota Democrat*, 14 June 1854, 2.

9. "Famous author," Keillor, *Grand Excursion*, 179-80, 246-48; *Putnam's Monthly Magazine*, September 1854, 321-22.

10. "Catharine Sedgwick," *Putnam's Monthly Magazine*, September 1854, 321-22.

11. "followed lines of latitude," D. W. Meinig, *Continental America*, 237-38, 264-73; June Drenning Holmquist, ed., *They Chose Minnesota: A Survey of the State's Ethnic Groups* (St. Paul: Minnesota Historical Society Press, 1981), 55-58, and Table 3.1 on 58.

12. "Historical geographer," D. W. Meinig, *Atlantic America, 1492–1800* (New Haven, Conn.: Yale University Press, 1986), 389-93.

13. "expressed these concerns," James Madison to Marquis de Lafayette, 20 March 1785, in *James Madison: Writings* (New York: Library of America, 1999), 25.

14. "Welcomes You," Keillor, *Grand Excursion*, 185.

15. "a lengthy period of settlement," Peter S. Onuf, *Statehood and Union: A History of the Northwest Ordinance* (Bloomington, Ind.: Indiana University Press, 1987), 54-58.

A State Must Be Built on Land

Puritans arrived in Massachusetts with considerable freedom because the English government needed them to settle and colonize a distant corner of its empire. Settlers coming to the Upper Mississippi region in the 1840s came to a land already controlled by a strong national government that welcomed them but did not need them to fend off enemies. They had less freedom to shape their new society—less risk and less reward.

The U.S. government had not always controlled this land. The Treaty of Paris (1783) ended the American Revolution, granted the United States its independence, and transferred to the new nation its northwestern corner—an area east of the Mississippi River and south of the fur trade route along the chain of lakes and rivers from Grand Portage to Lake of the Woods. Truth be told, it was hard for the infant nation to control an area whose borders were unclear and geographically wrong. Like carpenters several feet off at the corner of a building, the treaty negotiators drew a border from Lake of the Woods westward to the Mississippi River when no one knew if the river extended that far north. It didn't, and the line proved to be an impossible one. The government was too weak in the 1780s and 1790s to kick the British traders off of this land, and the Federalists who ran it were too uninterested in the West and too tied to Britain economically and diplomatically to make the effort.

The Nation Designs Two Ordinances
to Shape New Frontier Societies

Yet this young nation had a grand, near-utopian vision of its future, and the West was part of that. Migrants to the West were part and parcel of the Founders' vision and were not free to dream up a new one from scratch. The Founders' New Order of the Ages (*novus ordo seclorum*) provided an orderly way of surveying and describing land, an ordered process for making frontier regions into states equal to the old ones, and rules for keeping order among rough pioneers in the meantime. These orders came in the Northwest Ordinance of 1787 and the related Land Ordinance of 1785, shaped by the ideas of James Madison and Thomas Jefferson, and applied to the land north of the Ohio River and east of the Mississippi. These Ordinances set out a process of building ordered states on ordered sections of land. They solved the problems of English colonization of the New World—confusion over land titles and land descriptions, failure to make colonies equal parts of the mother country eventually, and disorder in frontier regions caused by a distant government's neglect of them.

The Land Ordinance required government surveyors to divide Western lands into townships of 36 square miles, each containing 36 square-mile sections, with the sections to be numbered in a set order. Each section had 640 acres and could be subdivided into a half section (320 acres), a quarter section (160 acres), and so forth. Later, the system was perfected so that each township had its unique identifying number on the national rectangular grid. For example, Township 113 North, Range 15 West was the 113th township north of a base line (latitude) in Arkansas and the 15th township west of the fifth principal meridian (longitude) running through eastern Arkansas and Missouri. That set of numbers would later describe Burnside Township west of Red Wing, and no other place. Every piece of land would be exactly described by a set of numbers, and every specific set of numbers would refer to only one piece of land.[1]

Land Ordinance of 1785 Reserves School Section

"The Surveyors, as they are respectively qualified, shall proceed to divide the said territory into townships of six miles square, . . . the surveyor [shall note], at their proper distances, all mines, salt springs, salt licks and mill seats . . . and also the quality of the lands. The plats of the townships respectively, shall be marked by subdivisions into lots of one mile square, or 640 acres . . . and numbered from 1 to 36. . . . There shall be reserved the lot N[umber] 16, of every township, for the maintenance of public schools, within the said township."[2]

The two Ordinances were more than a surveyor's manual. They sketched out a framework for a society and filled in some details. Rational order would encourage dense, compact settlements in which pioneers had close neighbors, local schools and churches, and local governments and courts— rather than attracting poor, isolated squatters raising illiterate children and hogs on the same feed corn. For example, the proceeds from the sale of Section 16 went to support a school; an earlier version included "support for religion," but that was dropped. The Northwest Ordinance specified that "[s]chools and the means of education shall forever be encouraged"—because "[r]eligion, Morality and knowledge [were] necessary to good government and the happiness of mankind." Churches would arise in the townships even if the government did not aid them financially.[3] In this system, settlement in the West would be more dense with more towns than in the South—not exactly like New England towns, for they would not control the initial sale of land, nor would farmers live in town and go out to work the fields.

'Township' is something of a pun here, for it means both a surveyed square piece of land (the so-called congressional township) and a unit of local government (the civil township). That double meaning expressed the double intention of the Ordinances—to divide up land so that the federal government could sell it and reduce the national debt, but also to unite and create new small societies on rural frontier lands. These were goals united into one vision—to create societies of religious, educated, self-governing, land-owning, and prosperous settlers. That was the intention, but often squatters arrived before surveyors and a period of confusion preceded true law and order.

The Nation Places the Minnesota Frontier Under the Two Ordinances

Jefferson's Democratic-Republicans won the presidential election of 1800, controlled the national government for the next quarter century, and included the Upper Mississippi region in their image of an agricultural nation stretching across the country. In 1803, they bought the Louisiana Purchase from France, bringing the west bank of the Mississippi under their control. In 1805, they dispatched Lieutenant Zebulon Pike and twenty soldiers up the Mississippi to find its source, make initial preparations for building a fort in the region, and shift American Indians' loyalties from Britain to the U.S.—partly by ejecting the British from their fur posts and their trade with the Indians. Pike signed an agreement with the Dakota for the purchase of land where the Minnesota River (then called the St. Peter's) flowed into the Mississippi and also a site at the mouth of the St. Croix River. The Democratic-Republicans nearly lost the region in their bungled War of 1812, but after escaping with a draw, they renewed their drive to control and utilize this district. In 1818, they solved the northwest boundary puzzle by agreeing with the British on a boundary line that ran south from the northwest corner (the Northwest Angle) of Lake of the Woods to the 49th parallel, the northern border of the Louisiana Purchase. In 1817, they sent Major Stephen H. Long to choose between Pike's two sites. He picked the location at the mouth of the Minnesota, and two years later two hundred soldiers of the Fifth U.S. Infantry regiment arrived to begin construction. Colonel Josiah Snelling supervised most of the building project, which was completed in 1824, and the fort was named after him.

The government made steady progress on the Upper Mississippi, but the region lay hundreds of miles north of American pioneers' main east-west route across the continent, and it lagged far behind in the start of pioneer settlement. In 1803, St. Louis had two hundred houses and a thousand inhabitants, while the falls and head of navigation six hundred miles upstream was as devoid of Europeans and their houses as when Father Louis Hennepin saw it in 1680.[4] The area would long be overshadowed by events to the south and often forgotten.

With its thick limestone walls, three substantial corner towers, and blufftop location, Fort Snelling "loomed above the wilderness like a medieval fortress . . . in an area accustomed to but small and temporary fur posts."[5] A successful Dakota or Ojibwe attack on it was a virtual impossibility. It was far stronger than necessary to protect the fur trade. The fort predicted—and protected—future waves of white pioneers coming to set up a farming empire. It symbolized a strong national government capable of controlling this frontier without the help of settlers—*it* would protect *them*—and, thus, able to enforce its rules for settlement. It need not bargain with pioneers to induce them to migrate there. Fort Snelling represented the opposite of the Selkirk colony of British and Swiss pioneers north of the 49th parallel, on the Red River, in what is now Manitoba, Canada. Arriving there in 1811–13 without effective protection from the British government or the Hudson's Bay Company that had welcomed them, they suffered a massacre in 1816 by the company's fur trade rivals, and many of them later drifted south to the shelter of Fort Snelling.

The small community of soldiers and civilian employees at the fort also became the 'seeds' of a new society, from which many firsts sprouted: the first school, first library, first play performed, and so on. One man who grew up there recalled, "we had a good library . . . then there was of course much sociability among the officers, and a great deal of playing of cards, dominoes, checkers, and chess. The soldiers too would get up theatrical performances every fortnight or so." The fort would not only protect a future society of settlers; it would start a society before they got there—one with a military tone. It jump-started economic and industrial activities: a saw mill at the Falls of St. Anthony, logging on the Rum River to supply the saw mill, the beginning of farming and gardening on a large scale. It witnessed the first religious revival among the whites in the region in 1835. By providing a terminal destination, it encouraged steamboats to start extending their routes to the Upper Mississippi. In 1823, the *Virginia* was the first of many to arrive at the fort's landing. The link by steamboat to towns on the lower river, in turn encouraged more settlement in the area and more economic activity.[6]

Yet the real sparks to white settlement were the two 1837 treaties with the Dakota and Ojibwe that resulted in the government's acquisition of a triangle of land east of the Mississippi, west of the St. Croix River and south of Lake Mille Lacs (including most of that lake). By that time, most of the Northwest Territory had successively passed through the stages outlined in the Ordinances, from district to territory to four new states (Ohio, Indiana, Illinois, Michigan). Wisconsin Territory had taken over these lands east of the Mississippi, and now lobbied for the treaties in order to expand its settlements into this area. Its governor, Henry Dodge, negotiated the 1837 treaty with the Ojibwe at Fort Snelling. (The Secretary of War negotiated the one with the Dakota.) The two-track machinery of the two Ordinances took much longer to cross the St. Croix. Government surveyors did not arrive until nearly ten years later. The section and township lines near Afton, Lakeland, and Stillwater in present-day Washington County—the first area to be substantially settled for agricultural use—were not completed until 1847–48. As usual, the settlers were well ahead of the surveyors, establishing town claims in Stillwater and farm claims near Afton in 1837-39.[7]

Frontier Residents for Whom the Two Ordinances Were Not Designed

Pioneer settlers coming to claim farmland in the rough triangle of land formed by the Mississippi and St. Croix rivers found that others had arrived before them. For the most part, these French Canadians, their Dakota and Ojibwe fur suppliers, and the biracial (Métis) descendants of French-Indian marriages were uninterested in the Ordinances' uniform, rectangular state-making machinery and had no experience in operating it. They were knit together with distant suppliers and fur marketers through an extensive network of rivers and lakes, with key points at Mackinac Island, Prairie du Chien, La Pointe, Mendota, and St. Louis. The purchase of lands far from water, the expulsion of the Dakota and Ojibwe who supplied the furs, and the drawing of surveyors' squares across this river-dissected landscape made little sense from their perspective and neither did the plan for self-government. The Dakota and Ojibwe had their own form of government; the fur traders were part of the American Fur Company, not a democracy but a corporation, and were used to the top-down, aristocratic but protective, rule of the *bourgeois* over his underlings. "The Métis, who considered themselves citizens of no country—*gens libre*—moved freely back and forth" across the U.S.-Canadian border.[8]

Given eighteenth-century prejudices and their specific near-utopian vision, the Founders who designed the Ordinances had not designed it for this mixed, fur trade population. An ordered state could not be built on long-distance, water-linked trading networks. In fact, the Ordinances were meant to prevent or to break up these widely-scattered clusters of French-speaking fur-gatherers of foreign birth living like Indians, intermarrying with them, and regarding themselves as independent of any nation and its laws.[9]

Louis Provençalle fit a Yankee settler's stereotype of this fur trade population. Born in Canada around 1780, this French-Canadian voyageur sided with the British in the War of 1812. Illiterate, he climbed the short promotional ladder of the fur trade to become a clerk who kept the books in "a system of hieroglyphics, understandable only to himself." His post at Traverse des Sioux was part of the American Fur Company network. Here, he knew the Dakota language and how to do business with the Dakota, who feared "his almost insane temper" and called him *Skadan*, 'little whitey.' He became an American citizen and was reasonably law-abiding. He obeyed the Indian agent's rules; however, his temperament was shaped by a fur trader's need to rule his post far from sheriffs or law courts. He might not have been the man to sit patiently through long deliberations of a township board or through a Yankee preacher's sermons—although he, his Dakota wife, and their children often went to Presbyterian missionary Stephen R. Riggs' services at Traverse des Sioux. This stereotype does not fit Joseph Rolette Jr., son of a prosperous French-Canadian trader in Quebec, educated at a New York City school, and a member of the territorial Council.[10]

A man who lived in Mendota in 1837 was ideally suited to be a broker between these two opposing worlds. Henry Hastings Sibley was a fur trader but one of Yankee stock with a good education and knowledge of the state-making goals and methods of Westward-migrating Yankees. Sibley was born in Detroit, Michigan, the son of prominent judge Solomon Sibley, who was a native of Massachusetts and a lawyer in Rhode Island before heading west. Solomon Sibley served in the Northwest Territory's first legislative body, became Chief Justice of Michigan Territory's highest Court, and helped make Michigan a state. Although Henry Sibley sought adventure in the fur trade at Mackinac Island, he did know some law, some Latin and Greek, and something about the territorial process. At Mackinac, he professed his conversion during a New England-style revival in 1830 but did not go to pray with the missionaries near Mendota. He fathered a biracial daughter there, and he well understood the Métis and their Dakota relatives. He learned French and could talk to the voyageurs but never dropped his Yankee culture. He could broker between the two societies.[11]

At six feet tall, well-built and athletic, "a master of the rifle, the fishing rod, and the canoe," and skilled "in the manly art of self-defense," Sibley possessed the personal qualities needed for leadership on the frontier, as well as the patrician air of superiority that his fur trade employees expected in their *bourgeois*. In 1837 he managed the fur trading post at Mendota as a junior partner in the American Fur Company's Western Outfit. His section of post along the Mississippi (north of Red Wing) and Minnesota rivers was called the Sioux Outfit; his contract did not allow him to trade with the Ojibwe.[12]

Even Sibley could not get fur traders and pioneers seeking farmland to get along without one common interest: Indian treaties. Traders needed them because the custom was that part of the treaty monies the government paid for American Indian lands in fact was paid to fur traders, not Indians, to settle Indian debts on the traders' books. Pioneers needed them to remove the Indian population and begin the process of surveys, land sales, settlement, and self-government. Sibley had traveled to Washington with Dakota leaders to negotiate the 1837 treaty, which gave $90,000 to the fur traders. Although the money was slow in coming, that treaty temporarily saved Sibley and his partners from financial disaster.[13]

Fur traders preserved the economy of the past, and Yankee settlers anticipated the economy and society of the future. A group of "squatters" mediated between the two—or blended them—in often illegal ways. The 1837 treaties invalidated American Indian ownership claims from the east bank of the Mississippi. Squatters settled on the east bank, five miles below Fort Snelling, at St. Paul's Landing. St. Paul's (earlier called Pig's Eye) exemplified the frontier society of free spirits that the Ordinances sought to avoid—and it started "in the most haphazard fashion" before they were applied to it. "A footloose and independent lot" of whiskey dealers, former Selkirk settlers, fur traders, fur trade employees, and discharged soldiers sought a "refuge from puritanism" and from Fort Snelling's Indian agent (Major Lawrence Taliaferro) with his rules against whiskey sales to Indians. They set up a makeshift village in constant flux that would contrast markedly with Yankee farm settlements nearby. They showed no interest in land as a source of stability. "With bewildering rapidity the settlers staked claims, traded them away for a barrel of flour or a few dollars, then claimed other sections." They had no plans to make this an urban center; they came to the area to escape civilization, not to build it. Quarrels were often settled not in court but "with fists, knives, or guns." Some of these people engaged in mercantile business, using squeaky Red River carts to reach the Selkirkers still up on Red River and steamboats to reach the downriver towns. Yankee farmers often had to do business with the St. Paul merchants they looked down on. Among the non-agricultural inhabitants were also the lumbermen who arrived west of the St. Croix after 1837. They were from New England but did not intend to farm; Stillwater became their center.[14]

Henry Jackson exemplified these squatters, although his business and his post as justice of the peace in St. Paul put him on a different side of the law than some of them. A native of Virginia but a westering wanderer, Jackson fought in the post-Alamo battles in Texas before moving to Green Bay and then Galena, Illinois, a major steamboat port, from which he could easily ship his goods upriver to St. Paul—a newer town with far fewer competitors— when his Galena business failed. Arriving in 1842, he bought three acres of unsurveyed land in what is now downtown St. Paul, built a crude cabin, and began to sell goods in "the Indian trade." A year later, Wisconsin's governor appointed him justice of the peace. Jackson sold liquor but presumably not directly to the Indians. A squatter who planned to stay, Jackson was well suited for the stable society to come, but he was no Yankee.[15]

William R. and Martha Boardman Brown typified the Yankee settlers (but where their ancestors lived is unknown). Martha A. Boardman was "a widow, who taught in the Methodist mission school at Kaposia," a Dakota village then located on the west bank of the Mississippi just downriver from St. Paul. In 1841, William Brown, a native of Ohio, arrived and helped construct mission buildings across the river at Red Rock. He married Martha and they settled on a farm near Red Rock. With no legal training, William acted as defense attorney in a case before Henry Jackson and disapproved of the Virginian's "partiality," misinterpretation of the law, and habit of denying defense motions. Like many Yankees, Brown disdained rough St. Paul. Showing a Yankee's moralism in his 1845-46 diary, he criticized a Stillwater woman's "playing at Back Gamon & cards." About a nearby wedding, he wrote, "They had Liquor & drank of which I disapproved." Martha made soap and helped with the garden. William cared for rutabagas, turnips, oats and wheat, and did other field work. Martha and William worked hard on agricultural land, which was the way to build a solid Yankee-style society.[16]

The missionaries occupied some precarious position between whites and Indians, and sometimes between Dakota and Ojibwe. In 1838-39, Presbyterians Frederick Ayer, William Boutwell, and Edmund Ely were making noticeable progress with the Ojibwe at their mission on Lake Pokegama, located in the treaty cession area about forty miles northwest of Stillwater. A government "farmer," Jeremiah Russell, was stationed there to teach agriculture and prepare the Ojibwe for the approaching farming frontier. That year Samuel Pond had a similar mission for the Dakota at Lake Harriet that had its own "farmer." His brother Gideon had joined Dr. Thomas Williamson at a mission far up the Minnesota River, at Lac Qui Parle, where the work of translating the Scriptures into the Dakota language was well underway. Stephen R. Riggs joined them in 1837, and the Gospels of Mark and John were finished by the end of 1839. There was also a Methodist mission to the Dakota below St. Paul's Landing. These missionaries greatly regretted the evil effects the whisky traders had on the Indians. They did not oppose the advance of white settlements but tried to prepare the Indians for that reality.[17]

Things became more complicated when Catholic Bishop Mathias Loras came in the summer of 1839 to launch a Catholic missionary effort among the Dakota. Catholic missionaries occupied a position between Protestant ones and American Indians—and Protestant missionaries, between Indians and Catholic ones. The Dakota may have played one side against the other. One Dakota chief, Little Crow III, told Bishop Loras that the Methodist Rev. Benjamin Kavanaugh neglected his agricultural duties to the Dakota and that "a minister of prayer ought to have neither wife nor children"—which sounds like telling the Bishop what he wanted to hear. Loras returned to Dubuque, but the Catholic presence remained on this frontier.[18]

A Road Not Taken: The Doty Treaties of 1841

The interests of all these groups were not identical, as shown by the two Doty treaties of 1841, a startling case of a road not taken that clarifies what road was taken. After the tragic removal of the Cherokee and other tribes from the Southeast in the 1830s by the Democrat Andrew Jackson, 'friends of the Indians' (mainly missionaries and their New England supporters in the Whig party) convinced the incoming Whig administration (1841) to work toward setting up a territory for the Indians in the Northwest that could become a state. Wisconsin Governor James D. Doty, a Whig, arrived at Fort Snelling in the summer of 1841 to negotiate with the Dakota. Sibley provided "indispensable aid" to Doty at his meetings with the Dakota at Traverse des Sioux and at Mendota, where two treaties were signed in late July and early August 1841. At the Dakotas' request, Riggs rode on horseback to Traverse des Sioux to assist them in the negotiations. Riggs reported favorably on the Traverse treaty to his mission agency's headquarters in Boston: "Whatever objectionable features it may have (and it doubtless has some) I have thought, on the whole it is a more favorable treaty than they or we had any reason to expect." Riggs hoped the attempt at providing a permanent home for the Dakota would succeed. Riggs approved of Doty's desire to advance Dakota education "as fast as possible." Yet some Dakota did not like the treaty "because they are unwilling to give up their mode of life."[19]

The Doty treaties represented a potentially revolutionary reversal of existing policies; white pioneer settlers could not enter this vast territory, the southern third of Minnesota plus much of eastern South Dakota; Indian residents would become U.S. citizens; the U.S. government would provide them with schools, roads, and other accoutrement of civilization; Indians would turn to a settled life of agriculture. "Every man who wishes to settle down has a field fenced and ploughed and a house built for him by Government," Riggs noted.

Payments to settle American Indian debts to the traders were part of the treaties, which almost guaranteed the support of the American Fur Company, which lobbied for their ratification in Washington. Many missionaries supported treaties that would place Indians in their own territory, "guarded by virtuous agents, where abstinence from vice, and the practice of good morals, should find fit abodes in comfortable dwellings and cleared farms." Local missionaries felt the treaties would move the Dakota fifty or one hundred miles west of Fort Snelling, thus creating a greater distance between Dakota and Ojibwe and ending the bitter battles between them. Samuel Pond hoped for ratification: "We are anxious to see an end of the hostilities between these two tribes. . . . If the late treaty is ratified the war will be stopped" due to the additional forts that would be built in the area. Among the Ojibwe, Frederick Ayer believed that when the Sioux left the Fort Snelling-Mendota area, his people would be able to return home safely.[20]

These terms were contrary to the long-term interests of white pioneers who wanted lands west of the Mississippi opened up for survey, sale, and settlement. However, the area between St. Paul and Stillwater had far too few pioneers to form a political bloc to defeat the treaties. The fate of the west bank was decided by national politics and Congressional debates, not by petitions from the St. Croix. The petitions were tabled by the Senate in September 1841 and taken up again in the spring and summer of 1842. Sibley's old fur trade boss at Mackinac, Robert Stuart, who had become a strong Christian and friend of missionaries, lobbied for ratification and tried to get Ayer and Pond's supervisor in Boston to lobby likewise. Stuart relied on the missionary societies for help; the Whig Secretary of War, who submitted the treaty to the Senate, thought this was "the very thing" to do. But the Boston missions leader refused to get involved in this political question, using the pretext of inadequate information—Riggs' description of the treaty's terms might be "hearsay." Senator Thomas Hart Benton of Missouri, the leader of Western Democrats, led the opposition to the treaty, and few Whigs wanted to run for reelection as defenders of American Indian self-government and land ownership against the interests of pioneer settlers. The treaty was overwhelmingly defeated in August 1842. Once again, policies were set in Washington without decisive input from the Upper Mississippi.[21]

Senator Benton expressed most Westerners' views, "I object, myself, to an Indian Territorial government anywhere."[22] Racial prejudice partly motivated such views, but they matched the 'one size fits all' approach in the Ordinances. Dakota and Ojibwe customs of communal land ownership, migratory hunting-and-gathering, and hereditary rights to leadership roles did not fit the one 'size' of farm families settled on sections of land and electing leaders.[23] These customs had gradually changed after a century of contacts with white fur traders and missionaries. By the mid-1840s, the Dakota chief Little Crow (Taoyateduta) was a skilled poker player, a trader who bartered liquor for buffalo robes among the Dakota farther west (competing with Sibley), a politician who used white tactics as chief, and a man literate in English and familiar with Christianity. He had one foot in both worlds. Still, Benton did not think he was qualified to lead a territory.[24]

It takes land to build a state. If the Doty treaties had been ratified, there would not have been enough land for white settlers west of the Mississippi to build a new state. The St. Paul-Stillwater area would have been included in Wisconsin, but it had as yet too little political clout to influence the ratification of the treaties. Its fate was decided by others. The decision not to take the road to an independent Indian territory meant that the road to a new territory and state dominated by white settlers would be taken at some point. Fur traders needed debt repayments from treaty proceeds. Settlers needed land, and settlers' use of the land was what the two Ordinances envisioned.

Senator Stephen A. Douglas Helps Minnesota Achieve the Status of a Territory

Settlers in the St. Paul-Stillwater area faced the probability that they would be included in Wisconsin, whose leaders assumed their state's western border would be the Mississippi River. St. Paul-Stillwater settlers opposed that fate. Over a hundred miles of wilderness separated them from Wisconsin's nearest settled area. Its capital, Madison, was nearly three hundred miles distant and had secured the choice plums of a new state—capital, university, penitentiary—with none left for the region beyond the St. Croix. Here again, their fate was decided by others, despite their petitioning and lobbying. In April 1847, Wisconsin voters rejected (for other reasons beside the border) a state constitution that set the border 15 miles east of the St. Croix River. The next proposed state constitution suggested a Rum River border as the "preference of the State of Wisconsin" but left the final decision up to Congress. Sibley helped obtain 350 signatures on a petition to Congress requesting a Chippewa River border east of the St. Croix, to no avail. Wisconsin voters approved this constitution but Congress disapproved both the Rum and Chippewa lines and set the St. Croix as the final border when it admitted Wisconsin in May 1848.[25]

Drawing state boundaries was not like surveyors drawing mathematical squares on the landscape. The push and pull of politics and land speculation twisted these lines away from mathematical consistency. A major player in Congress' decision was Stephen A. Douglas of Illinois. As chair of the House Committee on Territories in 1846 and 1847, Douglas kept the Iowa border well south of St. Anthony Falls, argued against a Wisconsin west of the St. Croix, and worked for a bill to form a "Minasota" territory. In the summer of 1848, after a smaller Wisconsin was admitted, he took a steamboat up the Mississippi and visited the area. From atop Pilot Knob overlooking Mendota and Fort Snelling, he admired the region's prospects and suggested that site for a capital. Douglas invested in real estate in Superior, Wisconsin, and hoped for a transcontinental railroad along a northern route from Lake Superior to Puget Sound. A senator by 1848 and chair of the Senate Committee on Territories, Douglas was well positioned to aid the St. Croix-St. Paul settlers in their efforts to persuade Congress to organize a new territory.[26]

In the summer of 1848, when Douglas visited them, they were 'squatters'—living on unsurveyed lands they only claimed and in an ungoverned area left out of the new state of Wisconsin and without any legal township, county, or state government. In late August, they acted to solve both problems at once. Many went on August 28, with Sibley as their leader, to the U.S. Land Office in St. Croix Falls, Wisconsin, to place bids for their lands at the land auction there and to intimidate anyone who might bid against them. Two days earlier, several dozen went as self-selected representatives to a "convention" at Stillwater to petition the President for the formation of a Minnesota Territory. Settlers feared that their other legalities were as much in jeopardy as their land claims, "that no sanction remained for the determination of rights, the punishment of crimes, the solemnization of marriages, the [inheritance] of estates, and the collection of debts." The convention chose Sibley to carry the petition to Washington and argue their case.[27]

Before Sibley left in November 1848, a scheme was concocted whereby settlers claimed Wisconsin Territory still existed, its former secretary became its 'governor,' he held an election to choose the territory's new delegate to Congress, and Sibley won the election. Thus, he arrived in Washington bearing two contradictory requests: that a territory-less region be made into a territory, and that he be seated as the delegate from the existing Wisconsin Territory. Knowing a bill to create Minnesota Territory would pass shortly, the House of Representatives seated him. Congressmen were impressed by him and by his speech. He was "of engaging presence and courtly manners," when some expected a figure in "buckskin, beaded belt, and moccasins." Instead, he dressed "in the height of fashion." His speech was lawyerly and persuasive, even if his contradictory causes and fictional status lent itself to pettifogging. His looks symbolized the fitness and readiness for self-government of these settlers west of the St. Croix.[28]

Sibley's Speech to Congress, December 22, 1848

"The region north and west of Wisconsin contains an area of more than 20,000 square miles, with a population of nearly, if not quite, 6,000 souls. Can a proposition be seriously entertained to disenfranchise and outlaw the people? Our beautiful country will become a place of refuge for depraved and desperate characters from neighboring States. The vast and varied agricultural and commercial interests of the country will be involved in ruin, and all security for life and property will vanish."[29]

Congress was not about to give them a territory just for looking fit and ready. Senator Douglas' legislative skills and political influence were needed. Douglas, a Democrat, persuaded the Senate to pass his bill creating Minnesota Territory—to "take effect upon its passage." However, the Whigs controlled the House, and their Zachary Taylor had won the 1848 presidential election and would take office on March 4, 1849. The House passed the Minnesota bill, but to take effect on March 10, to insure that Taylor appointed the territorial officials. The Senate refused to accept this clause, and the bill was stalemated. Douglas rescued it by threatening to block the creation of the Department of the Interior, which would also have officials for Taylor to appoint, if the House persisted. The Whigs backed down. The bill establishing Minnesota Territory passed the House on March 4, the last day of the session, which meant that it was too late for the outgoing Democratic President to appoint the territorial officials anyway.[30]

1. "divide Western lands," Onuf, *Statehood and Union*, 22-24, 38; Hildegard Binder Johnson, *Order Upon the Land: The U.S. Rectangular Land Survey and the Upper Mississippi Country* (New York: Oxford University Press, 1976), 42-45, 55-58, 72-75.
2. "Land Ordinance," Onuf, *Statehood and Union*, 22, 24.
3. "two Ordinances," Onuf, *Statehood and Union*, 22-24, 38-39, 63.
4. "St. Louis had two hundred houses," Meinig, *Continental America*, 60.
5. "Fort Snelling," William E. Lass, *Minnesota: A History*, 2nd ed. (New York: W. W. Norton,

1998), 86.

6. "small community of soldiers," Marcus L. Hansen, *Old Fort Snelling 1819–1858*, reprint ed. (Minneapolis: Ross & Haines, 1958), 99-100, 156-57; Gilman, *Sibley*, 65; Theodore C. Blegen, *Minnesota: A History of the State*, 2nd ed. (Minneapolis: University of Minnesota Press, 1975), 99-103.

7. "sparks to white settlement," Folwell, *History of Minnesota*, Vol. I, 159-60; W. H. C. Folsom, *Fifty Years in the Northwest*, 1999 Minnesota Territorial Sesquicentennial Edition (Taylors Falls, Minn.: Taylors Falls Historical Society), 34, 40-41, 50-51, 52, 356, 372.

8. "others had arrived before them," Gilman, *Sibley*, 29-35 and 93 (the quote regarding the Métis); Onuf, *Statehood and Union*, 31-32.

9. "not designed it for," Onuf, *Statehood and Union*, 31-32, 37-39.

10. "stereotype of this fur-trade population," Gilman, *Sibley*, 54; Blegen, *History of the State*, 133; Willoughby M. Babcock, "Louis Provençalle, Fur Trader," *Minnesota History*, Vol. 20 (Sept. 1939), 259-68; Bruce M. White, "The Power of Whiteness, Or, the Life and Times of Joseph Rolette Jr.," in Anne R. Kaplan and Marilyn Ziebarth, eds., *Making Minnesota Territory 1849–1858* (St. Paul: Minnesota Historical Society Press, 1999), 26-45, especially 37. In that special issue of *Minnesota History* is Carolyn Gilman's "A Day in the Life of the Gens Libres," 23-25.

11. "ideally suited," Gilman, *Sibley*, 3-8, 13-14, 17, 20-21, 23-27, 44-45, 63, 65-66, 75-76.

12. "Sibley possessed," Folwell, *History of Minnesota*, Vol. I, 161; Gilman, *Sibley*, 32, 37-38, 47.

13. "Indian treaties," Folwell, *History of Minnesota*, Vol. I, 160, 161, 165; Gilman, *Sibley*, 66-68.

14. "Squatters settled," Mary Lethert Wingerd, *Claiming the City: Politics, Faith, and the Power of Place in St. Paul* (Ithaca, N.Y.: Cornell University Press, 2001), 19-23 (quotes from 19, 20, 21); Folwell, *History of Minnesota*, Vol. I, 213-30.

15. "Henry Jackson," J. Fletcher Williams, *A History of the City of Saint Paul to 1875*, reprint ed. (St. Paul: Minnesota Historical Society Press, 1983), 117-118, 121.

16. "typified the Yankee settlers," Rodney C. Loehr, ed., *Minnesota Farmers' Diaries: William R. Brown, 1845-46 [and] Mitchell Y. Jackson, 1852-63* (St. Paul: Minnesota Historical Society, 1939), 2-4, 37-38, 39-41, 57, 77-81.

17. "The missionaries," Folwell, *History of Minnesota*, Vol. I, 170-212.

18. "more complicated," Leo J. Harris, "An Encounter at Kaposia: The Bishop and the Chief," *Ramsey County History* (Winter 2007), 28-32.

19. "the Doty treaties," Rhoda R. Gilman, "A Northwestern Indian Territory – The Last Voice," *Journal of the West*, Vol. 39, No. 1 (January 2000), 16-22; Folwell, *History of Minnesota*, Vol. I, 457-59; Gilman, *Sibley*, 79-81; Stephen R. Riggs to David Greene, 24 August 1841, "Correspondence July—December 1841" folder, Box 3, American Board of Commissioners of Foreign Missions (ABFCM) Papers, MHS. See also Alice E. Smith, *James Duane Doty: Frontier Promoter* (Madison, Wis.: State Historical Society of Wisconsin, 1954), 256-62.

20. "Many missionaries supported treaties," Folwell, *History of Minnesota*, Vol. I, 457-59; Gilman, *Sibley*, 79-81; Gilman, "Northwestern Indian Territory," 20; Frederick Ayer to David Greene, August 1841, and S. W. Pond to David Greene, 22 September 1841, both in Box 3, ABCFM Papers.

21. "fate of the west bank," Gilman, "Northwestern Indian Territory," 19-20; Robert Stuart to David Greene, 11 February 1842, and David Greene to Robert Stuart, 28 February 1842, both in Box 3, ABCFM Papers.

22. "Senator Benton," Gilman, "Northwestern Indian Territory," 20.

23. "Dakota and Ojibwe customs," Gilman, *Sibley*, 48-49.

24. "Dakota chief Little Crow," Gary Clayton Anderson, *Little Crow: Spokesman for the Sioux* (St. Paul: Minnesota Historical Society Press, 1986), 36-44, 52.

25. "included in Wisconsin," William E. Lass, "Minnesota's Separation from Wisconsin: Boundary Making on the Upper Mississippi Frontier," *Minnesota History* (Winter 1987), 309-320.
26. "major player," Lass, "Minnesota's Separation," 310-311; Rhoda R. Gilman, "Territorial Imperative: How Minnesota Became the 32nd State," in *Making Minnesota Territory*, 2-19, especially 5, 14-15; Gilman, *Sibley*, 107.
27. "acted to solve both problems," Gilman, *Sibley*, 105; Folwell, *History of Minnesota*, Vol. I, 235-237.
28. "he arrived in Washington," Gilman, *Sibley*, 106-107; Folwell, *History of Minnesota*, Vol. I, 238-243.
29. "Sibley's Speech," Theodore C. Blegen and Philip D. Jordan, eds., *With Various Voices: Recordings of North Star Life* (St. Paul: Webb Publishing Company, 1949), 86.
30. "Douglas's legislative skills," Folwell, *History of Minnesota*, Vol. I, 244-46.

Studying for Statehood

Illustrating how distant and isolated Minnesota was, the news that it was now a territory did not reach St. Paul until April 9, 1849, brought aboard the *Dr. Franklin-No. 2*, which waited until Lake Pepin's ice melted so it could proceed upriver. For a week people awaited the first boat of spring to bring word of their fate. Unlike 1858, the news was greeted with a great public excitement, as lawyer David Lambert described it in the first issue of the first newspaper published in the territory, the *Minnesota Pioneer*. Through an evening thunderstorm, people heard "the shrill whistle of a steamboat" and saw "the welcome shape of a steamboat just rounding the bluff, less than a mile below St. Paul. In an instant the welcome news flashed like electricity throughout the town, and . . . almost the entire male population dashed gallantly up to the landing." They boarded *Dr. Franklin-No.2* and bombarded the captain with questions and requests for newspapers until "[a]t length the news was known, and one glad shout resounding through the boat, taken up on shore, and echoed from our beetling bluffs and rolling hills, proclaimed that *the bill for the organization of Minnesota Territory* had become a law."[1]

That was a cumbersome clause to echo from the bluffs—one only a lawyer could shout in public—but some such cry of joyful news did resound in St. Paul. No wonder the legal profession rejoiced at territorial status that brought the chance to practice law before real courts under territorial laws—a more sophisticated and lucrative practice than that before a frontier justice of the peace like Henry Jackson. No wonder that the first newspaper came less than three weeks after news of territorial status, for frontier newspapers depended on government printing and lawyers' legal notices. A capital city depended on a newspaper to promote it. A native of New Hampshire, James M. Goodhue worked as lawyer and newspaper editor in southwestern Wisconsin. Hearing that Minnesota was a territory, he decided to start a paper in St. Paul. He thought to call it *The Epistle of St. Paul* but was convinced by friends that that name seemed to mock religion. Hence, the straightforward name, *Minnesota*

Pioneer, which identified the paper with its readers' daunting task of pioneering. "The people wanted no politics," Goodhue recalled, "and we gave them none; they wanted information of all sorts about Minnesota," which he gave. "We advocated Minnesota, morality and religion from the beginning."[2] Territorial years were this new society's school years as it studied for self-government under the tutelage of Congress and the President, who monitored its progress before graduating it to statehood. From a New England viewpoint, which dominated culture in these years, this period was also a schooling in morality and religion, the basis for self-government.

The territory's professionals were not necessarily or mainly cynical manipulators come to cash in on territorial status (although some undoubtedly were). The settlers genuinely needed an effective government, lawyers for a true judicial system, and newspapers to aid the former and to inform the people as they constructed a new society. The region had passed beyond the informal, traditional, military, and corporate systems of authority that had kept an approximate law and order: heads of Ojibwe and Dakota bands leading them, "Squire" Sibley ruling American Fur Company employees and those locals who appealed for his assistance, and the commandant enforcing military discipline on the troops at Fort Snelling. Incoming white settlers did not recognize American Indian, fur company, or military authorities as fit to rule them, and their arrival by the thousands pushed out the first two and made the third obsolete and limited. Absolutely necessary was a real local government that settlers would respect.

Imposing Morality and Order on a Rough Frontier Population

An incident in Henry Jackson's justice of the peace court in 1848 showed the dangers of frontier anarchy. Six jurymen were placed in a one-window room to discuss and decide a verdict. One was a fiddler. A Stillwater man came to fetch him for a ball that night. The jury was in fierce and long disharmony over the case. Impatient, the Stillwater man stood on a box by the window and talked to the fiddler, whose opponent in the jury debate accused him of illegally discussing the case "with an outsider." That charge provoked a fist fight "in which the whole jury were busily engaged . . . Chair and tables were broke to splinters, and two or three jurors were pounded badly." The fiddler's arm was dislocated. "The constable, justice and others rushed in to quell the fight, when the jurors who were able to go, broke out and ran away, and this ended the case"—without a verdict, evidently.[3]

That was a simple, locals-only dustup compared to the multiplying lawlessness that came ashore from the steamboats in the summers. "Sometimes eight or ten boats would be in [St. Paul] at once, each with large crews of low ruffians, who would roam about the city maddened with liquor, and committing excesses, and the small police force" was hard pressed to handle them. Once, a committee of vigilantes had to be set up. As real estate prices rose, the low ruffians became higher ones, "shysters . . . having no office but the sidewalk," where they spread out "a roll of town-site maps, and a package of blank deeds" and defrauded the unwary. It was as lucrative and easy as "coining money," and they spent it "as rapidly as made, on fast horses, fast women, wine and cards." That real estate craze came several years after territorial status, but it came on all Western frontiers, so Minnesotans had to prepare to control its lawless aspects. This largely-agricultural frontier was not as lawless as the California gold-mining district awaiting its Forty-Niners that summer, but it was not a quiet New England village either.[4]

Thus, Goodhue was likely being sincere when he claimed, "We advocated Minnesota, morality and religion," and not partisan politics. Pioneer society was relatively unified. Various functions, roles, and institutions were integrated into one whole rather than separated into specialized parts. The typical Yankee settler saw Christian religion as a foundation for public morality, which was a prerequisite for law and order. The territory could not pay for the police force needed if its population consisted of 'low ruffians.'

Coming up the Mississippi about a week after Goodhue, Rev. Edward Duffield Neill represented the organized Protestant religion that most white settlers looked to for moral guidance. Writing to his wife from on board the steamboat, Neill reported that "the Methodist preacher of Minnesota" said the winters were not so bad. "This new field will require on the part of both of us much more system than we had at Elizabeth [near Galena]." Goodhue's first issue announced that "Rev. Mr. Neill, a member of the Presbytery of Galena, is about removing to Saint Paul" and would "preach at the school house, on Bench street, next Sunday, (to-morrow,)" at 11 a.m. Neill's First Presbyterian Church of St. Paul was the region's first Protestant one that served mainly white settlers (there had been ones at the Dakota and Ojibwe missions, of course).[5] Rev. Neill and his wife named their oldest daughter Minnesota (her nickname was "Minnie"). Clergy would play a more vital role than editors in "advocating . . . morality and religion."

Taking a boat upriver a month after Neill was a representative of partisan politics, the territorial governor, former Pennsylvania Congressman

Alexander Ramsey, a Whig chosen by President Zachary Taylor as a reward for his help in the 1848 campaign. The straightforward, pragmatic Ramsey realized, like his fellow Whig Goodhue, that settlers "wanted no politics" of a bitter partisan variety. For a month, he and his family stayed at the house of the Democrat Sibley, who approvingly reported, "Our Governor takes well with the people. He is a plain, unassuming man of popular manners and much good sense." The two men from opposite parties became good friends who personified the 'no-party' consensus of the early pioneer years.[6]

The start of Ramsey's government was plain and unassuming. On June 1, 1849, four territorial officials, including Ramsey, sat on beds or trunks in an eight-by-ten-foot room in a St. Paul hotel and wrote on a washstand a First of

Alexander Ramsey, first territorial governor, second state governor, and U.S. senator, circa 1865.
From Edward D. Neill. A History of Minnesota *(1882).*

June Proclamation announcing that government was open for business and that residents were obliged to obey its laws. Ten days later, Ramsey set up three judicial districts, with a judge to preside in each one. Three weeks later, he set up legislative districts; voters elected nine councilors to the Council for two-year terms and eighteen men to the House of Representatives for one-year terms. The territory's secretary rented some rooms in the Central House—"a square log building" that had added "a frame upper story and attic" and then a wing on one end, so that it symbolized the different and competing branches of government—and it was here that the legislature first met on September 3. Rev. Neill gave the invocation.[7]

The House chamber was downstairs in the dining room; the Council chamber was upstairs in the ladies' parlor. The House had to adjourn for the hotel's meals. "After breakfast the dining room was cleared of its table and dishes, the desks of the members were brought in," and the House was in session. A half hour before noon, the hotel told the House Speaker "that the dining room was wanted." The House adjourned, members moved their desks to an office and stuffed their papers in their pockets, and the lunch table was set in place. The House moved back in for the afternoon, cleared out for supper, and came back in the evening if necessary. The Council was not nomadic, but at night its chamber became "a sleeping-room," with desks set to one side and the center floor "covered with straw ticks and Indian blankets" for members to sleep upon or under.[8]

Rev. Neill Describes Minnesota, September 21, 1849

"The Services on the Sabbath at the several points where I preach have been well attended. The people by their actions, often lead us to suppose that the motto of the present Territorial Seal 'Law, Liberty, Religion and Education' are not without significance. . . . The number of ministers in the Territory is on the increase. . . . If we do not 'walk as men' but closely imitate the pattern of the catholic Paul and know nothing but Jesus Christ and him crucified we and the people shall be blessed. . . . The legislature is still in session and will probably do something to promote Common School education and suppress intemperance."[9]

Fortunately, Minnesota became a territory when the philosophy of "home rule" for territories was strongest. Territories beyond the Missouri River and organized during and after the Civil War experienced long periods of heavy-handed federal rule. Home rule meant more power for elected legislators and less for appointed governors. Fortunately, the old Whig vs. Democrat partisanship was fizzling out. In 1851 Sibley noted, "lines of demarcation between the old parties are less plainly marked at this day, than they have been for the last fifty years." Voters in the West cared little for old issues of banking, currency, the tariff, and internal improvements (canals, railroads, turnpikes) that had long divided the parties. They cared about slavery coming to Western lands seized in the Mexican War, but the Compromise of 1850 appeared to solve that issue with "finality."[10]

A 'No-Party' Coalition Achieves Its Goal: Treaties with the Dakota

Due to that fizzling-out, politics was dominated by a 'no-party' or Territorial party coalition in the first four years. Minnesotans could not vote in presidential elections or send a voting congressman to Washington, so they were not compelled to take sides on national issues. There were too few Whigs to form a true opposition party. Many early Democratic leaders like Sibley were fur traders whose short-term goal was a treaty with the Dakota for the lands west of the Mississippi, with the usual sums set aside to pay debts they calculated the Dakota owed them. A treaty was not a partisan issue locally—all white settlers favored one—and traders' 'no-party' stance might keep it from becoming a partisan issue when it came up for ratification in the Senate. The task of starting a government from scratch could best be done if deep partisan splits were absent. The federal government was launched in the early 1790s absent political parties. Sibley and Ramsey personified this friendly cooperation in Minnesota Territory's early years.[11]

Attempts to ignite Whig-Democrat partisanship never took. In the fall of 1849, Sibley and his fur trade partner, Henry M. Rice, had a falling-out over Rice's use of fur company funds for real estate development (especially a hotel, the American House) and over "irregularities" in Rice's accounting books. Sibley and others filed a suit against Rice in the new territorial district court at Stillwater. It was settled out of court, but Sibley and Rice did not reconcile. Rice's friends retaliated by organizing the Democratic Party at the American House in October contrary to Sibley's 'no-party' policy. Rice Democrats had their own paper, the *Minnesota Democrat*. Editor Daniel A. Robertson was a political leader fresh from Ohio's partisan battles. In April 1850, Sibley's foes printed a parody:

> Address of the Hon. Hal Squibble, to the Dear People
> of Minnesota. Fellow Chickens: The time being at hand
> for the choice of a Delegate to represent the American
> Fur Company in the next Congress, I now . . . humbly beg
> your support.

For his part, Sibley termed Robertson "an individual who has been about six months in the Territory." Goodhue called him "a demagogue from Ohio, who came here to rule or ruin this territory." The Rice Democrats campaigned for three years to oust the Sibley-Ramsey Territorial party from power but blundered and failed, as long as the Dakota treaty and the naming of a territorial capital remained the main items on the agenda.[12]

Skillfully led by Sibley's aide, the "college-educated Scots-Canadian" Martin McLeod, the Sibley-Ramsey 'no-party' coalition held together and succeeded in the 1851 legislative session. Deciding the location of a capital, a prison, and a university were issues that set town against town, not one political party against another, and they were best handled by the 'no-party' group's ad-hoc log-rolling. St. Paul's ambition to be officially named the capital met with opposition from St. Anthony and the Crow Wing area. By giving Stillwater the prison, a Stillwater Whig the post of President of the Council, and a Stillwater Democrat the post of Speaker of the House, McLeod's faction secured Stillwater's votes for St. Paul as capital. St. Anthony received the consolation prize, a chartered university whose actual existence would be long delayed in a territory that did not possess a single high school.[13] This victory helped to prepare this coalition to succeed on the negotiation of the upcoming treaties with the Dakota for the lands west of the Mississippi—key to fur traders closing out their business in the black.

The story of these negotiations is complicated and sordid, but the outcome was almost preordained, given the pattern of prior U.S. treaties with American Indian nations and the failure to ratify the 1841 Doty treaties that would have changed that pattern. From July 18 to July 23, 1851, the first intensive talks with the western Dakota bands, the Sisseton and Wahpeton, took place at Traverse des Sioux. Representing the U.S. government were Luke Lea, Commissioner of Indian Affairs, and Ramsey. Delegate Sibley, his aide McLeod, various fur traders, missionaries Stephen Riggs and Thomas Williamson, St. Paul storekeeper Henry Jackson, the Mdewakanton chief Little Crow, editor Goodhue, an artist, a couple wishing to get married, and spectators were present to play the broker role or to enjoy the "carnival atmosphere." The usual gifts, champagne, arguments, and pressures were applied until the two bands agreed to sell their extensive lands in exchange for $1,665,000 (most of the money went into a trust fund and the annual interest was to be paid as an annuity) and a reservation on the Upper Minnesota River. At the signing ceremony, the chiefs were "pulled by the blanket" toward a barrel and induced to sign a "traders' paper" stipulating that some treaty proceeds would go to traders in payment of debts individual Dakota owed. Some chiefs likely did not know what they were signing. The same scenario was replayed at Mendota, where Lea and Ramsey negotiated with the Mdewakanton and Wahpekute bands from July 29 to August 5—with some time off due to intransigence on both sides. They sold their lands for $1,410,000 and a share in the same reservation, and signed a "traders' paper."[14] After Senate ratification, Minnesota Territory was almost entirely open to white settlers.

The Rise of a New Reform-Minded Republican Party

His task accomplished, Sibley did not seek reelection as delegate, and the Sibley-Ramsey 'no-party' coalition broke up. Taking center stage were religious and moral issues vital in forming a new society, especially the liquor issue. In 1851, Maine passed a law prohibiting liquor sales, and Yankees across the nation pressured their governments to do likewise. Feeling that liquor was a major cause of frontier disorder and a serious obstacle to building a moral society, Minnesota Yankees joined this crusade. On Monday, February 16, 1852, the largest procession yet seen in the territory marched in St. Paul, "reach[ing] nearly from one extreme of the town to the other, with banners streaming and drums beating." Marchers presented a petition with six hundred signatures demanding a Maine law. Whigs and Yankees in St. Anthony and the St. Croix valley favored such a law while Democrats and St. Paul leaders opposed it. (In 1850 St. Anthony held a dry

Fourth of July celebration in deliberate contrast to St. Paul's.) Three days later, a Maine-law bill was introduced in the House. Politicians tried to avoid the issue. The bill got lost. Council and House each insisted the other had it. A new bill had to be written. A hostile amendment adding the death penalty for a fourth violation was defeated, but one submitting the law to a popular referendum passed—the buck was passed to voters, who voted in favor of it in April. The territorial Supreme Court threw out the law as an illegal delegation of a legislature's powers to voters.[15] The 'student' legislators blundered or else they planned it that way—anti-liquor men would see legislators vote for the bill, but no law would result.

Democrats opposed to government interference in citizens' private lives opposed a temperance edict, but the Maine law movement persisted, led by the aptly named John Wesley North, who combined religious zeal for reform with the political views of the North's anti-slavery activists. The son of Yankees who migrated to upstate New York, a graduate of Wesleyan University in Connecticut, North burned with anti-slavery zeal that led him to Unitarianism and away from the trinitarian Methodists whom he accused of being soft on slavery. The Compromise of 1850 deflated the anti-slavery cause, and he turned to the fight against liquor. Coming upriver on the *Dr. Franklin* in November 1849, John and Ann North heard the screams of David Lambert, who had "jumped overboard" while intoxicated. At their home on Nicollet Island by St. Anthony Falls, Ann and John entertained visitors in a cultured, New England way and wrote letters recruiting hundreds of settlers for Minnesota. North portrayed St. Anthony as a fine moral place for Yankees; landowners "refuse[d] to sell lots to any one who will sell liquor. . . . I never knew so young a village, where there was so little vice. . . . We have already two schools, a public library, and regular preaching by Presbyterian, Methodist, and Baptist denominations."[16]

A wave of reform activity and utopian societies across the North impacted Minnesota's settlement. John North led reform-minded pioneers who started the town of Northfield. In 1853, seventy-five Yankees of the Northampton Colony arrived to find land, also on the Cannon River. They did not stick together, but many settled down here and there in places like Chanhassen, including their advance agent, Rev. Henry Martyn Nichols, who called Minnesota "the New England of the West." Excelsior, Zumbrota, Hutchinson, and Rollingstone were also founded by organized colonies, some short-lived. Nichols noted, "The settling in large companies with the expectation of each man being satisfied with his claim, cannot be accomplished." Settling in church-centered villages reproduced the New England ideal, whether families trickled in one by one or came all at once.[17] Nichols' sister Harriett came to Minnesota a year before him to teach at Frederick Ayer's school for Ojibwe children. Her letter to him from Sauk Rapids indicated a Yankee's priorities.

Harriett Nichols Wishes to be in New England

"Dearest Brother & Sister The latitude here is the same with the southern part of Maine. . . . I do indeed think of New England privileges, of her Sabbaths and Sabbath schools. Our society is so very small, there is little encouragement to try to have a meeting ourselves. Mr. [Jeremiah] Russell has sometimes read a sermon and had worship, but his workmen are all Catholics, and they won't come in. We have had preaching but twice since I have been here. . . . I wish sometimes I could fly across the lakes and prairies to New England and see friends a little while."[18]

Supported by Sibley and anti-prohibitionists, organized Democrats defeated the 'no-party' group in the 1852 election. They beat back attempts in the 1853 legislative session to pass a Maine law. Yet their future prospects were linked to those of Stephen A. Douglas and his Northern Democrats. Douglas blundered in early 1854 by pushing through the Kansas-Nebraska Act that re-ignited the slavery issue. A wave of anti-Nebraska-Act anger swept the North, led by Protestant clergy. In October 1854, John North and friends began the *Minnesota Republican,* with the Rev. Charles Gordon Ames as editor, as the first step toward a new political party. A Free Will Baptist pastor until North convinced him to become a Unitarian, Ames addressed "the Christian Public" in that first issue: "the character of a government has much to do with the morals of the people," but in "our country and Territory . . . multitudes of nominal Christians are implicated and engaged in the general and unscrupulous scramble for place and plunder," thus damaging Christian witness. "We must have a system of politics agreeable to the maxims of the word of God," namely, a Maine law, a strong anti-slavery Minnesota, and a rejection of anti-Catholic nativism or any "efforts of Pope or Priest to gain possession of government." North's home by the Falls was headquarters for a drive to organize the new party. A convention was held at St. Anthony's Methodist church in late March 1855.[19]

Douglas disliked clergy meddling in politics, but his Kansas-Nebraska Act was what opened convention hall doors to clergymen. Once this new Republican party was formed, there was no return to a no-party territory. Territorial Republicans had a new system of politics to create, a new government whose character was unshaped, and thus no need to address only national issues. In their laissez-faire approach to politics and citizens' character traits, Democrats often used political office for economic-development and speculative purposes. That left them vulnerable in the early 1850s, a time of disgust with corruption in the old parties. Also aiding the new party were thousands of Norwegian and Swedish immigrants who, leaning Republican, also opposed Catholicism, liquor, and slavery. The distance to Minnesota and the absence of any Scandinavian settlements prior to 1849 meant the earliest such immigrants often came in organized groups. They established Protestant churches that dominated village life—very similar to Yankee towns begun by colonization or by a trickling-in process. Swedish immigrants started towns at Chisago Lakes (1851) and Vasa (1854). Rev. Eric Norelius served the latter town, started the *Minnesota Posten* (1857), and editorialized for the Republicans.[20]

Democrats received reinforcements from across the Atlantic. A flood of German immigrants tended to vote Democrat in reaction to Republican calls for prohibition and in suspicion that Republicans did not really oppose nativist restriction on immigrants. A Dutchtown of German sawmill workers arose "just north of Stillwater" after 1853. They may have sparked Rev. Nichols to grumble in his diary (October 10, 1854), "Territorial election. . . . Rum democracy triumphed by 40 majority." That summer, advance parties of German Catholics arrived in Stearns County, which became their bastion. They came too late to join the parochial-school debate at the 1853 legislative session—an attempt to let public school monies go to church schools was also defeated by Protestants who saw it as a Catholic move—but that became their issue and a reason to vote Democrat. Some Germans voted Republican, including the freethinking Turners of New Ulm.[21]

In largely Democratic St. Paul, Protestant business leaders welcomed Catholic priests and nuns (many were French or French Canadian) and their churches. These were needed to control what the elite saw as undisciplined French Canadians, Irish, and Métis who would not listen to Nichols' grumbling about rum but might heed a priest with a similar message. In 1850, the first Catholic Bishop, Joseph Cretin, arrived to great enthusiasm and "the familiar strains of the *Te Deum* and the *Magnificat* echoed across the river." The Sisters of St. Joseph started a school for girls and St. Joseph's Hospital. Cretin vowed to "neglect nothing to promote education and morality in St. Paul."[22]

Public Education as a Foundation
For a Law-Abiding New Society

For all ethnic and religious groups, education was key to shaping a new society, but it was also controversial. Schools kept squatters from forming wild societies, the Founders thought, so the Land Ordinance set aside Section 16 "for the maintenance of public schools," and the Northwest Ordinance provided that schools "shall forever be encouraged." Minnesota had twice the encouragement, for Sibley obtained two sections per township for the schools. The proceeds from selling the sections funded the schools. Probably aided by Neill, the Democrat McLeod authored the 1849 law providing free tax-supported "common schools" for students from four to twenty-one years old. A township became a school district too, until Minnesotans demanded smaller neighborhood districts and got them. School buildings appeared. Just west of Red Wing, in a largely Methodist township, sections 16 and 36 were "school" sections. Two small districts were set up by June 1855. Two months later, Minnesota's first frontier camp meeting was held outdoors here. Settlers built a log school house that also served as a Methodist church.[23]

Controversy swirled around what should be taught in public schools. Jefferson saw them as alternatives to religious education, with children memorizing "facts from Grecian, Roman, European, and American history" to prepare them for the task of self-government. McLeod advocated teaching "sublime truths and precepts of Christianity."[24] Red Wing's Methodists saw different truths than did German Catholics of Stearns County or Swedish Lutherans in Vasa. Local control of schools might mean each group's schools taught different facts or precepts. But these differences did not necessarily hinder the shaping of a new society if all taught a general morality and obedience to law.

John North's House education committee chided the territory in 1851 for not having a college yet—Massachusetts founded Harvard when it had half Minnesota's population. North authored the 1851 law chartering the University of Minnesota and locating it at St. Anthony. Local promoters like Franklin Steele used the institution to raise St. Anthony real estate values. Reform-minded Republicans like North started its educational mission with a preparatory school run by the clergy; Minnesota youth were not ready for college work nor were academic professionals ready to teach at a fledgling academy. Education and religion were hardly separated: the university's first building housed the First Congregational Church and its first teacher preached at the Methodist Church. Enrollment increased to 170 by 1855, and promoters (mainly Democrats) commenced building a "Renaissance palace of stone," 277 feet by 81 feet, until the Panic of 1857 left it unfinished and empty, and the bonded debt unpaid.[25] First to offer college classes was the Methodists' Hamline University in Red Wing, founded in 1854.

Population Growth Leads Toward Statehood for a North-South State

Population growth was phenomenal—from 4,500 (1850) to 40,000 (1855) to 150,000 (1857).[26] It caused feverish land speculation and railroad promotion, as did the need to select sites for towns and rail lines. Very visible, typical of frontiers, these signs of boom times were the froth atop a steady, substantial formation of a new society driven by stable motives—a desire to start families, sustain them on good farms or with prosperous businesses, anchor them in church-taught religion and morality, and secure them by government-maintained law and order. Growth raised real estate values but was not dependent on values remaining high. Much attention was paid to railroad and real estate dramas: the chicanery surrounding the Minnesota and Northwestern Railroad Company, an attempt to move the capital to St. Peter for speculative gain that was stymied by Joe Rolette's hijacking the bill, bankruptcies and out-migration that hit St. Paul after the Panic. Yet settlers arrived, couples married, families grew larger, more land was cleared and plowed and planted, and the work of building a new society continued.[27]

DeWitt Clinton Cooley Parodies Legislators ("Sovereigns")

Sovereign Hudibras rose to a question of privilege. He read an article . . . charg[ing] that this meeting had been gotten up for the purpose of creating a prejudice between the city and the country, that would eventuate in the removal of the 'capitol' from this city. . . . Sovereign Cruikshank alluded to the impossibility of removing the 'capitol' even were it our purpose. Why, there were more than three hundred thousand bricks in that building; and all the money in the Territorial treasury, and all the money in the hands of the Secretary, and all the jackasses in the Territory, combined, would not be able to effect such a purpose."[28]

Considerable anti-St.Paul feeling stirred at the legislature and in the southeastern farming districts of Minnesota—partly due to rural prejudices that it was too Catholic, too fur-trader-dominated, and too Democratic. Americans had long distrusted prominent capital cities with their "architecture of authority" as symbols of aristocracy and monarchy, of empire, of a privileged class displaying its rule over the rural provincials. For this reason, they moved the nation's capital to a new unformed city, Washington D.C., and kept it primitive for decades.[29] The Northwest Ordinance said nothing about a capital for a new Western state, although it was presumed. In some states created under that Ordinance, rural-dominated legislatures moved the capital twice, as if to show who was in charge and to forestall urban domination. Rolette's hijacking of the bill to move the capital to St. Peter—though the bill had legally been passed—forestalled those rural efforts in Minnesota, for the time being. The illegal means used only increased the anti-St. Paul sentiment in rural areas.

Population growth led to applying for statehood. Remaining a territory had benefits: the nation paid the territory's expenses, including the cost of a territorial capitol building in 1853. Yet a state could issue bonds, receive a federal land grant, vote in presidential elections, have voting members of Congress, etc. Graduation to statehood was the normal goal for settlers forming a new society. One question helping to determine what *kind* of society was: where would the borders be? Not all the Territory to the Missouri River would be in the state. Would a north-south state extend to the Canadian border but not to the Missouri? Or would an east-west one extend to the Missouri but only north to a given line of latitude?

This question appeared to involve the fate of political parties and different towns. Yet the fate of parties rested on who lived in the state and what they did for a living—thus, on the shape of the society. The fate of politicians debating this question rested on the opinion of voters who had no ambition to hold office or to own speculative lots in a promising town. Many voters favoring an east-west state were Republicans—because they favored the free-soil, Yankee-style, farm-based society that party was seen to favor.

The rock outcroppings and pine forests of the northern region would not support a society of farm families like the one in the south. That society resented the political dominance of former fur traders like Rice and Sibley, merchants and speculators of St. Paul, and lumbermen in Stillwater—who wanted their northern hinterland included so as to offset the farming south's growing strength. Historian William Watts Folwell summarized the southerners' desire to "exclude" a north "never to be permanently settled, but to be roamed over by 'a sort of *omnium-gatherum*' of trappers, miners, hunters, and lumbermen, from whom no taxes could be exacted."[30] This roaming band seemed precisely the loose collection of wanderers and squatters the Founders felt was unsuited to self-government. Farmers in the south knew the Ordinances favored an agricultural people like themselves.

The Ordinances did not let people select their state's borders. The precedent was that Congress passed an enabling act setting terms of the 'final exam' whereby the area graduated to statehood—one term being borders. Existing states, sections (North and South), and political parties had a major stake in how many new states were created and exactly where. "Local officials and citizens" usually wanted larger states, but "they might be induced to accept a smaller size to avoid a lengthy delay in acquiring statehood."[31] In the bitter North-South partisanship of the late 1850s, Minnesotans who wanted an east-west state worried about lengthy delay—the South was not eager to admit a new state whose senators might vote against it, while the Democrats in control in Washington did not want a new state to be Republican.

Minnesotans had no say in the final decision. Delegate Rice, a Democrat, worked with Douglas, the driving force behind Western legislation, to push through an Enabling Act specifying a north-south state with its western border at the Red River, past Lakes Traverse and Big Stone, and then on a line due south to the Iowa border. Steamboats and trains carried Minnesota leaders to Washington in December 1856 and January 1857 to lobby for and against this border, but there was little opponents could do to stop it.[32]

The Act's main requirement was that a Minnesota constitutional convention draw up a constitution and submit it to the voters for approval—in effect, to Congress also, for Congress' vote to admit the new state might hinge on the document's acceptability. In setting out the rules for electing delegates and for holding the convention, the 'student' legislature again blundered. Confusingly, it did not follow the Act's rules for the number of delegates nor did it set a time of the day when the convention was to convene. To add to the chaos, election fraud occurred, some delegates' right to participate was contested, and partisanship was so bitter that Republicans and Democrats could not agree on an hour for the convention to assemble on July 13, 1857—the 70th anniversary of the Northwest Ordinance, as it happened, but this was not a scene bringing honor to that document.[33]

Republicans called in major national figures to campaign for their candidates for the delegate slots, while Democrats did not. The newer, moralistic party was more zealous to shape a state and society than were the Democrats, who had a laissez-faire preference for letting society shape itself. Zeal paid off, as fifty-nine Republican delegates attended the convention and only fifty-five Democrats attended. But all were not necessarily legally elected, since more showed up to the affair than the legislature had invited.[34] No agreement was reached between the two sides regarding delegate contests, an hour to meet, or other disputed points. Sibley and North "journeyed together from Northfield to Mendota" shortly before the convention and "freely conversed" about the "vexed questions," but they could not or would not strike a deal binding on their parties.

A Divided Convention Does Write a Constitution (or, Two Drafts of One)

On Sunday night, July 12, suspicious Republicans arrived at the capitol to prevent a Democratic takeover at midnight. July 12 was the traditional Irish Protestant celebration of their victory over Catholics at the Battle of the Boyne, and some Republican delegates alluded to it in a show of anti-Catholic feeling certain to make Monday less harmonious. They camped out in the House chamber overnight to forestall a takeover. At 11:45 a.m., the Democratic delegates marched into the hall and the confusion commenced as two rival conveners (North, for the Republicans) mounted the platform to call the meeting to order. The Democrats' convener put to a vote a motion to adjourn, which he ruled to have carried. North nominated a Republican to chair the convention, and Republican delegates elected him. Neither party voted on the motions put by the other. Democrats walked out of an adjourned convention to meet later in the Council chamber; Republicans stayed in their un-adjourned convention in the House chamber. And never the twain shall meet—they met separately for the next month and a half. When word reached them of the unfavorable impression this split created in the East—that Minnesota was as bitterly divided as Kansas and its admission might be delayed too—the two sides named a compromise committee to arrive at one document. That was done. A brief outburst led to the former Democratic governor, Willis Gorman, caning a Republican over the head, as a South Carolina Democrat had caned Republican Charles Sumner in the Senate in 1856.[35]

Unseemly as things appeared, no bloodshed occurred as it had in Kansas. A Democratic delegate correctly denied being "in a state of anarchy" and claimed that "a feeling of kindness exists" between the two sides. They knew they had to form rules for *one* new society. "Southerners" in both conventions tried to specify borders shaping an east-west state. Republican Thomas Wilson of Winona insisted "[t]he southern portion" was "all agricultural" and "[t]he interests of its inhabitants are diverse from those of Saint Paul, and from those of the northern sections of the Territory." Manifesting the Yankee and farmer suspicion of St. Paul, he implied that St. Paulites dominated by acting "as rowdies and blackguards." Democrat Charles Flandrau of St. Peter argued that an east-west state would enjoy "the advantages of the navigation of the Mississippi River on the one side, and of the Missouri on the other." John North countered that changing Congress' borders would delay admission, that Congress' split over slavery would exacerbate that delay, and that Republicans "should feel an interest in the northern section of the Territory." A former east-west supporter, Gorman stated the Congressional railroad grant necessitated a north-south state.[36] Rice's *fait accompli* in having Congress specify a north-south state could not be undone.

Constitutional details indicated what kind of society both sides envisioned. A lottery was banned, as was imprisonment for debt. The state legislature could not grant divorces (the territorial one could). The Bill of Rights included a statement of religious liberty and a ban on establishing one church or making a "religious test" for holding office. Republicans insisted the preamble say Minnesotans were "grateful to God for our civil and religious liberty" and it did, despite some feeling that it was unnecessary to be stated. The right to vote defined who was in this political society—antebellum Americans assumed only males voted but that did not exclude women from society's other functions. Needing immigrants, the state granted the vote to non-citizens who filed a declaration of intention to become U.S. citizens and set short residency rules—one year in the United States, four months in Minnesota, and ten days in the election precinct. Some Republicans wanted to give the vote to free blacks, but Democrats were opposed and other

Republicans feared voters would reject such a constitution. American Indians were in a more ambiguous position. Those who were biracial Métis could vote if they had "adopted the customs and habits of civilization," of white society that is. Full-blooded American Indians had to "have adopted the language, customs, and habits of civilization"—they had to know English—and a district court must examine them to see that they met those requirements. Residing on a reservation did not affect the right to vote but neither did it exempt anyone from taxation. Education was stressed, perhaps to qualify immigrants and Indians for citizenship in the end. Because "the stability of a Republican form of government depend[ed] mainly upon the intelligence of the people," the state needed to provide public schools. The capital "R" was unwise, and some in Congress feared they were admitting a Republican state, but they did admit Minnesota on May 11, 1858.[37]

While the delegates met, the Territory's champion, Senator Douglas, came to St. Paul on a steamboat from Prairie du Chien. He was a guest at Henry Rice's house. A large group of local Democrats, led by Sibley, marched with a band to Rice's residence on the bluffs. They gave nine "hearty cheers" as Douglas stood outside to receive them. Former Governor Willis Gorman thanked him in flattering terms for his aid to Minnesota in Congress. Douglas modestly admitted to "feel[ing] a great interest in the prosperity and welfare of Minnesota" and cited an earlier visit he had made when St. Paul supposedly "contained two or three houses and—a grocery [saloon]. (Laughter and cheers.)" Douglas "claim[ed] no special gratitude" for paying attention to the Territory, for he had taken "care of seven of the Territories of this Union, prior to their admission as States." He then "mainly" credited Rice, for "the great results which have been accomplished for Minnesota." The ongoing convention illustrated "that great fundamental principle" of popular sovereignty by which Americans in different areas had "the right to form and regulate their own domestic institutions to suit themselves. [Loud cheers.]"[38] That term "domestic institutions" had a double meaning: at the convention it meant suffrage and schools; in the South, slavery.

On Monday, August 17, Douglas visited the Democratic convention, which took a one-hour recess in his honor. The next day, they voted to appoint a five-man committee to meet with a similar delegation of Republicans to agree on a single constitution. It is likely that Douglas told the Democrats that the admission of Minnesota might be jeopardized by the continued split. Minnesota could choose her "domestic institutions," but there must be only one set of them. Douglas' visit showed several things: the

Illinois senator still championed Minnesota's admission despite rumblings of Republican power at the convention; Democrats were still in charge in the territory's and the nation's capitals; Democrats in Congress were highly unlikely to object to any "domestic institutions" in Minnesota's constitution; however, debate over the South's "domestic institutions" might continue as loudly as ever.

1. "David Lambert described it," *Minnesota Pioneer*, 28 April 1849; J. Fletcher Williams, *A History of the City of St. Paul to 1875*, reprint ed. (St. Paul: Minnesota Historical Society Press, 1983), 206.

2. "the first newspaper," Williams, *City of St. Paul*, 208-211; Folwell, *History of Minnesota*, Vol. I, 251; George S. Hage, *Newspapers on the Minnesota Frontier 1849–1860* (St. Paul: Minnesota Historical Society, 1967), 1-5. Technically, the first Minnesota newspaper might be the *Minnesota Register*, whose first issue was dated 27 April 1849, but that issue was printed in Cincinnati, its first editor never made it to Minnesota, and its first issue printed in Minnesota came on July 14, 1849; Hage, *Newspapers*, 1, 138.

3. "justice of the peace court," Williams, *City of St. Paul*, 180-81.

4. "multiplying lawlessness," Williams, *City of St. Paul*, 364, 380.

5. "Rev. Edward Duffield Neill," Williams, *City of St. Paul*, 212-13; Edward D. Neill to his wife, 24 April 1849, "Correspondence, undated, 1827–1855" folder, Box 1, Edward Duffield Neill and Family Papers, MHS.

6. "Alexander Ramsey," Folwell, *History of Minnesota*, Vol. I, 248-49; Gilman, *Sibley*, 109.

7. "start of Ramsey's government," Williams, *City of St. Paul*, 223, 235-36; Folwell, *History of Minnesota, Vol. I*, 252, 253; William Murray, "Recollections of Early Territorial Days and Legislation," *Minnesota Historical Society Collections, Vol. 12*, 103-30, especially 110.

8. "House chamber," Murray, "Recollections," 110.

9. "Rev. Neill Describes," Blegen and Jordan, eds., *With Various Voices*, 246, 247.

10. "became a territory," Jack Ericson Eblen, *The First and Second United States Empires: Governors and Territorial Governments, 1784–1912* (Pittsburgh, 1968), 3-4, 138-41, 158-70 [Minnesota seems to fall in his First Empire, supposedly ending in 1848]; *Minnesota Pioneer*, 22 May 1851, 2 (quoting Sibley); *St. Anthony Express*, 31 May 1851, 2; Henry Hastings Sibley to Alexander Ramsey, 14 April 1850, Roll 4, Alexander Ramsey Papers, MHS.

11. "Territorial party coalition," Steven J. Keillor, "Decline of the Second Party System: Legislative Elections and Sessions in Minnesota Territory, 1849–1854," unpublished paper (1988) in author's possession; John C. Haugland, "Alexander Ramsey and the Birth of Party Politics in Minnesota," *Minnesota History*, Vol. 39, No. 2 (Summer 1964), 37-48.

12. "Attempts to ignite," Gilman, *Sibley*, 109-12; Haugland, "Alexander Ramsey," 44; Henry Hastings Sibley, "To the Public," in *Minnesota Pioneer*, 22 May 1851, 2; Hage, *Newspapers*, 34-35; *Minnesota Democrat*, 10 December 1850, 1, 2; Governor R. Wood to President-elect Franklin Pierce, 15 February 1853, copy in Daniel A. Robertson Papers, MHS.

13. "Skillfully led," Jane Lamm Carroll, "The McLeods, an Anglo-Dakota Family in Early Minnesota," *Minnesota History*, Vol. 60, No. 6 (Summer 2007), 219-33 (quote from 220); Keillor, "Decline of the Second Party System," 30-32. For the logrolling and maneuvering, see William Holcombe to Henry Hastings Sibley, 8 January 1851; William Henry Forbes to Sibley, 14 January 1851; Martin McLeod to Sibley, 4 and 28 January, and 4 February, 1851; and Benjamin W. Brunson to Sibley, 30 January 1851, all in Roll 8, Sibley Papers, MHS;

Minnesota Pioneer, 10 April 1851, 2; and the *Minnesota Chronicle and Register*, 6 January 1851, 2.

14. "story of these negotiations," Folwell, *History of Minnesota*, Vol. I, 277-87; Anderson, *Little Crow*, 58-64; *With Pen and Pencil on the Frontier in 1851: The Diary and Sketches of Frank Blackwell Mayer* (St. Paul: Minnesota Historical Society, 1932), 145-50, especially note 5 on 146.

15. "the liquor issue," Folwell, *History of Minnesota*, Vol. I, 264; Williams, *City of Saint Paul*, 323-24; Merlin Stonehouse, *John Wesley North and the Reform Frontier* (Minneapolis: University of Minnesota Press, 1965), 47, 65-66; *Minnesotian*, 21 February 1852, 2; House *Journal* (1852), 113, 122, 127, 181-82.

16. "aptly named John Wesley North," Stonehouse, *John Wesley North*, 4-10, 14, 19, 26-27, 30, 36-39, 49-52.

17. "Minnesota's settlement," Stonehouse, *John Wesley North*, 87; E. S. Seymour, *Sketches of Minnesota, The New England of the West* (New York: Harper & Brothers, 1850), see especially xii; June Drenning Holmquist, ed., *They Chose Minnesota: A Survey of the State's Ethnic Groups* (St. Paul: Minnesota Historical Society Press, 1981), 63; Charles W. Nichols, "Henry Martyn Nichols and the Northampton Colony," *Minnesota History*, Vol. 19 (June 1938), 132-47, and "The Northampton Colony and Chanhassan," *Minnesota History*, Vol. 20 (June 1939), 140-45, and "New Light on the Northampton Colony," *Minnesota History*, Vol. 22 (June 1941), 169-73.

18. "Harriett Nichols," Harriett S. Nichols to Dearest Brother & Sister, 18 February 1852, Box 1, Henry Martyn Nichols and Family Papers, MHS.

19. "Supported by Sibley," Keillor, "Decline of the Second Party System," 38-41, 43-44; Stonehouse, *John Wesley North*, 82; *Minnesota Republican*, 5 October 1854, 2; *Minnesotian (St.Paul)*, 4 April 1855, 2; *St. Anthony Express*, 31 March 1855, 2.

20. "earliest such immigrants," Holmquist, ed., *They Chose Minnesota*, 249, 252; Hage, *Newspapers*, 71.

21. "flood of German immigrants," Kathleen Neils Conzen, *Germans in Minnesota* (St. Paul: Minnesota Historical Society Press, 2003), 14, 20-22, 43-45, 63; Henry Martyn Nichols, entry for 10 October 1854, Vol. 7, Box 2, Nichols Papers, MHS; *Minnesotian* (St. Paul), 27 September 1853 and 1 October 1853, both 2; *St. Anthony Express*, 8 October 1853, 2. German Catholics in Stearns County discovered they could control local school boards and obtain the education they wanted without funding parochial schools.

22. "welcomed Catholic priests," Wingerd, *Claiming the City*, 23-27 (quoting Cretin on 26).

23. "education was key," Onuf, *Statehood and Union*, 24, 39, 63; Folwell, *History of Minnesota*, Vol. I, 256; Folwell, *History of Minnesota*, Vol. IV, 135-36; Steven J. Keillor, "Burnside!: A Biography of a Township, A History of America," unpublished manuscript in author's possession, Chapter 3 (28), Chapter 4 (15), Chapter 8 (122).

24. "Controversy swirled," *Jefferson: Writings*, 272, 274, 1150, 1226, 1399; Folwell, *History of Minnesota*, Vol. IV, 136.

25. "University of Minnesota," Folwell, *History of Minnesota*, Vol. I, 261; Stonehouse, *John Wesley North*, 55-57; Norene Davis Roberts, "An Early Political and Administrative History of the University of Minnesota, 1851-84," Ph. D. diss. (University of Minnesota, 1978), Vol. I, 34-37, 43, 57-59, 65-69.

26. "Population growth," William E. Lass, *Minnesota: a History*, 2nd ed. (New York: W. W. Norton, 1998), 107, 120.

27. "railroad and real estate dramas," Folwell, *History of Minnesota*, Vol. I, 327-50, 362-64, 381-87.

28. "Parodies," DeWitt Clinton Cooley, *Journal of the second sitting of the third session of sovereigns,*

Saturday evening, Feb. 16, 1856 (St. Paul: S. Smith, 1856), 11, copy at MHS.

29. "distrusted prominent capital cities," Meinig, *Continental America*, 177, 350, 441. The phrase "architecture of authority" is Meinig's.

30. "Folwell summarized," Folwell, *History of Minnesota*, Vol. I, 406-07; William Anderson, *A History of the Constitution of Minnesota* (Minneapolis: University of Minnesota, 1921), 44-47; Gilman, *Sibley*, 148-49.

31. "wanted larger states," Meinig, *Continental America*, 432-41 (quote from 435).

32. "an Enabling Act," Folwell, *History of Minnesota*, Vol. I, 390-93; Anderson, *History of the Constitution*, 52.

33. "setting out the rules," Anderson, *History of the Constitution*, 73, 77, 79; Folwell, *History of Minnesota*, Vol. I, 395-98; Gilman, *Sibley*, 150; Stonehouse, *John Wesley North*, 96, 97-98.

34. "Zeal paid off," Folwell, *History of Minnesota*, Vol. I, 402.

35. "Sunday night, July 12," here and above, Folwell, *History of Minnesota*, Vol. I, 397-420; Anderson, *History of the Constitution*, 78-82, 88-104; Stonehouse, *John Wesley North*, 95-99; Francis H. Smith, reporter, *The Debates and Proceedings of the Minnesota Constitutional Convention* [Democrats] (St. Paul: Earle S.Goodrich, 1857), 492 (Sibley on his meeting with North).

36. "tried to specify borders," Anderson, *History of the Constitution*, 92; *Debates and Proceedings* [Democrats], 296, 298-99; *Debates and Proceedings of the Constitutional Convention for the territory of Minnesota* [Republicans] (St. Paul: G. W. Moore, 1858), 21, 22, 24.

37. "details indicated," Folwell, *History of Minnesota*, Vol. I, 412-13; Anderson, *History of the Constitution*, 208, 209, 210-11, 217, 218, 229-30, 231, 232, 252. For the capitalizing of Republican, see Smith, *Debates and Proceedings* [Democrats], 664, and 653, 658-59, 663, 670 for other provisions.

38. "Territory's champion," here and below, *St. Paul Pioneer & Democrat*, 15 August (3) and 16 August (2), both 1857; *Debates and Proceedings* [Democrats], 520-23.

3

Trials & Tribulations

The editor of the *Winona Republican* could not have known how right he was in cautioning that "heavy responsibilities" came with statehood, that Minnesota's "character for ability, honesty and integrity" must be established anew "in her State capacity," that these qualities must be tested "in the most severe struggle." However, the "beggings and petitionings" would come from the Federal government, asking for the state's support. The state's "credit [was] to be tried by the exacting money-lenders of the nation," but Minnesota would not emerge from "the ordeal with untarnished honor."[1] One reason to become a state was to be able to issue bonds and borrow money (a territory could not) to jump-start railroad construction, which would promote economic development, increase real estate values, encourage immigration, and rescue political leaders' investments and speculations. The aftermath of the Panic of 1857 was a poor time to risk the state's credit to build railroads, for the 1850s railroad boom was over, and Minnesota had already missed the bonanza.

The Five Million Loan for Railroads Tarnishes the State's Fiscal Reputation

The story of the "Five Million" railroad loan of 1858 is complex. However, the moral is simple enough: a people went into debt at the wrong time to obtain assets they felt they needed *right then*. The constitutional conventions had voted to forbid this very thing by stating in the constitution that "[t]he credit of the state shall never be given or loaned in aid of any individual, association or corporation." Another provision limited state borrowing to the one purpose of "extraordinary expenditures" and to the amount of $250,000. In the Democratic convention, Sibley spoke in favor of that maximum. Yet little progress was made toward building railroad lines, which Minnesotans badly wanted in order to market their crops and to enjoy other benefits of a railroad-based society and economy that other states enjoyed. The first state legislature (meeting before Congress admitted Minnesota) submitted to the voters, and they approved in April 1858, a constitutional amendment allowing "special bonds of the state" up to $5 million to be issued to railroad companies "for the purpose of expediting the construction of lines of railroads." The lines were not expedited, for the national recession was the wrong time to market the bonds of a new state or to launch ambitious construction projects on the nation's frontier.[2]

The April 1858 "Five Million" amendment was supported by some leaders in both parties and opposed by some in both. Voters approved it by a four-to-one margin. Sibley neither supported nor opposed it. John North opposed it, although Sibley and he were officers in one railroad company that stood to benefit by it. It cannot be blamed on one party, but it continued the heedless economic development policies of the territorial Democrats, still in power in 1858, and a similar bonding fiasco occurred under the Democratic regents who controlled the state university. Minnesota was one society despite partisanship, and antebellum Americans saw progress as one undivided concept that included for-profit railroads, Westward expansion, social reform, and religion. Rev. Neill delivered a sermon on railroads as promoters of "pure and undefiled religion" because they would bring good Yankee-type immigrants to Minnesota and would bring the clergy around to minister to frontier residents. His text was Isaiah 40:3 ("Make straight in the desert a highway for our God"). North promoted railroads as part of his social reforms, colonization efforts (Northfield), and investment interests. He saw no contradiction: railroads would build a better society. Yet he felt the state's credit should not be risked to aid private companies.[3]

Rev. Edward D. Neill on Railroads

"Secondly: They aid religion by proving antidotes to bigotry. When the wagon drawn by oxen was the mode of conveyance to a new country, but few penetrated the wilds of the west. . . . Far away from all refining influences, they rapidly degenerated; their children, debarred the knowledge of the common school, grew up without education, and were semi-barbarous. . . . Through the influence of railways and steam carriages, this state of things has been almost dissipated."

Yet it was. Around $2.25 million in state bonds were issued, but their value to the railroads rapidly dwindled to nearly nothing, as the market value of the bonds declined to the vanishing point. As president of the Minneapolis and Cedar Valley Railroad (Sibley was on its board of directors), North hurried to New York City in November 1858 to sell the M&CV's bonds (whose value rested on the state bonds' value). New York's "exacting money-lenders" were fast losing faith in the new state's credit, as were its newspaper editors. The *New York Evening Post* had banner headlines: "THE GREAT FIVE MILLION DEBT, BANKRUPTCY OF THE STATE OF MINNESOTA." At North's urging, Governor Sibley rushed to New York to reassure investors, but to no avail. Back home, lack of investor confidence meant a lack of funds to pay contractors and laborers, and a halt to railroad construction. Minnesota's railroads were bankrupt. The voters felt they had been tricked in April 1858, and they passed a new constitutional amendment in November 1860 that stated the 1858 one "only purport[ed] to be an amendment" and thus erased it from the constitution. Voters repudiated the bonds and their prior vote, and the new state's credit was badly tarnished.[5]

By then, there was not a single mile of functioning rail service in the state. The state government foreclosed on the railroad companies, thereby recovering the lands it had granted them, plus "240 miles of graded roadbed, somewhat the worse for flood and frost." The St. Paul attorney and satirist DeWitt Clinton Cooley mocked that "the general railroad superintendent of the State" said that "the present rolling stock, on the various and zig-zag lines under his supervision, consists at present of diverse Jersey wagons, propelled by sundry crumpled horned oxen, yearling bulls and other quadrupedal machinery, engaged in locomoting wood" stolen from public lands.[6]

Minnesota's First Presidential Election Looks Like the Union's Last

The new state would have to redeem its honor on the battlefield, and the war's federal deficit spending would have to revive the nation's and the state's economies. First came the 1860 presidential election that caused the conflict—the first one in which Minnesotans could vote. The excitement of a fateful campaign hit the new state. For the Mississippi River towns, it came by steamboat as did most excitements. New York Governor William H. Seward toured Minnesota on behalf of the man who beat him for the Republican nomination, Abraham Lincoln, and arrived in Red Wing one "dark and rainy" Saturday night, September 15, on board the *Milwaukee*, the same boat that brought the news of statehood two years earlier. The local unit of Republicans' national marching group, the Wide Awakes, fired a salute, and he made a few remarks at a local hotel. Days later, the Wide Awakes paraded through town, 108 strong, as did a rival group, the Little Giants, supporting Douglas for President. A Republican presidential elector and a future governor, Stephen Miller, debated a Democratic elector, Christopher C. Andrews, but the "rival companies" showed a friendly spirit toward each other.[7]

Despite all that Douglas had done for Minnesota, the election was no contest here. Sibley went as a Democratic delegate to the Charleston and Baltimore conventions that saw the fatal division between Douglas' Northern supporters and the Southern Democrats—both ran presidential candidates and neither had much hope of winning the national race. John North went to the Republican convention, visited Lincoln in Springfield, campaigned hard for him in Illinois and Minnesota, and hoped for a government position. Both parties had been correct in seeing a rising Republican tide in the state. Lincoln won Minnesota's four electoral votes by a nearly two-to-one margin over Douglas. Lincoln appointed North to a post in the territory of Nevada, and he never resided in Minnesota again. Alexander Ramsey had become the state's second governor (after Sibley) by winning the October 1859 election that heralded Lincoln's triumph a year later.[8]

Lincoln's election triggered South Carolina's secession from the Union on December 20, 1860, and then a winter-long crisis in which Minnesota and its leaders played little role. The Union was in grave danger. The older Eastern states that had created and maintained it would have to rescue it or else abandon their eighty-year investment. Border states like Virginia and Kentucky led a last-ditch attempt at compromise while Republicans in New England, New York, and the Midwest set limits on how far the new party would compromise. Three-year-old Minnesota had almost no say in the political maneuvering. Yet Governor Ramsey happened to be in Washington on the weekend of April 12-14, 1861, when Confederate forces fired on Fort Sumter in Charlestown harbor. He was the first governor to offer Lincoln a regiment to put down the rebellion. Lincoln accepted his offer—Lincoln needed armed men willing to risk their lives for the Union, and ones from a new Western state would do just as well as Easterners.

The Nation Learns of Minnesota by Seeing Its Volunteer Soldiers

Ramsey's being first with his offer was coincidental, but the rapid recruitment of volunteers for the regiment was no accident. News of Fort Sumter awakened anger and outrage at this insult to the nation's government, flag, and army. By then, telegraph lines had reached Minnesota. Ramsey's telegram reached Lieutenant Governor Ignatius Donnelly on Monday, April 15; that evening volunteers began to sign up in St. Paul. At the start, this was a war motioned, seconded, and carried by a frontier democracy in public meetings; it was more than a top-down creation in which a president sent orders down a chain of command. Goodhue County held its meeting on Friday evening, April 19, at its courthouse. "[T]he people were there in astonishing numbers," according to the *Red Wing Sentinel*, and they "swept like a black torrent" into the court room, erupted in "rapturous applause and deafening cheers" when the Star Spangled Banner was brought into the room, and wept when an aged judge told of the American Revolution of his childhood. Adjourning their partisanship, they chose both Republicans and Democrats to preside and passed a motion to "bury forever the political hatchet." After the speeches, an enlistment roll was set out and the call given for "all who wished to volunteer to come forward and sign it on the drum head." Forty volunteers did so that evening.[10]

An equally democratic enthusiasm accompanied the volunteers to Fort Snelling, where they trained from late April until mid-June and where crowds came to watch dress parades or to visit friends and relatives in the regiment. Or, soldiers went to the crowds, to a picnic dinner at Nicollet Island not far from the North home, and to St. Paul where Anna Ramsey presented a flag and aptly spoke the state's feelings.

Anna Ramsey on the First Minnesota's Destiny

"To you is reserved a proud destiny . . . the solicitude and love of the entire state will follow you. From this [c]apitol to the most remote frontier cottage, no heart but shall send up a prayer for your safety and success, no eye but shall follow with affection the flutterings of your banner as you cover it with

glory. In your hands we feel that the honor of our young state
is safe. To you—with firm faith—we commit its virgin and
unsullied fame."[11]

On June 22, the First Minnesota boarded two steamboats for the trip to
La Crosse and the battlefields of Virginia.[12] They marched down Chicago's
streets from one train station to another. The *Tribune* was impressed.
"Gallant Minnesota deserves high credit for her noble sons. . . . There are few
regiments we have seen that can compare to the brawn and muscle with these
Minnesotans, used to the axe, the rifle, and the setting pole."[13]

When they arrived in Washington, the nation's capital got a look at
them, and they, at it. Camped a half-mile from the Capitol, they held "a dress
parade each evening" that citizens watched. Lincoln reviewed them. And he
visited them "unheralded—and probably without knowing what regiment it
was—riding in a carriage . . . where he sat for a time shaking hands and
talking with the boys as anyone might have done." Now chaplain of the First
Minnesota, Rev. Neill saw Lincoln and his cabinet at "a flag raising in the
park" near the White House. "The President is a long, thin & somewhat
sallow man," he observed, "in manner a little lacking in dignity. Mrs.
Lincoln's figure is as round & plump as her husband's is angular." Soldiers
thought Washington lacked dignity. Pigs ran wild in muddy streets, and the
canal stank. "With the exception of the Public Buildings," Private Jasper
Searles noted, "it is a second or third class city." Residents had no idea where
or what Minnesota was. When an Irish fellow asked them where they were
from and was told "Minnesota," he asked, "Yes, I know the name, but where
are you from?" Hearing the same reply, he reworded his question, "Yes, I
know it's Minnesota, but *what State?*"[14]

At Bull Run, on July 21, the regiment was in the center of the heavy
fighting on Henry House Hill and did maintain the young state's honor
by fighting bravely and retreating in an orderly fashion amidst the
tarnishing of the North's honor by the pell-mell retreat to Washington. An
American diplomat in Belgium ordered three rifled cannon sent to the
regiment to reward their "conspicuous valor."[15] In the regiment, and at
home, the rout at Bull Run revealed that the war would be lengthy,
bloody, and possibly a defeat.

More Minnesota regiments would be needed for a lengthy conflict, and
more left Fort Snelling—the Second (October 14, 1861), the Third

(November 17, 1861), the Fourth (April 20, 1862), and most of the Fifth (May 24, 1862; part was kept in the state for frontier duty).[16] Unlike later American wars, the Civil War was fought by military units drawn from individual states, and their performance reflected honor or dishonor on their state. When the First Minnesota was under heavy fire at Savage's Station (June 29, 1862), Lieutenant Colonel Stephen Miller rallied them by saying, "Minnesota, stand firm! Don't run, Minnesota!"[17] Corporal James A. Wright recalled, "We had lots of State pride and I certainly believe that 'Minnesota' was the magic word that encouraged us to stand and face that terrible storm of bullets that swept our line." Reinforcing them, two other states' regiments cried, "We are with you, Minnesota!" Men from a single county or city often made up a company, so soldiers fought alongside neighbors and honored their locality. Other forms of unit identification resulted: over one hundred African Americans served in the "colored" regiments of this segregated army (in this case, segregation did mean black soldiers received full credit for the bravery shown by their units); the Third Regiment had one Swedish-American company. Some dishonor came as well: Colonel Henry Lester surrendered the Third Minnesota to the Confederates on July 13, 1862, at Murfreesboro, Tennessee, over his subordinates' protest.[18]

The State Rallies Its Citizens to Aid the National Government in Crisis

The national government did not communicate directly to Minnesota citizens but called on the state to furnish a regiment. The state called on its counties and townships to carry out the details. A state had the accoutrement of a sovereign nation, with a governor as commander-in-chief and an adjutant general as its military head. Governor Ramsey appointed officers. Politics entered into it, as Democrat Daniel Robertson's recruited regiment was bypassed and its companies diverted into a new regiment under a different colonel. The state failed to recruit soldiers to fill up the ranks of older regiments whose desirable officer positions were taken. Men preferred to be colonels and majors and captains by organizing new regiments. After the Fifth was formed, the well ran dry. The young unmarried men who did not own businesses or farms had already enlisted. New recruiting would cut deeply into the key roles in the state's society and economy. When the state tried to fill a sixth regiment, it only secured one-fourth of one by August 1, 1862. The War Department issued an order: if any state failed to raise its quota (Minnesota's was 5,362) in two weeks, men would be drafted from its militia units. Restating that threat, Ramsey called for the sixth to be filled and five more regiments created by August 22nd; appointed local officials to list likely recruits and to conduct a draft if needed; and assigned a quota to each county and township. To prevent flight to avoid the draft, the adjutant general decreed that no one was to leave the state "without a pass from the attorney-general" or to leave their county "without a pass from the sheriff." Local pressure—and bargaining over who went and who would assume their home duties—helped Minnesota meet the quota.[19]

In Burnside Township west of Red Wing, the quota of twenty-six men was more than met (thirty-two men served). In early August, the Red Wing newspapers beat the editorial drums for volunteers and pointed to the bounty offered to recruits; the community pledged to raise nearly $2,500 to aid "the families of Volunteers who have or may enlist from Red Wing." A local Republican politician raised a company for the Sixth Minnesota, and a 26-year-old single farmer named Kingsley Wood enlisted in it—perhaps in place of his married brother Willard and their married neighbor Marshall Cutler. After being mustered in at Fort Snelling on Thursday, August 14, he was given a furlough to finish his harvesting.[20]

Soldiers' families did need the assistance. James Wright's mother Amelia had three sons in the Union Army, a ten-year-old son and seven-year-old daughter to care for, a 340-acre farm to run (100 of those were 'improved' acres-cleared and some planted), a dozen cows and a dozen swine to look after, and a $475 mortgage. The 1861 harvest must not have gone well for her, because in late September 1861 her creditor forced a sheriff's sale and took ownership of the farm. James sent $8 of his $11 monthly soldier's pay to his mother, but that "meager pay offered no solutions." In the summer of 1862, she took out a new mortgage and reacquired the farm but was still in financial danger. James reported that "letters from home" that fall "were often discouraging in tone" due to wartime inflation, the war's duration, "the cold season coming on and no adequate provision for the winter. What were they to do? How could they manage?" Prior to the battle of Fredericksburg, he lost sleep over his mother's poverty not over war's dangers. By February 1864, Amelia Wright gave up and moved to Red Wing, "her health poor." She could hardly afford to hire labor, for farm wages that had been 50 or 65 cents a day had "soared" to "between three and four dollars a day."[21]

The Young State's Own Crisis
Threatens to Unravel Its Ordinance-Based Society

Kingsley Wood never harvested his last twelve acres, for violence broke out on the Dakota reservation on Monday, August 18th. The causes were many and complex. Partly, the sordid and squalid aspects of the 1851 treaties and of an 1858 treaty came home to roost. White settlement advanced much closer, much quicker toward the Dakota than anticipated; traders' insistence on a nearby Minnesota River site was ill-advised. Dakota were angered over these treaties and the government's failure to live up to all the terms. In the 1858 treaty, negotiated in Washington to separate older chiefs from younger, more anti-white Dakota, the chiefs sold the half of the reservation north of the Minnesota River. And yet, treaties for the communal sale of communally-owned land were not a grievance to the growing faction of 'cut-hair' Dakota who were abandoning traditional dress, adopting farming, converting to Christianity in some cases, and leaving the teepee for the frame or brick house. Partly, a deepening split between them and the traditional 'blanket' faction caused the hostilities. Partly, it was due to the patronage system in which victorious Republicans installed inexperienced Thomas J. Galbraith as Indian agent in place of the experienced Democrat, Joseph R. Brown, who had led a successful drive to reward 'cut-hair' farmers and increase their numbers. Galbraith lacked the skills needed to continue that campaign. Partly, conflict was due to the severe 1861-62 winter that caused food shortages, which the traders refused to alleviate by selling food on credit before the late summer harvest. Partly, the cause was a lengthy delay in shipment of the treaty annuity money that would have financed food sales. The crisis seemed over by August 12, due to a food distribution, some trades for food, and an "abundant" harvest in sight. Missionary Riggs and Agent Galbraith reported calm on the reservation.[22]

Seeing the Dakota on their reservation as "not within the jurisdiction of the State of Minnesota," and as a federal responsibility, the state government played almost no role in these events.[23] That proved short-sighted. Its citizens were settling near the reservation, hunting game, depriving the Dakota of their game, and angering them in other ways. They would then look to the state to protect them from the Dakota, with Washington preoccupied by the Civil War. Brown County citizens petitioned Ramsey on August 14th that their militia not be recruited and sent East until the annuity had been paid and the Dakota "appeased."[24]

The 'blanket' Dakota's hunting-and-warring culture was cornered and confined on a reservation too small to support it, surrounded by an opposing white farming culture, and threatened by more Dakota converting to that culture. Whites had racial prejudices against Indians, but the 'deep-seated animosities' were between farmers and hunters as well. The key, dangerous development was the transformation of 'soldiers lodges' from committees in charge of the hunt to young warriors meeting in secret, defying tribal and band councils often controlled by cut-hair farmers, and discussing warfare against whites. The spark that ignited this anger into action occurred on Sunday, August 17th, when four young hunters murdered five white settlers in Acton Township, forty miles north of the reservation. One hunter taunted another with being a coward afraid of whites. A similar taunt provoked the Mdewakanton leader Little Crow to agree that night to lead a war against the whites. Tribal councils were not consulted, and the Dakota were badly divided from the start. Recent Civil War recruiting, the departure of new recruits for the East, and news of Union defeats had led some Dakota warriors to believe victory was possible, but Little Crow knew long-term victory was not. The war seemed like insulted honor lashing out more than a strategy.[25]

It erupted on Monday morning, August 18th. Dakota Warriors killed about twenty whites at the Lower Sioux Agency, sent the rest fleeing to nearby Fort Ridgely, and ambushed a detachment from that fort at the ferry crossing. Several hundred Dakota divided into raiding parties and headed to nearby German and Scandinavian settlements to kill their inhabitants. The Warriors could have seized the fort that day. Killing women and children was customary in warfare between American Indian peoples who were traditional enemies living apart from each other. This sudden assault departed from custom. Many Dakota opposed it, and the councils had not been consulted, thus casting doubt on the war's legitimacy. Some whites living at the agency were relatives, albeit ones who treated the Dakota badly. Nearby settlers, unlike the Ojibwe, thought they were at peace with the Dakota, and many of those killed were unarmed or defenseless. By warning some whites to flee, Little Crow and others indicated some guilt about this killing (and personal regard toward those warned), perhaps based on long acquaintance with other norms of warfare. By urging warriors to "make war after the manner of white men," Little Crow showed he had lived near whites for decades and knew their view of the proper 'manner.' Soldiers lodges threatened fellow Dakota—cut-hairs and chiefs—with death. From the Iowa border to counties near the Mississippi to the state's southwest corner, some 800 white civilians were killed. One historian termed it "the largest massacre of whites by Indians in American history." The killing panicked settlers into a mass flight that depopulated twenty-three counties, an area fifty by two hundred miles. Excusing the slaughter as customary Dakota warfare is problematic, for much about the war did not match their customs.[26]

The process of building a state upon surveyed, settled farmland started to unravel. The western half of this state society was washing away in a flood of refugees. A group of lawless whites looted the abandoned farmsteads. "As the people fled from one town, the inhabitants of town or country beyond [farther west], fleeing also, came in and plundered the houses."[27] Law and order disintegrated. With the national government preoccupied with the Civil War, the state had to assume a government's burden, and highest priority, of defending its own citizens—thus, its own legitimacy. At the same time, it had to assume its burden of sending new recruits to the Union army.

The State Must Raise Its Own Army to Defend Its Existence

Governor Ramsey received the news around noon on Tuesday, August 19th, and he went to Henry Sibley's house at Mendota to ask his friend to lead a state force to relieve Fort Ridgely and to defeat the Dakota. He gave Sibley "the rank of colonel in the state militia," for this would be a state army and "a Minnesota state war" at first. He could not wait for federal action, which was not soon forthcoming. Fortunately, the Sixth Regiment had not yet been mustered into the U.S. Army or shipped east, so that Kingsley Wood and others could be recalled from furlough to report to Fort Snelling. Wood's Red Wing unit arrived at the fort on the 21st and headed up the Minnesota River to join Sibley's green "army" that absorbed militia units as it went but was short on ammunition and supplies. Uncertain what Dakota force lay ahead of him, lacking adequate mounted cavalry to fight a mounted foe, Sibley moved slowly and cautiously, which aroused anger among the state's citizens, yet he needed to stop to give aid and assurance and some of his scarce supplies to fleeing citizens. Sibley was appalled by their reports of devastation, saying, "unless we can now and effectually crush the rising, the State is ruined."[28]

Aided by three cannon, soldiers from one Fifth Minnesota company plus other units and civilians narrowly beat back Dakota attacks on Fort Ridgely, on Wednesday the 20th and Friday the 22nd. Bypassing the fort, Little Crow's forces attacked New Ulm on the 23rd and came close to taking it. A state supreme court justice, Charles E. Flandrau, commanded 250 white civilians (including Dr. William W. Mayo of Le Sueur who worked on the injured), gave a speech to encourage the men to keep fighting, and chased two defenders back to duty. Around 800 Dakota repeatedly assaulted first one section of town and then another, but buildings were set on fire to create a cleared space around the central four-block stronghold, which did hold out. Over 1,000 white refugees and townsfolk huddled in the basements and buildings while their defenders fought. After Little Crow's men retreated, the town was evacuated on Monday the 25th. After their three defeats, the Dakota withdrew up the valley amidst growing dissension and the formation of a soldiers lodge of peace advocates, mainly Sisseton and Wahpeton led by Little Crow's cousin, Paul Mazakutemani. He chastised the warriors for attacking civilians, not just white soldiers, and tried to seize the white captives.[29]

Sibley's state army of some 1,400 men reached Fort Ridgely on August 28th. After a burial detail was severely cut up by the Dakota on September 2nd at Birch Coulee, Sibley became aware of the captives and of Dakota divisions—both reasons for continuing his slow pace, for the peace party might bring about the captives' release. Ramsey telegraphed Washington, "This is not our war; it is a national war." But Washington sent only the defeated Union general, John Pope. Not until October 5th did the first non-Minnesota unit from the U.S. Army (the 25th Wisconsin Regiment) arrive to relieve the state militia. A month before then, an organized petition drive began to urge Ramsey to call a special session of the legislature in order to pass "an efficient militia law," for the federal government was too absorbed in the Civil War "to give sufficient attention to the affairs of a remote frontier people," so we must "provide for our own defence, and do so promptly." Ramsey did call the special session for mid-September, and the legislature voted to borrow money to assist refugees. For 45 days, it was "a Minnesota state war."[30]

The Pioneer & Democrat Asks, Who is Responsible?

"Minnesota is the victim of the most astounding calamity that has ever befallen any State of the Union. . . . Was there any one whose duty it was to have foreseen the danger and provided against it? . . . Than Governor Ramsey, no one better knows the causes of complaint and irritation for years past existing among Minnesota's bands of the Dakota Nation. . . . He ought to have known, from this and other causes, that for many years there has been danger at every payment, of a Sioux war; which has been prevented on several occasions only by a display of military force."

St. Paul Pioneer & Democrat, 10 September 1862, 1

The state infantry trudged up the valley from Fort Ridgely to the Lower Sioux Agency and beyond, in pursuit of Little Crow's mounted force. Sibley was now in touch with the Dakota peace party, whom he reassured that if they came to his camp "under a flag of truce" he would not punish those who had not murdered whites. On September 23rd, as Sibley was nearing the Upper Sioux Agency, the Dakota warriors set an ambush, but a potato-foraging party prematurely triggered the fighting at Wood Lake. The state army's greater numbers and its artillery forced Little Crow to retreat after this last battle in Minnesota. The peace party freed the white captives. The war party crossed into Dakota Territory to winter on the Great Plains. Without cavalry, Sibley could not pursue them.[31]

Although he now was appointed a Brigadier General in the U.S. Army, Sibley's duties turned from the military to the judicial. He set up "a military commission of five officers to conduct trials." After hasty and irregular trials, it condemned 307 Dakota men (of nearly 400 tried) to death, including those who had fought only against armed white soldiers at the fort. Truth be told, there was little chance of a fair and adequate trial. State courts could not handle so many cases. Also, the state's citizenry would likely attack defendants on their way to trials farther east and would attack any sign of leniency by Sibley or Ramsey, architects of the 1851 treaties who were a bit suspect now. The U.S. government was too absorbed by the Civil War to set up four hundred judicial proceedings. Under tremendous pressure from the citizens whom it had failed to protect, the state government was not about to show the Dakota warriors any mercy.[32]

Fortunately, other voices intervened. A government whose citizens have been killed does not forgive like a church can—but several missionaries felt misgivings over Sibley's tribunal, and one churchman, Episcopal Bishop Henry B. Whipple, courageously went to Lincoln that fall to inform him of valid Dakota grievances against the Indian agent, the government, and the traders that led to the violence. Lincoln reported, "[Whipple] talked with me about the rascality of this Indian business until I felt it down to my boots." Lincoln insisted that General Pope send him the trial records. State leaders like Ramsey pressured him by warning that mobs would execute the condemned if Lincoln didn't, but he "refused to be stampeded" and cut the list of condemned down to thirty-nine (one was later reprieved). As rumors spread that Lincoln might pardon them all, furious Minnesotans held a public meeting in Mankato near the prisoners' camp and about 150 headed toward the camp on December 4th in a disorganized attempt at a violent capture, but the military guards halted it. On December 26th, the thirty-eight condemned Dakota were hung at Mankato in "the largest public execution in American history." The following May, after a bitter winter at Fort Snelling, around 1,300 cut-hair and other Dakota were shipped to Crow Creek in Montana. Few Dakota were left in Minnesota.[33]

The First Minnesota Regiment
Establishes the State's Military Reputation

The First Minnesota Regiment read of the August 18th outbreak in New York newspapers while marching toward Second Bull Run. The news "awaken[ed] anxious thoughts among those whose homes were in the western part of the state," recalled James Wright, "and we would all gladly have hurried to the defense of the state we represented."[34] The War Department would not gladly hurry them there, however, so they marched north to participate in heavy fighting at Antietam. They saw little action at Fredericksburg (December 1862) or Chancellorsville (May 1863), but the Confederates drove north into Pennsylvania after their two victories. The Union Army marched north to stop them.

Around 2 a.m. on July 2, 1863, they were aroused from sleep to march the final few miles to Gettysburg—to Cemetery Ridge south of town, for the Union Army had retreated from the town the prior day. They could not suspect, Wright noted, "that that day was to be the saddest, bloodiest, grandest, and most glorious day in the history of the regiment." Stationed on the ridge, the men watched as General Daniel Sickles moved his Third Corps a half mile in front of the rest of the army, got sharply attacked for his troubles, and many of his regiments broke apart and came rushing back past the Minnesotans. "Crashing, crushing, stunning discharges of artillery made the earth vibrate beneath [them]." Wright's company was sent off as skirmishers to deal with

Confederates to the left. The rebel infantry were set to charge through a hole in the Union line. General Winfield S. Hancock rode up to assess this crisis. Seeing that he must gain five minutes so that hurrying reinforcements could plug the hole, he ordered Colonel William Colvill to lead the regiment's meager 289 men in a charge on the advancing rebels, who outnumbered them perhaps five to one. "Every man realized in an instant what that order meant—," Second Lieutenant William Lochren recalled, "death or wounds to us all; the sacrifice of the regiment to gain a few minutes' time and save the position, and probably the battlefield." The young state's reputation and possibly the nation's fate rested in their hands. They charged three hundred yards into three Alabama regiments. Over 220 of them were killed or wounded, but the Union line was saved on July 2nd—and the First Minnesota helped save it again the next day by aiding in the repulse of Pickett's Charge. Of the First's charge, Hancock later said, "There is no more gallant deed recorded in history." The young state's honor was safe with them.[35]

Minnesota's troops in the Western theater fought bravely on many battlefields. At Chickamauga on September 20, 1863, after the Confederates had driven through a hole in the Union line and sent half the Union Army fleeing for Chattanooga, the Second Minnesota joined General George Thomas' remnant holding Snodgrass Ridge and preventing a complete debacle. They suffered 162 casualties out of their 384 men. Two months later, they and others in Thomas' army climbed four-hundred-foot Missionary Ridge and seized that Confederate stronghold. In December 1864, four Minnesota regiments in Thomas' command participated in the assault that overran Hood's position at Nashville "and virtually ended the war in the West."[36]

By then, the First Minnesota had been mustered out, its three-year term of duty expired. By being the state's first regiment, serving in the Eastern theater that received better press coverage, and by saving the second day for the Union Army at Gettysburg, the First garnered more honors than the state's other units. The state's representatives and senators gave a banquet for the regiment at Washington's National Hotel on February 6, 1864, before they headed home. The nation's notables gathered—Vice President Hannibal Hamlin, Secretary of War Edwin Stanton, two other cabinet members, and three senators from other states. "The immense dining room was profusely decorated with flags, flowers, and evergreens," James Wright marveled, and "long tables were loaded with a line of choice dishes." Speeches praised the heroes. Seriously wounded at Gettysburg, Colonel Colvill was carried into the room as a surprise to the men, who had not seen him in the seven months since the charge. The *Chronicle* of Washington reported that the First was "the senior regiment in the service"—likely due to Ramsey's being first to offer a regiment—and the veteran of "a score of brilliant battles." The Minnesotans living in the nation's capital had raised $1,000 for the banquet, which showed "true Minnesota go-a-headativeness."[37]

After a train trip through Harrisburg, Pittsburgh, and then Chicago to La Crosse, the First came home in true Minnesota fashion—up the frozen Mississippi aboard sleighs "filled with straw and cross-seated with boards," equipped with "buffalo robes" to ward off the zero-degree winter night winds—their "first sleigh ride in the service." They came in from the cold for a series of welcoming banquets in the next three days in warm, bright, fire-heated halls in Winona, Red Wing, and St. Paul. At the capitol "there was an immense crowd which welcomed us with shouts and cheers, and bells were ringing and whistles blowing," according to Wright. The parade to the Atheneum was over a mile long. At that hall, food burdened the tables, the Great Western Band played "martial music," and Governor Stephen Miller—who had commanded the First—"welcomed us on behalf of the state." With that, they could consider themselves home at last.[38]

The state could look forward to peace and the end of relentless trials that marked its first seven years. Federal wartime deficit spending lifted the economy out of recession. Even the hefty wartime inflation eased the burden of 1857 debts off many a shoulder. The wartime labor shortage and high farm-labor wages stimulated the manufacture and sale of farm machinery. The state now had 210 miles of functioning railroad track and a ten-mile passenger service between St. Paul and St. Anthony. The 1862 Homestead Act offered 160 acres of virtually free land to immigrants claiming a farmstead on the frontier. The state was well-positioned for economic growth and free of Dakota warriors near its towns and farms. It would not have its progress further blocked—as its admission had been—by Southerners in Congress. Yet the defeat of Southern states' rights lessened the Northern states' sphere for independent action too. The new state society formed in the mid-1850s could not dream of a unique identity like seventeenth-century Massachusetts, but that vision was even more impossible a decade later. The national government discovered its strength and its identity in the course of defending its existence. The states would have to respect the power of this new American nationalism and gingerly carve out their own niche within it.

1. "The editor," *Winona Republican*, 19 May 1858, 2.

2. "railroad loan of 1858," Folwell, *History of Minnesota*, Vol. II, 41-51; Anderson, *History of the Constitution of Minnesota*, 240-43; *Debates and Proceedings* [Democrats], 395.

3. "supported by some leaders," Folwell, *History of Minnesota*, Vol. II, 48-49; Roberts, "Early Political and Administrative History," 57-59, 67-72, 124-25; Gilman, *Sibley*, 155-56; Stonehouse, *John Wesley North*, 74-75, 105-06.

4. "Neill on Railroads," Edward Duffield Neill, *The History of Minnesota from the Earliest French Explorations to the Present Time* (Philadelphia: Lippincott, 1873), 601-02.

5. "North hurried," Gilman, *Sibley*, 158, 220; Stonehouse, *John Wesley North*, 107-12; Anderson, *History of the Constitution of Minnesota*, 243.

6. "satirist DeWitt Clinton Cooley," Folwell, *History of Minnesota*, Vol. II, 328; DeWitt C. Cooley, "Tri-ennial Message of the Governor of the Sovereigns of Minnesota … February 8th, 1860," 7, MHS.

7. "arrived in Red Wing," *Goodhue County Republican*, 21 September (2) and 28 September (3), both 1860; *Red Wing Sentinel*, 31 October 1860, 2.

8. "no contest here," Gilman, *Sibley*, 162-65; Stonehouse, *John Wesley North*, 120-27, 131.

9. "Ramsey happened to be," Kenneth Carley, *Minnesota in the Civil War: An Illustrated History* (St. Paul: MHS Press, 2000), 14.

10. "rapid recruitment," Carley, *Civil War*, 14; *Red Wing Sentinel*, 24 April 1861, 2; *Goodhue County Republican*, 26 April 1861, 2.

11. "Anna Ramsey," James A. Wright, *No More Gallant a Deed: A Civil War Memoir of the First Minnesota Volunteers* (St. Paul: MHS Press, 2001), 29.

12. "democratic enthusiasm," here and above, Carley, *Civil War*, 6; Wright, *No More Gallant a Deed*, 23, 25, 29.

13. "down Chicago's streets," Wright, *No More Gallant a Deed*, 38.

14. "the nation's capital," Richard Moe, *The Last Full Measure: The Life and Death of the First Minnesota Volunteers* (New York: Henry Holt, 1993), 34-37; Wright, *No More Gallant a Deed*, 40-41, 43; Edward D. Neill to 'My dear Nan,' 29 June 1861, Box 2, Edward D. Neill Papers, MHS.

15. "At Bull Run," Moe, *Last Full Measure*, 61-62; Wright, *No More Gallant a Deed*, 56-60, 65, 124-25. One of these cannon is at the military museum at Camp Ripley.

16. "Minnesota regiments," Carley, *Civil War*, 197-99.

17. "Miller rallied them," Wright, *No More Gallant a Deed*, 151.

18. "unit identification," Carley, *Civil War*, 68-69, 80-81, 84-87.

19. "state called on," Folwell, *History of Minnesota*, Vol. II, 88-90, 100-05 (quote from 104).

20. "Burnside township," Keillor, "Burnside!," 105-08; *Goodhue Volunteer*, 6 and 13 and 20 August 1862, all 2.

21. "Amelia had three sons," Keillor, "Burnside!," 111-12; Frederick L. Johnson, *History of Goodhue County, Minnesota*, 77-78.

22. "causes were many," This summarizes the narrative/analysis in Anderson, *Little Crow*, 89-130. Riggs' and Galbraith's statements are in Adjutant General's *Annual Report* – 1862 (State Archives), 416.

23. "Seeing the Dakota," *St. Paul Pioneer & Democrat*, 14 September 1862, 1 (quoting Ramsey).

24. "Brown County citizens," John C. Rudolph, et al., to Governor Ramsey, 14 August 1862, Governors Papers, Box 111.E.20.4F, State Archives, MHS.

25. "cornered and confined," Anderson, *Little Crow*, 81-82, 116-19, 129, 130 (quoted), 131-34; Folwell, *History of Minnesota*, Vol. II, 234-36, 239-41, 415-17; Gary Clayton Anderson and

Alan R. Woolworth, eds., *Through Dakota Eyes: Narrative Accounts of the Minnesota Indian War of 1862* (St. Paul: Minnesota Historical Society Press, 1988), 12-13, 25-26.

26. "It erupted," Folwell, *History of Minnesota*, Vol. II, 109-25, 127; Anderson, *Little Crow*, 135-39, 141; Gilman, *Sibley*, 174; David Herbert Donald, *Lincoln* (New York: Simon & Schuster, 1995), 392 (quoted).

27. "lawless whites," Folwell, *History of Minnesota*, Vol. II, 248 (quoting Stephen Riggs).

28. "ask his friend," Gilman, *Sibley*, 172-75; Folwell, *History of Minnesota*, Vol. II, 147-49, 171, 176, 186 (quoted); Keillor, "Burnside!," 108-09; Adjutant General's *Annual Report* – 1862, 419 (quoting Sibley).

29. "beat back Dakota attacks," Folwell, *History of Minnesota*, Vol. II, 126-32, 135-44; Anderson, *Little Crow*, 144-46, 151-53; Judith Hartzell, *I Started All This: The Life of Dr. William Worrall Mayo* (Greenville, S.C.: Arvi Books, 2004), 57-59.

30. "Sibley's state army," Gilman, *Sibley*, 178-81; Anderson, *Little Crow*, 156-59; Folwell, *History of Minnesota*, Vol. II, 170, 186-87 (quoted), 244. For the petition drive, see, e.g., A S. Whitney, N. H. Miner, et al., to Governor Ramsey, n.d., in Governors Papers, State Archives, Box 111.E.20.4F. Numerous identical petitions are in the box also.

31. "trudged up the valley," Gilman, *Sibley*, 180-83; Anderson, *Little Crow*, 157-61.

32. "from the military to the judicial," Gilman, *Sibley*, 184-85; Anderson, *Little Crow*, 184.

33. "other voices intervened," Donald, *Lincoln*, 393-95; Folwell, *History of Minnesota*, Vol. II, 208-09, 259; *Mankato Weekly Review*, 6 December 1862, 2, and 13 December 1862, 2; Gilman, Sibley, 191.

34. "read of the August 18th outbreak," Wright, *No More Gallant a Deed*, 180.

35. "July 2, 1863," Wright, *No More Gallant a Deed*, 291, 295; Moe, *Last Full Measure*, 268-75, 297 (quoting Hancock); Brian Leehan, *Pale Horse at Plum Run: The First Minnesota at Gettysburg* (St. Paul: Minnesota Historical Society Press, 2002), 36-98, and 169-77 (on the number of casualties); Folwell, *History of Minnesota*, Vol. II, 310-11.

36. "the Western theater," Folwell, *History of Minnesota*, Vol. II, 316-26; Carley, *Civil War*, 201-03.

37. "mustered out," Wright, *No More Gallant a Deed*, 400-01.

38. "came home," Wright, *No More Gallant a Deed*, 409-17.

Railroads & Regions

After the Civil War, Minnesotans expanded their society beyond its core area at the junction of the St. Croix, Minnesota, and Mississippi rivers. The war revived the national economy, and, with it, railroad construction. Business leaders in this core area (St. Paul, St. Anthony, Minneapolis, Stillwater) had a strong motive for laying rail tracks: to avoid being absorbed into Chicago's trade network and becoming merely a five-minute whistle stop on the way to the Windy City. Already, the state had granted lands and specified routes for four railroads leading into and out of this core: 1) the St. Paul and Pacific (SP&P) main line along the Mississippi to St. Cloud and Crow Wing, thence to Pembina on the Canadian border; 2) an SP&P branch line west to the Red River at Breckenridge; 3) the St. Paul and Sioux City (SP&SC) road southwest toward Sioux City, Iowa; and 4) the Minnesota and Cedar Valley (M&CV) through Northfield and Faribault on its way to Iowa's Cedar River valley. During the war, Congress and the state legislature granted lands to the Lake Superior and Mississippi (LS&M), which was to run from St. Paul to a site on the Minnesota shore of Superior—thus giving Duluth its start. Two routes did not pass through the core—the Winona and St. Peter (W&SP) that also continued west to the Dakota border, and the Northern Pacific (NP), a transcontinental railroad chartered by Congress in 1864 to link Lake Superior and Puget Sound.[1]

The Core Area (the Twin Cities)
Versus the Rest of the State

Core area leaders had to appease southern Minnesotans by agreeing to plans for the W&SP, which was certain to funnel commodities to Chicago and Milwaukee, not Minneapolis or St. Paul. Promoters outside Minnesota pushed for the NP that also bypassed the core. The LS&M was the core area's tactic for shipping Minnesota's commodities via the Great Lakes, thus bypassing Chicago and its domineering merchants and manufacturers. State government acted as a

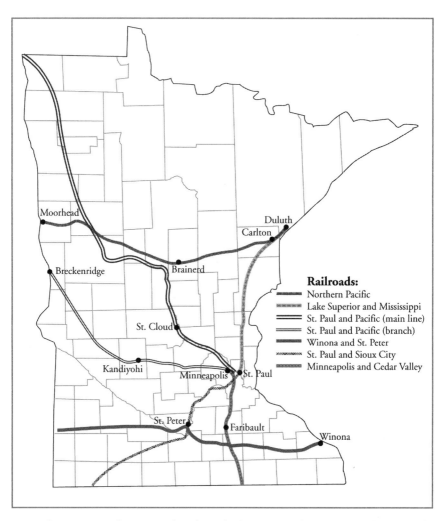

Map of Minnesota showing railroads with their original names: Northern Pacific
Railroad from Duluth via Carlton and Brainerd to Moorhead; Lake Superior and
Mississippi Railroad taking approximately the route of I-35 from St. Paul to Duluth;
St. Paul and Pacific Railroad Main Line through St. Cloud, and its Branch Line to
Breckenridge; Winona and St. Peter Railroad between those cities; St. Paul and Sioux
City Railroad running southwest to the Iowa border; and Minneapolis and Cedar
Valley Railroad heading south through Northfield and Faribault to Iowa.
Adapted from map in W. W. Folwell's A History of Minnesota, *Vol. II.*

broker and facilitator only. Michigan's failed attempt at state-owned railroads in the 1830s and 1840s foreclosed any similar attempt by its younger western sibling. Although unavoidable by 1860, the sight of a state legislature granting state lands to private companies (to build and operate highly profitable and monopolistic public highways) in return for stocks and favors for the legislators would surely have made the Ordinances' idealistic authors gasp.

After the war, wood ties and iron rails made progress toward the horizon. The SP&SC reached Sioux City in 1869, the year the M&CV touched the Iowa border. The SP&P branch made it to St. Cloud in 1866, and its main line arrived in Breckenridge by October 1871. The NP made it (barely) to Moorhead by the end of 1871. In the rail boom years, the Milwaukee & St. Paul was built to Winona in 1871, and direct rail connections to Chicago and the East were begun. Zealous to escape St. Paul's rail dominance, Minneapolis millers built a short line to connect directly to the LS&M that same year (1871), the year the LS&M completed its line to Duluth. A Southern Minnesota (SM) Railroad went west from La Crescent across the southern tier of counties.[2]

Leaders in the core area realized railroads were the key to postwar settlement. In a brief but bitter dispute over another capital-removal proposal, in February and March of 1869, they spoke of government as the key. The dispute reveals much about postwar assumptions. The constitution allowed the legislature, without a vote of the people, to move the capital to lands Congress gave the state for that purpose—lands later located in Kandiyohi Township in Kandiyohi County.[3] Other states moved their capitals from a territorial site near their eastern or southern border to a site nearer the frontier or the geographical center. The rural-dominated 1869 legislature quickly passed a bill to move the capital away to Kandiyohi. A city of only 13,000 inhabitants, Minneapolis lagged far behind St. Paul, and the *Minneapolis Daily Tribune* supported the bill, stating that "a great commercial metropolis" was not necessary or desirable "for the seat of government." The *Tribune* also wrote, "Let not the rural districts be overruled by the metropolis." Early settlers had always intended to take the capital away from such an eastern site. The *St. Paul Daily Pioneer* countered that Kandiyohi was "a howling wilderness" unsuited for the social and cultural status of a capital; keeping it at St. Paul "would tend to build up a brilliant commercial metropolis at the head of navigation of the great Mississippi."[4]

Governor William R. Marshall vetoed the bill. One issue was the future growth of the state. Marshall argued that a west-central capital was inappropriate, for the NP would develop "the northern section," a "large commercial city" would arise at or near Duluth, and "the mineral resources of Northeastern

Minnesota" would result in its growth—and, "[t]he western treeless districts" west of Kandiyohi would be slow to grow—so it was premature to place the capital there. The *Tribune* objected that his public skepticism about the prairie hindered the recruitment of immigrants to that area, and that "[a] vast region of northeastern Minnesota is almost uninhabitable by white men, and will not be populated for a thousand years." Moving the capital to Kandiyohi would aid in recruiting immigrants and pushing the frontier of settlement farther west. The capital-removal scheme failed, and the various regions were settled, skeptics notwithstanding. The railroads, not the location of a capital, played the key role.[5]

Rail construction through settled areas and an existing society brought different effects than in regions where it helped to create the society. The existing wheat-raising farms gave it outgoing freight from the start. The railroad company linked existing towns but did not plat or found new ones. The W&SP, M&CV, and SM lines through southeastern wheat areas met opposition from farmers used to governing their localities and angered at the local monopoly a railroad enjoyed. Railroads soon got out of wheat-buying and wheat-storage but made sweetheart deals with men who would undertake those tasks. The SM gave special freight rates to Jason Easton and helped him acquire a virtual monopoly of the wheat trade on that line.[6] Farmers happy to have train service grew accustomed to it and began to complain about its costs. Competing points like Owatonna, where the M&CV crossed the W&SP, benefited from lower freight rates than non-competing points that were not rail junctions.[7] In 1870, a St. Paul lawyer named Cushman K. Davis traveled this area delivering a speech, "Modern Feudalism," that accused the railroads of reducing this self-governing society to a near-feudal dependence on their monopoly power. The several rail lines were "an irresistible force like an invading army advancing through a conquered country in parallel columns" spaced far enough apart "so that each may forage on the tributary country without stint."[8]

Newly-Constructed Railroads Open Up Settlement of Areas Unsuited to Agriculture

Foraging was mighty thin in the unsettled north. The U.S. government negotiated a series of treaties with the Ojibwe that opened this area to survey, sale, and settlement. The 1854 Treaty of La Pointe purchased the North Shore of Lake Superior and inland areas thought to contain deposits of copper. Signed in Washington, the 1855 treaty acquired the upper Mississippi and its headwaters, for loggers not miners, for this area

Ojibwe leaders met with representatives of the federal government to sign the Old Crossing treaty in 1863. Carl Mose's bronze statue *Chippewa Brave* stands at the signing site on the banks of the Red Lake River near the village of Huot.
Courtesy of Moira F. Harris.

contained valuable stands of timber. Less valued tracts in the Red River Valley and along the Rainy River were conveyed to the United States in 1863 and 1866. An 1867 treaty promised the Ojibwe perpetual ownership of a reservation at White Earth, a fertile and tillable area east of the Red River where the Ojibwe could be encouraged to settle into agricultural ways. Gradually, members of the Mississippi bands moved to this area, for their prior village sites were not suited to the large-scale farming that whites thought necessary for agriculture.[9]

The crews that surveyed, graded, and laid track through the ceded Ojibwe lands found a landscape unsuited to the section-and-farm society the Ordinances intended. A crew surveying the NP route left Ottertail City in 1870 and traversed "a dense growth of timber some 40 miles wide—full of lakes, swamps, marshes, and mosquitoes," Edward Jordan noted. West of Duluth, the *St. Paul Weekly Press* reported "the direct line" to be "a pretty crooked one . . . it winds about among the sloughs, and lakes, and bogs, and wooded and sandy ridges of a curiously broken and barren country." About 180 miles west of Duluth, Jordan's crew was still not out of the bogs. The tamarack swamps were "floating forests of trees, and beneath the network of roots and moss there is generally a mud lake from ten to 20 feet deep." The only way across was to step gingerly on the roots. A misstep would cause the "occasional disappearance of everything but the head of some unlucky chap," who had to be hauled out of the mud. The NP's management was as crooked as its route, and contractors used such shoddy fill on its roadbed that when the executives took their first train ride, "the cars were separated by means of long [chain] links" to avoid putting too much weight on one spot, "and the passengers were asked to walk around the sink hole." Railroads also had to be built on land.[10]

In other areas, the broken country and wooded ridges contained timber and mineral resources far more valuable than twenty feet of mud. Ramsey and others knew the area north of Duluth contained minerals, including iron ore. Prospecting parties traversed the area after the Civil War. State geologist Newton Winchell recalled that there were two possible routes—canoeing the lakes along the old fur trade route bordering Canada or "walking from Duluth over the old Vermilion lake 'trail' which led through swamps and forests, over mountains and through gorges . . . through the interminable swamps infested with insect pests."[11] As for Duluth and other sites along Lake Superior, the ridge of rock outcroppings rising from the beach to a height of eight hundred feet in three miles, the short and rapids-filled rivers tumbling down to the lake, and a shortage of good harbors to protect against the raging nor'easters all challenged those who hoped to put the land to some economic use. South of Duluth, an Eastern newspaperman noted in June 1869, "The Superior and Mississippi [rail]road runs mostly through a heavily timbered country containing some very handsome pine timber, a heavy growth of maple, some birch, and in some places tamarack abounds." Future travelers would "thank God for the sight of a railway car," to replace the present "road of heavy clay mud, haunch deep to horses, and hub deep to wheels; rocky, full of pit-holes, broken corduroy timbers, and [plagued by] swarms of mosquitoes."[12]

Kentucky Congressman J. Proctor Knott on Duluth

"Duluth! The word fell upon my ear with peculiar and indescribable charm. . . . But, where was Duluth? Never in all my limited reading, had my vision been gladdened by seeing the celestial word in print . . . this map, kindly furnished me by the legislature of Minnesota, . . . illustrate[s] the position of Duluth in the United States . . . [and] its relations with all created things . . . . Duluth is pre-eminently a central place . . . that is so exactly in the center of the visible universe that the sky comes down at precisely the same distance all around it. (Roars of laughter.)"—January 1871, in Congress

Off-target were Southern Minnesotans' fears that this North Country was "to be roamed over by 'a sort of *omnium-gatherum*' of trappers, miners, hunters and lumbermen from whom no taxes could be exacted."[13] Economic wealth susceptible to taxation was there. Railroads meant these profit-seekers need not "roam" but could economically harvest and transport the area's resources. Yet vast stretches of this area were "never to be permanently settled" in the farm-and-section way they associated with permanence and settlement and the land laws required for land ownership.

The Homestead Act and other laws were designed for farmers, not lumbermen or miners or railroaders, who became scofflaws as they acquired land for their enterprises. The Homestead Act provided virtually free (apart from fees) 160-acre farmsteads to actual settlers who cleared and plowed land, built residences, and stayed for five years (they could buy the land after six months for $1.25 per acre). This law was unsuited to mining regions, and in 1872 Congress passed a mining land law but with the proviso that it did not apply to Michigan, Wisconsin, and Minnesota—where the old laws remained. In obtaining enough pine and mineral lands for large-scale, economical operations, lumber and mining company owners committed, and hired others to commit, fraud and perjury on an enormous scale. Hired to investigate, former Governor William R. Marshall reported in 1882 that he had traveled to "ten or more townships" on the Vermilion range and "did not find any actual settlers" (with a few exceptions), for the "land is situated in a forest region of rocks, swamps and marshes, and is not suitable for farming purposes." In one township on the Mesabi range, he "reported forty-seven fraudulent pre-emption entries" made by persons hired to claim land and to construct phony residences—"pens 4 poles high, 10 feet square, without floor or roof, and a hold 20 inches by 30 inches for a door." Another special agent estimated that "less than one-thirtieth of the claims" of land in the Duluth district "are taken for actual settlement."[14]

If these were just land-law technicalities, then violating them might have few real consequences. However, land laws were integral parts of a holistic system for forming a new society whose economic, family, religious, educational, and political aspects intertwined. When a few entrepreneurs obtained huge swaths of land for exclusively economic uses, the system was thrown out of balance. At the start, settlers were too few to establish schools, churches, and functioning governments. Migrants were often single males or temporary residents, not independent citizens but employees controlled by landowners with a narrowly economic interest in the area. They built colonial regions that shipped raw materials out to more advanced ones and depended on other areas for finance, management, and leadership—what the Founders tried to avoid. "Region" comes from the Latin *regio*, to rule, but colonial regions were the ruled, not the rulers. A farming society is not the only good one—land laws could have been redesigned for areas unsuited to agriculture—but that was not done at the start and had to be painfully worked out for decades. So optimistic in their 1850s society-forming zeal, Republicans had lost much of their idealism after a grueling Civil War and frustrating society-reforming work in the postwar South. Yet colonial regions were sure to have bitter grievances, which Republicans who would not prevent dependency would have to deal with for decades to come.

Railroads created economic regions by lowering freight-hauling costs—from nearly fifteen dollars per ton per mile by wagon down to three or four pennies per ton per mile by rail—enabling shippers to market their iron ore, flour, butter, or lumber in distant cities that earlier were beyond their reach.[15] Year-round rail service overcame Minnesota's prior isolation due to its distance from eastern markets and due to the annual five-month winter freeze-up. For prairie and pines areas beyond navigable waters, the trains made economic exports possible. If all had been farm areas, then railroads would have created one region by evening out the disparities in transportation—making river-less farms equal to river-served ones. Minnesota's varied landscapes meant different natural resources; trains enabled each area to specialize in its resource, to use its comparative advantage in some crop or mineral or tree, and to import needed goods that other areas could better produce. Railroads created economic regions.

That posed a problem. Ideally, a state was a union of interests; for example, Iowa was agricultural in almost all its corners. Minnesota was not a homogeneous landscape. When railroads enabled different areas to specialize, irreconcilable regions were created not so dissimilar from the North and South that fought the Civil War.

The economic imbalance of concentrated land ownership also contributed to the rapid depletion of the state's natural resources. The state's future generations were a 'region' not represented in its current politics. A large firm owning thousands of forested acres had a strong economic interest in clear-cutting it and letting it go back to the government as tax-delinquent land—unlike parents intent on passing on a small acreage as an inheritance to sons and daughters. A local society with schools, churches, and other institutions to perpetuate might have insisted that the long-term future of the forest resource be protected. Large companies, often owned by Minneapolis or St. Paul investors, had few such concerns. The peak of Minnesota's lumber production came as early as 1905, followed by a long decline.[16]

A Survey of the State's Dissimilar Regions: 1) The Dairy Region

A clockwise 'swing around the circle'—starting in Southeastern Minnesota—will achieve a survey of these regions. What brought southeastern farmers into wheat raising was not the railroads but the wartime increase in the price of wheat from about 50¢ in 1861 to $1.50 in 1866. The census showed wheat production in 1869 concentrated in the counties just west of the Mississippi (Houston, Winona, Wabasha, Goodhue, Dakota) and in the interior counties of Fillmore and Olmsted.[17] An article in *Harper's Monthly Magazine* (January 1868) described the intense activity of wheat harvest in St. Charles (western Winona County) in August-September 1867, as migratory farm laborers poured in on the train, townspeople went to the fields to help, crop yields approached 22 bushels an acre, "150 wagonloads of wheat" came into town per day, and the railcars had to carry out up to 8,000 bushels of wheat per day to prevent the town's grain elevator from overflowing. Profits of 90¢ per bushel did push St. Charles society to frenzied economic activity for a month or so—the author noted that the migratory hands swore to drown out their Methodist farmer-employer's dinner prayer— but the income supported a balanced society that returned to religious, social, cultural, and political pursuits in other months.[18]

This southeastern region did not remain with wheat but turned to dairying in the late 1870s and early 1880s. By then, twenty years of one-crop farming had exhausted the soils and lowered yields to eleven bushels an acre, locusts swarmed over the wheat fields in the mid-1870s, and railroads to the Red River Valley brought competition from these new farms on virgin soils.[19] Farmers in upstate New York, Ohio, Illinois, and Wisconsin had set the pattern of switching old wheat areas to dairying with this innovation: many farmers delivered milk to their association's cheesemaking or buttermaking factory. In the early 1880s, the centrifugal separator was introduced to separate cream from skim milk in higher volumes more efficiently. Urban growth in the East meant potential purchasers; the railroad could bring dairy products to them. Wisconsin had seized the cheese market, but the younger state could specialize in butter.[20]

Yet, this southeastern society had to move collectively to dairying in order to gain from these new opportunities. The religious, law-abiding, self-governing society the pioneers formed now became essential to its economy, as its members had to sacrifice some short-term personal interests, take economic risks in forming cooperatives, obey milk-handling and cow-feeding rules, participate in tiresome meetings and elections, and trust neighbors to do the same. The success of dairy cooperatives often depended on intangible social virtues more than on soil fertility or proximity to markets. The state's model cooperative creamery at Clarks Grove began in the Danish Baptist church and was greatly aided by ethnic and religious solidarity. Each for its own reasons, the University of Minnesota and the

Republicans used Clarks Grove and other models to urge farmers to form cooperative creameries. Nearly 150 existed by 1894—most in southern Minnesota. In this dairy region, farmers escaped dependency on Twin Cities business leaders by forming cooperatives, controlling the making and marketing of butter and cheese, starting crossroads communities every five or six miles that they also ran, and retaining the dense settlement needed to support schools, churches, and ethnic institutions. When land ownership alone did not suffice, due to the risks and failures of wheat, the society shaped by the Ordinances' land laws survived by using cooperatives' by-laws to create its own local economic units, which worked alongside family, school, church, and government.[21]

A distinctive landscape and lifestyle marked this region: numerous farms of 80 or 160 acres, red barns dotting the landscape, small herds of one or two dozen milk cows heading to the barn twice a day to be milked, horse-drawn wagons filled with milk cans heading to the crossroad creamery whose smokestack could be seen in the distance. At the creamery, wagons waited to unload, the buttermaker hurried here and there, and departing wagons brought skim milk home to feed to pigs or calves. A crossroads store nearby did not need to sell on credit, for its customers received a monthly check from the creamery for their milk. The cooperative's own wagon loaded with butter tubs left each week for the nearest railroad depot to ship the butter to commission merchants in Philadelphia or New York. Late in the month, the cooperative's "officers me[t], figure[d] up the amount of milk received, the butter made, and the money received and expended, all for the previous month. Each patron receives a check in proportion to the amount of milk furnished" by that farmer. In January, members went to a nearby hall or schoolhouse for their annual meeting to elect officers. Talk was in German, Danish, or Norwegian, for the five-mile-limit on hauling milk by wagon (lest it spoil) meant that a creamery's area often coincided with an ethnic enclave.[22]

2) The New Wheat-Growing Region in Western Minnesota

Wheat-raising migrated to the west and northwest to form a second region in and near the Upper Minnesota and Red River valleys. Unlike the dairy region, this one was created by the railroads and often ruled by them. Settlement would have come slowly, eventually, but railroads needed to sell their land grants quickly to finance further construction. They could not wait. The SP&P and NP distributed promotional literature in Europe, sent agents like Hans Mattson to Scandinavia to recruit immigrants, often gave free or reduced rail tickets to settlers, built dormitories to house new arrivals, and provided rail-construction jobs that helped immigrants raise funds needed to buy land and build houses. The "two railroads employed more than five thousand construction workers in the Red River Valley during 1872."[23] Inadvertently aiding their efforts were the flour millers of Minneapolis who were innovating a new process method of milling spring wheat that raised the value of spring wheat compared to winter wheat. Its winters were too severe to grow winter wheat, so the Red River Valley 's fertile black soils had to grow spring wheat, and the millers made what had been spring wheat's disadvantage into a plus. Minneapolis mills now had an almost insatiable demand for spring wheat.[24]

The NP added a promotional strategy the Ordinances surely never envisioned: the encouragement of gigantic 'bonanza' wheat farms as very visible signs "that capital could be engaged as successfully in raising wheat as in cotton growing or in sugar plantations." But crooked management, shoddy construction, and excess expenditures landed the NP in bankruptcy and the nation in depression in 1873. To rescue itself, the NP offered its bondholders an irresistible deal: exchange bonds worth only $20 for $110 worth of NP land. Large bondholders acquired thousands of acres and hired managers and workers to raise wheat on a hitherto-unimagined scale. Many bonanza farms were in Dakota Territory. Some were in Minnesota: Donaldson's 33,000-acre farm near Kennedy yielded a quarter of a million bushels of wheat in 1885, railroad magnate James J. Hill had two farms totaling 20,000 acres in Kittson County, and several investors had smaller ones.[25] These bonanza farms showed the value of the new horse-drawn, steam-powered machinery out on the prairie, where there was nothing to block the plowing, harrowing, seeding, harvesting, and threshing. President Rutherford B. Hayes visited a bonanza farm in September 1878, bringing the valley to the attention of the nation's writers and journalists, who seemed to love exaggerated tales of miles-long furrows. All these factors— railroads, new-process milling, farm machinery, and promotion—turned the valley and much of western Minnesota to commercial wheat farming from 1876 to 1878.[26]

This small-grains economy yielded a landscape and lifestyle of distance. Farms of 160 to 320 acres, with a few over 500 acres, took advantage of the fertile and flat lands that were easily cleared by the horse-drawn machines.

Seen from miles away, they looked like children's toys, scattered and idyllic; the two-story wooden houses, small horse barns, and sheds looked like dry-goods boxes scattered on the horizon. Every seven miles or so along the rail line, a wooden grain elevator might be glimpsed, but it might not signal a true trading town—farmers came several times a year, not daily. Between rail lines it might be ten miles to an elevator because grain could be hauled long distances. Schools and churches were not always at elevator sites—they had to be closer than seven or ten miles apart, and the sparse population might not support the number needed to build an educated, churched society. School terms were three to five months, mostly in winter when parents had less need for their children's farm labor. Farming did not run in daily cycles, like dairying, but in yearly cycles. Plowing began in the fall and might be finished the next spring when harrows broke up the clods to prepare for seeding in late April or in May. Oats were harvested in late July, wheat in August, and a small farmer waited to hire a threshing crew and steam-powered threshing machine in September or October (threshers gave bonanza farms first crack) unless he joined others in a 'ring' to buy and run their own machine. He then drove the yellow grain to town, and this once-a-year payday had to retire a year's worth of debts to merchants.[27]

Storage, transport, and milling of the wheat farmers' crop were controlled by what looked like an interlocking set of monopolies. Often, only one railroad served a given area, or its rival was a prohibitive distance away. That railroad preferred the predictability offered by a 'line' elevator company that owned dozens of elevators along one rail line—perhaps the only one in a given town. Railroads did not suffer by the loss of grain-buying competition, but gained by having a reliable, proven grain-handler to partner with during the hectic harvest season. Minneapolis' flour millers did not want competition driving up the price of wheat. They owned parts of the lines, including the Pillsbury and Hurlbut line, "the most powerful in the state" around 1880, and through their Millers Association (1876-86), they cooperated in purchasing wheat so as not to bid against each other and drive up the price. Farmers could sell to elevators on the NP that shipped to Duluth, but there were NP line elevators. This second region felt "ruled"—an "invading army" set up forts every seven miles and foraged on the "tributary country."[28] Vesta's farmers were soon to get an independent elevator, but "a locomotive and a caboose full of men appeared alongside" the half-built structure. "Cables were hastily attached to the timbers, the locomotive began panting. . . . The building was soon a wreck."[29] Railroads ruled.

Englishman Charles Beadle Visits Minnesota, 1887

"On the train from Winnipeg to St. Paul we met a very intelligent Scotch farmer . . . he had just bought a section, 640 acres, on the northern border of Minnesota, which he cropped entirely with wheat. He said he and his four sons did most of the work; that they ploughed with four horses eleven hours a day, turning a 14-inch furrow; that in the flat country there was nothing to hinder the cultivation."[30]

3) The Rough-and-Tumble Logging Region of Northern Minnesota

As it headed east to Duluth, the NP cut through the third region, the logging one. To lumbermen, the king of trees was the white pine, growing 100 to 160 feet tall and up to three feet in diameter, with straight-grained wood that could be easily sawn or split for siding, planks, beams, or shingles. Lightweight, it would float downriver to sawmills. The most and best white pine grew in a 30-mile-wide swath, a crescent that began near Duluth, then ran 100 miles southwest and around the south shore of Mille Lacs Lake, then back north 100 miles through Brainerd and up toward Grand Rapids. The NP crossed the crescent twice—at Brainerd and at Carlton.[31] Lesser stands of white pine were scattered throughout the coniferous area, and the entire area (less the iron ranges) formed the logging region.

Railroads had not created this logging region. The search for the king of trees began well before the Civil War along the upper reaches of major streams such as the St. Croix and the Rum rivers. After the war, lumbermen pushed up into the tributaries. Logging was a winter activity: swampy lands were accessible then; horses could pull sleds laden with whole logs down ice roads to a piling area near a stream, where they awaited the spring thaw and a tumultuous "drive" downriver to a sawmill. Areas near streams could be logged this way, but extensive logging of the entire region depended on logging railroads—the first was built near Carlton in 1886—to bring logs to mills where no river reached. In addition, regular railroads made possible sawmills in interior areas, for the boards could be economically shipped out by rail to distant markets. It did not pay to build a regular railroad just for logging, but with the NP and, later, the mining railroads built for other purposes, lumbermen could use the already-existing cars and the railroad could use the income. A sawmill was stationary and led to an inhabited town, but lumber camps moved and employed a transient male, mainly bachelor workforce that had little inclination to settle down, own a home, or start schools and churches—not at the moment anyway. So railroads through this region did not create new towns every few miles.[32]

Buried deep in dense woods, the lumber camp's few log buildings were not noticeable parts of the landscape unless you stood by them. Several dozen to several hundred lumberjacks lived there for nine months, eating prodigiously, obeying the company's strict rules, playing cards, telling stories, sleeping their eight hours, then heading out to the snowy woods to chop down trees, cut away branches, saw them into 18½-foot lengths, load them onto horse-drawn sleds, and lead the horses to the piling area. Then it was back to camp for more grub. In the spring, they boarded a wanigan, a wooden house boat "about ten feet wide by twenty-five feet long" that housed twenty-five lumberjacks for the downriver 'drive.' They often only

Logging on the St. Croix River at Taylor's Falls, 1865. Stereopticon photograph by B. F. Upton. *Courtesy of Moira F. Harris.*

slept in it, because they worked wet, dangerous, fast-paced days directing a torrent of trees, breaking up logjams, and helping to float the white 'cork' pine safely to the boom area or the sawmill.[33]

Small towns grew up around many sawmills, and the inhabitants likely wished they had not when the laid-off lumberjacks poured in during late spring. If some residents had created a religious, moral society, it had to go into hiding for a few weeks as 'jacks' spent their winter's wages at the saloons and brothels that the moral residents could not eliminate. "Townsfolk kept children indoors" at one northern town, "and respectable women avoided the [illicit] 'business districts'. . . . [t]he prone forms of lumberjacks sleeping off benders littered haylofts, horse stalls, alleys, sheds, and even the foul, muddy gutters."[34]

Cloquet was one such sawmill town, located at Knife Falls on the St. Louis River. Its population soared from 93 in 1880 to 911 in 1885 and then to 2,530 in 1890. It began nearly as a company town, as C.N. Nelson & Company ran "two large sawmills," had "vast drying yards," and became the Upper Midwest's "ninth largest lumber producer" by 1888. This was a noticeable landscape— "the river choked with logs, sprawling mill sites with smoke belching . . . huge piles of drying lumber, a persistent whine of the great saws cutting wood, punctuated by the scream of mill whistles." Nelson and another mill owner tried to dry out Cloquet by preventing landowners on both sides of the St. Louis from selling alcohol, but a fellow bought an island in the middle and marketed lots to saloonkeepers, madams, and boarding house operators. Walking across floating logs was more difficult on the inebriated return trip from the island. The permanent residents on the south bank worked for an educated and moral society; by 1890, Cloquet had two schools and Catholic (1882), Presbyterian (1884), and Swedish Lutheran (1888) churches, but the banks of good taste and morality were seasonally flooded by lumberjacks on a spree.[35] Much the same could be said of other urban centers in the logging region—Virginia, Bemidji, Little Falls, Grand Rapids.

4) The Early Iron Mining Region of Northern Minnesota

Railroads serving sawmill towns and enabling the lumbermen to reach the interior were first built to haul iron ore from the Vermilion and Mesabi ranges, the fourth region, to Lake Superior. Railroads made this iron region possible; the two ranges were more than fifty miles from usable harbors on Superior, and no navigable rivers could float ore-laden barges to the lake. Developed by Pennsylvania investor Charlemagne Tower, the Vermilion came first, and its

Open-pit iron ore mine at Biwabik, Minnesota, 1895.
Courtesy of the Minnesota Historical Society.

first ore went out on the Duluth and Iron Range (D&IR) railroad to the new
port of Two Harbors on July 31, 1884. Ironically, grading crews had exposed
the "Red Pan Cut" at Mesaba Station where the D&IR crossed the Mesabi
range. This obvious iron ore deposit encouraged exploration on the Mesabi.
The Mesabi's more horizontal, soft deposits close to the surface (and
occasionally on it) did not fit geologists' stereotype of deep veins of hard-rock
ore—the Vermilion had fit that model—and development was delayed. Not
until 1892 did Duluth's Merritt brothers transport the first ore from their
Mountain Iron mine via their Duluth, Missabe, and Northern (DM&N)
railroad to Superior. A year later, they were using docks they built in Duluth.[36]

The two ranges exhibited different types of mining. At the Vermilion's
Soudan mine with its vertical vein of iron ore, crews used dynamite to
excavate deep shafts that ultimately reached 2,000 feet below ground, then
dug or dynamited the ore loose, and brought it up through "a main hoisting
shaft." On the Mesabi, a thick strata of glacial drift, including boulders,
covered the horizontal deposits. Once crews removed the drift, a steam shovel
could load the "soft powdery ore" and place it in rail cars right at the open-
pit mine. Underground shafts were also dug here, but open pits with terraces
and rail tracks bringing cars into the pit became the characteristic Mesabi
method. It was also the cheapest. Open-pit mining cost only five cents to ten

cents to remove one ton of ore, while the underground mining cost thirty-five to fifty cents per ton. Low cost and ease of mining made the Mesabi the "poor man's range" that "attracted hundreds of mining firms to the newly opened Mesabi, where opportunities for explorers with limited capital seemed promising." The seven Merritt brothers began capital "poor" compared to Tower. The Mesabi might have become an egalitarian, locally-run, balanced society not unlike the small-farm dairy and wheat regions, but the Panic of 1893 drove the Merritts and smaller operators to the wall. By 1900, four companies headed by a group of ten men (only three were Minnesotans) controlled the Vermilion and Mesabi ranges.[37] This region was ruled from 'overseas'—Cleveland and Pittsburgh across the Great Lakes.

Their landscapes differed, but the mining lifestyle was similar on both ranges. Transient exploration camps of tents became semi-permanent mining camps of log buildings—bunk houses and cooks' shanties—until a few miners' families arrived and mining companies constructed company towns, called 'locations,' with wood-sided, two-story houses for married workers to rent. Except for its own stores, the company kept out businesses and also saloons and brothels. Away from locations, profit-minded men platted town sites and sold lots to saloonkeepers, boarding house operators, and others who catered to a population of single males.[38] In 1885, there were 250 men in this area for every 100 women; in some ethnic groups the sex ratio was 25 men to 1 woman. Whether bachelors and men who had temporarily left their wives in Europe, many men were so-called "birds of passage" planning to return to Europe.[39] Early Hibbing had "mud streets, plank sidewalks, high upon cedar posts; upon which passed miners, lumberjacks, prospectors, gamblers and camp followers of various sorts." One street in Eveleth was "almost a solid row of large boarding, tenement and bath houses . . . nearly all over crowded, with a number of home laundries . . . and a row of cow sheds and much used privies" near the alley. Dysentery and diphtheria ravaged the towns.[40] Neither camps, locations, nor towns made for a settled, moral society.

For its first twenty years (1884–1904), this fourth region seemed easily ruled by the iron mining companies and railroads. They planned to stay while many of their workers did not; their managers spoke and wrote English while the polyglot workforce lacked English-language skills and, thus, the ability to cooperate to form unions. Most workers were transient renters and wage workers who had no resources to stand up to the company, and the range towns were dependent on the companies for their existence.

5) *The Twin Cities Rule Other Regions Together But Do Not Resemble Each Other*

The fifth region, the urban core, ruled the others—except the mining region, which was ruled from 'overseas' Cleveland and Pittsburgh. The Mississippi River had created this core region; the great river's effective head of navigation became St. Paul, and its waterfall spawned St. Anthony and Minneapolis on its east and west sides. Nearby, incoming tributaries brought logs down the Rum and St. Croix rivers and various commodities down the Minnesota. Water-borne advantages remained important. The waterpower of St. Anthony Falls made Minneapolis first the nation's number one sawmilling city and then its chief flour-milling city. Several industries grew up to supply the mills and use the waterpower: a hydroelectric plant, a woolen mill, iron works companies making mill machinery, coopers, and bag makers. The grain exchange provided a forum for the purchase and sale of wheat. Professional and service businesses developed around the milling industry as well: printers, lawyers, bankers, brokers. A canal to channel tumbling waterpower to more sites on the west bank was built and expanded from 1857 to 1885.[41] By comparison, the east side of the river stagnated, and Minneapolis absorbed St. Anthony in 1872.

The 1880 census showed the new city with a population of 46,000— about 5,000 more than St. Paul, which was displeased. These were not identical twins; feelings between them were often not even fraternal. On September 3, 1883, they staged rival shows for NP President Henry Villard to celebrate the NP's completion to the Pacific, and Nicolaus Mohr was there from Germany to witness both shows. Ten years later, they celebrated the completion of Hill's Great Northern line to the Pacific Coast.

Nicolaus Mohr Visits Minneapolis for the NP Festival

"Today President Arthur, former President Grant, and various secretaries and American state officials of the highest rank were a part of our Villard party. . . . Each [city] has tried to demonstrate that it will be capable of dominating the massive extra territory which the railroad is now opening up. Thus any cooperation between the cities on this venture was rendered impossible. So there was a parade in St. Paul and another parade in Minneapolis . . . . 'Wheat is king and the Northern

Pacific its throne' was the motto used to introduce the industries of Minneapolis. . . . I simply cannot enumerate all we saw . . . and my hand was lame from taking notes."[42]

St. Paul's economy focused on wholesaling. In the early 1870s it had "ninety wholesaling houses specializing in dry goods, grocery, and hardware" plus eighty-eight factories selling goods to wholesalers. St. Paul's wholesalers freed Minnesota from being reliant on Chicago's. Railroads took wholesalers' traveling salesmen out to the small towns of western Wisconsin, Minnesota, and Dakota, and brought retailers and buyers in to St. Paul, which offered eight hundred saloons and "a lively nightlife" to help attract the men away from home. Contributing to the capital's prosperity, several railroads were headquartered in St. Paul.[43]

Minneapolis gained by milling's multiplier effects, including the creation of auxiliary industries to supply the mills—hiring more workers led to more personal income in the city and to more consumer spending at its stores, who then had to hire more workers, etc. With the new-process method, the city's 1890 flour output was thirty-five times its 1870 output. Up to 40 percent of the flour was exported, as Minneapolis' brands gained a reputation in Europe. The city became the nation's (and the world's) largest flour-mill

Robert Zins presented the history of South St. Paul in his 2006 outdoor mural. Railroads brought cattle to the stockyards and the Armour meatpacking plant. Cattle sellers deposited their cash in the Stockyards National Bank, shown in the center of the painting. *Courtesy of Moira F. Harris.*

Early flour mills on Hennepin Island, at St. Anthony Falls, 1860.
Courtesy of the Minnesota Historical Society.

center. Railroads granted millers a 'milling-in-transit' privilege: one freight charge from the elevator to the eastern market for the flour—not one charge for the incoming wheat and a second one for outgoing flour. Still dissatisfied, the millers built their own Soo Line railroad to Sault Ste. Marie in order to bypass Chicago railroads and St. Paulite James J. Hill's railroad to Duluth. In 1882, the *London Times* reported that Minneapolis' mills produced 28,000 barrels of flour per day and ground 20 million bushels of wheat per year, from 1.25 million acres of farmland.[44]

The urban landscape expanded. In St. Paul, the better residential districts headed west on stylish Summit Avenue toward the distant Mississippi and the cross-river rival. In Minneapolis, the prosperous moved away from the dusty mills and also southwestward (not east toward St. Paul!), toward the finest housing district along a chain of lakes from Cedar Lake and Lake of the Isles to Calhoun and Harriet (it took decades to reach the latter). Both cities' cultural life flowered, as orchestras, libraries, art collections, country clubs, and theaters transformed the crude frontier towns into would-be sophisticated cities. The hard material underpinnings of their prosperity were not hidden. A line of rail facilities, switching yards, and roundhouses connected the two cities and filled in part of the un-built area between them called the Midway district. The social atmosphere of a sawmill city appeared in Minneapolis' Gateway District next to the sawmills and flour mills and near the Union Depot. Here, the seasonal and migrant workers from several Minnesota regions—farm laborers laid off for the winter, lumberjacks with an idle summer on their hands, railroad workers between jobs—drank at bars, slept in cheap rooming houses, and generally caroused.[45] This core region ruled the others, but its working class was ruled also by the elites who ran the wholesaling houses, flour mills, railroad headquarters, and factories.

1. "granted lands and specified routes," Folwell, *History of Minnesota*, Vol. II, 38 and map on following page; Blegen, *Minnesota*, 296-97. The names indicated are different than the 1857 ones.

2. "made progress," Blegen, *Minnesota*, 297-99; Wills, *Boosters, Hustlers, and Speculators*, 116-17, 133, 135; M. John Lubetkin, "'Twenty-Six Feet and No Bottom,': Surveying and Constructing the Northern Pacific Railroad," *Minnesota History*, Vol. 60, No. 1 (Spring 2006), 15.

3. "state constitution allowed," Article 15, Section 1 ("Seat of government") of state constitution.

4. "passed a bill," Folwell, *History of Minnesota*, Vol. III, 8-10; *Minneapolis Daily Tribune*, 25 February (1), 28 February (1), both 1869; *St. Paul Daily Pioneer*, 25 February (1), 5 March (2), both 1869.

5. "future growth of the state," *Minneapolis Daily Tribune*, 6 March (2) and 7 March (1), both 1869.

6. "special freight rates," Margaret Snyder, *The Chosen Valley: The Story of a Pioneer Town* (New York: W. W. Norton, 1948), 302-10.

7. "began to complain," Steven J. Keillor, *Cooperative Commonwealth: Co-Ops in Rural Minnesota, 1859–1939* (St. Paul: Minnesota Historical Society Press, 2000), 65-66.

8. "a St. Paul lawyer," this speech is in Box 11 of the Cushman K. Davis Papers, MHS.

9. "negotiated a series of treaties," Folwell, *History of Minnesota*, Vol. I, 305-07, map facing page 324; Blegen, *Minnesota*, 171-73; Melissa L. Meyer, *The White Earth Tragedy: Ethnicity and Dispossession at a Minnesota Anishinaabe Reservation, 1889–1920* (Lincoln, Nebraska: University of Nebraska Press, 1994), 35-43.

10. "a crew surveying," Lubetkin, "Twenty-Six Feet and No Bottom," 4-17.

11. "Winchell recalled," Newton H. Winchell and Horace V. Winchell, *The Iron Ores of Minnesota, Their Geology, Discovery, Development, Qualities and Origin, and Comparison with Those of Other Ranges* (Minneapolis: Harrison & Smith, 1891), 166. For early knowledge of iron ores, see William Watts Folwell, *History of Minnesota:* Vol. IV, revised ed. (St. Paul: Minnesota Historical Society, 1969), 2-4, 8; and David A. Walker, *Iron Frontier: The Discovery and Early Development of Minnesota's Three Ranges* (St. Paul: Minnesota Historical Society Press, 1979), 18-20.

12. "South of Duluth," Theodore C. Blegen and Philip D. Jordan eds., *With Various Voices: Recordings of North Star Life* (St. Paul: Itasca Press, 1949), 231, 232, 233.

13. "to be roamed over," Folwell, *History of Minnesota*, Vol. I, 406-07 (also, "never to be

permanently settled").

14. "Hired to investigate," these reports are quoted and summarized in Fremont P. Wirth, *The Discovery and Exploitation of the Minnesota Iron Lands* (Cedar Rapids, Iowa: Torch Press, 1937), 91, 95, 143-44. From maps showing the townships' location, see Walker, *Iron Frontier*, 55, 92-93. Marshall's report is also quoted in Folwell, *History of Minnesota*, Vol. IV, 14 (he describes the 1872 mining law on 13 and other land-claim abuses on 15). For the same frauds in the pine land region, see Folwell, *History of Minnesota*, Vol. II, 332-33.

15. "freight-hauling costs," Willard W. Cochrane, *The Development of American Agriculture: A Historical Approach* (Minneapolis: University of Minnesota Press, 1979), 216, 220.

16. "1905," Thomas J. Baerwald, "Forces at Work on the Landscape," in Clifford E. Clark, Jr., *Minnesota in a Century of Change: The State and Its People Since 1900* (St. Paul: Minnesota Historical Society Press, 1989), 33.

17. "wartime increase in price" and "census," Edward Van Dyke Robinson, *Early Economic Conditions and the Development of Agriculture in Minnesota* (Minneapolis: University of Minnesota, 1915), 59, 62, 65.

18. "An article," G. W. Schatzel, "Among the Wheat-Fields of Minnesota," reprinted in Blegen and Jordan, eds., *With Various Voices*, 143-64 (especially 151, 155, 160-61, 162).

19. "did not remain with wheat," Robinson, *Early Economic Conditions*, 76.

20. "set the pattern," Keillor, *Cooperative Commonwealth*, 100-09.

21. "move collectively to dairying," Keillor, *Cooperative Commonwealth*, 112-17, 119-22, 123-24, 130-31, 133-36, 144-46.

22. "distinctive landscape and lifestyle," based generally on Keillor, *Cooperative Commonwealth*, 112-46 (quoting Lt. Governor John Gibbs on 139).

23. "this one was created by the railroads," Stanley Norman Murray, *The Valley Comes of Age: A History of Agriculture in the Valley of the Red River of the North, 1812–1920* (Fargo: North Dakota Institute for Regional Studies, 1967), 65-68. Of course, some workers were employed on the Dakota side of the river.

24. "aiding their efforts," Henrietta M. Larson, *The Wheat Market and the Farmer in Minnesota 1858–1900*, reprint ed. (New York: AMS Press, 1969), 128-31.

25. "added a promotional strategy," Murray, *Valley Comes of Age*, 104-08, 132-33, 136.

26. "bonanza farms," Murray, *Valley Comes of Age*, 109, 121, 139-41; Hiram M. Drache, *The Day of the Bonanza: A History of Bonanza Farming in the Red River Valley of the North* (Fargo: North Dakota Institute for Regional Studies, 1964), 70-71, 119-22.

27. "a landscape and lifestyle of distance," this description is based on Drache, *Day of the Bonanza*, 119-22; Hiram M. Drache, *The Challenge of the Prairie: Life and Times of Red River Pioneers* (Fargo: North Dakota Institute for Regional Studies, 1970), 180-86, 253-58, 295-98; Murray, *Valley Comes of Age*, 134 (Table V).

28. "an interlocking set of monopolies," Larson, *Wheat Market and the Farmer*, 132-36, 142-44; Keillor, *Cooperative Commonwealth*, 191-201.

29. "Vesta's farmers," Keillor, *Cooperative Commonwealth*, 191 (quoting the *Cottonwood County Citizen*). Vesta is in Redwood County.

30. "Charles Beadle," "An Englishman in Minnesota, 1887," *Minnesota History*, Vol. 6 (1925), 46-48.

31. "the king of trees," Lass, *Minnesota*, 170, 314 (map showing "white pine crescent"); Francis M. Carroll, *Crossroads in Time: A History of Carlton County, Minnesota* (Cloquet, Minnesota: Carlton County Historical Society, 1987), 131.

32. "search for the king of trees," Lass, *Minnesota*, 170-73; Carroll, *Crossroads in Time*, 129-31, 135, 137, 141; Jeff Forester, *The Forest for the Trees: How Humans Shaped the North Woods* (St. Paul: Minnesota Historical Society, 2004), 26-27, 68-80; Michael Williams, *Americans and*

their forests: A historical geography (New York: Cambridge University Press, 1989), 210-17.

33. "Buried deep in dense woods," *Forester, Forest for the Trees*, 68-84.

34. "Small towns grew up," Forester, *Forest for the Trees*, 68, 84-85.

35. "Cloquet," Carroll, *Crossroads in Time*, 140-41 (quoted), 144 (quoted), 205, 210, 212-14; Paul Gerin Fahlstrom, *Old Cloquet, Minnesota: White Pine Capital of the World* (Baltimore: Gateway Press, 1997), 20, 27, 63.

36. "iron region possible," Walker, *Iron Frontier*, 49, 57-58, 76, 87, 88, 105-06, 116-17.

37. "The two ranges," Walker, *Iron Frontier*, 68, 85, 131-34, 138, 202.

38. "mining lifestyle," Walker, *Iron Frontier*, 89; Arnold R. Alanen, "Years of Change on the Iron Range," in Clifford E. Clark, Jr., *Minnesota in a Century of Change: The State and Its People Since 1900* (St. Paul: Minnesota Historical Society Press, 1989), 155-94.

39. "250 men," Holmquist, ed., *They Chose Minnesota*, 387-88.

40. "Early Hibbing," Alanan, "Years of Change," 163.

41. "St. Anthony Falls," Shannon M. Pennefeather, ed., *Mill City: A Visual History of the Minneapolis Mill District* (St. Paul: Minnesota Historical Society Press, 2003).

42. "Mohr visits," Nicolaus Mohr, *Excursion Through America* (Lakeside Classics, 1973), 70-72, 83, 84, 85, 94.

43. "St. Paul's economy," Wills, *Boosters, Hustlers, & Speculators*, 142, 143 (quoted); Wingerd, *Claiming the City*, 49 (quoted).

44. "milling's multiplier effects," David B. Danbom, "Flour Power: The Significance of Flour Milling at the Falls," *Minnesota History*, Vol. 58, Nos. 5 & 6 (Spring/Summer 2003), 273, 278; John Storck and Walter Dorwin Teague, *Flour for Man's Bread: A History of Milling* (Minneapolis: University of Minnesota Press, 1952), 271; *London Times*, 3 February 1882, 3.

45. "social atmosphere," Pennefeather, ed., *Mill City*, 60.

A State of Many Nations

Creating economic regions meant populating them with farmers and laborers doing tasks needed for any economic activity. In 1865, the line of settlement had not progressed much beyond the Blue Earth River from Blue Earth City to Mankato, then northwest to New Ulm and north to Hutchinson and St. Cloud.[1] Many settlers who fled the Dakota warriors had not returned to those areas. In May 1865, Indians murdered a farm family just east of the Blue Earth and panicked pioneers on this frontier again.[2] Competing with other states to attract settlers, Minnesota was handicapped by its location to the north of the major east-west migration routes; its competitors pointed to its harsh winters and their balmier climates to sway migrants' decisions. Yankees and New Yorkers were used to cold winters, but that migration dried up after the Civil War.[3] Minnesota had to seek immigrants from northern Europe. Yet the state's leaders seemed confident that ethnic regions could be 'ruled' as easily as economic regions—by a dominant Yankee class, its Republican party, and its dominant core area of St. Anthony-St. Paul-St. Croix.

Hans Mattson's activities in 1866-71 show how the state's leaders, railroads, and ethnic groups already in the state cooperated to recruit immigrants. A farm boy from Skåne in southern Sweden, he pioneered in Vasa, served in the Civil War, and became the Third Minnesota's Colonel, earning the respect of Old Stock leaders in his Republican party. Hearing that rival states enticed Scandinavian immigrants arriving at Chicago or Milwaukee, Governor Marshall appointed Mattson to go there in July 1866 to protect them from dishonest agents and to "advise and assist [them] on to Minnesota." People without knowledge of English or America were cheated, and honest Mattson did aid them—partly by giving them free railroad tickets to Minnesota , which the railroads donated. Reporting to Marshall, Mattson called for a state agency to promote immigration and protect immigrants.

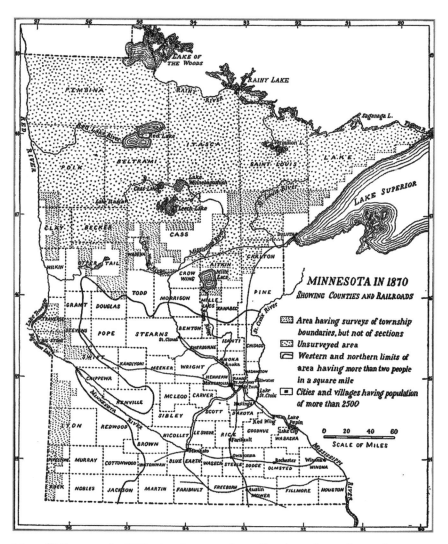

Map of Minnesota in 1870, showing counties, railroads, and population density. *From W. W. Folwell,* A History of Minnesota, *Vol. III.*

The State Board of Immigration was set up in 1867. Marshall appointed Mattson as its secretary. One of his first tasks was to organize a relief effort to save Scandinavian settlers near the Upper Minnesota River from starvation. An 1866 drought and lack of seeds for the 1867 crop year threatened to peel back a swath of sections-and-townships settlement. The state government hastened to prevent that.

Secretary Mattson's main task was to bring in new immigrants. At first, he wrote articles for Scandinavian-language newspapers stressing free government land under the Homestead Act located where the St. Paul & Pacific Railroad was laying track—thus offering immigrants future markets and present jobs. The SP&P's president informed Mattson that he wanted 1,000 Scandinavian workers for spring 1867 to work under "their own supervisors, not mixing them with the Irish." Through its agent's articles, the state offered them detailed advice: form cooperating groups to clear land and build cabins, bring at least $100, buy land near compatriots and do it by May 31, the first year have three men work for the railroad while the fourth plows land, and then the 'company' could be safely disbanded in the fourth year. Calling for a farm-making cooperative, the state gave far more detailed advice than the Ordinances had, and it enlisted the railroad's aid.

In fall 1868, Mattson went to Sweden to recruit in person. His trip was financially backed by the state, the SP&P, a steamship line, and a Chicago Scandinavian bank. As a farm boy made Colonel, he was a walking advertisement for Minnesota, and Swedes thronged to see him. "People come from far away to see me as if I were a miracle." When he attended his uncle's funeral, "immense hordes of people had gathered by the houses along the road to see me." At a New Year's Eve party, the servant girls drew lots for the honor of serving him coffee, but the winner came back to the kitchen disappointed: "Oh, pshaw! He looks just like any other man!" Mattson encouraged this attention, for he was a walking 'pull factor' too, whose apparent wealth, rise in social standing, and public critique of Swedish conservatives and the Swedish army personified freedoms emigrants sought in America and suggested the opposite 'push factors' or reasons not to remain in Sweden—military service, dislike of the official class and aristocracy, rigid social-class inequalities, and widespread poverty following some disastrous harvests of the late 1860s. Eight hundred emigrants went to Minnesota with him the next spring.[4]

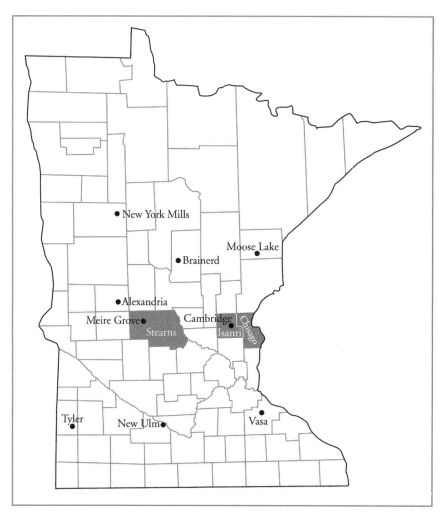

Map of Minnesota showing towns and counties that correlated to ethnic regions. Ethnic enclaves and settlements in Minnesota found Germans in New Ulm, Stearns County (especially Meire Grove), St. Paul, and in towns along the lower Mississippi River. Swedes settled in Vasa, Chisago and Isanti counties, and in both of the Twin Cities. Norwegians immigrated to Alexandria, southeastern Minnesota, the Twin Cities, and along Lake Superior's North Shore. Tyler was a Danish enclave, while New York Mills and Brainerd attracted Finnish immigrants.

The Germans: The Largest & Most Disunited Ethnic Group

Despite Mattson's considerable success, Germans were Minnesota's largest single immigrant group, if they were a single group at all, since Germany was not a unified nation until 1870-71. Many German speakers lived in other nations, and Germans were the most religiously divided ethnic group. Yet they had been longer established in the Eastern states than others, and a failed 1848 revolution brought hundreds of educated, skilled Forty-Eighters to the United States as migration to Minnesota began. For Mattson's role, the state cast two Forty-Eighters, friends Albert Wolff and Eduard Pelz, the state's immigration agent to Germany in 1869-71 (Wolff) and its main German-language pamphleteer and publisher (Pelz). They saw firsthand the push factors motivating Germans to emigrate. In German provinces where all heirs inherited equal shares of the family's land, a 'dwarf economy' of tiny farms forced many to contemplate emigration. Elsewhere, younger sons left with no land to inherit did likewise, as did males subject to the military draft. The failed revolution brought political refugees, joined by a patchwork of religious refugees fleeing the various churches dominating various districts, plus freethinkers fleeing religion in general. A 'German triangle' of Cincinnati, St. Louis, and Chicago-Milwaukee provided immigrants with stopping-off points and centers of supportive German institutions.[5]

German Minnesota was not a unified region.[6] German Americans studying English at a Chicago night school founded the society that founded New Ulm, the single most visible German city in the state and a center for freethinking anticlerical Turners. Minnesota's most visibly German rural area was the heavily Catholic Stearns County, whose founder, Father Franz Pierz, warned migrants that "to prove yourselves good Catholics do not bring with you any freethinkers, red republicans, atheists or agitators." German Catholics invaded New Ulm and made it "a center of Catholicity" by 1905, but the Turners did not penetrate Stearns County. A third group, German Lutherans, came to New Ulm and founded Dr. Martin Luther College in 1884. German Lutherans were not unified religiously but divided into six competing synods by 1882, as synods from Buffalo, Missouri, Iowa, Wisconsin, and Ohio came to start churches. The sixth, the Minnesota Synod, tried to unite Lutherans but succumbed to the invaders. There were German Methodists, Baptists, Presbyterians, and much else. Converting to an American church like Methodism—nonexistent in Germany and favoring a prohibition directly counter to German beer-drinking culture—meant partly abandoning German ethnicity. All this disunity made Germans less influential than their numbers suggest.[7]

German Minnesota began with Germans in the sequence of Mississippi River towns—Winona, Wabasha, Red Wing, Hastings, and St. Paul—supported by their rural compatriots in some inland townships in the southeastern counties. More resided in the lower Minnesota River towns of Shakopee, Jordan, Le Sueur, and St. Peter, and in the adjacent townships. New Ulm was their center on the upper river. North of the Minnesota a zig-zagging series of townships bearing names like Moltke, Bismarck, and Frankfort, and containing hamlets like Cologne, New Germany, and Hamburg linked the southern core to the Crow River Valley, then northwest to Stearns County. Farther west, isolated German concentrations developed near Millerville and southern Otter Tail County, also by the Dakota border at Nassau, and at scattered places elsewhere in the wheat region.[8] In the state's core area, St. Paul received the most German immigration, and it was as religiously diverse as elsewhere—six Catholic parishes for Germans, churches of the Lutheran synods, plus four German Methodist congregations, two Baptist churches, and a Turner presence. Minneapolis had this variety in smaller doses. Similarly, Stillwater's Dutchtown was a company town for workers at the Schulenberg and Boeckeler sawmill.[9]

The Ordinances' sections-and-townships system was well suited for the creation of German religious principalities across the rural landscape. If one group outnumbered other settlers even in one township, it could control a rural church or two, a public school, and perhaps a crossroads community with creamery and general store. Given the Catholic predominance in Stearns County (85 percent of its church members were Catholics by 1906), settlers allocated different townships to German Catholics from different provinces. Westphalians predominated in St. Augusta Township; Lower Bavarians, in Albany Township; Oldenburg settlers, in Grove Township; and Luxembourgers, in Luxemburg Township.[10] Concentrated German population helped maintain the use of the German language. Since "language saves the faith," Catholic churches and German Lutheran synods encouraged its use. In parts of Stearns County, one rarely heard English and rarely needed it for daily life.[11]

Central and eastern Stearns County thus became the state's most noticeable ethnic enclave, an area forty miles by thirty miles dominated by one church, one ethnic group, and one language. The cheap land, sure land titles, and local control of the Ordinances' system did result in the creation of an ordered rural society. Unexpectedly, historian Jon Gjerde notes, immigrants ordered it so as to "cordon themselves off from the developing American tradition," and to perpetuate Old World traditions seemingly at odds with the American one.[12] Dozens of smaller German enclaves (listed above) soon stretched across the dairying and wheat regions. 'Enclave' meant a place surrounded by immigrants from another nation; neither the Founders nor the state's leaders intended ethnic localities to perpetuate foreign traditions, but the settlements' leaders intended just that. As if to mark its territory, the Catholic Church set up 14-foot-high crosses around Stearns County in the 1860s that bore the words "Blessed is he who perseveres to the end"—encouragement to Catholics but an implied rebuke to Protestants whose ancestors left the Church. Protestant farmers did not even persevere on the land. They sold out and the county became even more a German Catholic enclave.[13]

Meire Grove in Stearns County illustrates the organic unity of the ethnic enclave. Settled by Catholics from Oldenburg and other provinces in northwest Germany, St. John the Baptist parish covered some thirty-three sections south of the town of Melrose. Some families from the British Isles and from Eastern states lived there in the 1860s, but they gradually sold out, and German Catholics owned 100 percent of the land by 1896. No other church existed in this area, and virtually all its people belonged to the Church of St. John the Baptist, whose services were conducted in German, as were the ordinary affairs of the people. Public school classes were taught in German by seminary-trained teachers overseen by the priest. The public school taught religion. The elected school board of Catholic men would hardly have it otherwise. Sons and daughters did not go on for higher education, which was seen as useless for farm families.

As the priest supervised the community, so the father ran the family and ordered his wife and children's farm work. Farmland was the foundation of the family and must not be risked by speculation, gambles in wheat, debts, a son's rebelliousness, or idleness. Fathers bought land from departing Protestants in order to distribute parcels of adjacent land to their sons. The railroad came to Melrose in 1871 and opened a market for wheat, but German farmers disliked wheat's wild price swings and Minneapolis millers' control. As dairying began in the 1880s, they switched to milk cows, especially purebred Holsteins. Their conservative, patriarchal discipline was well suited for the slow, steady accumulation of assets by the year-round grind of twice-a-day milking and constant care of herds. In 1897, they formed a cooperative creamery and secured control of the making and marketing of their crop, free from outside influence. The village of Meire Grove now offered the essential services a farmer needed: harness shop, blacksmiths, general stores, shoe shop, stables, and saloon. This self-contained enclave needed nothing from non-German non-Catholics and so could not be contaminated by their ways, languages, or beliefs.[14]

Such enclaves had not been the Ordinances' intent nor were they desired by many non-Germans. Assuming Anglo-Saxon ethnicity, English language, and Protestantism, the Founders had been very terse in the Ordinances, which negatively defined liberty as freedom *from* strong central governments, high taxes, and a landlord class. Taking for granted religion as a means to "Morality and knowledge," they had not foreseen an active religion forming a local society, warding off all secularism, and making the Ordinances a freedom *for* the creation of a European parish in America. They hoped families farming cheap land would build the *state*, not a church-ruled enclave. They assumed family ties but provided no means for strengthening these; their schools and state governments might weaken family. They sought stable, permanent settlers not speculators or temporary squatters, but, ironically, German Minnesotans so outpaced Yankee pioneers at stability and love of the land that the latter became squatters by comparison—eager to sell out to the land-hungry Germans. German Minnesotans achieved an initial victory but would have to watch out that the state, its schools, and its University did not reclaim lost ground and weaken the Catholic parish to achieve some broader American goal.[15]

The Scandinavians: Swedes, Norwegians & Danes, Whom Outsiders Saw As One

The second-largest immigrant group, the Swedes, did not deliberately organize such self-contained colonies. They emigrated from a cohesive nation religiously united by a shared Protestantism, even if pietist and Baptist dissenters opposed the Lutheran state church. A Protestant heritage of individual religious choice, based on an individual's own view of Scripture, combined with the American tradition of religious freedom and the Swedish state church's disinterest in actively organizing churches in Minnesota—all made the idea of a Swedish religious colony unlikely. Swedish immigration was less collective and corporate, as families came alone or in small groups.

In 1851, Per Andersson led a small group to the Chisago Lakes area thirty miles north of St. Paul, settling near Center City. With Isanti County next door, this 'Swedeland' became the most heavily Swedish rural district in the United States.[16] No one set out to make it that, but this land on the border between hardwood and pine forests was not desired by other groups, so Swedish settlements had room to expand. Religious disunity aided expansion, for dissenters led the early Swedish emigration and brought more Swedes here. Baptists who met opposition in Lutheran Chisago Lakes moved to Isanti, which became the most Baptist county in Minnesota. The issue of infant versus believers' baptism became the most divisive one among the state's Swedes, especially in Isanti where the two sides were evenly matched. The Lutherans' Augustana Synod dropped the state church's formalism but never became as low-church as the Baptist, Mission Covenant, or Free Mission people, and its pastors feared the periodic dissenter revivals that swept this rural area.[17]

Neither Baptist nor Lutheran pastors steered the local economy toward self-sufficiency to protect Swedish religious ways. Immigrant farmers soon switched from the barley grown in Sweden to the American crops of wheat, oats, and corn—and from draft horses to oxen for farm work. Isanti's sandy soils were ill suited to wheat. Potato growing for a local starch factory in Isanti County finally put agriculture on a firm foundation. Swedish-American farmers turned to dairying and cooperative creameries in the 1890s, but the resulting crossroads communities were not linked to the churches as Meire Grove was—in fact, their more secular halls competed with churches. The market town of Cambridge had Yankee merchants, so Swedes had to learn English. Faith and language were preserved in 'Swedeland,' but it was more open to outside influence, for its individuals pursued economic gain apart from the group.[18] Separated by only thirty miles, Stearns' Catholics and Isanti's Baptists were about as far apart on issues of baptism, salvation, church hierarchy, and liquor as any two groups in the state. Isanti was the most pro-prohibition county. Both groups would have to eye each other and the state warily.

Other Swedish rural settlements were boxed-in by rival ethnic groups and never grew to the size of a 'Swedeland' or a Stearns County. Rev. Norelius' and Mattson's Vasa was the nucleus of a seven-township Swedish area. After the Civil War, Vasa acquired a fine brick (Lutheran) church, an orphanage, stores, a creamery, and the state's first successful rural cooperatives—the first retail and wheat-marketing cooperatives, and a farmers' mutual fire insurance company. German and Norwegian settlements blocked its expansion.[19] Other Swedish areas were smaller, covering one or two townships or less: Vista (Waseca County); Carver, Waconia, and Swede Lake (Carver County); New Sweden, Lake Prairie, and Bernadotte townships (Nicollet County). The construction of railroads across western Minnesota opened up new sites. Mattson worked with the SP&P to recruit Swedish settlers for its lands near Cokato (Wright County); Dassel, Litchfield, Grove City (Meeker County); Atwater and Willmar (Kandiyohi County). The SP&P main line attracted settlers to Lund Township (Douglas County).[20] It was clear who farmed in the 1880s in Svea and Skane townships near James J. Hill's St. Paul, Minneapolis & Manitoba railroad in the state's northwestern-most county, Kittson. Farmers named their townships. The railroad picked names for rail towns it platted—Kennedy for investor John S. Kennedy and Donaldson for bonanza farm manager Hugh Donaldson.[21]

Coming from a timber-producing nation, some Swedes found jobs in the lumbering region in eastern Minnesota. Even as farmers, their best early markets for produce were nearby lumber camps, and they could supplement their farm income by working at the camps in the winter. Immigrants from northern Sweden used to such conditions started small farms in the cutover areas of Kanabec and Mille Lacs counties. After 1880, more single, male Swedes arrived who were even better candidates for logging camps, iron ore mines, sawmills, Duluth or Two Harbors docks, or seamen's jobs on Lake Superior. If they stayed at such jobs and did not marry, they tended to lose their culture and language rapidly.[22]

Post-1880 immigration also funneled many Swedes into the St. Paul-Minneapolis area. By then, the best farmland was taken and the two cities were expanding rapidly, offering thousands of unskilled jobs in railroad shops, flour mills, and factories to single males. 'Swede girls,' valued for their cleanliness and work ethic, took positions as domestic servants in Yankee mansions along St. Paul's Summit Avenue or in Minneapolis' Kenwood district. If they respected the marriage boundary and married within their ethnic group, as most did, they might start a family in a crude house in *Svenska Dalen* (Swede Hollow) along Phalen Creek, near the railroad and several mills where husbands could find work, and then move up the hill to a better East Side dwelling. They shopped at Swedish-speaking merchants' stores on Payne Avenue, St. Paul's Snoose Boulevard (*snus* meant snuff). Cedar-Riverside was the Minneapolis equivalent, and Swedish immigrants could walk from there to the flour mills, sawmills, and railroad yards near downtown. Wives or sisters cleaned offices downtown. In this growing city, however, a general Scandinavian neighborhood arose, and Swedes had to share Dania Hall and other entertainment or cultural sites with Norwegians and Danes. Churches were started, but a purely Swedish ethnic enclave was impossible in such an urban setting.[23]

The state's third largest group, the Norwegians, disliked being lumped with Danes and Swedes in a mongrel Scandinavian category. Both nations had ruled them—Norway was in a Swedish-run joint monarchy from 1814 to 1905—and they sought to establish their own identity. Intense nationalism toward outsiders co-existed with an intense localism toward each other. They remained loyal to the western fjord or central valley of their origin. They were from Telemark, Hallingdal, Sogn, or Gudbrandsdalen. The forests and mountains that kept each of these small patches of arable land isolated from its neighbors instilled in its people an intense land hunger; once installed on a large swath of cheap farmland, they were not easily detached from it. Once in America, they tended to settle near other immigrants from that district (*bygd*) and to form a *bygdelag* or Norwegian regional society. Local loyalties caused a staged, chain migration: Muskego, Wisconsin, was a mother colony of Telemark migrants, some of whom went on to Mound Prairie (Houston County) once Muskego land was taken; this daughter colony filled up, and groups headed for Moland in Clay County. Ties of marriage, business, church, and correspondence continued to link the points into one chain of Telemark ethnicity.[24]

One humorous anecdote shows the localism felt across oceans, sections, and townships. The Talla brothers from Sogn came to Goodhue County with other Sognings and liked the land, so they "roamed about and put their names on all the [government] surveyor's posts over a wide area." The Sognings agreed to tell any intruding land seekers "that Minnesota law allowed them to hold land for relatives coming later." They aimed to control two townships. Along came a massive Telemark man, Big Sven Norgaarden, with a group from the Koshkonong (Wisconsin) area. Going from one Sogning-marked section to the next, they soon realized what had happened. With no lawyer to consult the statutes, Big Sven defeated the Tallas with sticks and fists to open the land for Telemark pioneers.[25]

Likewise, Norwegians were intensely intolerant of outsiders such as Catholics (they were known for anti-Catholicism) but religiously divided internally—splitting into twice as many synods as the German Lutherans. Hans Nielsen Hauge's pietist movement let low-church folk in Norway protest high-church formalism without leaving Lutheranism. Disputes over predestination, lay preaching, liturgy, and rules for behavior meant many Lutheranisms and Norwegian Lutheran churches in one town. That prevented the clergy from centering a community's economic and social life officially in the church. Yet the laity may have been more loyal to the split-off church they *chose* to join. On Sundays, people gathered at rural churches, "trading horses, assigning road work, hiring thrashers, or hearing the latest news" and preparing to worship. Splits may have strengthened Norwegian-American Lutheranism.[26]

A dispute in the Norwegian Synod over public versus parochial schools showed that they were not as successful as German Catholics in Stearns or the Missouri Synod Lutherans in forging a church-run community. Swedes in Isanti sent children to public school, supplemented by a Swedish-language summer school that taught religion.[27] Some Norwegian Synod ministers wanted to go further and have parochial schools compete against public schools: the latter did not teach much, and very little on the Christian faith, but educated Norwegian children away from their ancestral language and culture—so the minister thought. The Stearns solution of taking over the public schools seems not to have been suggested—perhaps because Protestant counties had a supervising county school superintendent who would not allow ethnic, sectarian schools.[28] Goodhue's Horace B. Wilson would not even allow Pastor Bernt Muus' private critique of public schools to go unanswered but attacked this "foreign priest" for encouraging Norwegian Americans "to perpetuate in this land of their adoption, a foreign language, a foreign sentiment, and foreign institutions." Utilizing Protestant dislike of dominating "priests," some Norwegian-American editors' anti-clerical views, and farmers' dislike of pastors' higher social status, Wilson defended public schools as "purely State institutions, established for the protection and safety of the State," and successful in teaching the morality the State needed in its young. Muus replied that a general, ethical Christianity taught in the non-sectarian public school did not yield the public morality produced by a school teaching specific Biblical doctrines. To the English-hearing ear, Wilson seemed to win in a battle that hardly occurred in Stearns County. Norwegian parents sent children to public schools, and pastors' role was limited.[29]

Unlike the Swedes of Chisago and Isanti, Norwegians found no early center with room for expansion—Goodhue County had other groups; Houston County's forested ravines and bluffs resembled Norway in lack of tillable land. They leapfrogged over other ethnic enclaves in the 1860s and

1870s to establish their own near Hanska-Linden, Lakefield-Heron Lake, Walnut Grove, and Canby. The upper Minnesota River Valley offered about thirty townships in Yellow Medicine, western Renville, Chippewa, Swift, and Lac Qui Parle counties—from the Upper Sioux Agency to the Dakota border at Ortonville, and from ten to twenty miles on either side of the river. Pastors from older settlements, like Rev. Muus, labored to bring church services to this area. It was a wheat and small grains region, but land-hungry Norwegian farmers would take those risks. Farther north, Lars K. Aaker and his protégé Knute Nelson encouraged a band of Norwegian farms along the SP&P branch line from Alexandria to Ashby to Fergus Falls to Moland Township by the Buffalo River, then to townships on the Red River—Hendrum, Halstad, Scandia, Vineland, Bygland. Here was elbow room. If the flat land did not resemble Norway, neither did the high soil fertility, absence of stones, and lack of trees to clear. Some Norwegians worked in the lumber camps, while others made up the vast majority of commercial fishermen along Superior's North Shore.[30]

Nelson was only a part-time farmer, but he illustrated the Norwegian pattern. Emigrating from Norway with his mother, he grew up in the Koshkonong settlement south of Madison, Wisconsin, where Aaker had lived also before moving to the daughter area of Goodhue County. Koshkonong nurtured Nelson as other Wisconsin and Illinois mother settlements nurtured others. He acquired an academy education, fought in the Civil War, served in the Wisconsin legislature, 'read' law, and practiced it. Also a Civil War veteran and a long-time Minnesota legislator who had moved from the Goodhue area, Aaker invited Nelson in Spring 1870 to come to Alexandria, where there was "good Prairie Land" for only $1.25 per acre. "I think you could do better here than in Wis. You could get yourself Land near the line of the new RR and practice your profession at the Land Office and act as Land Agent. Think of it." This invitation fit Aaker's role as president of the Scandinavian Emigration Society (and helper to Mattson) that sought to recruit Scandinavians to Minnesota. As register of the U.S. Land Office at Alexandria and a leading Republican, Aaker offered Nelson more specific rewards—a lawyer with ties to the land office could handle cases and file claims, and a man with ties to Aaker could aspire to Minnesota's legislature. Norwegians proved adept at politics, perhaps because immigrants from a land ruled by others simply *wanted* political power more than others.[31]

Nelson also illustrated how influential dissent against the Lutheran clergy helped prevent Norwegian ethnic enclaves from "cordon[ing] themselves off" as fully as Stearns' enclaves did. For the 1880-81 U.S. tour of Norwegian author and anticlerical freethinker Bjørnstjerne Bjørnson, Nelson set up a lecture in Alexandria while informing him, "The clerical influence is against us." Nelson had close ties to anticlerical editor Luth Jaeger in Minneapolis but not with that city's controversial Unitarian minister and author, Kristofer Janson. A regent of the University of Minnesota, Nelson sailed into a storm when the 1883 legislature set up a professorship in Scandinavian language and literature. Who should they hire? One Swedish paper wondered, "What is meant by the 'Scandinavian' language? Is that Swedish, or Norwegian, or maybe Icelandic?" Another worried that Norwegians "as always will certainly push themselves forward and get one of their own appointed." A Norwegian paper saw this as typical Swedish condescension toward Norsemen. Then there was the religious question. Could a freethinker like Jaeger or Janson be chosen? A Norwegian-language paper warned Nelson that "he dare not offend the people's religious beliefs by appointing anyone who denies God and his Word to teach the young at the University." In the end, a scholarly former pastor and college teacher got the nod.[32]

Although Norwegian Unitarian churches existed at rural places like Underwood and Hanska, and Minneapolis had strong Lutheran churches and institutions, the urban areas were destinations for rebels against the disciplines of farm and *menighet* (church). There, Norwegians tended to melt into a broader Scandinavian and sometimes secular life on Snoose Boulevard or in middle class fraternal groups like Sons of Norway. A greater percentage of Norwegians than of any other ethnic group remained in rural areas.[33]

A third Scandinavian group, the Danes, joined this urban mixture and mixed with others in rural areas too. By 1895, there were some 16,000 Danish-born Minnesotans—100,000 fewer than the Swedish-born. Denmark's strong dairy sector supported its rural population, and its industrializing cities employed those rural folk who did leave the land. Many Danes melted into Norwegian America, for the two peoples shared a history and their written languages were nearly identical. The best safeguard for Danishness was religious dissent or an organized colony. If Danes assembled in a colony, rather than dispersing among other groups, they could preserve their language, educate their children, enable their offspring to marry fellow Danes, and maintain their group identity. In April 1885, a Danish Lutheran committee and a land agent for the Winona & St. Peter Railroad contracted that 35,000 acres be sold only to Danes for an average of seven dollars per acre, with free rail travel to those who bought 160 acres. By 1889, about two hundred Danish families lived near Tyler. South of town a campus-like 'Danebod' overlooked the lake and included a three-story wooden folk school flying the Danish flag, a gymnastics hall, a stone hall, a two-room parochial school for young children, and a beautiful church with handcrafted woodwork and a model ship suspended from the ceiling in the Danish style. This was the state's most visibly Danish enclave. Youth learned Danish culture in the Danish language; coeducation led to marriages between Danes; the next generation was groomed to lead Danish-language churches rather than tempted to switch to Scandinavian churches or American ones.[34]

British: The Group So Like Old Stock Americans, They Were Hardly Ethnic

Merging with other English speakers as Danes did with Norwegians, the state's fourth largest group was barely noticeable—British Canadians from Ontario and the Maritimes. Their most famous member was Ontario's James J. Hill, the railroad "empire builder." Lumbermen from New Brunswick and Nova Scotia had joined their neighbors, the Maineites, in the lumber region before the Civil War. As rail connections improved, more British Canadians came, especially after the Canadian Pacific railroad reached Winnipeg in 1885. This New-World, English-speaking group erected no flag-flying 'Canada Hall' to encourage Canadian culture and Canadian marriages. Their only sizeable, concentrated settlement was in Kittson County along the barely noticeable U.S.-Canadian border; many hardly knew on which side of it they lived. Here, the very noticeable Hill had his sizeable Northcote farm, amidst his compatriots' farms.[35]

Also outnumbering Danes were immigrants direct from the British Isles. Celtic ones like the Welsh and Scots preserved their ethnicity in rural enclaves. Three rural colonies for the English at Fairmont, Furness, and New Yeovil failed, for the settlers were new to farming. At one colony, they planted wheat one seed at a time! Competent Welsh farmers, however, succeeded south of the great bend in the Minnesota River—in townships west and south of Mankato. They had distinctions to preserve: the Welsh language so unlike English, their own Calvinistic Methodist denomination, and their four-part singing and literary recitations at *eisteddfod* gatherings. A similar concentration of Scottish farmers formed a dozen miles south of the Welsh, near Mapleton, and a [Robert] Burns Club, Scottish pipe band, and clan gathering testified to their Celtic identity. Scots also gained a visible presence in Duluth, where they were managers in business affairs, residents of Glen Avon neighborhood, and leaders in two Presbyterian churches. If they began as lowly clerks, English speakers had the advantage of steady promotion within companies—something non-Anglo groups often did not enjoy. On the Vermilion range, experienced Cornish miners began the underground mining but then rose to become managers while non-Anglos took their place in the deep shafts.[36]

The Irish came from the British Isles, but troubles with the British and negative views of them set them apart. Irish settled in southeastern Minnesota and in St. Paul before the Civil War, and Senator James Shields organized one Irish colony in western Rice County. Postwar railroad construction brought a thousand Irish workers to Minnesota, and many settled on farms amidst other ethnic groups. Bishop John Ireland of St. Paul headed the most visible effort— the Catholic Colonization Bureau—to create Irish Catholic enclaves on SP&P railroad lands in western Minnesota in the 1870s. The Americanized Bishop Ireland—a Civil War chaplain, a Republican (unlike most Irish) with ties to business leaders like Hill, a zealous advocate for temperance, a national leader in Americanization of ethnic Catholics—did not want the Irish to "cordon themselves off" from American society. He resisted German Catholics' efforts to do so. He hoped to free poor Irish from American ghettoes and Irish tenant farms, but he mainly attracted Irish Americans who could afford a farm's start-up costs. His colonies further Americanized the Irish by making them take the plow like most Americans and take the pledge to abstain from alcohol. They were to stay Catholic. The first man in a colony was a priest, who served as local land agent. The church was the first construction project. Parochial schools supplemented public ones. The plan worked in De Graff, Clontarf, Graceville, Currie, Avoca, Iona, Fulda, and Adrian. Other ethnic Catholics joined the Irish and at Ghent, Belgians proved the best farmers. The public failure of a few desperately poor Connemara settlers in 1880-81 grieved Ireland but did not alter his colonizing success.[37]

Groups Too Late for the Best Land: Finns & Other Eastern Europeans

Finns were the Scandinavians' Irish—a people geographically within Scandinavia but whose language was so different as to set them apart, aided by some Scandinavians' stereotypes of them. Being late to arrive was the

Finns' main problem in Minnesota. A few Finnish settlers came in the 1860s when good homestead land was available and started small communities near Cokato and Holmes City, but it was Finns working in the lumber camps near Brainerd who started the largest agricultural settlement at New York Mills in the mid-1870s. That sawmill town was on the NP line. For the next twenty years it attracted Finns weary of the low wages and seasonal work in northeastern Minnesota's lumber camps and mines. Several thousand Finnish Americans farmed nearby or worked in town. Others moved east to cutover lands near Sebeka and Menahga, but there never was enough good farmland for all the miners and loggers who wanted to farm.[38] Being too late for the best farmland meant some Finns grew disillusioned with America and its low wages, corporate dominance in mines and mills, company towns, lack of unions, and barriers to advancement. Being late meant they left Finland after the Socialist movement took off there. Some arrived with socialist notions little appreciated in the United States. The logging and mining regions they came to were regions where land ownership was concentrated in the hands of a few men who ruled a lower class.

They were very divided over religion, with early settlers who found farmland often Laestadians—pietists who set up an Apostolic Lutheran Church in many Finnish towns—while later arrivals were often single males who found work in Duluth or in mines or mills or logging camps, sympathized with socialism, and left the church. As with other ethnic groups in these regions, the Finnish temperance societies, missionaries, and cultural groups had to work to establish a family-based, sober, orderly society amidst the disorderly culture of saloons, brothels, and boarding houses that a single, male workforce encouraged. Twenty-one temperance clubs, mainly Finnish, were formed on the Mesabi Range from 1890 to 1900, before splits over religion and socialism weakened the movement. The temperance hall was a church away from church, with similar fraternal and social activities. The later Socialist halls were temperance-minded and tried likewise to build some self-disciplining morality apart from religion.[39]

Some Single-Male Disorder Among Finns

"In many Finnish areas of settlement conditions had gone to wrack and ruin. . . . The majority of immigrants from Finland were young, unmarried men. . . . This restless life centered in the saloons, into which newcomers from Finland were so often

drawn, threatened not only to destroy numerous promising young men but also threatened to brand the Finns as a whole."
Hans Wasastjerna in *History of the Finns in Minnesota*

Similar social disorder characterized the first years as other ethnic single males came to the iron ranges and logging camps. Southern Slavs reported very high ratios of men to women: for Serbs, 25 to 1 on the Mesabi in the early years; for Croats and Slovenes, over 5 to 1 for the first decade or so. Some men planned to return to a wife in Europe once they earned a 'nest egg.' They came in large numbers for the new mining jobs. In 1888, about 25 percent of the population of Tower on the Vermilion Range was Slovenian, Father Joseph Buh estimated. Father Buh sought to build a religious and organizational life—working with two congregations on the Vermilion and running America's first Slovenian newspaper—before he switched his society-building efforts to the new Mesabi. The boardinghouse, saloon, and ethnic store were key institutions for this male-worker society of Southern Slavs, as they were for the Eastern Slavs who came later to the Mesabi—Russians, Ukranians, and others. It would be years before the Catholic and Orthodox churches, the temperance societies, and other institutions among Eastern and Southern Slavs reached the mature stage of the earlier Finns, but they eventually tamed this rough society.[40]

In the last decades of the nineteenth century, these ethnic groups largely lived in peace in their enclaves. In rural areas, a dozen miles might separate one from another. Even in Minneapolis and St. Paul, one group dominated its neighborhoods and allowed others to dominate theirs. Yet fights could not be always prevented when liquor, weekend nights, and crowds of young off-duty male workers all mixed. On Christmas Eve 1869, "some forty or fifty Swedes" building the Lake Superior and Mississippi Railroad "collected at a saloon at Moose Lake, and after drinking freely," headed for a camp of Irish and French-Canadian workers and "badly whipped" two of them. The next day, the two sides met at a saloon in town "where whiskey flowed freely." A Swede hit "an Irish boy" and sparked "a general fight" in which the Swede "was knocked down and killed outright." Nearly fifty men fought using "clubs, pistols, &c." for nearly three hours and two more men were killed.[41] In late July 1872, in the new NP railroad town of Brainerd, a hundred railroad workers gate-crashed a "Swede dance" at the Hotel Svea on a Saturday night. "[U]nacquainted with the round [folk] dances which were going on," they demanded more familiar ones "which they could join in." The dance "managers" agreed to a few such dances but when the railroaders' demands for more were refused, they threatened to "just clean out the Swedes." "A bloody fight ensued, in which pistols, knives, bottles, &c., were freely used, until the furniture and windows were a complete wreck." The railroaders retreated with two wounded comrades, one of whom was stabbed through the lung. A militia company was in town to guard against another lynching in Brainerd, and the soldiers and county sheriff restored order.[42]

When different ethnic groups rubbed shoulders, violence could result. Especially when a person in one group injured or killed a member of another group, the latter might not wait for the state's justice to work. But, for the more sober and older members of ethnic groups, it took a controversial social or political or religious issue to spark the confrontation—which hopefully was more reasoned and orderly than the ones in Brainerd and Moose Lake. There were enough controversial issues to keep the arguments going, even on weekdays, in the daytime, among women and children as well as men, and in cities as well as small towns or hamlets. A state of many nations was sure to have a few wars.

1. "line of settlement," Lass, *Minnesota*, 137.
2. "May 1865," Folwell, *History of Minnesota*, Vol. II, 346-50.
3. "dried up," Holmquist, ed., *They Chose Minnesota*, 58, 59.
4. "Hans Mattson's activities," Here and above, see Lars Ljungmark, *For Sale—Minnesota; Organized Promotion of Scandinavian Immigration, 1866–1873* (Chicago: Swedish Pioneer Historical Society, 1971), 11, 22-24, 28-29, 35-37, 87, 95, 100-09; Hans Mattson, *Reminiscences: Story of an Emigrant* (St. Paul: D. D. Merrill, 1892), 97-99, 109.
5. "largest single immigrant group," this paragraph is based on Hildegard Binder Johnson, "The Germans," in Holmquist, ed., *They Chose Minnesota*, 153-61; Kathleen Neils Conzen, *Germans in Minnesota* (St. Paul: Minnesota Historical Society Press, 2003), 4-12; and Lass, *Minnesota*, 146-47.
6. "not a unified region," Hildegard Binder Johnson, "The Most Diversified Ethnic Group," in Clarence A. Glasrud, ed., *A Heritage Deferred: The German-Americans in Minnesota* (Moorhead: Concordia College, 1981), 32-33.
7. "German Americans," Johnson, "Germans," 164, 166, 170; Conzen, *Germans*, 47-48, 50; Karl J. Fink, "German Lutherans in Minnesota," in Clarence A. Glasrud, ed., *A Heritage Fulfilled: German-Americans* (Moorhead: Concordia College, 1984), 156-67.
8. "German Minnesota," Johnson, "Germans," 163 and maps on 155, 156, 157.
9. "the state's core area," Johnson, "Germans," 169-73; Conzen, *Germans*, 14.
10. "different townships," Johnson, "Germans," 167.
11. "the German language," Johnson, "Germans," 169; Conzen, *Germans*, 44; Fred W. Peterson, *Building Community, Keeping the Faith: German Catholic Vernacular Architecture in a Rural Minnesota Parish* (St. Paul: Minnesota Historical Society Press, 1998), 25.

12. "Unexpectedly," Jon Gjerde, *The Minds of the West: Ethnocultural Evolution in the Rural Middle West, 1830–1917* (Chapel Hill, N.C.: University of North Carolina Press, 1997), 7.

13. "mark its territory," Peterson, *Building Community*, 14.

14. "Meire Grove," here and above, Peterson, *Building Community*, 12-29, 40-41, 56.

15. "Such enclaves," I am greatly indebted to Gjerde, *Minds of the West*, and Onuf, *Statehood and Union*.

16. "the most heavily Swedish," John G. Rice, "The Swedes," in Holmquist, ed., *They Chose Minnesota*, 250.

17. "Religious disunity," Rice, "Swedes," 253-54; Robert C. Ostergren, *A Community Transplanted: The Trans-Atlantic Experience of a Swedish Immigrant Settlement in the Upper Middle West*, 1835–1915 (Madison: University of Wisconsin Press, 1988), 49, 116-17, 213-15, 279-80.

18. "local economy," Ostergren, *Community Transplanted*, 194-202, 248-50, 254-55

19. "the nucleus," Rice, "Swedes," 252; Johnson, *Goodhue County*, 41-44; Keillor, *Cooperative Commonwealth*, 18-20, 81-82.

20. "Other Swedish areas," Rice, "Swedes," 253, 258, 260.

21. "picked names," here, and elsewhere, the derivation of place names is taken from Warren Upham, *Minnesota Geographic Names: Their Origin and Historic Significance*, reprint ed. (St. Paul: Minnesota Historical Society, 1969).

22. "Some Swedes," Rice, "Swedes," 260-61; Ostergren, *Community Transplanted*, 195.

23. "the St. Paul—Minneapolis area," David A. Lanegran, "Swedish Neighborhoods of the Twin Cities: From Swede Hollow to Arlington Hills, From Snoose Boulevard to Minnehaha Parkway," in Philip J. Anderson and Dag Blanck, eds., *Swedes in the Twin Cities: Immigrant Life and Minnesota's Urban Frontier* (St. Paul: Minnesota Historical Society Press, 2001), 39-56; H. Arnold Barton, "Why Minnesota, Why the Twin Cities?," in *ibid*, 34-35.

24. "the Norwegians," Carlton C. Qualey and Jon A. Gjerde, "The Norwegians," in Holmquist, ed., *They Chose Minnesota*, 220-28; Odd S. Lovoll, *Norwegians on the Prairie: Ethnicity and the Development of the Country Town* (St. Paul: Minnesota Historical Society Press, 2006), 4, 65-71.

25. "humorous anecdote," Joseph M. Shaw, *Bernt Julius Muus: Founder of St. Olaf College* (Northfield: Norwegian-American Historical Association, 1999), 80-83.

26. "religiously divided," Qualey and Gjerde, "Norwegians," 227, 234-35; Lovoll, *Norwegians on the Prairie*, 109-18.

27. "Swedes in Isanti," Ostergren, *Community Transplanted*, 229.

28. "Some Norwegian Synod ministers," Shaw, *Bernt Julius Muus*, 211-21, 228-32; Gjerde, *Minds of the West*, 277-78.

29. "Goodhue's Horace B. Wilson," Shaw, *Bernt Julius Muus*, 223-27; Johnson, *Goodhue County*, 112-14; *Goodhue County Republican* (Red Wing), 5 May (1), 2 June (2), 16 June (1), 7 July (1, 2), all 1870.

30. "leapfrogged over," Qualey and Gjerde, "Norwegians," 222, 227-31; Shaw, *Bernt Julius Muus*, 153-82.

31. "Nelson was only," Millard F. Gieske and Steven J. Keillor, *Norwegian Yankee: Knute Nelson and the Failure of American Politics*, 1860–1923 (Northfield: Norwegian-American Historical Association, 1995), 51-56, 69-70, 74-75; Lars K. Aaker to Knute Nelson, 29 March 1870, Knute Nelson Papers, MHS; Lovoll, *Norwegians on the Prairie*, 40; Qualey and Gjerde, "Norwegians," 228.

32. "Nelson also illustrated," Keillor and Gieske, *Norwegian Yankee*, 125-27.

33. "the urban areas," Qualey and Gjerde, "Norwegians," 233-34.

34. "the Danes," Ann Regan, "The Danes," in Holmquist, ed., *They Chose Minnesota*, 277-83;

Henrik Bredmose Simonsen, *Kampen om Danskheden: Tro og nationalitet i de danske kirkesamfund i Amerika* (Aarhus, Denmark: Aarhus Universitetsforlag, 1990), 43-44, 67-70, 92-94; Steven J. Keillor, *Hjalmar Petersen of Minnesota: The Politics of Provincial Independence* (St. Paul: Minnesota Historical Society Press, 1987), 9-10.

35. "British Canadians," Sarah Rubinstein, "The British: English, Scots, Welsh, and British Canadians," in Holmquist, ed., *They Chose Minnesota*, 111, 113, 121-22.

36. "from the British Isles," Rubinstein, "British," 115-17, 119-21, 123-24; Walker, *Iron Frontier*, 55, 62.

37. "Irish settled," Ann Regan, "The Irish," in Holmquist, ed., *They Chose Minnesota*, 130-38; James Shannon, *Catholic Colonization on the Western Frontier* (New Haven: Yale University Press, 1957), 7, 36, 43-49, 51-53, 54-60, 136, 150-51, 176-77, 190-92, 202.

38. "A few Finnish settlers," Timo Riippa, "The Finns and Swede-Finns," in Holmquist, ed., *They Chose Minnesota*, 296-302; Hans R. Wasastjerna, ed., *History of the Finns in Minnesota* (Duluth: Minnesota Finnish-American Historical Society, 1957), 146-47.

39. "very divided," Riippa, "Finns and Swede-Finns," 306-08; Wasastjerna, ed., *Finns in Minnesota*, 147-48, 359-64, 372-75.

40. "other ethnic single males," June D. Holmquist, Joseph Stipanovich, and Kenneth B. Moss, "The South Slavs," 381-91, and Keith P. Dyrud, "East Slavs," 410-11, both in Holmquist, ed., *They Chose Minnesota*.

41. "Christmas Eve 1869," *Duluth Minnesotian*, 8 January (3) and 15 January (3), both 1870; I am indebted to Gjerde, *Minds of the West*, 243, for this and the following incident, plus newspaper sources.

42. "the new NP railroad town," *St. Paul Daily Press*, 31 July 1872, 4. The editor of the *Brainerd Tribune* (3 August 1872, 1) made a feeble, unpersuasive attempt to defend the town's reputation by minimizing the row.

Regions Make for Conflict

In the 1860s, immigrants had not begun to challenge Old Stock Americans for control of political parties or to be chosen as candidates for major state offices. They started farms, organized churches, learned English, and adapted to a new economy. Their success in outdoing Old Stock pioneers at settling, so that they looked like wavering squatters by comparison, aroused Old Stock jealousy—in Oliver H. Kelley, for example. A Yankee from Boston, Kelley came west in territorial days and pursued many callings: legislative staffer, newspaper editor, town site speculator, founder of agricultural societies, and farmer. He grew disgruntled at farming's low status and poor earnings, and partly blamed his immigrant competitors. Kelley wrote, "Our foreign population seem[s] to get ahead in the west in the business . . . but a Yankee can't do it." In 1866, he complained, "In German neighborhoods, males and females, old and young, are busy digging potatoes . . . and in a few instances I see girls holding the plow." Women in the fields suggested a low-status European peasantry. Would German success lower all farmers' status?[1]

Farm Protest Movements Result in Conflict: 1) The Grange

Kelley's answer was to organize the Grange (Patrons of Husbandry) in 1867-68, with Daniel Robertson (Sibley's old nemesis) and aided by the Fall 1868 Minnesota State Fair. A year later, 36 local granges existed in the state. This national movement grew from 1,000 granges (1872) to 5,000 (1873) to nearly 9,000 (1874). Township-level granges met in local halls, used a secret ritual, held social events like picnics to reduce rural isolation, gave tips on farming and gardening methods, and cooperated to win higher wheat prices and lower store prices. Politics was kept out of township granges, but county and state granges paralleled the hierarchy of governments and did discuss politics. Its exclusive nature (members voted to admit new members), secret ritual (putting members above unknowing non-members), church-like ceremonies (Bible lessons, but in its ritual female members were cast as Roman goddesses like Ceres and Pomona), and in-group sociability created an occupational ethnic group. Grangers hoped it would raise farming's social status. To Old Stock Americans who didn't feel ethnic in America, the Grange gave an identity and a pride to help them persevere on the land and not sell out to immigrants. "The clans gathered from Elmira, Dover, Quincy, Viola," a Rochester newspaper noted in June 1873, and a gathering of these Old Stock towns did make for an ethnic festival of sorts.[2]

The regular ethnic groups and their clergy complained. Vasa's Rev. Eric Norelius asked, "Can any Christian woman act as—and let herself be called—a goddess?" Lutheran and Catholic clergy objected to the secret rites and oaths. Two local Grangers attacked Norelius as a "priest" meddling in secular matters and wishing Swedes to remain peasants "follow[ing] the well beaten paths of labor and drudgery" in the same "blissful ignorance" as their ancestors. Many immigrant farmers sensed Grangers' condescending superiority and lacked Old Stock alarm at farming's status. They did not join the order.[3]

Meeting of the Grange in Northfield, Minnesota, 1875. Edward Newall James, photographer. *Courtesy of the Minnesota Historical Society.*

Rochester-area Grangers attacked railroads more than reverends. It cost five cents more to ship wheat by rail forty-five miles from Rochester (non-competing point) to Winona than to ship it twice as far from Owatonna (competing point) to Winona. A local doctor, William W. Mayo, served as secretary of an "Anti-Railroad Convention" in Rochester on December 1, 1870, that led to two 1871 "Granger" laws that declared railroads "public highways," set maximum passenger fares and freight rates, and created the office of railroad commissioner to investigate railroads and enforce maximum charges. Railroads refused to comply on grounds that the laws were unconstitutional. A Rochester discount retailer, John D. Blake, added to his popularity with Granger customers by serving as their defendant in a test case. The Minnesota and U.S. Supreme Courts ruled the laws constitutional in 1873 and 1876, but hard times following the Panic of 1873 lowered rates below the maximum charges, so the legislature continued to tinker with railroad regulation.[4]

Dr. William W. Mayo on the Railroads

"If I could treat this railroad company in my profession, I would give them such a puke [emetic] as would bring their corns from their toes through their stomachs."[5]

Hard times hurt Granger cooperatives—stores, flour mills, grain elevators, fire insurance mutuals—but these failed largely because Old Stock Grangers were not a united ethnic group but individualists with "no bonds of union except that of buying cheap." Faced with similar hard times, Scandinavians ran successful stores and mutuals in the 1860s and 1870s. Yankees proved poorer cooperators.[6] Minnesota farmers were hit by economic reverses in the 1870s: swarms of Rocky Mountain locusts devastated crops in 1873-77; the national government's policy of deflation hurt debtors and lowered wheat prices; Minneapolis millers sought to control wheat prices; and depression halted railroad construction so that frontier farmers lacked transportation for their crops. The Grange went into a steep decline that further shook Old Stock confidence in farming.[7] Land-hungry immigrants with new farms and without other economic opportunities weathered the storm better than the Old Stock who could more easily move to a city or a trade.

They could move to the trade of politics, since they dominated county offices, the legislature, and executive offices. That began to change. Goodhue County's Norwegians, like Aaker, led the Scandinavian charge into politics. Many immigrants were too focused on starting farms and too embarrassed at their poor English to do more than vote, but an Americanized Knute Nelson—educated at a New England-style academy—jumped in quickly. In 1874, he was elected to the state senate, where he helped James J. Hill secure laws enabling Hill's group to take control of the SP&P and to add new track in the late 1870s as the St. Paul, Minneapolis, and Manitoba (SPM&M). Lawyer Nelson brokered deals with farmers who sold right-of-way land to the SPM&M. In 1882, Nelson was ready to run for Congress, but Old Stock leaders did not cede control without a fight.[8]

Nelson's 1892 campaign against Charles Kindred in the new Fifth District of central and northern Minnesota was the most rough-and-tumble one in the state's history—politics with all the bark still on. Partly, it pitted the Old Stock against Scandinavians whom Mattson, Aaker, and Nelson had recruited to the SPM&M line; partly, the NP's logging region was pitted against the SPM&M's wheat-raising region. As chief NP land clerk, Kindred had snatched a fortune of $250,000 in the NP's crooked business culture. Money and muscle, he hoped, would get him to Congress. At the Republican convention in NP Detroit Lakes, streets, hotels, and convention hall were packed with Kindred men, and he footed the bill. In the hall, fists were used, pistols were drawn and nearly used, and chaos led to a split in the group; one side nominated Kindred, the other Nelson. Kindred offered voters jobs, subsidized or started a dozen newspapers, and promised to build a railroad from St. Paul to Brainerd to win votes. Eggs were thrown at Nelson in one NP town. When he spoke at the NP's Brainerd, twenty friends with pistols sat with him on the platform to offer protection. Nelson won, but Kindred collected 3,000 fraudulent votes in logging camps and railroad camps, whose workers voted more than once. A company-run logging region was no home to farmers' self-governing, Ordinance-style democracy.[9]

Public Education Results in Political Conflict in an Immigrants' State

Education was also a contentious issue and a major reason ethnic groups entered politics. State government moved to control and finance local public education: in 1878, it began state aid ($400 to each high school); in 1885, it made education compulsory for children ages 8 to 16 (a law hard to enforce); in 1887, it levied a state school tax, the monies to be paid to school districts based on the number of pupils; in the late 1890s, state aid went to elementary schools too. Wisconsin had a terrific fight over its 1889 compulsory education law that also required the key subjects to be taught in English, but Minnesota's legislature did not challenge foreign language enclaves in this way. Yet religion in the public schools sparked battles like the 1870 Muus-Wilson debate. An 1877 constitutional amendment outlawed public funding for schools teaching sectarian doctrines. The attorney general interpreted it to outlaw the reading of Scripture in any translation in the public schools. He was ignored. Many citizens believed doctrines like that of a Judgment Day, which others thought sectarian, were needed to teach morality. Others believed religion unnecessary for morality. Their views appeared in an 1881 law allowing teachers to instruct in "elements of social and moral science"—which led to thirty-one virtues that the law named. Did science or Scripture best promote morality?[10]

This debate reflected the growing influence of Darwin's theory of evolution and of late-nineteenth-century skepticism. More than dry academic arguments were involved. Some nineteenth-century males, like Nelson and John Lind, went into politics and the law partly because their skepticism about orthodox Christianity made them unsuited for—and disinterested in—the main rural profession: the ministry. The state's first Swedish-American congressman, Lind, lived in New Ulm, where he joined freethinking Turners, served as county school superintendent, and supported the Turners' fight against Bible reading in New Ulm's public schools.[11] Nelson had moved to Minnesota partly due to his opposition to the Norwegian Lutheran clergy in Koshkonong, but he had not openly sided with agnostics and skeptics as Lind did.[12] The Granger, Anti-Monopoly, and Populist politician, Ignatius Donnelly, was the son of an Irish immigrant who left Catholicism, and Donnelly kept on leaving it as he pursued politics.[13] Also active in politics and elected to the state senate, Dr. William W. Mayo acted as Rochester's feisty evolutionist, lecturing and writing letters-to-the-editor to defend Darwin.[14]

This debate swirled around the University. Its first president, William Watts Folwell, had wrestled with doubts at the University of Berlin. He disliked the prevailing church-college model of chapel, religious instruction, and tight discipline. Preferring a secular German model, he proposed a "Minnesota Plan," with high schools teaching freshmen and sophomores, and students entering the University as juniors. With only older, mature students, the University would be freed from moralizing, disciplining duties in order to undertake the advanced one of teaching science. Factional war erupted on campus, as high schools opposed duties delegated to them, clergymen-professors opposed Folwell's secular approach, and students disliked having their education be unlike that in other colleges. University enrollment stagnated. The Plan was never implemented. Student pranks and vandalism against Folwell led to a professor accidentally shooting a student in May 1882. Two months later, knowing his days as president were numbered, Folwell gave a speech, "The Secularization of Education," to the National Education Association. Denying theology was needed for morality, he argued, "The public school assuming the essential goodness in human nature, is in the best position to inculcate a sound morality . . . moral training can be fully separated from the religious and sectarian instruction of the family and the church." Most critical of Catholic education but linking Protestant clergy to it by calling them "priests," Folwell repeated this talk in Catholic Stearns County, but a winter blizzard cut attendance and thus muffled its inflammatory impact.[15]

The University President in Court

"After the usual grist of criminal business had been ground out in the Municipal court this morning, three cases . . . were called. The three prisoners, who were none other than President Folwell and Profs. Pike and Moore of the state university, . . . by the court officers [were] directed to take seats which the criminal gang that had just gone out, had vacated, which they did. The cases all grew out of the shooting of the student Paine, on Monday night. . . . The president toed the scratch, smiled blandly, bowed to the court, and said he preferred to see his counsel before pleading."[16]

As the home of the University and its Yankee leaders, Minneapolis was the main site of this debate. A Minneapolis Liberal League sponsored forums and printed booklets critical of the clergy's doctrines. Minnesota Academy of Natural Sciences lectures explored Darwinism. The city's Gale family personified disunity: Amory was a Baptist missionary, his brother Samuel a Unitarian Liberal Leaguer—one Thanksgiving dinner featured "a violent theological debate" between them; their nephew Harlow became a brain-cell-dissecting psychologist and agnostic at a German university before teaching at the University and then being fired. When Folwell's problems erupted, the "Father of the University," Minneapolis businessman John S. Pillsbury, had finished his third term as governor. Concerned about the school's irreligious image and low enrollment (222 students in 1882-83), he recruited a fellow New England Congregationalist, Professor Cyrus Northrop of Yale, as the next president. A skilled orator, sensitive to parents' concerns, kindly toward students, Northrop increased enrollment to over 5,000 by the end of his 27-year tenure in 1911. Yet he could not halt a slow, internal secularization that further encouraged the ethnic groups to found their own private religious colleges.[17]

Partly they did so to educate their future clergy, and even a devout state university may never have met their expectations, but Folwell's certainly did not. Each Norwegian Lutheran synod started its own college and seminary: the Conference's Augsburg Seminary and College (1872); the Norwegian Synod's (later, United Church's) St. Olaf College (begun in 1874 as an academy) founded by Pastor Muus; the Hauge Synod's Red Wing Seminary (1879); and the United Church's Concordia College in Moorhead (begun in 1891 as an academy). Most began as academies and grew into colleges. Swedish Lutherans' Augustana Synod's academy moved to St. Peter in 1874 and had its first college graduates in 1890; it became Gustavus Adophus College. Swedish Baptists' Bethel Academy (St. Paul) became a college also by the early twentieth century. German Lutherans' Dr. Martin Luther College in New Ulm mainly educated teachers for their parochial schools. Stearns County's Catholic institutions—St. Benedict's for women, St. John's for men—became a college and a university. Old Stock Americans founded colleges—Methodists' Hamline revived in St. Paul in 1880; Presbyterians' Macalester founded by Rev. Edward D. Neill, and Congregationalists' Carleton in Northfield—but these lacked the mission of foreign-language preservation that partly marked the others.[18]

Different Ethnic, Cultural Views on Liquor Result in Political Conflict

Liquor was a more inflammatory issue than language or liturgy—not on campus, for an 1876 law forbade alcohol sales three-fourths of a mile from the University, and colleges opposed student drinking.[19] Minnesota

Republicans could not escape liquor battles—too many of their Yankee and Scandinavian supporters fought for prohibition, and the most visible Catholic Republican, Bishop Ireland, organized temperance societies. Pressured by the Prohibition Party that agitated this issue, the GOP compromised in 1886 and called for high fees for saloon licenses, but the Democrats nearly won the governor's race by opposing this move. The 1887 legislature set a $1,000 fee for saloons in larger cities; that cut the number by one-third but confirmed brewers' backing for the Democrats, and dissatisfied prohibitionists still doubled their vote at the next election in 1888. Many Norwegian Minnesotans favored prohibition, and Swedish Baptist Isanti County gave a higher percentage of its votes to that party than did any other county. Republicans' appeal to these prohibitionists caused German and Irish voters to cling tighter to Democrats.[20]

Pressured by anti-liquor forces on its right, so to speak, Republicans also lost thousands of Scandinavian votes to agrarian protesters on its left. Actually, the two issues were not on opposite poles. Both centered on saving the family and family farm—which could be lost through low crop prices and foreclosure or through a father's alcoholism. To maintain party loyalty, Republicans used Civil War issues: Lincoln's party saved the Union, while Confederate *Democrats* shot and killed Union soldiers. The war was still vividly remembered. In September 1887, a great battlefield reenactment was held at the State Fair grounds in St. Paul; about 6,000 men participated and more than a dozen cannon were fired.[21] Civil War service counted for much when running for office, as Nelson knew. However, debt-laden farmers grew weary of Republicans 'waving the bloody shirt' to remind voters of the war.

Farm Protest Movements Result in Conflict:
2) Farmers' Alliance

The Farmers' Alliance replaced the Grange as *the* farmers' organization in the 1880s. It too had township groups (suballiances) that met in halls (schoolhouses) and formed county and state units to set up cooperatives, purchase goods jointly, and elect candidates. The Alliance recruited immigrants, for it was not a secret society, had no ritual, and was not Old-Stock-dominated. More immigrants were comfortable at English-language public meetings now, fifteen years after the Grange began. There were 438 Minnesota suballiances by 1886, and nearly 1,200 four years later.[22]

Ignatius Donnelly, lieutenant governor, two term member of U.S. House of Representatives, and author. Carte-de-visite photograph by C. A. Zimmerman, circa 1880. *Courtesy of the Minnesota Historical Society.*

Like a snowball rolled downhill, agrarian protest accumulated more issues and supporters until it was a formidable movement by the early 1890s. Ignatius Donnelly personified it, for he was active in its successive stages. The Grange had contributed the monthly social functions, the basic cooperatives (store, grain elevator, joint-purchasing rings), and the drive for railroad regulation. Donnelly joined the Greenback Party that added the demand for inflation, first through paper money and later through more silver coinage. In 1878, he ran for Congress against miller William Washburn and added the issue of millers' alleged cheating when grading wheat. By the mid-1880s, a wheat region existed in the Red River and upper Minnesota River valleys. The Alliance was strong here; an interlocking system of railroads favoring 'line' elevators shipping wheat to Minneapolis millers was most powerful here and stirred the most anger. In some areas, the Alliance protested against county seat towns which were now more prosperous and controlling than fifteen years earlier. By placing their stores or newspapers there, Alliancemen aided a rival town against a county seat: Adrian against Worthington (Nobles County), Clarkfield against Granite Falls (Yellow Medicine), Sleepy Eye against New Ulm (Brown), and Henning against Fergus Falls (Otter Tail). In writing their 1886 platform, Donnelly added old issues to the snowballing agrarian protest.[23]

Whatever the party or movement or moment, Donnelly was ever the vigorous Irish orator. He was a short stocky man with a large dark-haired head, often a stovepipe hat atop it, blue eyes, and high-pitched voice. When he addressed the 1890 Alliance convention, "his hand pressed over his heart," the farmers "shouted themselves hoarse." He was no blushing moderate. "The word radical means that which goes to the root of things," he told them. "Remember the French Revolution," he shouted. "The fact is, my friends, that a wrong has no rights, except the right to die—and die at once."[24] Small-town merchants, Catholic priests, and Minneapolis millers did not welcome his rhetoric.

In 1890, the Alliance became a third party, running candidates. The editor of *Farm, Stock and Home*, Sidney Owen, ran for governor, won over 58,000 votes, carried nearly all wheat-region counties, beat Republican William Merriam two-to-one in Nelson's Douglas County, and left Merriam with a 2,267-vote victory over the Democrat. Alarmed Republicans saw defeat coming across the prairie. University regents Pillsbury and Nelson visited the University of Wisconsin's dairy school to recruit a dairy instructor and former aide to Republican governors, Theophilus Haecker, to start a Minnesota dairy school. The University did its land-grant duty by teaching agriculture and dairying. This offered a non-political solution to wheat farmers' problems that might help Republicans stop the Alliance. Old Stock leaders gave up control of the governor's office to avert defeat. In 1892, they ran Nelson for governor, hoping his appeal to an ethnic Scandinavian region outweighed the Alliance's appeal to an economic wheat region. Farming near Alexandria shielded him from rural suspicion of a domineering St. Paul and Minneapolis. Old Stock criticism of Nelson surfaced, but party regulars felt they had little choice. Now known as the People's Party, the Alliance chose Donnelly to run against Nelson. Democrats ran St. Paul lawyer Daniel Lawler, who assured Catholic voters of his support for parental rights in education.[25]

Knute Nelson Leads a Republican Drive to Defeat Populism

The national Republican party helped out by holding its 1892 national convention in Minneapolis for a reason of its own—to stem the Populist tide in the West. Due to its efforts to outshine St. Paul, Minneapolis had the fine Exposition Hall seating 11,000. This June 1892 event introduced the Flour City to the nation's elite. Scouting out this venue in advance, a *New York Times* reporter disliked the city's restaurants, especially one that was a "big log cabin . . . built after the style of the logging camps" and offering the "regular lumberman's dinner," that is, pork and beans. Convention organizers planned to bake huge amounts of beans in pits near the Hall. Despite some grumbling, the national convention was held without serious deficiencies.[26]

Delegates, Alternates, and Visitors all had badges for entrance to the Republican National Convention in Minneapolis, June 7, 1892.
Courtesy of Leonard Nadasdy.

G. O P. IS IN TO STAY.

STATE
CAPITOL

The Populist "Munk" (to the Democratic Jackass)—"Don't seem to be room for us to get in, does there?"

Political cartoon from *Minneapolis Tribune*, October 20, 1894.

Nelson headed to the wheat region to speak sense to his straying Scandinavian brethren. At Elbow Lake, annoyed by noise and heckling, he stormed into the audience and grabbed an Allianceman by the collar. Barnstorming Red River Valley towns during the campaign's final week, he calmed down (he did best as a reasoned, fact-reciting speaker) and offered disgruntled wheat farmers some concessions, like a law compelling railroads to offer side-track service to farmers' elevators. Nelson won and became the state's first foreign-born and first Scandinavian governor. Ethnic appeal trumped economic grievances. Nelson received 20,000 votes more than Merriam, carried all but five of the twenty-three wheat counties Owen won in 1890, and cut Donnelly's total to nearly 20,000 less than Owen's. An Old Stock Republican complained, "Whenever we have elected a Scandinavian to an office, they have ever after claimed a warranty deed to it, and you couldn't get them out with a stump-puller."[27]

In office, lawyer Nelson began writing up the warranty deed by aiding Haecker's cooperative dairying drive and by pushing legislation to regulate grain elevators and to force railroads to serve cooperative elevators. Running for reelection in 1894, he delivered a major speech at Argyle in the Red River Valley wheat region—quoted at length in the *New York Evening Post* as nearly the definitive Republican answer to Populism. Suggesting the answer was dairying, Nelson compared Freeborn County (dairy region) to Polk County (wheat region): Freeborn's twenty-four creameries and fine herds produced butter in demand on the market, paid a dependable cash income, and supported 900 people per township; Polk had two creameries, its wheat brought low prices due to "a glut in the foreign market," money was "quite scarce," and wheat farming supported only 400 people per township. Populist "I-told-you-so reformers" who blamed Polk's problems on Republican government were setting "class against class" and calling the farmer "the neglected stepson of organized society," but Republicans truly aided wheat farmers and University experiment stations aided those who wanted to escape wheat and enter dairying.[28]

Many farmers made the switch. Using Clarks Grove's creamery as his model, Haecker traveled the state and circulated his farm-school bulletins promoting cooperative dairying. In December 1894, the state had 149 cooperative creameries; by 1898, there were 560. The dairy region expanded from its original core in south-central Minnesota northward to central and west-central areas that had been wheat-raising counties.[29]

Despite hard times following the Panic of 1893, Nelson easily won reelection in 1894, added nearly 40,000 votes to his 1892 total, and split the wheat counties with the Populist candidate, Sidney Owen. Still, Owen more than doubled Donnelly's 1892 total, and Populism was not dead but was gaining strength for the 1896 showdown.[30]

State Senator Donnelly won partial revenge in 1893, when the legislature investigated decades-old frauds in the logging region linked to Republicans. Lumbermen had long acquired government lands fraudulently, conspired with state officials to underestimate the timber they cut from state-owned lands, and thus woefully underpaid stumpage fees due the state. Tree harvests were "five to ten times greater than what the surveyor general reported." Wielding their ability to expose lumbermen's frauds, Republican state officials, the surveyors general, charged exorbitant "scaling fees" for doing the estimating—which they hardly did at all—and pumped the revenues into the party's campaigns. Nelson had gained from these campaign funds but joined Donnelly in exposing this loss of millions in state revenue. The pineland probe foreshadowed a Progressive movement that replaced Populists' class-based issues with issues of good government, fair elections, and an honest civil service. Populists' demand for lower interest rates helped debtors and hurt creditors or investors; their call for higher wheat prices helped farmers but hurt millers or consumers of flour. Such demands were often just but aroused opposition. When the 1895 legislature acted to end pine-land abuses, no significant class was unjustly hurt.[31]

Nelson asked the 1895 legislature to elect him to the U.S. Senate instead of incumbent William D. Washburn of the Minneapolis flour-milling family. Before 1912, legislatures elected senators; direct popular election was a procedural issue pushed by Populists and Progressives. A candidate for the U.S. Senate influenced legislative elections by seeking commitments from legislative candidates, funneling support and money to those pledged to aid him, and working to defeat the others. Washburn relied on federal employees who owed their jobs due to his influence, especially the Minneapolis postmaster. Such friends (and others) then offered campaign contributions to pro-Washburn candidates. Another Progressive demand was for merit-based appointments to government jobs—civil service reform. Working behind the scenes, Governor Nelson used his appointees, especially state oil inspectors, to push for legislative candidates who favored him.[32]

Geographical, ethnic, and class divisions also drove the Nelson-Washburn fight. Minneapolis demanded its *own* U.S. senator—the other one, Cushman K. Davis, lived in St. Paul. The two cities' rivalry was at its peak. St. Paul police officers arrested Minneapolis' census-counting committee in 1890 for

When Republican delegates came to Minneapolis for the 1892 nominating convention, they saw the Mississippi River at St. Anthony Falls, crossed by the Great Northern Railroad's Stone Arch Bridge, and flanked by nearby flour mills, 1900. *Courtesy of the Minnesota Historical Society.*

"alleged census fraud," and the Mill City retaliated by charging St. Paul with fraud. Both were guilty: the Mill City inflated its true count by 11 percent; the capital city, by 7 percent. How could one senator represent two quarreling cities? Old Stock leaders sought to retain both Senate seats. A native of Maine, the millionaire Washburn personified the aristocratic style. His ten-acre Fair Oaks estate in Minneapolis boasted the city's finest sixty-foot-high mansion with mahogany and walnut finery, "marble floor with Washburn's monogram" and "onyx fireplaces." Each New Year's Day, he allowed his common constituents to pay $1 to come in and shake hands with him. "Uncle Knute," the Alexandria Norwegian living in a nine-room house and farming 120 acres, hobnobbed with farm families at country fairs. This stark contrast worked in Nelson's favor with voters, but they had no vote here. Furious lobbying began once legislators arrived for the 1895 session. Bribes, job offers, petitions, appeals to Scandinavian pride, pressure from constituents—all were reportedly thrown at legislators for three weeks until Nelson became the nation's first Scandinavian-American senator. They couldn't get him out with a stump-puller, and he served until he died in 1923.[33]

The 'Free Silver' Issue
Provokes the 1896 Battle of Armageddon

The other major Scandinavian politician, John Lind, was unlike Nelson. Also a lawyer linked to the land office and the first of his ethnic group elected to Congress (1886), Lind won more as a personable Republican than as a Swede. He lived in German New Ulm and Old Stock Tracy; his Congressional district had only one heavily Swedish area. In 1886, he faced no fireworks as Nelson had in 1882. His fight came in 1890 when he survived the Alliance tide with less than 500 votes to spare. Like Nelson, he retired after three terms in the House. What drew him back into politics and away from his party was the issue of bimetallism, the coinage of gold *and* silver to increase the money supply. Defenders saw this as an antidote to the deflation that was raising the value of each dollar and the burden of each debt. Detractors saw it as dishonest inflation letting debtors repay loans with dollars worth less than ones they had received. Lind's friend from Congress, William Jennings Bryan, pushed silver coinage to the forefront in 1894-96. A Silver Republican, Lind supported the cause. When his party went for gold only, he left it and ran for governor in 1896 as the Fusion candidate of Silver Republicans, the People's Party, and the Democrats. Bryan was the Fusion candidate for President.[34]

Only men could vote (women could vote for school offices and, after 1898, for library offices), so late-nineteenth-century campaigns were male, almost military, affairs. Two or three sides mobilized their armies at the

Political buttons became popular by the end of the nineteenth century. John Lind, Democrat and Populist candidate for governor, needed different versions for his 1896, 1898, and 1900 campaigns.
Courtesy of Leonard Nadasdy.

township level. Local captains talked to each voter. County colonels commanded newspapers and sent out pamphlets by the thousands. Party generals in St. Paul plotted strategy, picked candidates, and employed tricks of the trade. When a candidate visited a small town, bands and parades excited the party faithful and impressed the undecided. When Nelson came by train to Argyle in 1894, a crowd met him at the depot, the Argyle Cornet Band played, and it led a march down the street to the hall.[35] Nothing matched the 1896 Battle of Armageddon: William McKinley's Gold-standard Republicans against Bryan's Silver Democrat-Populist coalition. McKinley stayed home in Canton, Ohio, but campaign money flowed into Minnesota. Republican editors and spokesmen hinted a Bryan-Lind win would lead to depression, bankruptcies, joblessness, and a loss of the state's credit. The *St. Paul Dispatch* pounded Lind for agnosticism, membership in the Turners, and his role in the New Ulm school fight. Several Swedish-American spokesmen and papers opposed him, and he lost Lutheran Chisago County by a three-to-one margin. Bryan came to the Twin Cities in October and spoke to 10,000 at the St. Paul Auditorium and thousands at other halls and the Minneapolis Exposition Hall. Bryan lost the national election and Lind, the state one.[36]

The rhetoric cried that civilization was at stake, but not all the action was serious. Politics was free or low-cost entertainment in an age that had less of it. For the last day of the Carlton County fair at Barnum, organizers invited the Silver Republican congressman, Charles Towne, to debate J. Adam Bede, a humorist and newspaperman who favored the gold standard. Four hundred Duluthians—gold bugs and silverites but few neutral—came down on a special train and marched behind a band to the fairgrounds, paid their quarter to enter, and went to the grandstand where nearly a thousand people gathered. Men stood while ladies sat on hay bales for the two-hour debate. The serious Towne began with ancient Rome while Bede gave "witticisms" about the two being exhibited "like pumpkins and hogs. Suppose hogs and cows were made legal tender, we'd pay our debts in hogs"—bad money (silver) drove out good money (gold), the gold bugs asserted.[37]

Stressing agrarian issues, Bryan failed to appeal to urban workers or the middle class. Rural-only reform could not succeed in an urbanizing nation. Defeat did not halt the snowballing reform drive, which just added urban issues to its weight as it rolled into a Progressivism that added new demands to old Populist ones.

Progressivism Uses Science to Craft Municipal Ordinances to Govern Cities

The Founders had never written an Ordinance for establishing and governing cities, which grew with little organized attention to forming a balanced, family-centered, moral society. In the 1880s, Minneapolis grew by 251 percent to reach a population of 165,000. St. Paul grew by 221 percent to a size of 133,000. Home ownership was unaffordable for many workers while manufacturing, wholesaling, and retailing firms earned fortunes for their owners. In Swede Hollow, Italians came to live in shacks vacated by the Swedes and Irish; outhouses perched on stilts over Phalen Creek; the city provided no water or sewer services; on the bluff, brewer Theodore Hamm's mansion overlooked the shacks of several hundred poor immigrants. Could the property-less be real citizens and vote against their wealthy employers' wishes? Ward bosses provided city jobs, handed out gifts at holidays, aided a stricken family, protected the neighborhood saloonkeeper from the law, and were predictably reelected. Turn-of-the-century Minneapolis' city-wide boss, Mayor Albert Ames, led a crooked regime that became nationally notorious. Any one family was powerless to end corruption; any one church counted for little amidst so many denominations; the elementary and secondary schools could hardly educate adult ward-heelers to change their corrupt ways. Who could reform and govern the cities?[38]

In the mid-1880s, the national labor movement, the Knights of Labor, tried to give working men political and economic clout similar to what farmers had in their Alliance. Coopers making barrels for Minneapolis flour mills formed the nation's largest, most successful Knights cooperatives. By 1886, eight barrel-making cooperatives did $1 million in annual business and employed over 60 percent of the city's coopers. More than money was involved. The cooperatives formed a community of family-oriented, home-owning, frugal, drink-avoiding workers who socialized together across ethnic lines and formed something "like a small town." Strikes, discord, and firings ended this attempt.[39]

The *Minneapolis Tribune* editor who wrote about the coopers, Albert Shaw, was a leading student of European municipal governments, which Progressives saw as models unencumbered by Americans' stress on rural life, liking for weak governments, and belief in laissez-faire freedom for businesses to do as they pleased. Now professor of political science at the

University, Folwell used Shaw's *Municipal Government* in his seminar. With its thousands of students and a hundred faculty experts, the University was the one urban school that could aid in solving urban problems. Its blueprint was secular. Folwell and other faculty stressed science. Progressivism's scientific spirit preferred the nonpartisan expert in a commission over the partisan alderman or legislator. It never matched the University of Wisconsin's close ties to that state's Progressive government, but when sociologist George Vincent replaced Northrop as its president in 1911, he expanded its services to the state by adding county agents and extension weeks in small towns. University experts were already spearheading a League of Minnesota Municipalities.[40]

Lincoln Steffens exposed Mayor Ames as "The Shame of Minneapolis" in *McClure's Magazine* (1903), after Ames was indicted by the grand jury. Old Stock leaders sprang into action. They had insisted on laws ending prostitution and gambling, and regulating saloons, but Ames and his police fined offenders, pocketed much of the money, and let illegal businesses continue. Citizens formed the Minneapolis Voters' League in 1904. Reformers ran for city council seats. The streetcar and telephone companies had joined in corrupting the city council, so reformers demanded that the city own utilities and hold at-large elections to the council to end ward bosses. In 1906, these leaders formed the Saturday Lunch Club, a group of civic-minded professional men and academics who met to hear talks and discuss issues at noon on Saturdays—the 5½ day workweek ended then. The club shaped liberal opinion on issues for decades thereafter.[41]

In urban areas where social problems were more complex, in an age revering science and increasingly skeptical of traditional religion, the church and the family were no longer unanimously seen as the adequate and necessary basis of morality and public order. Other institutions might have to supplement or even replace them, for some issues.

Progressives sought to purify politics and reform cities by giving women the right to vote. The Grange admitted women as members, and the Women's Christian Temperance Union had fought against saloons for decades. Women were mainstays of many a rural and urban church. The urban crisis of the 1880s and 1890s gave women a new field of action in which their public speaking and organizing could be justified (to the skeptical) as an extension of their duty to protect the home and family, now threatened by the saloon, unsanitary conditions, gambling and prostitution, and joblessness. In 1881, women started the Minnesota Woman Suffrage Association (MWSA). The 1890s saw a multiplication of women's clubs, which became forums for women to hone their skills in researching issues, forming a consensus, and lobbying city councils or legislatures. Some clubs offered the intellectual stimulation which upper-class women who had not attended college enjoyed. MWSA had twenty-four branch clubs by 1912, but its "organizational mainstay" was the Political Equality Club of Minneapolis, and its leaders tended to be Minneapolis Unitarians like Clara Ueland, Nanny Jaeger, and Maud Stockwell, or University faculty like Francis Potter and Mary Peck. Unitarians had their own church and some University faculty were religious, but both groups stressed scientific rationales for reform. Like male partisan politics, the female world of reform causes became more secular after 1890.[42]

Male Progressives thought woman suffrage would add new Progressive voters. Most married women were not employees whose vote could be swayed by a corporate boss or a ward boss. Justice and morality would lead them to fight bosses, patronage, corruption, and officials' tolerance of prostitution and gambling. Progressives relied on women's support in the fight against saloons and liquor. Woman suffrage advocates used this role of purifying politics as an argument for their cause. Clara Ueland urged women to get the vote to battle "the three evils of the day—liquor, prostitution and war." High license fees had not solved the liquor problem, so by 1908 Progressives favored county option—allowing voters in a county to decide whether liquor sales would be allowed or outlawed in that county. The county option battle drove the state's politics for the next seven years. Enlisting woman suffrage supporters to battle liquor also recruited opponents to the anti-suffrage cause—especially German Minnesotans who felt their beer-drinking culture was threatened.[43]

Progressive Reform Alienates German Americans & Iron Miners

Progressivism reconciled some ethnic groups. The Old Stock middle class joined the Scandinavian and British-American middle class on most issues. Yet conflict between those groups and Germans was heightened. Several issues intertwined, Progressives felt. They used the German word *plunderbund* to describe their foes—brewers and liquor distillers (often of German ancestry) who fought county option by appealing to their customers, bribing city councils, aiding political machines to control the legislature, fighting the primary election and nonpartisan rules that might end machines, opposing woman suffrage, and allying with any anti-Progressive faction.[44] Progressivism was the consensus. Republicans or Democrats could be Progressives. So could Main Street merchants who feared mail-order competition from Montgomery Ward or Sears. Scandinavian farmers were Progressive, even in the wheat region. Populism was dead, and rural cooperatives were their main hope now that government intervention was ruled out. Labor was Progressive barring other options. Germans were the main group outside the consensus.[45]

The personable small-town editor John A. Johnson, governor from 1905 to 1909, personified this consensus. A Democrat from St. Peter, Johnson was lukewarm on Bryan in 1896, for he disliked "the alignment of class against class and section against section, which Bryan had so clearly called for." A small-town editor often must work with people of all classes. In 1904, Johnson won due to a Republican factional fight and the lingering effects of the pine-lands scandals. He was inaugurated in the new state capitol, the state's third, designed by architect Cass Gilbert and opened in 1905. He got along with the Republican-controlled legislature and achieved several Progressive goals: an end

Official postcard depicting Governor John A. Johnson and the Minnesota seal.
Courtesy of Moira F. Harris.

Political buttons for Governor and possible Presidential candidate John A. Johnson, circa 1905.
Courtesy of Leonard Nadasdy.

to free rail passes long used to influence public officials; passage of a "wide-open" constitutional amendment freeing state government to use innovative taxes like the income tax; a law allowing cities to own utilities; and more rules on sales of state timber lands.[46]

Sometimes one class aligned itself against another class and one region pitted itself against another region. Progressives were least able to handle zero-sum conflicts where there was no expert scientific solution, where better procedures would solve nothing, and where compromise seemed impossible. The 1907 Mesabi strike pitted thousands of workers led by the Western Federation of Miners against Oliver Iron Mining Company, part of U.S. Steel Corporation. Strikers held rallies and armed themselves. The middle class of Range businessmen, Oliver foremen, and skilled employees armed themselves, some as deputies. The company and the county sheriff asked Governor Johnson to send troops to maintain order—in effect, to break the strike. Johnson toured the Range to speak to strikers, strike leaders, company officials, and government officials. The former editor collected his facts by listening carefully. Johnson could not bring the two sides together, bring himself to send troops, or do anything to resolve the impasse. The company ended the strike with strikebreakers. About 75 percent of the strikers were Finns, so nearly 1,200 Finns were blacklisted from mining employment, forced to seek work in logging or farming, and further radicalized. Around 1,000 Montenegrins came in as strikebreakers. The 1907 strike created volatile conditions for further labor unrest, despite Johnson's best efforts.[47]

Governor John A. Johnson with James J. Hill and others, seated behind the railing, circa 1905. *Courtesy of the Minnesota Historical Society.*

Progressivism Largely Ignores American Indians, But Not Forest Conservation

American Indians were a class ignored, except by reformers like Bishop Whipple. State government regarded reservations as a region not in Minnesota but under federal jurisdiction. In the late nineteenth century, white interest in their lands led to a push to concentrate the Ojibwe in one area, and reformers opted for the White Earth Reservation, which had the best farming potential. There, reformers hoped an Ordinance-style allotment policy that gave each family a farmstead and a rural society of farms, schools, and churches would assimilate the Ojibwe into American society. However, lumber companies committed the usual land-claim and stumpage frauds, and white farmers or real-estate dealers used liquor and other means to get Ojibwe to sell their allotted land and give up the Ordinance-like design for a new Ojibwe society, which was unfamiliar to many of them. The state did not halt this Ojibwe impoverishment but successfully litigated its claim to swampland at White Earth.[48] The Ojibwe at Red Lake and other sites kept their former status, and Dakota families returned to Minnesota in small groups to southern and western Minnesota. Progressives' reforming zeal did not significantly aid the state's American Indian population.

Progressives did tackle the rapid depletion of the state's forest resources, and their approach summarizes their ideas and methods. As with other issues, they built on earlier efforts—the pioneering forestry work of Christopher C. Andrews, a Yankee and a Civil War general who warned in 1856 of lumbermen defrauding the government of its timber land. Typically, the reformer Andrews had been to Europe (as U.S. minister to Sweden from 1869 to 1877), and he pointed to a superior European example—Swedish iron manufacturers' reforestation projects to protect their charcoal supply. He stressed the science of forest management and fought for a school of forestry at the University, but the legislature acted only after the Hinckley fire of 1894 killed over four hundred people—and it stressed fire-fighting rather than science. Its 1895 law utilized the old systems of government by making the state auditor act as the state's forest commissioner and township supervisors act as the fire wardens—and Andrews became the chief fire warden to serve under the former and to supervise and educate the latter. The frugal legislators set aside only $6,000 a year to protect a $100 million resource. Still, the reformer had a toehold.[49]

Fueled by "slashings," the dried branches and unusable trunks left after logging, the Hinckley fire was a "catastrophic fire" feeding on the gasses it created and racing along the canopy in unlogged areas. Afterwards, white pine did not re-grow, for the seed stock had burned. Forestry could not confine itself to fire-fighting. Andrews got his duties expanded to forest investigations. Then he promoted the creation of new forest reserves that would be scientifically managed and reforested—the Cass Lake reserve (1902) that led to the Chippewa National Forest, and the Superior National Forest that Progressive President Theodore Roosevelt created in February 1909. Andrews enlisted Progressives in the Minnesota Federation of Women's Clubs to lobby for these reserves. Typically, this reformer's office grew also—into the Forestry Commissioner (1905), then the Forestry Board (1911) that hired experts, a state forester, and his assistant to manage the work. Forestry reform and scientific management were placed on a firm foundation, at least in districts set aside for future reforestation and management, but Progressives had not overturned the logging system in most districts that was based upon misuse of the Ordinances' land laws. This imbalanced exploitation of forested land had nearly finished its job by the time they succeeded in ending it at a few sites—lumbermen were already looking to move their operations to the Pacific Northwest. Andrews, the forestry sheriff, performed a splendid service, but he arrived with partial legal powers only after the property had been mostly stolen.[50]

On October 12, 1918, fueled again by slashings, two huge fires hit Cloquet and environs and the Kettle River-Moose Lake area. Over 450 people were killed, 11,000 families forced from their homes, and $30 million in property destroyed. Ten towns, including the city of Cloquet, were entirely burned. The U.S. fleet in the North Atlantic saw the smoke blown eastward, but the great 1918 fire commanded less attention in Minnesota than had the 1894 fire, for the state was preoccupied with the Great War.[51]

1. "Oliver H. Kelley," Thomas A. Woods, *Knights of the Plow: Oliver H. Kelley and the Origins of the Grange in Republican Ideology* (Ames: Iowa State University Press, 1991), 76, 170; Keillor, *Cooperative Commonwealth*, 35, 39.

2. "organize the Grange," Woods, *Knights of the Plow*, 94-96, 104, 112-14, 117, 150-51, 165-76; Keillor, *Cooperative Commonwealth*, 35-39.

3. "complained," Keillor, *Cooperative Commonwealth*, 38-39; *Red Wing Argus*, 8 May (1) and 22 May (4), and 24 July (4), all 1873.

4. "attacked railroads," "Report of the Proceedings of the Anti-Monopoly Convention held at Rochester, Minn., Dec. 1st, 1870," pamphlet in MHS; *Rochester Post*, 3 December 1870, 3 (calling it an "Anti-Railroad Convention"); Folwell, *History of Minnesota*, Vol. III, 32-33, 39-57; Hartzell, *I Started All This*, 85, 102.

5. "Dr. William W. Mayo," Hartzell, *I Started All This*, 85.

6. "Granger cooperatives," Keillor, *Cooperative Commonwealth*, 11-99.

7. "economic reverses," Folwell, *History of Minnesota*, Vol. III, 93-111, 141

8. "Americanized," Gieske and Keillor, *Norwegian Yankee*, 27-29, 66-68, 77-83, 89-90, 92-96, 99.

9. "Nelson's 1892 campaign," Gieske and Keillor, *Norwegian Yankee*, 97-119. As it neared Moorhead, the NP also passed through the wheat region, but most of its Minnesota line passed through non-farming areas.

10. "a contentious issue," Folwell, *History of Minnesota*, Vol. IV, 143-73; Paul Kleppner, *The Cross of Culture: A Social Analysis of Midwestern Politics 1850–1900* (New York: Free Press, 1970), 158-68.

11. "Lind lived in New Ulm," George Stephenson, *John Lind of Minnesota* (Minneapolis: University of Minnesota Press, 1935), 16, 21, 23, 122-29.

12. "Nelson had moved," Gieske and Keillor, *Norwegian Yankee*, 62-67, 126-27.

13. "Ignatius Donnelly," Martin Ridge, *Ignatius Donnelly: Portrait of a Politician* (Chicago: University of Chicago Press, 1962), 3, 4, 5, 12, 265-67.

14. Hartzell, *I Started All This*, 79-80, 87-88.

15. "debate swirled," Steven J. Keillor, "Premodern, Modern, Postmodern: A History of Ideas at the University of Minnesota, 1869–1984," Chapters 1-2, unpublished manuscript in author's possession. The main sources are Folwell's diary (MHS), his inaugural and NEA speeches, and papers in the University Archives.

16. "President in Court," *Minneapolis Journal*, 16 May (1) and 17 May (4), both 1882.

17. "site of this debate," Keillor, "Premodern, Modern, Postmodern," 22, 26-27, 34-39, 47, 49-55.

18. "they did so to educate," Johnson, "Germans," 166-67, and Rice, "Swedes," 265, and Qualey and Gjerde, "Norwegians," 235, all in Holmquist, ed., *They Chose Minnesota*; Blegen, *Minnesota: A History*, 415-19; Shaw, *Bernt Julius Muus*, 233-55; Merrill E. Jarchow, *Private Liberal Arts Colleges in Minnesota: Their History and Contributions* (St. Paul: Minnesota Historical Society, 1973), 13-15, 17-20, 25-29, 41-43.

19. "an 1876 law," Keillor, "Premodern, Modern, Postmodern," 20.

20. "liquor battles," Lowell J. Soike, *Norwegian Americans and the Politics of Dissent 1880–1924* (Northfield: Norwegian-American Historical Association, 1991), 62-68; Folwell, *History of Minnesota*, Vol. III, 172-79; Conzen, *Germans*, 61-61, 66.

21. "reenactment," *Minneapolis Tribune*, 7 August 1887.

22. "Farmers' Alliance," Keillor, *Cooperative Commonwealth*, 147-68; Gieske and Keillor, *Norwegian Yankee*, 148.

23. "a formidable movement," Ridge, *Ignatius Donnelly*, 168-73, 183-87, 246-47; Keillor, *Cooperative Commonwealth*, 155-58, 191-97.

24. "the vigorous Irish orator," Ridge, *Ignatius Donnelly*, 278 (quoting Donnelly), 398.

25. "a third party," Folwell, *History of Minnesota*, Vol. III, 188-89; Bruce M. White, et al., comps., *Minnesota Votes: Election Returns by County for Presidents, Senators, Congressmen, and Governors, 1857–1977* (St. Paul: Minnesota Historical Society, 1977), 166; Gieske and Keillor, *Norwegian Yankee*, 150-51, 154, 160; Keillor, *Cooperative Commonwealth*, 134-35.

26. "1892 national convention," June Drenning Holmquist, "Convention City: The Republicans in Minneapolis, 1892," *Minnesota History*, Vol. 35, No. 2 (June 1956), 64-76.

27. "Nelson headed," Gieske and Nelson, *Norwegian Yankee*, 161, 165-68, 170.

28. "a major speech," White, et al., *Minnesota Votes*, 167-68; Gieske and Keillor, *Norwegian Yankee*, 177-80, 194-96; *New York Evening Post*, 6(?) August 1894, clipping in Box 5, Nelson Papers, MHS; *Warren Sheaf*, 9 August 1894, 4.

29. "farmers made the switch," Keillor, *Cooperative Commonwealth*, 124, 135-36.

30. "Nelson easily won reelection," White, et al., *Minnesota Votes*, 168-69.

31. "the legislature investigated," Gieske and Keillor, *Norwegian Yankee*, 181-84; Folwell, *History of Minnesota*, Vol. III, 500-15.

32. "Nelson asked," Gieske and Keillor, *Norwegian Yankee*, 201-06. The 16th Amendment to the U.S. Constitution requiring direct election was adopted in 1913, but the state legislature had already acted to require the 1912 vote to be by direct election.

33. "Nelson-Washburn fight," Wingerd, *Claiming the City*, 13-16; Gieske and Keillor, *Norwegian Yankee*, 199-220.

34. "John Lind," Stephenson, *John Lind*, 23-26, 31-43, 61-63, 66, 79, 83, 101-11.

35. "When Nelson came," *Marshall County Banner*, 2 August 1894, 1.

36. "the 1896 Battle of Armageddon," Ridge, *Ignatius Donnelly*, 362-63; Stephenson, *John Lind*, 117-29; White, et al., *Minnesota Votes*, 169.

37. "Carlton County fair," *Duluth Herald*, 26 September 1896, 1, 2, 4; *Duluth News Tribune*, 26 September 1896, 1, 2; *Cloquet Pine Knot*, 26 September 1896, 1, 8.

38. "governing cities," Wingerd, *Claiming the City*, 16, 79-82; Barbara Stuhler, *Gentle Warriors: Clara Ueland and the Minnesota Struggle for Woman Suffrage* (St. Paul: Minnesota Historical Society Press, 1995), 24; Langran, "Swedish Neighborhoods," 45, in Anderson and Blanck, eds., *Swedes in the Twin Cities*; Rudolph J. Vecoli, "The Italians," 453, in Holmquist, ed., *They Chose Minnesota*; Lincoln Steffens, "The Shame of Minneapolis," in *McClure's Magazine*, Vol. 20, No. 3 (January 1903).

39. "Coopers making barrels," Steve Leikin, "The Cooperative Coopers of Minneapolis,"

Minnesota History, Vol. 57, No. 8 (Winter 2001-02), 386-405.

40. "Progressives saw," Daniel T. Rodgers, *Atlantic Crossings: Social Politics in a Progressive Age* (Cambridge, Mass.: Harvard University Press, 1998), 40-43, 132-35; Keillor, "Premodern, Modern, Postmodern," 59, 85-91.

41. "sprang into action," William P. Everts, Jr., *Stockwell of Minneapolis: A Pioneer of Social and Political Conscience* (St. Cloud: North Star Press, 1996), 142-48, 165-71; Carl H. Chrislock, *The Progressive Era in Minnesota 1899–1918* (St. Paul: Minnesota Historical Society, 1971), 26.

42. "women started," Stuhler, *Gentle Warriors*, 28-29, 48-50, 51-53, 62-67.

43. "thought woman suffrage," Chrislock, *Progressive Era*, 3; Stuhler, *Gentle Warriors*, 61-63, 75, 107.

44. "issues intertwined," Chrislock, *Progressive Era*, 31-32; Conzen, *Germans*, 66.

45. "consensus," Chrislock, *Progressive Era*, 22-35.

46. "John A. Johnson," Chrislock, *Progressive Era*, 18-19; Winifred G. Helmes, *John A. Johnson, The People's Governor: A Political Biography* (Minneapolis: University of Minnesota Press, 1949), 87, 152-53, 168, 173-75.

47. "the 1907 Mesabi strike," Helmes, *John A. Johnson*, 218-24; Riippa, "Finns," 309-10, and Holmquist, et al., "South Slavs," 392-93, both in Holmquist, ed., *They Chose Minnesota*; Chrislock, *Progressive Era*, 30-31.

48. "concentrate the Ojibwe," Melissa L. Meyer, *The White Earth Tragedy: Ethnicity and Dispossession at a Minnesota Anishinaabe Reservation* (Lincoln, Neb.: University of Nebraska Press, 1994), 49-52, 137-40, 142-56, 212-13; Gieske and Keillor, *Norwegian Yankee*, 137-43.

49. "pioneering forestry work," Folwell, *History of Minnesota*, Vol. IV, 386-89; Christopher C. Andrews, *Recollections: 1829–1922* (Cleveland: Arthur H. Clark Co., 1928), 222, 275-78, 285-87; Forester, *Forest for the Trees*, 103-14.

50. "got his duties expanded," Forester, *Forest for the Trees*, 16-17, 21, 113-15, 118-19, 123-28; Folwell, *History of Minnesota*, Vol. IV, 388-95; Andrews, *Recollections*, 286-98.

51. "two huge fires," Francis M. Carroll and Franklin R. Raiter, *The Fires of Autumn: The Cloquet— Moose Lake Disaster of 1918* (St. Paul: Minnesota Historical Society Press, 1990), 3-6.

Progressive Order
Leads to Disorder

Like other Americans, Minnesotans were shocked when the assassination of Archduke Franz Ferdinand on June 28, 1914, led to European powers' exchanging ultimatums, mobilizing armies, and then declaring war in August. Many University faculty, including President Vincent, were on summer study tours of Europe at the time. Some had difficulty securing emergency passage home. They shared most Minnesotans' neutralist views. Immigrants had left Europe to escape its wars and opposed U.S. involvement in them.[1] The war threatened the Progressives' consensus on domestic affairs, and the consensus would not hold on foreign policy, which was an emotional, moral subject very unlike their rational, procedural issues.

A rural society of weak governments and local control was not designed to mobilize a state to support the nation in a European war. Progressives built a second story of stronger agencies atop the old ones to tackle problems of large cities, new industries, and big corporations. The state had new commissions to regulate railroads and industry, new taxes beside the real estate tax, more control over schools, and new election laws to limit bosses' power. The Australian ballot, voter registration, primaries, a nonpartisan legislature, and popular election of U.S. senators existed by 1914. With 5,000 students and 100 faculty members, the University was a strong institution whose professors gave social-scientific advice to the state and whose county agents taught better farming methods and promoted rural school consolidation and other 'scientific' solutions to reluctant farmers.[2] Experts' ideas of city reform and municipal utilities were adopted. Ames' machine was driven out of Minneapolis. In 1914, Democrat Winfield Hammond won the governorship—a win for Progressives and a defeat for Edward Smith's Republican machine.[3]

The most bitterly-opposed reform—thus, the greatest victory—was county option, which the legislature passed and Hammond signed into law in February 1915. By mid-summer, forty-three counties voted themselves dry. Political parties were weakened by the seven-year fight over liquor. As part of that battle, the 1913 legislature prohibited the use of party labels by legislative candidates and county officials.[4] Progressivism was a nonpartisan movement that seemed to regard political parties as opportunists who seized on the flaws of the Ordinance system of local control and weak government in order to increase their own power. Now the parties were weakened and Progressivism triumphant.

Credit the editors, for this era was the heyday of the rural newspaper editor in Minnesota. John A. Johnson was the most famous, but others improved their papers, stressed editorial independence, cut their dependence on political parties, and crusaded for reform. Editors like Victor Lawson of the *Willmar Tribune*, Gunnar Bjornson of the *Minnesota Mascot*, and Frank Day of the *Fairmont Sentinel* were powerful voices in print. Rural readers could receive all their news from weekly papers, which had "patent insides" of national news and ads that were distributed by a regional syndicate.[5] Along with the county agent, the editor served as a broker translating the unfamiliar ideas of the University expert or a state commission into ordinary language understood in village and township. The experts' science was universal and cosmopolitan. It expanded the idea of democracy beyond a simple means to govern localities and made it a scientific principle for resolving distant, abstract, or enormous problems hard for ordinary citizens to visualize or analyze, from governing a city to regulating international relations. It often disregarded common-sense opinions or religious beliefs influential in ethnic enclaves. The editor translated science into common sense.

Progressives' scientific agencies and language did not solve conflicts of economic and ethnic regions. Wheat farmers still fought Minneapolis millers, railroads, and grain elevators. Iron miners were still nearly powerless dependents of the mining companies. A vast inequality of wealth and power still separated workers and management in the Twin Cities. Science could not conceal the fact that some had power and some did not.

Challenges to the Progressive Consensus: 1) The 1916 Mesabi Strike

The first conflict to erupt and shake Progressives' consensus occurred in the mining region. By 1915, the new Cuyuna range that ran seventy miles northeast from Brainerd was being mined. During World War I, steelmakers came to value its iron ore's high manganese content. Taxation of the mining industry divided all three ranges from the other regions—the other regions wanted mines to bear more of the state's tax burden while the mining region feared high taxes might threaten its economy. The initial (1881) tax of a penny per ton of ore was declared unconstitutional in 1896. Mines were then taxed at their assessed value like other real estate. Progressives favored a tonnage tax on grounds that the state lost a natural resource as each ton was mined, and should be compensated. Governor Johnson vetoed a tonnage tax bill in 1909 as an unjust form of double taxation. An implicit deal emerged: U.S. Steel Corporation built a steel plant in Morgan Park (creating a company suburb of Duluth) that opened in 1915, employed 3,000 workers, and made wire, posts, and ties for sale to farmers—and the legislature backed off from adding more taxes on iron ore.[6]

Tensions remained between workers and Oliver Iron Mining, a division of U.S. Steel, on the Mesabi range. Workers were paid by a piecework rate based on the amount of ore mined per day. That penalized those who worked harder on more obstructed ore veins and left all miners uncertain of their monthly pay. Dangerous mines, poor living conditions, and long hours were grievances too. A spontaneous strike began at Aurora on June 2, 1916. Hundreds of miners—Finns and miners from southern and eastern Europe—marched down the Mesabi to spread the strike and demand an hourly wage and bimonthly paychecks. They met in Finnish socialist halls. The Industrial Workers of the World (IWW) sent organizers, including the aptly named Sam Scarlett, to head an increasingly militant strike of 8,000 workers. Refusing to negotiate, Oliver Mining hired a private army of guards who went beyond protecting mine property to attacking picketers in streets and residential areas. On June 21, the sight of a red flag in front of a strike parade caused anti-strike forces to attack the marchers. Three men were killed in the next two weeks. A parallel battle raged as the strikers harassed strikebreakers brought in by the company.[7]

Governments could not maintain law and order. The range towns tried to mediate, but Oliver officials refused their offers. Larger than some states, St. Louis County was dominated by Duluth, and its government did not side with the towns. Its sheriff deputized Oliver guards, who joined in one gunfight that led to two deaths. Strike leaders were blamed, and legal proceedings against them were held in Duluth, not in the range towns. The Progressive governor, J. A. A. Burnquist, supported the sheriff's private army, did not disband Oliver's private army, and failed to call out the state militia. Progressives and other citizens viewed the IWW as a violent, irresponsible group. That enabled Burnquist to delegate the state's law-and-order duties to a county and a company. Oliver waited until the hungry workers had to return to work.[8]

Challenges to the Progressive Consensus: 2) The Nonpartisan League

Next, tensions intensified in the wheat region. Farmers had created cooperative elevators in the preceding twenty years, but their impact was limited and local. Many farmers' elevators operated on credit furnished by Twin Cities grain commission firms that insisted they market their grain at the Minneapolis Chamber of Commerce (MCC), a grain exchange run by flour millers. In 1908, the new American Society of Equity started a cooperative grain exchange to give farmers' elevators a better price at the terminal market in Minneapolis. A bitter eight-year war between the two exchanges followed.[9]

In July 1916, the Nonpartisan League (NPL) crossed the Red River to hold its first Minnesota meeting eight miles from East Grand Forks. North Dakota farmers resented being a colonial grain region run by the Twin Cities' milling, railroad, and elevator giants. Their state government did not have true political-economic independence from these giants. Their farmers' elevators were not truly independent of the MCC. A bankrupt flax farmer, ex-Socialist organizer, and native Minnesotan, Arthur C. Townley combined Socialists' idea of a disciplined group of dues-paying members with Progressives' primary election. Busy farmers gave up time-consuming meetings, let Townley and his NPL leaders make key decisions, paid $16 membership dues, and promised to vote for NPL candidates in the Republican primary. The NPL-elected legislators and governor would pass reforms to end the state's weakness vis-á-vis the giants: state-owned terminal elevators and flour mills to bypass the MCC, state rules for grading grain, and a state-owned bank. Townley's initials were ACT: don't wait for reform to trickle up from the Ordinance-designed system; the NPL will organize a top-down command. The NPL won in 1916, took control of North Dakota, passed the reforms, and moved on to Minnesota.[10]

In the fall of 1916, nearly ninety NPL organizers in their Model T Fords rolled into Minnesota. In June 1917, NPL speakers came for all-day picnics and indoor meetings. Total attendance at four events exceeded 10,000. "There were games, band music, singing, an abundance of speech-making, and plenty of good food" at the picnics. The wheat region welcomed the NPL, as 95 percent of farmers in some townships joined. Some Main Street merchants aided it.[11]

Minnesota had four other regions, whereas North Dakota was one grain-growing region. An IWW-led strike hit the logging region in late December 1916 and shut down mills in Virginia and International Falls but the companies broke the strike before the NPL could even sympathize with it.[12]

To win Minnesota, the NPL had to forge a farmer-labor alliance against strong opposition from the Twin-Cities-based giants and their allies, whereas few North Dakotans had favored the economic colonizers headquartered outside that state.

Townley was an ex-Socialist, for Socialism was suspect in church-centered areas of North Dakota (Minnesota too); however, Socialists dominated the Minneapolis labor unions' Trades and Labor Assembly and maintained strong locals in that city's wards where workers felt as much antagonism to the corporate giants as the prairie farmers did. In city elections, candidates for council and mayor ran without party designation; in Milwaukee and elsewhere "sewer Socialism" stressing municipal services gained popularity in those years. As a result, machinist and Socialist Thomas Van Lear was elected mayor of Minneapolis in 1916—alarming the city's business leaders nearly as much as the NPL triumph in North Dakota that year.[13]

Challenges to Progressive Consensus: 3) Debate over U.S. Entry into World War I

The war set some ethnic regions at odds with Old Stock Twin Cities business leaders. A British Navy blockade of Germany and Germans' retaliatory submarine blockade of Britain violated U.S. neutral maritime rights. Germany's sinking of the *Lusitania* in May 1915 angered Americans, which led Germany to end unrestricted submarine warfare. Yet that conditional promise could be revoked at any time. East Coast business, political, and cultural leaders like Theodore Roosevelt pushed for military preparedness and then for U.S. entry on the side of Britain. University Dean Guy Stanton Ford went in early 1916 from the neutral-minded Midwest to pro-Ally Harvard for his sabbatical; he arrived "in *terra incognito*" and asked a fellow historian, "What country is this I'm in?" Twin Cities bankers and businessmen joined Eastern colleagues in the National Security League to advocate a pro-Ally preparedness. In reply, the German-American press launched a pro-neutrality drive. Ethnic groups lined up on one side or the other. As an immigrants' state, Minnesota became one of the most deeply divided states.[14]

In an editorial ("The Hyphen Must Go"), the *Minneapolis Journal* reacted to immigrants—German Americans, Swedish Americans, etc.—taking a stand on U.S. foreign policy based on its impact on their homeland. The *Journal* spoke in generalities about the nation, but Minnesota's ethnic enclaves were among its chief targets. The U.S. 'melting-pot' would not work where "unmelted lumps . . . are permitted to endure." The *Journal* wrote that in many areas there were "old men who came here from Europe many years ago, yet who cannot carry on a conversation in English." Why was that? "There are newspapers published in some foreign language, schools, clubs, various organizations and social societies made up of 'hyphenated' Americans in every city. The various Continental languages are taught in the home and schools with almost religious regard for the traditions of many fatherlands." In the enclaves, English was the foreign language. With such splintering, the United States could not become a "great nation."[15]

Enclaves and their separate-ness threatened Minnesota's reputation in the nation, some spokesmen felt. In February-March 1916, Congress debated the Gore-McLemore resolutions that cautioned Americans not to travel on the ships of the warring nations if their routes entered war zones. Supporters of neutrality pushed these resolutions while preparedness advocates sought to table them as a craven surrender of America's rights on the high seas. All ten of the state's congressmen voted against tabling Gore-McLemore, as did Senator Moses Clapp. Only Senator Knute Nelson voted to table. *The New York Times* impugned the state's patriotism: "The Minnesota delegation in Congress consists of eleven Kaiserists and one American [Nelson]. . . . [The eleven] voted against the President, against the upholding of American rights. The German-American Alliance of Minnesota urged or bullied these eleven weaklings to the course they followed." The *Minneapolis Journal* and other papers seconded this opinion.[16] As in the Civil War, what was at stake was the state's good name—as judged by opinion-making Eastern elites and their press.

Pro-Ally, pro-preparedness leaders hoped voters would eject the "eleven weaklings" in 1916. Yet no congressman lost, save one beaten by a stronger neutralist, Ernest Lundeen of Minneapolis. St. Paul lawyer Frank B. Kellogg replaced Clapp only because several neutralist candidates ran in the primary and general elections. Kellogg won less than 50 percent of the vote in both elections. Becoming governor after Winfield Hammond's death in December 1915, the 37-year-old Swedish-American Burnquist

Political Button for J. A. A. Burnquist, who became governor when his predecessor died. He was running for that office in 1918. *Courtesy of Leonard Nadasdy.*

had "a kind of presumptive right" to be the Republican candidate in 1916. As a candidate for governor, he did not need to take strong stands on foreign policy nor did voters assess him on it. The Democrats suffered a meltdown opening the door for the NPL: an unknown Minneapolis boilermaker became its candidate and won fewer than 24 percent of the votes.[17]

Soon after the winners were sworn into office, Germany revoked the pledge on January 31, 1917, and inaugurated a foreign-policy crisis. Wilson cut off diplomatic relations with Germany. Events spiraled downward toward an early-April special session of Congress to vote on war with Germany. One ethnic enclave, New Ulm, sent people to Washington to argue against that course, in vain. Three Minnesota congressmen from districts with sizeable German enclaves voted against the declaration of war (as did Lundeen).[18] Holding its biennial session, the legislature debated bills that focused on how Minnesota could best mobilize to aid the nation in the war. The state constitution limited the legislative session to ninety "legislative days," which meant adjournment by mid-April, and prevented it from holding a regular session again until January 1919—although the governor could call a special session "on extraordinary occasions."[19] Legislators felt they should create some agency to supervise the war effort for this two-year period.

An Agency to Impose Order: The Minnesota Commission of Public Safety

Amidst rumors of enemy sabotage and the excitement of the nation's first European war, against the homeland of the state's largest ethnic group, legislators considered four bills: 1) to clamp down on the IWW; 2) to register aliens; 3) to create a public safety commission to organize the state's war mobilization; and 4) to prohibit public speech that would discourage Minnesotans from enlisting in the nation's armed forces. The alien-registration bill proved the most controversial; a reporter termed the debate "one of the most bitter in the history of the Legislature." Equity leader and state representative Magnus Johnson, a Swedish American, complained, "I was born in Europe and am a citizen of this country by choice. . . . I am willing to shoulder a gun to defend the United States and I am not a copperhead." The bill went nowhere. Aimed at the IWW, the bill prohibiting the championing of violence and sabotage for political purposes passed, as did the bill prohibiting seditious speech tending to discourage enlistments.[20]

The bill creating the Minnesota Commission of Public Safety (MCPS) passed as well. Progressives created state commissions to handle problems that weak local governments and state agencies could not handle—war mobilization was one such problem. One House member and no senators voted against the bill. Johnson and Henrik Shipstead, the Glenwood dentist who favored just treatment of the NPL, voted for it. Amendments gave the MCPS greater powers: to oversee local officials and a Home Guard, a new state army to guard public property and factories. A House amendment to subject MCPS actions to the governor's veto failed in the senate. Other states had "councils of defence" to implement federal orders; Minnesota had a commission to formulate a state's mobilization policy. It could even be a de facto state government not subject to a governor's veto or to a court that might declare it unconstitutional.[21]

The *Minneapolis Journal* noted that the MCPS bill "would gather the sovereign powers of the State in a few responsible hands for quick and effective use in case of need."[22] And, few officials who saw themselves as responsible would end up saying they did not need the sovereign powers that the legislature had so thoughtfully given them.

Soldiers and Sailors Serve, *Some in Minnesota Units, Some Simply as Americans*

While the legislature created the MCPS, Minnesota men enlisted in the military, as they had done in prior wars. Actually, many had already done so. The state had three infantry regiments: the First, largely from the Twin Cities; the Second, headquartered at Faribault and recruited from southern Minnesota; the Third, drawn from northern and central areas and headquartered at Duluth—plus a field artillery regiment in the Twin Cities and a naval militia unit in Duluth. The National Defense Act (1916) made these units subject to overseas duty, if the president so ordered. Also, the University had a cadet corps and compulsory military drill for all male students. Once war was declared, National Guard units recruited new members—the artillery under the slogan "Go with the Gopher Gunners"— citing the advantages of serving with one's neighbors instead of in the U.S. Army, in companies made up of men from many different states. Registration for the national draft took place on June 5, 1917, with the first drawing of names on July 20. These men would be placed in national units with no state identity.[23]

Canteen workers of the St. Paul chapter of the American Red Cross, with U.S. Army volunteers at the Union Station, St. Paul, 1917. *Courtesy of the Minnesota Historical Society.*

Great patriotic enthusiasm accompanied this early recruiting. On August 18, the First Infantry Regiment and field artillery regiment reenacted part "of the battle of Vimy Ridge at the state fair grounds." Fort Snelling became an officers' training camp that summer. The heights across from the fort witnessed "Battles of Pilot Knob"—troops going across the Minnesota River by ferry, then marching up "a steep road to the top," a sweaty duty that did no damage to the enemy but "helped to rid a number of [soldiers] of many pounds of weight." Three governors (Iowa, North Dakota, South Dakota) came to witness the final exam, an infantry attack under a fake artillery barrage.[24]

The three National Guard infantry regiments trained at Camp Cody, New Mexico, as part of the 34th Division. Two remained intact as units of Minnesotans—which greatly pleased the soldiers, whose band led them on a parade, "cheering and singing until late at night" after they heard the news. A large number of drafted Minnesotans trained at Camp Dodge, near Des Moines, Iowa—a site chosen, allegedly, because Iowa was a dry state. One of them wrote, "You must see it to fully realize it. . . . [The] 'National Army' [is] the melting pot, so to speak of our National Manhood." Many were in the 88th Division.[25]

At various times, mainly in the spring and summer of 1918, these units were shipped to France. Brigadier General Frederick Resche, the officer in command of the three National Guard regiments, was not allowed to accompany his men to France, presumably because he was a German American who "had served in the German army." Many Minnesota soldiers had never sailed across the Atlantic before. The trip aboard transport ships, with convoying naval vessels and daily lifeboat drill and nightly blackout, offered excitement, although the risk of submarine attack was quite small. Once landed in France, troops were transported by train in the famous "48" box cars (*40 Hommes, 8 Chevaux*—40 men, 8 horses), usually to a training site for several weeks before going to a quiet spot on the front lines, then to a hot spot. Marching to the front, the soldiers moved only at night to avoid German airplane attacks.[26]

One Minnesota Soldier Describes France

"France is all hills and it seems that where ever you go you are always going up hill and never down. There doesn't seem to be farm houses like in the U.S. The farmers all live together in these little villages and farm around the towns. Almost every time I go on the street I have to step aside to let a herd of cows or sheep go by. A lot of the people wear wooden shoes. It is just like you read about, and see in the movies. There seems to be every thing grown here that there is in the U.S. except corn."

Tracy Gray Cassidy to Dear Family, July 19, 1918 [27]

The 34th Division with its three Minnesota regiments did not finish its training in France in time to see combat, and some units of draftees in the 88th Division saw only limited action. Other Minnesotans were in the thick of it. A sizeable contingent of recruits from the University of Minnesota had joined the 6th Marine Regiment, which fought sharp actions at Chateau-Thierry, Belleau Wood, St. Mihiel, and the Argonne Forest. The National Guard field artillery regiment, which had become the 151st Field Artillery Regiment, was "the most distinctively Minnesotan unit to reach the front."

It helped to halt the German advance at the Marne River, then fought north of Chateau-Thierry, in the St. Mihiel salient, and in the Argonne Forest. In October 1918, the 151st "hammered at and slowly advanced upon the Germans . . . in the fiercest fighting the regiment had known . . . [against] one of the strongest points in the whole German line of defense."[28]

Nearly 3,500 Minnesota servicemen died during World War I, out of nearly 119,000 who served in the army, navy, and marines. Close to 4,500 were wounded in the army alone.[29] Despite concerns that an immigrants' state of hyphenated Americans would not do its part, Minnesota came to the nation's aid, even on Europe's battlefields.

The MCPS: A Progressive State Agency Used for Conservative Purposes

Historians have tried to distance the MCPS from Progressivism, but in essence and in origins it was a Progressive agency. An MCPS member *ex officio*, Burnquist gave the most Progressive inaugural address to date in January 1917. The other *ex officio* member, Attorney General Lyndon Smith, was also a Progressive, as were two men Burnquist named to the

Members of the Minnesota Commission of Public Safety, 1918.
Courtesy of the Minnesota Historical Society.

five appointive slots—ex-Governor John Lind and Anton Weiss, a Duluth journalist who joined Lind to support Woodrow Wilson in 1912—and the MCPS legal counsel, Ambrose Tighe. More conservative were Charles March, a Litchfield lawyer, and Charles W. Ames, West Publishing Company executive, board member for St. Paul corporations, and philanthropic leader in that city. Most conservative was John McGee, an Irish immigrant's son who sought to appear as Americanized as the Old Stock executives his Minneapolis law firm served. Minneapolis "banking, grain, and milling circles" wanted him on the MCPS, McGee boasted. He made vitriolic, quotable statements that make the MCPS appear reactionary from the start. He came to play a leading role in it, which no one foresaw in May 1917 and neither the governor nor the legislature intended. Another sign of Progressivism was the professional experts on the MCPS—five lawyers, one editor, and a law publisher—and no farmers or workers.[30]

Replying to a complaint of no farmers, Burnquist displayed the Twin Cities' sense that they should rule. A rural-dominated legislature that delegated its powers to a body meeting in St. Paul made such rule possible. A St. Paul lawyer, Burnquist, saw farmers in their occupational role, not their role as citizens. He had appointed farmers to a committee overseeing the production of food. He searched for a farmer for the MCPS but none "was in position to give up his work at this time of the year." The MCPS met often and without compensation. "It was therefore desirable to have men who are living in or near the Twin Cities and who can come to the meetings without great expense or loss of time." These Twin Cities men had traveled around the state on business and were "familiar with conditions in every section"; that guaranteed other regions' interests would be looked after, or so Burnquist thought. He thought of them as "the farm districts." The part-time, seasonal, and local nature of Ordinance governments had enabled farmers to participate in government as equals. Progressives' stronger second-story system did not.[31]

The legislature created a parallel government empowered "to do all acts and things non-inconsistent with the constitution or laws" of Minnesota or the United States, "so that the military, civil and industrial resources of the state may be most efficiently applied" in the war effort. The MCPS could use eminent domain to acquire property, could subpoena persons, could investigate public officials, advise Burnquist to remove them from office, and recruit "a home guard." First meeting at the capitol on April 23, 1917, seven MCPS commissioners set up the parallel government. They recruited a 7,000-man home guard. To investigate charges of disloyalty in ethnic enclaves and radical groups, they hired Pinkerton agents and others. Thomas G. Winter, a Minneapolis grain trader, headed this "intelligence bureau." His wife (Charles Ames' half-sister), Alice Ames Winter, ran the MCPS Women's Auxiliary Committee that pushed the food-conservation drive, recruited women for work in war plants, led efforts to Americanize immigrants, and aided the campaigns to end prostitution. The main MCPS and Winter's auxiliary set up county branches—Burnquist appointed the county CPS directors, who chose a county auxiliary leader or deferred to Alice Winter's choice. The county CPS and its auxiliary tried to set up township, village, or city-ward branches. County-elected officials and legislators were apparently not consulted in selecting local MCPS leaders, who were not accountable to citizens. Elected officials had deniability: they weren't responsible for what they didn't control. (Some joined in MCPS actions.)[32]

Many of its creators did not intend that the MCPS be seized by conservatives like McGee. Yet the Twin Cities "banking, grain and milling circles" were highly organized in April 1917—e.g., the National Security League's local branches, the St. Paul Patriotic League, and the Minneapolis Civic and Commerce Association. They had the strong motives of ensuring that Minnesota earned a good reputation for wartime loyalty and of defeating the NPL, Socialists, and IWW. They had the money and the time to participate in this parallel government staffed by volunteers, and they had a statewide network of local bankers, insurance agents, and traveling salesmen to staff the MCPS. Mobilization for war must be done quickly, and they had a network in place. The Minnesota Bankers Association helped the MCPS find county directors; six were bankers or bank directors. Some volunteers had local enemies to attack or grudges to avenge. No elections held them to account. In Ramsey and Hennepin counties, poorly-funded CPS units could go to business leaders' groups to raise funds. The state had few full-time salaried government officials; statutes regulated what township, city, county, and state officials could do. The MCPS was temporarily and relatively free from statutory limits or judicial interference.[33]

Progressives endorsed many MCPS programs. They saw the war as a crusade against German militarism that would "not end with the overthrow of Prussian autocracy" but would turn to "our own tyrannies—to our

Colorado mines, our autocratic steel industries, our sweatshops, and our slums." That had begun, as the MCPS fought the anti-county-option *plunderbund*—closing some saloons and restricting hours to 9 a.m.-to-5 p.m. for others, and by ordering wet Red Lake County to go dry. Alice Winter was a prominent suffragist, founder of the Minneapolis Woman's Club, and Progressive. Her auxiliary enlisted women in the war effort to strengthen the case for woman's suffrage. Working from her home near Lake of the Isles, Winter fought for the Progressive goals of child welfare, an end to prostitution, and Americanization of immigrants. The MCPS regulated food prices to thwart war profiteers—a Progressive program and goal.[34]

The war invigorated weak governments, and Progressives applauded that change and used it to reach long-sought goals—including women's suffrage and prohibition.[35] In Minnesota, they used it to "nationalize" the state—making a regionally-divided state at the northern margins of the United States fit national norms by Americanizing its ethnic enclaves, persuading its immigrants to support the nation's foreign policy, and combating the radicalism caused by the dependent status of mining, logging, and wheat regions. Lacking a professional, politically-neutral civil service, they relied on Twin Cities business networks—executives in touch with national leaders and able to travel by train to Chicago, New York, or Washington, and managers or salesmen in touch with small-town bankers or businessmen and able to travel to Willmar, Albert Lea, or Fergus Falls. "Farm districts" were seen as provincial areas resistant to a nationalizing drive. The president of Northwestern National Bank and of the Minneapolis unit of the National Security League stated, "We want especially to get at the farmers and people in the rural districts . . . [to] get the people thinking about the country as a whole."[36]

The University was the other extensive network they used—both nationally and locally. In the nation's capital, Dean Guy Stanton Ford headed a key war propaganda agency, the Division of Civic and Educational Publications within the Committee on Public Information (CPI). Ford recruited University faculty, especially historians, to write CPI pamphlets.[37] Its faculty could be sent around the state. In June 1917, Richard Price, head of the extension division, listed for Charles Ames "the patriotic meetings for which we have supplied speakers." To a St. Paul business leader and MCPS supporter, Price wrote that a regionally, ethnically divided state needed University faculty to "mobilize an efficient and intelligent public opinion."[38]

Richard Price on Minnesota's Weakness in War

"In the United States as a whole, and in Minnesota in particular, we are a widely scattered people divided by lines of clique, lodge affiliation, religion, politics, and race. We must learn to function as a people and not as a heterogeneous conglomeration of unsympathetic human units."

History Professor August Krey edited CPI pamphlets for Ford, read Midwestern German-language papers to gauge German-American opinion, and gave a patriotic speech in the ethnic enclave of Mountain Lake in July 1917. "They all speak German, low-German chiefly, are thrifty, have voted the town dry regularly for the past five years." Older residents were "stolidly pro-German" while "younger and progressive elements are patriotic." Krey conversed mainly with the latter. "But picture to yourself the scene," he wrote Ford. "A public square band-stand occupied by the village band & the speakers, a crowd of Low-German Americans of all ages & sexes to the number of about 300 seated around the square. Then imagine me explaining why we are at war to a Pro-German pacifist group." He used CPI propaganda pamphlets in his talk.[39]

University faculty and other professionals tended to be Progressives eager to aid this reinvigorated government. Their concerns about its infringements on civil liberties came later, in hindsight. Their CPI pamphlets, monitoring of newspapers, and patriotic speeches helped produce a climate of opinion supporting such infringements.

The Intelligence-Gathering Activities of the MCPS

MCPS undercover detectives also visited German enclaves. After a complaint about a German-American doctor on the draft exemption board, A.K.F. went to Melrose, a few miles northeast of Meire Grove. He talked to maids at the hotel who "had overheard the conversations of men who roomed" there. He attended a barn dance that a suspect might also attend (he didn't), talked to dancers, but discovered the doctor was no longer on the board. He was told the St. Cloud bishop "deserved credit for the decrease of pro-German sentiment in Melrose, as he had made the priests preach English, and for this country." Agent 83 tailed Rev. Adolph

Ackermann, president of the Wisconsin Synod's Dr. Martin Luther College in New Ulm, who was in St. Paul for a synod event. Ackermann took the streetcar, went to a church for the event, bought items at a store, watched *Battle of the Somme* at a movie theater, went to a baseball game between St. Paul and Indianapolis, visited Mounds Park, and took the train home. "As he went through the gate I heard him mention New Ulm to the gateman"— not surprisingly.[40]

Intelligence-gathering had serious consequences. In July 1917, an MCPS informant at the University reported that nearly the entire German department was "disloyal," as were the dental school dean and William Schaper, the German-American political science chair. McGee complained to the Board of Regents. The dean and the department satisfied the regents of their loyalty. Schaper was summoned to appear before the board with little warning that September. He exchanged angry words with regent Pierce Butler and was fired. At the time, professors emphasized academic freedom from church colleges' demands for religious orthodoxy, not from the government that was seen as Progressives' ally. There were very few protests at the time from Schaper's faculty colleagues.[41]

In February 1918, after an MCPS agent spent a day in Paynesville, several prominent citizens were brought before a "Federal officer" and accused of "disloyal and seditious remarks, failure to encourage the purchase of [war] bonds, threatening to blow up bridges [and] farm buildings, burning crops, and discouraging the raising of crops." The citizens included the president and vice president of a bank, the pastor of a church, the manager of an Equity cooperative, a merchant, and several farmers.[42] That month, the MCPS required aliens to register, to list their property, and to explain why they had not filed papers to become U.S. citizens. In the state's ethnic enclaves, such as Meire Grove, the concentration of one ethnic group using a foreign language for daily business indirectly encouraged alien residents to regard citizenship as a formality. The war changed that. Registering raised the implicit threat of a confiscation of the listed property, and encouraged residents to become U.S. citizens to avoid that danger.[43]

The MCPS Assault on the Nonpartisan League and Its Rights

1918 was the year the NPL's primary-election tactic would be tried in Minnesota, and business interests running the MCPS were determined that it not succeed. Accusing the NPL of not backing the war effort was their

Certificate of contribution to the National Nonpartisan League, 1918, signed by A. C. Townley. *Courtesy of the Minnesota Historical Society.*

tactic. Prudence might have led the NPL to suspend its drive during the war: Townley's sharp, profane talk and his socialist organizers' distaste for war were likely to set patriotic tinder ablaze. The war gave its enemies a tool to use against it. Yet the NPL drive was underway when the war began; the NPL had a constitutional right to proceed; and the state had the duty to defend its rights. The NPL used the war effort for its goals by arguing wealth should be conscripted also. Progressives disliked this disciplined dues-paying machine, hardly 'non-partisan' to them. It used their reform, the primary, for its class-based purposes and stirred farmers' anger against Main Street. After Wisconsin Senator Robert La Follette minimized American grievances against Germany at an NPL conference in St. Paul in September 1917, businessmen met in St. Paul on October 7 to organize an anti-NPL drive.[44]

Business leaders' grievances were national and local. The NPL was "cast[ing] odium on the North Star state" in the nation's eyes. "[W]hen residents of this state get outside the state they are uniformly asked, 'What's the trouble in your state, has Germany and the enemies of the government . . . got Minnesota by the throat?'" Locally, businessmen faced "boycott[s] by league members if they say anything against Townley and the organization." Business leaders feared "[t]hat the commercial life of Minnesota will be attacked by legislation" if an NPL victory in the upcoming 1918 elections gave the group "a large voice in the next senate and house." German enclaves endangered the state's good name and were NPL hotbeds. University President Marion Burton was shocked at the situation in German counties and was placed on a committee to plan a loyalty convention. The group considered a call to ban foreign-language papers but rejected it.[45]

Banning NPL meetings began in the fall of 1917: Main Street leaders pressured men renting halls to the NPL to rescind the deals or county sheriffs prohibited them. Moving to a smaller village or hamlet, NPL speakers urged listeners to contribute to the Red Cross, buy Liberty bonds, and increase crop acreage. The MCPS still regarded the NPL as disloyal. Farmers sometimes boycotted the towns that denied them the right to meet—and this economic conflict caused the MCPS to oppose the NPL all the more. The MCPS did not itself explicitly prohibit all NPL meetings; however, it informed county sheriffs and city police that they should not allow "seditious" meetings or any

Buttons signifying donations made to the various Liberty Loan drives, 1917–1918. *Courtesy of Moira F. Harris.*

Charles A. Lindbergh Sr., candidate of the Nonpartisan League, with onlookers, 1918.
Courtesy of the Minnesota Historical Society.

that might lead to violence. "Loyal" MCPS volunteers and Main Street leaders then organized a riot-in-the-making, or threatened one, and the sheriff called off the NPL meeting.[46]

The NPL still ran candidates for state offices and the legislature, mainly in the Republican primary. Former Congressman Charles A. Lindbergh Sr. became the NPL candidate for governor, against Burnquist, in the primary on June 17, 1918—and, thus, anti-NPL vigilantes' most visible target. Spring 1918 brought a political campaign of violence and intimidation unlike any in the state, even worse than the Nelson-Kindred campaign of 1882. Lindbergh was hung in effigy, denied the right to speak in many localities, attacked with stones and eggs, and his car was hit by shotgun pellets in Rock County. Supporters had NPL banners stolen off their cars. Near Hinckley, a farmer and NPL organizer, Nels Hokstad, was tarred and feathered. Nineteen counties prohibited NPL meetings. State government failed to perform its most basic function—maintaining law and order so that a fair election could be held to select its own officers and legislators. Its surrogate, the MCPS, campaigned for Burnquist, who announced he would make no political speeches but only "patriotic addresses"—and the MCPS secured such invitations for him while its publicity machine promoted a positive image of him.[47] The MCPS parallel state government helped elect the new governor and legislature that would replace it in January 1919.

Ole Gunderson of Dalton Complains to the Governor

"How do you stand for persons offering cigars to *minors* for picking of banners from cars owned by persons who are heavy subscribers to Liberty Loan, Red Cross and War Savings stamps! If a person has got a banner, is that his property or does the banner come under noxious weed law!"[48]

In the state's southwest corner, Rock County illustrated the state's failure to maintain law, order, and fair elections. A Great Northern lawyer in St. Paul took the lead in early May 1917 to find a county MCPS director. The editor of the *Rock County Herald*, A. O. Moreaux, helped choose Luverne lawyer C. H. Christopherson, a cautious man who felt "agitation was unwise" and avoided "local animosities" and "stirring up local feelings." He called a meeting for the court house in Luverne; two hundred people came to elect local leaders and organize an association. Moreaux was the local MCPS secretary. The association's work was prosaic, but outside of it, at least formally, a "vigilance committee" was begun in August 1917. Suspected German sympathizers were reported to it—including two school board members. An MCPS agent reported that Rock's "only bad spot" was the area around Hardwick, a village eight miles north of Luverne that was NPL "headquarters" and the center of "a strong German settlement." Typical evidence of disloyalty was a woman listening in on a party-line phone conversation in which a school board member's wife said, "The rulers of this country are as bad as the kaiser."[49]

The NPL organized for the election. Tensions mounted. A Luverne Loyalty Club was a vigilante group doing things the local MCPS could not do. In late May, local NPL leaders started the *Rock County Leader* to promote Lindbergh and the NPL legislative candidates. On June 11, Townley came to hold a meeting on a farm southeast of Luverne. He missed a tar-and-feathers party of fifty that awaited him at the depot, but the presence of two hundred men at the farm to prevent the meeting caused the deputy sheriff to prohibit it on the grounds that a riot would ensue. The NPLers drove across the state line to Iowa to meet in a pasture. A local NPL farmer's house was painted yellow. On the evening of June 13, a crowd gathered in Luverne outside the *Leader*'s building to destroy its machinery. "Wiser counsel prevailed" and the paper was given two days to cease and desist. On Saturday the 15th, after another crowd gathered as the deadline was to expire, the mayor consulted with Christopherson (the county attorney), ordered the paper shut down, and erected a sign that read, "Permanently discontinued as a Nonpartisan Paper." Meanwhile, the crowd hunted for W. C. Coates, "nonpartisan league organizer," who was reported to be hiding at a home near Hardwick. An automobile posse futilely searched for him. A crowd of two hundred roughed up the farmer who had sheltered him and threatened to tar and feather the man, who took the train to St. Paul, complained to Burnquist's secretary, and asked for protection (in vain).[50] Coates escaped.

The war-effort loyalists objected to a township near Hardwick hiring John Meints, an elderly German-American farmer accused of disloyalty, to do road work with his tractor. Meints stopped his work. After Burnquist won the primary and won Rock County by a four-to-one margin, emboldened loyalists drove door-to-door to intimidate farmers into signing a pledge renouncing their NPL membership. These groups acted as if they had legal powers: "registering" NPL members, holding hearings, questioning NPL members, accusing Meints of "false testimony" when he wrongly denied NPL membership, and deporting him to Iowa after he refused to sign the pledge they demanded of him. He was "required to get into his own automobile and drive to the Iowa state line," followed by vigilantes.' All NPL members who refused "to disavow their membership" by midnight Saturday, June 22, were to "leave the state." When Meints returned in August, he was tarred and feathered and deported to South Dakota. The *Rock County Herald* claimed there was "no violence or disorder" at the first Meints deportation, but the entire action was illegal disorder and the later tar-and-feathers treatment was certainly violent.[51]

In the short run, the MCPS, its business allies, and the local vigilantes won. The NPL lost the primary, its Farmer-Labor candidate (David Evans) lost the general election, and Burnquist was reelected. In the long run, a strong Farmer-Labor party emerged as a coalition of those victimized by the MCPS. They won women's suffrage and prohibition by U.S. constitutional amendments, but Progressives also suffered a long-term setback, for the MCPS partly discredited them. Their efficient wartime government had proven unable to handle the hot wartime issues. Their support for the war advanced their other goals, for patriotism was a strong argument for Progressivism that ordinary people understood. Yet the flip side of that case—that failure to aid the war effort was unpatriotic and perhaps treasonous—proved powerful among ordinary citizens and hard to limit or control. Progressives had no plan for controlling vigilantism. Progressives' drive to make Minnesota more like the rest of the nation and to restore its good reputation by patriotic war endeavors backfired. State government, the key tool for Progressives, was tarnished by its failure to perform its most basic state duties of maintaining law and order, upholding its laws, protecting its citizens, and conducting fair and free elections.

1.   "were shocked," Chrislock, *Progressive Era*, 66-70, 75-76; Keillor, "Premodern, Modern, Postmodern," 91. For examples of study tours available that summer, see Rodgers, *Atlantic Crossings*, 269.
2.   "county agents," Keillor, *Cooperative Commonwealth*, 264-67.
3.   "machine was driven out," Chrislock, *Progressive Era*, 26, 38-39, 83.
4.   "bitterly-opposed reform," Chrislock, *Progressive Era*, 60-61, 85-86.
5.   "the heyday," Keillor, *Hjalmar Petersen*, 22, 32-33; Chrislock, *Progressive Era*, 22; Keillor, *Cooperative Commonwealth*, 240, 254.
6.   "occurred in the mining region," Walker, *Iron Frontier*, 246-55; Folwell, *History of Minnesota*, Vol. IV, 27, 53-57; Chrislock, *Progressive Era*, 20, 178; Helmes, *John A. Johnson*, 290-91; Clark, ed., *Minnesota in a Century of Change*, 169, 231.
7.   "Tensions remained," Neil Betten, "Riot, Revolution, Repression in the Iron Range Strike of 1916," *Minnesota History* Vol. 41 (Summer 1968): 82-93; Peter Rachleff, "Turning Points in the Labor Movement: Three Key Conflicts," in Clark, ed., *Minnesota in a Century of Change*, 196-200; Chrislock, *Progressive Era*, 116-18.
8.   "could not maintain law and order," Betten, "Riot," 86-89, 91, 92.
9.   "the wheat region," Keillor, *Cooperative Commonwealth*, 208-11, 227-31.
10. "crossed the Red River," Robert L. Morlan, *Political Prairie Fire: The Nonpartisan League 1915–1922*, reprint ed. (St. Paul: Minnesota Historical Society Press, 1985), 22-27, 29, 106, 230-31; Chrislock, *Progressive Era*, 109-11, 112.
11. "rolled into Minnesota," Morlan, *Political Prairie Fire*, 126-27; Chrislock, *Progressive Era*, 112-13.
12. "IWW-led strike," Carl H. Chrislock, *Watchdog of Loyalty: The Minnesota Commission of Public Safety During World War I* (St. Paul: Minnesota Historical Society Press, 1991), 32-34.
13. "Socialists dominated," Morlan, *Political Prairie Fire*, 23-25; Chrislock, *Progressive Era*, 114-15; Millard L. Gieske, *Minnesota Farmer-Laborism: The Third-Party Alternative* (Minneapolis: University of Minnesota Press, 1979), 20-21.
14. "war set some ethnic regions," Chrislock, *Progressive Era*, 89-98; Keillor, "Premodern, Modern, Postmodern," 91.
15. "an editorial," *Minneapolis Journal*, 29 May 1915, 4. For this reference, I am indebted to Chrislock, *Watchdog of Loyalty*, 21.
16. "threatened Minnesota's reputation," Chrislock, *Progressive Era*, 104-05.
17. "hoped voters," Chrislock, *Progressive Era*, 119-22, 125-27; White, et al., comps. *Minnesota Votes*, 34-35, 182-83.
18. "New Ulm," Chrislock, *Watchdog of Loyalty*, 47; Chrislock, *Progressive Era*, 134-35.
19. "state constitution," Article IV, Section 1, and Article V, Section 4.

20. "legislators considered," Chrislock, *Watchdog of Loyalty*, 51-60.
21. "bill creating," Chrislock, *Watchdog of Loyalty*, 52-60. Chrislock (60-64) musters many signs of 1917 hysteria to explain why the legislature passed the bill, without discussing the simplest explanation – that the state's governments were too weak to mobilize for war a state divided into contesting regions.
22. "the MCPS bill," quoted in Chrislock, *Watchdog of Loyalty*, 52.
23. "enlisted in the military," Franklin F. Holbrook and Livia Appel, *Minnesota in the War with Germany*, Vol. I (St. Paul: Minnesota Historical Society, 1928), 67-75, 84-88, 136, 139
24. "patriotic enthusiasm," Holbrook and Appel, *Minnesota in the War*, Vol. I, 92, 175, 188-90.
25. "trained," Holbrook and Appel, *Minnesota in the War*, Vol. I, 260-61, 268-70, 307-09, 312, 346.
26. "shipped to France," Holbrook and Appel, *Minnesota in the War*, Vol. I, 270, 275, 348-50, 352-53, 357.
27. "Describes France," Tracy Gray Cassidy to Dear Family, 19 July 1918, Tracy Gray Cassidy and Family Papers, MHS.
28. "see combat," Holbrook and Appel, *Minnesota in the War*, Vol. I, 356-69.
29. "during World War I," Holbrook and Appel, *Minnesota in the War*, Vol. I, 374.
30. "tried to distance," Chrislock, *Watchdog of Loyalty*, 55 (quoting McGee), 68-85, 93. To distance Progressivism from the MCPS, Chrislock highlights the wartime hysteria, as exemplified by McGee, and interprets Burnquist as only seemingly Progressive.
31. "a complaint," Burnquist to S. B. Qvale, 25 April 1917, in April 1917 Correspondence folder, Box 10, J. A. A. Burnquist Papers, P448, MHS.
32. "a parallel government," Chrislock, *Watchdog of Loyalty*, 89-90, 99-104, 107-09, 116-22, 126-32, 227-30.
33. "seized by conservatives," Chrislock, *Watchdog of Loyalty*, 44, 53, 102-03; Chrislock. *Progressive Era*, 94.
34. "MCPS programs," Chrislock, *Progressive Era*, 15-36; Chrislock, *Watchdog of Loyalty*, 206-11, 212-21, 227-38; Stuhler, *Gentle Warriors*, 48, 50, 148. Stuhler ignores Winter's MCPS activities.
35. "applauded that change," Rodgers, *Atlantic Crossings*, 278-79.
36. "The president," Keillor, *Hjalmar Petersen*, 40.
37. "Dean Guy Stanton Ford," Keillor, "Premodern, Modern, Postmodern," 94-97.
38. "Richard Price," here and below, Richard Price to E. M. McMahon, 11 December 1917, "Oct.—Dec. 1917" folder, Donald R. Cotton Papers, MHS; Richard Price to C. W. Ames, 16 June 1917, MCPS Papers Box 103.L.8.3B, MHS.
39. "History Professor August C. Krey," Keillor, "Premodern, Modern, Postmodern," 95; August C. Krey to Guy Stanton Ford, July 1917, Folder 32, Guy Stanton Ford Papers, University of Minnesota Archives (UMA); *Mountain Lake View*, 6 July 1917, 1.
40. "MCPS undercover detectives," "A.K.F. Reports," 27-29 June 1917; "W.G.S. Reports," 4 August 1917; and "#83 Reports," 20 August 1917, all in MCPS Papers, Box 103.K.20.13(B), State Archives, MHS. The Ackermann incident is also described in Chrislock, *Watchdog of Loyalty*, 153.
41. "serious consequences," Keillor, "Premodern, Modern, Postmodern," 97-99.
42. "an MCPS agent spent a day," *Melrose Beacon*, 21 and 28 February 1918, both 1.
43. "MCPS required," Chrislock, *Watchdog of Loyalty*, 277-80; *Melrose Beacon*, 21 February 1918, 1.
44. "their tactic," Chrislock, *Watchdog of Loyalty*, 164-76; *Duluth News Tribune*, 8 October 1917, 1, 12.
45. "Businessmen's grievances," *Duluth News Tribune*, 8 October 1917, 1, 12.

46. "Banning NPL meetings," Morlan, *Political Prairie Fire*, 152-59; Chrislock, *Watchdog of Loyalty*, 178-82.

47. "a political campaign of violence," Bruce L. Larson, *Lindbergh of Minnesota: A Political Biography* (New York: Harcourt Brace Jovanovich, 1971), 235-39; Morlan, *Political Prairie Fire*, 159; Chrislock, *Watchdog of Loyalty*, 304-07.

48. "Ole Gunderson," Ole Gunderson to J. A. A. Burnquist, 12 June 1918, "June 12-14" folder, Box 14, Burnquist Papers, MHS.

49. "Rock County illustrated," A. L. Janes to John Pardee, 7 May 1917; Christopherson to MCPS, 21 May, 29 June, 2 July, all 1917, and 10 January 1918; Ambrose Tighe to Henry W. Libby, 29 April 1918; A. O. Moreaux to MCPS, April 22, 1918, all in "Rock County" folder, Box 103.L.10.2(F)   Correspondence with Counties, Ramsey to Yellow Medicine, MCPS Papers; Report of Organization of the Rock County Public Safety Association, "Rice to Stevens" folder, "Reports on Organization of Local Public Safety Committees and Assns," Box 103.L.7.1(B), MCPS Papers, MHS; "Chronological Events of Rock County," in *Rock County in the Great War 1917–1918–1919*.

50. "Tensions mounted," Chrislock, *Watchdog of Loyalty*, 290; *St. Paul Daily News*, 23 June 1918, 1; *Rock County Herald*, 14 June (1, 2) and 21 June (1, 2, 12), both 1918.

51. "John Meints," Chrislock, *Watchdog of Loyalty*, 290; *Rock County Herald*, 28 June 1918, 1, 2; *St. Paul Daily News*, 23 June 1918, 1.

8 Face Off Between Two Sections

In November 1922, the new Farmer-Labor party's candidate for U.S. Senate, the Glenwood dentist and former legislator Henrik Shipstead, won 45 percent of the vote to defeat the Republican incumbent, St. Paul lawyer Frank B. Kellogg (34 percent), and the Democrats' Anna Dickie Olesen (17 percent). A suffragist leader and orator from Cloquet, Olesen was the first woman to run for this office, in the second state election in which women could vote. In German-American counties, Shipstead won big over Kellogg: nearly 4-to-1 in Brown; nearly 3-to-1 in Scott; and nearly 2-to-1 in Stearns. Two Farmer-Labor candidates were elected to the U.S. House of Representatives, and over twenty to the state senate. Less than four months after they were sworn into office, Knute Nelson died, and a special election was set for his Senate seat. His protégé, Governor Jacob A. O. Preus, was similarly beaten by dirt farmer, Equity leader, and legislator Magnus Johnson, a former Swedish glassblower whose strong lungs were now to be heard in the Senate chamber. Johnson won nearly 3-to-1 in Brown and Scott, and 2-to-1 in Stearns. With the help of German-American voters, a muscular Farmer-Labor party would be heard for two decades in Minnesota.[1]

Conservatives' wartime tactics backfired (Kellogg had won the three German-American counties' total vote in 1916). Yellow paint, tar and feathers, deportations, and denials of farmers' and workers' rights to free speech and public assembly cemented a farmer-labor alliance—and added the normally conservative German-American vote. The Farmer-Labor party was an MCPS-victims' coalition of German Americans, wheat farmers, iron miners, Twin Cities and Duluth laborers, and farmers of the cutover area. Outlawing dissent replaced several economic and ethnic regions with one outlier section now politically united. Far from ensuring Minnesota's respectability in the nation's eyes, wartime repression led to the twin 1922-23 results that left the state perceived as radical for having a pair of third-party U.S. senators.

This section was also created by a sharp drop in farm prices from June to December 1920, that left the farm district an 'outlier' exception to the national boom of the 1920s. The price of wheat plummeted from $2.58 per bushel in June 1920 to $1.43 on December 1, 1920. High prices and strong demand during the war caused Minnesota's farmers to borrow money to expand their acreage and buy more machinery. Then crop prices dropped, the price of machinery did not drop comparably, freight rates increased, and so did real estate taxes. The farm economy did not fully recover for two decades. The Republicans were able to help their dairy region as they had in the 1890s. After a fall in butter prices from 70¢ per pound in April 1920 to 30¢ per pound in May 1921, Governor Preus' agriculture department used the county agents to drum up support for a meeting in the House chamber on June 7, 1921, to organize a federation of cooperative creameries. The federation became Land O' Lakes, which produced uniform high-quality butter under one nationally-known brand name and gained dairy farmers a higher price. Similar attempts to form cooperative federations to control wheat marketing failed.[2]

A sharp drop in the persuasive value of Progressive rhetoric proved a harder problem to solve. Rhetoric had been debased when converted into vigilante action. The Senate's refusal to ratify the peace treaty or allow the United States to join the League of Nations, the most visible fruit of all that wartime sacrifice, embittered some Minnesotans and led to cynicism and historical revisionism that claimed the bankers and munitions makers forced the nation into war to protect their loans and profits—just as Lindbergh and some NPLers had charged. The outlier section of MCPS victims seemed to be vindicated.

Prohibition led to outlaws and outlier areas. The wartime need to save grains for food and the animosity toward (beer-drinking) German Americans pushed the anti-liquor crusade over the top. The 18th Amendment went into effect in January 1920, after Minnesota Congressman Andrew Volstead of Granite Falls authored the Volstead Act that set up the rules for prohibition. Beverages containing more than .5 percent alcohol could not be legally made or sold. Individuals could consume alcohol in their homes, but it was hard to acquire any legally. As with most illegal acts, how much moonshine was made and how much smuggled liquor was sold is very hard to quantify. When federal agents raided throughout Stearns County in October 1930, they caught 115 persons flouting the law. One famous Stearns brand of moonshine was named "Minnesota 13" after the hybrid corn variety.

Violating this law in German-American enclaves was partly defiance against governments that harassed them during World War I. The law was also defied in urban areas and among other ethnic groups.[3]

The other successful Progressive reform, woman suffrage, encountered more apathy than opposition. Minnesota's suffrage leaders, like Clara Ueland of Minneapolis, were disappointed at women's voter turnout, at the four women elected to the legislature in 1922 (Ueland wanted twenty), and at the low number joining the League of Women Voters, which replaced the suffrage groups. The social issues of liquor, child welfare, and prostitution that women had used to gain the vote proved to have much less traction in the 1920s, and women were divided over the proposed new issue, an Equal Rights Amendment.[4] Basic economic issues predominated in the 1920s and 1930s, and women voters did not take positions on these issues markedly different than the male members of their families.

The Two Sections: One Inside, One Outside the Nation's 1920s Culture & Economy

No new state consensus arose after the Great War to replace the Progressive pre-war one. Instead, a jumble of competing outlooks emerged out of the wartime bitterness and post-war disillusionment. Only the rival Farmer-Labor and Republican parties were able to muster them into two political armies that clashed. However, one insider section participated in the nation's culture and 1920s prosperity while the outlier section did not participate—albeit the latter was internally divided on many other points.

Any one town or enclave could fit into this outlier section for one of seven reasons: 1) many of its residents might still speak and write a foreign language; 2) its churches might belong to denominations outside the American mainline ones; 3) its churchgoers might be conservative, pious, and opposed to the 1920s national culture of Hollywood, radio, and jazz; 4) much of its business might be done through cooperatives rather than private, for-profit companies; 5) thus, some residents might hold radical anti-capitalist views outside the U.S. political mainstream; 6) its economy might be depressed so that residents could not afford the new consumer goods of the 1920s; or 7) it might be geographically isolated from the state's urban centers and the nation's culture. In general, lack of electricity left rural areas outside the twenties' consumer culture of electric lights, central heating, running water, indoor plumbing, and electric appliances like refrigerators or washing machines; only 12 percent of Minnesota's farms had electricity as late as 1935.[5]

Finnish-American New York Mills (Otter Tail County) fit into this outlier section. It was a center of Finnish-language publishing, with the NPL and farmer-radical newspaper *Uusi Kotimaa* printed there until 1931 and the independent and non-political *Minnesotan Uutiset* replacing it in 1932. Presses turned out Finnish-language pamphlets, hymn books, stories, novels, and calendars. Twenty to thirty percent of the residents, or more, spoke Finnish in their homes. The Apostolic Lutheran Church was independent and outside the main Lutheran synods. Its members were pious teetotalers who did not need Prohibition to keep them sober. In this dairying area, the New York Mills cooperative dairy produced butter. Other cooperatives flourished: a farmers' elevator, fire insurance company, publishing company (it put out *Uusi Kotimaa* for several years), livestock shipping association, general store, and gas station. Even the state bank was cooperative. In this anti-capitalist enclave speaking a foreign language, a private businessman might hesitate to invest money to build a store. New York Mills' ethnic, religious, political, and cooperative identity isolated it.[6]

Exemplifying the largely urban insider section was Minneapolis' lake district of Lake of the Isles and Lakes Calhoun and Harriet. By the 1920s, dredging projects had created usable shorelines of beaches, parkland, and lakeside boulevards for Isles and Calhoun, which in turn attracted middle-class and upper-class residential housing to the area. The streetcar lines made it possible to commute to the downtown offices. Mainline churches—Congregational, Methodist, Episcopal, Presbyterian, and Unitarian—served an Old Stock and English-language population. Reflecting the national prosperity and these local advantages, Hennepin Avenue became a high-status shopping and service location. Professional offices of lawyers, architects, doctors, and dentists moved into the second floors above the specialty stores—Abdallah's for the candy lover, Hove's grocery (the Lunds of the twenties), the New Rainbow Café, Schlampp's fur store—while the Grenada and Lagoon theaters showed the latest Hollywood films. Only a mile toward downtown, a cluster of automobile dealers on Hennepin sold the cars that were partly causing the Booming Twenties. The Calhoun Yacht Club offered sailing, and the Minikahda Club on Calhoun's west side had an 18-hole golf course by 1923. The twenties' sporting and shopping culture prospered in the lake district. There was no anti-capitalist protest.[7]

In Minneapolis, Jewish residents were an outlier enclave within an insider section. The Mill City was known for anti-Semitism: Jews were excluded from the housing market in certain neighborhoods, from some clubs, and from employment in certain banks, stores, and factories. In St. Paul, families of German Jews who had been in the city since the Civil War faced little discrimination and, in fact, shared some of the class prejudice against the poor Eastern European Jewish immigrants who came later.[8]

A home for outlaws, St. Paul was in the insider section, for elites did not ostracize Prohibition lawbreakers. Since the 1880s, St. Paul had long hosted a "vice economy" of "alcohol, gambling, and prostitution," promoted by wholesalers eager to lure buyers into the city. In 1900, Police Chief John J. O'Connor began his "O'Connor System" of granting criminals safe haven in the city if they reported their arrival to police, paid the police money, and committed no crimes within city limits. That Minneapolis objected to outlaws fleeing to St. Paul raised the system's popularity at home. Prohibition brought many more ships seeking safe harbor: perhaps 75 percent of St. Paul's residents made alcoholic beverages in 1922; some entered the business of selling them; speakeasies proliferated; an Irish and Jewish network of bosses ran this industry and paid protection money to police, councilmen, and judges. On North Wabasha, the Green Lantern Saloon hung a sign reading "Dapper Dan, The Hot Dog Man," which was a front; inside, a false wall concealed the Blue Room, "a speakeasy where the underworld enjoyed liquor, piano music, slot machines, and nude dancers." The Hollyhocks Club Casino on Mississippi River Boulevard "was filled with tuxedo-clad businessmen and their wives sipping fine liqueurs and rubbing elbows with the most wanted gangsters in America." Looked up to like movie stars, gangsters like John Dillinger and the Barkers sought refuge in St. Paul and earned it national disrepute, even after Prohibition ended in 1933.[9] The nation's thirst for scandal and celebrity meant this was not all negative publicity. Still, a city was a creation of a state government charged with law enforcement, not to be absolved of all responsibility when one of its cities refused to deliver criminals over to another.

Twenties' images are stereotypes with some truth. The urban economy recovered from the 1920-21 recession and enjoyed 2 percent annual growth and low inflation and unemployment rates for eight years. The number of radios and cars that were made tripled; the number of refrigerators rose by 150 percent. The new medium of radio plus older print media became sites of massive national advertising campaigns for such products. Minnesota companies joined in the rush to innovate and advertise: 3M invented masking tape (1925) and Scotch brand cellophane tape (1930); the Washburn Crosby Company introduced Wheaties, changed its corporate name to General Mills (1928), and invented an ideal homemaker-adviser named Betty Crocker to promote its goods; Honeywell thermostats became a recognized brand name, as did Land O' Lakes butter with its Indian maiden trademark. Washburn Crosby's WCCO and Stanley Hubbard's KSTP eventually linked up with the national networks of CBS and NBC, respectively, but also mirrored the old Minneapolis vs. St. Paul rivalry. In 1929, WCCO became a 'clear channel' station at 50,000 watts, able to reach rural Minnesota. Urban and small-town theaters allowed Hollywood to reach the state with its star-making, dream-forming powers. In darkened auditoriums, Charlie Chaplin, Douglas Fairbanks, Mary Pickford, and Rudolph Valentino induced Minnesotans to dream of life in southern California, Arabian deserts, New York City, or another locale distant in time and place from 1920s Minnesota, rural or urban.[10]

One former Minnesotan suddenly erupted as a twenties' stars, albeit not through Hollywood. The son of the congressman and 1918 gubernatorial candidate, Charles A. Lindbergh Jr. made the first solo flight across the Atlantic on May 20-21, 1927. Nicknamed "Slim," the "Lone Eagle," and "Lucky Lindy," the boyish 25-year-old Lindbergh was wildly welcomed as a simple, rural homespun hero by people who feared the nation was being corrupted by money-grubbing, bootlegging, jazz, movies, and urban decadence. Raised in the rural outskirts of Little Falls, "Slim" seemed to personify the outlier section's distance from national culture—he did not smoke or drink and had never danced with a woman—but he refused to be turned into "a tin saint," and he had ties to St. Louis, San Diego, and Wisconsin, so he could not be turned into a pure-and-simple Minnesotan. Yet there was irony in the son of the vilified candidate becoming the state's most famous native son.[11]

Twenties' youth culture centered on colleges, fraternities and sororities, their social events and the Saturday football game. President George Vincent had remarked that he knew of no "college or university in which social life is run on the 'wide-open' schedule" as at the University of Minnesota. There was a dance or a banquet every night of the week, some ran past midnight, and some were off-campus, away from the dean's eyes.

Two Minnesota writers brought new ideas to American culture in the 1920s. The Nobel Prize went to Sinclair Lewis for his portrait of small towns (*Main Street*) and of evangelist Elmer Gantry. F. Scott Fitzgerald's short stories and novel, *The Great Gatsby*, depicted the Jazz Age for many readers. Lewis is shown at work in Minneapolis, 1919, while F. Scott and Zelda Fitzgerald were photographed in Dellwood, 1921. *Courtesy of the Minnesota Historical Society.*

The annual pajama parade from the University Avenue fraternities to the 10th Avenue sororities drew disapproving publicity each May. Journalist Harrison Salisbury recalled that his University class was "the last generation of the Ski-U-Mahs, crazy about football, . . . Bronko Nagurski, the Little Brown Jug, Stutz Bearcats (there wasn't one on the campus), . . . pom-poms, rumble seats, homecoming bonfires and booze—the last of the 1920s." University student and trombonist Carl Warmington recalled Homecoming, when a crowd "paraded behind the marching band down University Avenue—'Go Gophers' pennants waving, cloche-hatted coeds decked with gold pom-poms" and some headed to "Sorority Row on 10th Avenue—a stretch almost impassable with parked sport roadsters and Model T Fords in driveways and on the lawns." The unlucky uninvited

Frank Kellogg and his wife (on left) are shown with President and Mrs. Coolidge (center) and Governor Theodore Christianson (far right) at Union Depot, arriving for the Norse-American Centennial Celebration, 1925.
Courtesy of the Minnesota Historical Society.

stood outside to hear live jazz music and see dancers doing the Charleston. A victory usually added to the festive atmosphere, as Bernie Bierman's Golden Gophers won national championships in the 1930s at Memorial Stadium. On University Avenue, the state's college-age youth could experience twenties' youth culture.[12]

In the state's outlier section, they could not or would not, due to religious scruples, lack of funds, or sheer isolation. On Moorhead's 8th Street, students attending Concordia College, a Norwegian-American Lutheran institution that attracted students mainly from the Red River Valley, largely missed the stereotypical campus life of flappers, flasks, and fraternities. Although Moorhead had nearly thirty speakeasies, Concordia's presidents during the twenties were clergymen—Rev. J. A. Aasgaard and Rev. J. N. Brown—who enforced bans on tobacco, liquor, card-playing, dances, and visits to pool halls or to the opposite sex's dormitory. The doors to the dorms were locked at quarter past ten every night. Aasgaard diagnosed the twenties' ailment as "the amusement problem," and his Christian college offered the home-like amusements of chapel, Tuesday night Bible Study, a choir, and a college Christmas celebration. One student appreciated this chance "to rid ourselves of the jargon of the flapper and frequenter of pool halls." Colleges of other ethnic groups and denominations followed a similar pattern.[13]

Despite the agricultural depression, the outlier section, and the outlaw flouting of Prohibition, the Republicans restored their dominant position after the 1922-23 setbacks. The small-town editor from Dawson, Theodore Christianson seemingly carried on the Progressive tradition and won three terms as governor (1925-31) on a platform of government efficiency and low taxes. The most consequential Republican program was the building of state highways—70 state highway routes covering nearly 7,000 miles—that enabled trucks to take over farm-to-market hauls, made obsolete the crossroads communities of horse-and-wagon days, opened lakes and forests to tourism and weekends spent at the lake. Highways created a recreational geography in which landscapes had new uses from those of the railroad-created economic geography of the 1880s and 1890s.[14]

Depression Brings Farmer-Labor Rule of a State Temporarily United by Necessity

When the stock market crashed on Black Thursday (October 24, 1929) and Black Tuesday (October 29), lost 33 percent of its value in a month, and helped sink the nation into the Great Depression, Minnesotans were mainly innocent bystanders. Their commodity-producing state had no corporations that were prominent in the wild stock speculation leading to the Crash. The local high-stakes speculator was an outsider, Wilbur Foshay, whose holding companies were like Ponzi schemes dependent on constant income from new sales of utility stocks to keep the dividends flowing out to shareholders. His 30-story Foshay Tower in Minneapolis, high above more conservative bank buildings, symbolized his zeal to take higher risks than Mill City bankers thought prudent. Foshay's office chair was hardly warm before the Crash led the bankers to foreclose on his new tower, loans, and stocks. He went to Leavenworth prison on a 15-year sentence for mail fraud. Yet he was an exception; Minnesota was largely blameless of causing the Crash.[15]

Dedication ceremonies for the Foshay Tower of Minneapolis, 1929. Shown is the garden court with Harriet Frishmuth's *Scherzo* fountain sculpture. (Later, *Scherzo* welcomed visitors to Charlie's Café Exceptional in Minneapolis.) John Philip Sousa was the featured guest at the ceremonies. *Courtesy of the Minnesota Historical Society.*

The state suffered the effects. Farm prices sank even lower: wheat, to 38¢ per bushel and corn, to 32¢. The specter of bankruptcy and farm foreclosures loomed. In Otter Tail County, Oscar and Martha Hegge and their four kids had to make do on $20 per month in cream checks, extra money from cutting wood, and plenty of self-sufficiency in food and clothing; the Tosos raised nine children on a forty-acre farm and some day labor for other farmers; Hans Ronnevik's farm was mortgaged and he lost it. On the Iron Range mining slowed; in 1932, it "came to a virtual standstill." Three thousand Hibbing men sought government assistance. An April 1930 survey showed 5,700 jobless in Duluth, "the highest rate of unemployment in the nation." By March 1932, that number rose to 11,700, "more than 30 percent of the labor force." In 1931, over 60 percent of the state's manufacturers showed a loss, and in 1932, that rose to 86 percent. Accurate unemployment statistics were not kept by the government, and certainly not state-by-state; however, in 1933 the national unemployment rate was estimated at 25 percent, and Minnesota's was likely in that range. These crushing consequences were not immediate or obvious in October 1929.[16]

Nor did the Crash change the basic relationship of outlier and insider sections—as seen in the life of Elmer Andersen, who came to Minneapolis in 1928 as a salesman for a company making school furniture. With his headquarters at Minneapolis' Curtis Hotel, he traveled the state submitting bids to school boards—in Starbuck, North Branch, and other towns—and trying to sway their decisions before his competitor did. Rural outlying school districts had the political right to decide, but salesmen had the power of inside information. Off duty in the Mill City, he heard John Philip Sousa's band at the opening of the Foshay Tower, watched Jimmy Durante's vaudeville act at the Orpheum Theater, listened to jazz at a Hennepin Avenue café, and attended First Baptist to hear William Bell Riley preach. A month before the Crash, he entered the University's School of Business Administration, while continuing to work part-time. He worked as hard as any small-town employee but also benefited from the insider section's personal networking: the Dean became his friend; he married the daughter of the owner of a lumber company; a tip from a business friend led to a job with the H.B. Fuller Company, a maker of school pastes and other adhesives. He became active in Republican politics, which was almost part of this insider's job ladder.[17]

Campaign headquarters, with signs urging veterans to vote for Franklin Roosevelt and Floyd B. Olson, 1932. *Courtesy of the Minnesota Historical Society.*

The immediate gainers from the Crash were Farmer-Laborites, whose spokesmen "sold short" during the twenties by predicting this disaster, and their 1930 candidate for governor, Floyd B. Olson, who won with 57 percent of the vote. "He stood well over six feet with broad shoulders," his biographer writes. "A pair of restless, half-defiant blue eyes dominated a masculine countenance." Olson roughly bridged the divide between the two sections; politically, he represented the outlier section. Born, raised, and residing in Minneapolis, he dressed stylishly and socialized with insider tycoons like Charles Ward of Brown & Bigelow. He personified the rebel's disdain for Prohibition and rule-making. He loved to take the new highways to Pelican Lake north of Brainerd, to Breezy Point Lodge, owned by Captain Billy and Annette Fawcett, who published the raunchy *Capt. Billy's Whiz Bang* and entertained literary celebrities and Hollywood stars to jazz band music. Trombonist Carl Warmington recalled dances, bootleggers' whiskey fresh from Canada, and gangsters who requested "Sing You Sinners." The gregarious, fun-loving Olson could socialize with them all and then go to a Finnish town or a St. Paul union hall to anathematize the capitalism that fed the Fawcetts and their lodge.[18]

Cover of *Capt. Billy's Whiz Bang*, 1923. This magazine, published by William Fawcett, launched his publishing career. *Courtesy of Moira F. Harris.*

Olson was consistent in being a rebel. The targets of his rebellion just changed—moralizers, capitalists, or killjoys—depending on which audience he was winning over.

A Personable Olson Laughs with His Foes

"After his [1931] inauguration, he went to his Office and sent for state Sen. A. J. Rockne of Zumbrota, the staid, conservative watchdog of the state treasury. . . . Olson explained, 'I wanted to know what you thought of my inaugural address.' Rockne paused for a moment, and then answered, 'I'd have to tell you, Governor, that if we did one half of the things you proposed, we'd drive this state into bankruptcy.' Olson leaned back in his chair and laughed heartily and said, 'That's why I've sent for you, Senator. If you let me make the speeches, and you keep the state finances sound, we'll get along just fine.' "[19]

A governor had to be agile in the Depression's first years. The crisis was grave; voters demanded answers; Washington seemed to have none; state government still relied on the real estate tax; yet a state leader couldn't just say he had no answer. Olson's Farmer-Laborites faced added problems. Legislative candidates ran without party labels, so it was hard to take over the legislature. Republicans had a strong network of county-seat leaders and businessmen, while Farmer-Laborites had a few popular leaders at the top like Olson and thousands of ordinary voters but a weak organizational structure in between to link them. Progressives' reforms made it harder for a party to develop such a structure, and farmers' interests conflicted with those of workers at several points.

President Herbert Hoover did not see it as the federal government's duty to find work for the unemployed, or food and shelter if there was no work. So the unemployed and the farmers looked to Governor Olson in St. Paul. In January 1931, his capitol reception room "became a glorified employment bureau with forty to sixty applicants waiting at all times." He had little to offer them. He persuaded the legislature to authorize $15 million in bonds for highway construction. The Highway Department became Olson's major tool for providing jobs for the unemployed—it offered unskilled jobs; paving highways was not make-work but clearly useful and popular with voters. In

Tear gas being used against strikers during the Minneapolis truckers strike, 1934. *Courtesy of the Minnesota Historical Society.*

1933, the legislature increased the state highway network by 65 percent, and federal funds became available for more road construction jobs.[20]

Olson addressed a broader range of issues and achieved successes in his first two terms: reforming the state's farm lending agency, tightening up its securities laws, creating its first state income tax (dedicated to school aid), passing a mortgage moratorium law that gave delinquent debtors two years to catch up and avoid foreclosure, instituting a tax on chain stores, strengthening the state conservation agency, and creating new state forests out of the vast areas of tax-delinquent farms in northern and central Minnesota. Olson failed to get legislators to pass an unemployment compensation law. The state income tax was a key long-term victory, for it opened up a sizeable new source of revenue for state government. For these victories, Olson relied on votes from Republican legislators with Progressive, good-government views. Farmer-Laborites had no majority in either house. Some state agency heads were Republican Progressives.[21]

Farmer-Labor 'Outlier' Section Abuses Power; 'Insider' Section Ends That Rule

Despite successes, despite Olson's political skills, and despite the favorable situation from January 1931 to March 1933 of a state government committed to using all its resources to fight the Depression while the national government could not do so due to the ruling Republicans' political philosophy—still, the Farmer-Laborites were not quite able to fashion a new state identity for Minnesota as an exception to the national rule, as North Dakota had been under the NPL. That failure was not inevitable, although international events and Democrats' national takeover did make a unique state identity problematic.

Farmer-Laborites did take *the state* (the state government) seriously. After winning reelection in 1932, Olson allowed Farmer-Laborites to use state government jobs to build a political party machine. Fatefully, Republican Progressives in the 1920s had failed to pass a civil service law mandating merit-based, not politics-based, hiring of state employees. Progressives had created a strong commission, the "Big Three," to run state government: personnel director, commissioner of purchases, and budget commissioner. Farmer-Laborites on the "Big Three" took over state agencies and hired Farmer-Laborites. A party activist from Brainerd, I. C. "Dutch" Strout, became personnel director and turned state government into a "glorified employment bureau" for loyal party workers. Strout's network of oil, hotel, grain, and bank inspectors traveled the state contacting Farmer-Labor clubs, starting new ones, handing out campaign literature, and replacing the Republicans' old network of county-seat editors, bankers, and lawyers. Strout created state jobs for absentees—state-paid publicists who really worked at the party's Educational Bureau writing literature the inspectors distributed. His detectives checked out state employees' party loyalty.[22] The state government that the Progressives reformed in order to weaken political parties became the base for a strong party.

State jobs as inspectors or as highway workers were more vital in the outlier, rural section where private sector jobs were scarcer than in the Twin Cities. In Farmer-Labor northern and central Minnesota, the party's state bosses had economic clout over people. Membership in the Farmer-Labor Association (FLA) soared from 7,500 (1930) to 20,000 and as high as 30,000 (1934-36).[23] This outlier section departed further from the national norm, as more of its labor force worked for cooperatives—including rural electric cooperatives that began in the mid-1930s—or for a state government run by a third party successful only in Minnesota. In this outlier section, a young man could rise from laborer to manager or another white collar job by being promoted to manage a local cooperative or its regional wholesaler or by campaigning for the FLA and earning a state job—apart from the normal job ladder followed by Elmer Andersen that required a college degree, middle-class habits, obedience to the boss, and respectable Republican political views.

The result was a political machine. The Farmer-Labor administration could hire and fire about 10,000 state workers on the basis of their political views and activities. That increased membership in the dues-paying FLA, which relied for its campaign expenses and its newspaper's funding on monies raised by state government supervisors who asked their employees for a 'voluntary' donation of 3 percent of their salary to the party. Those who paid the piper picked the tune. State employees dominated the FLA and its choice of candidates—including the choice of a governor to head the next administration, which would retain workers, so they could donate their 3 percent and keep the machine going.[24]

Amidst the economic crisis, this Farmer-Labor machine scored impressive wins: five of the state's congressmen were Farmer-Laborites in 1933, as was Senator Henrik Shipstead; a sizeable liberal caucus now existed in the state house of representatives. Franklin Roosevelt's New Deal programs sounded radical enough to vindicate the Farmer-Labor ideology—Shipstead had used the term "New Deal" before FDR did. At its 1934 convention, an emboldened FLA pronounced capitalism a failure, called for "a new sane and just society," and proposed state ownership of banks, "mines, hydroelectric power plants, transportation, communications, packinghouses, public utilities, insurance, and all factories except" cooperative ones. Olson encouraged this radical platform by giving a rousing speech before it was considered: "I am not a liberal. I am what I want to be—I am a radical. . . . I want a definite change in the system." Well, he was fundamentally a rebel who soon rebelled against the platform and replaced it with an interpretation of the platform that merely called for more cooperatives. Olson survived the storm over the platform to win a third term in November 1934, albeit with a lower victory margin.[25]

Vince Day on Minnesota's Identity

"The Cooperative Commonwealth is Minnesota's American solution to the American problems brought on by a predatory, ruthless capitalism."[26]

Farmer-Labor rule and the thirties' openness to alternative economics caused some cooperators to stress radical consumers' cooperation over cautious farmers' cooperation. This drive, which could have made Minnesota's economy quite unique, was led by Midland Cooperative Wholesale, which had 201 oil cooperatives in its network by 1938. Producers' cooperatives sought a better price for crops that farmers marketed through the for-profit system. An ideology influential nationwide in the mid-1930s held that consumer-owned retail and wholesale outlets selling what consumers demanded could replace a system of producing what best earned a profit. Cooperative wholesalers would run their own factories, as in England. Midland enlisted Farmer-Laborites in state government to survey Minnesota's cooperatives and thereby advance Midland's goal. Midland hosted the national convention of the Cooperative League of the U.S.A. at Glenwood, Minnesota, in July 1936, and the picnickers and paraders drew national media attention to what a *New York Times* reporter termed "the nation's most cooperative state." Midland's ideas enabled Republicans to appeal to dairy cooperatives, to farmers who supplied the Twin Cities milk market, and to Farm Bureau members (the Farm Bureau ran its own cooperatives)—in short, to cautious farmers whom Midland was offending.[27]

Olson had kept a good relationship with the Farm Bureau, which had close ties to the county agents and the University and supported his income tax bill. Olson died of pancreatic cancer six weeks after the Glenwood convention. Lieutenant Governor Hjalmar Petersen filled out the final four months of Olson's third term. Olson's real heir was Elmer Benson, a Norwegian American from the Norwegian enclave along the upper Minnesota River, a former bank cashier in Appleton, and Olson's former banking commissioner. Benson was filling out the term of a deceased U.S. senator that summer while he campaigned for governor. A true son of the outlier section, Benson had climbed its job ladder—so unlike Elmer Andersen's—by working for a farmers' elevator and cooperative livestock shipping association. Benson fought for Farmer-Labor policies with a moralistic zeal quite unlike Olson's skill at socializing and rebelling. The outlier section would sorely miss Olson's insider political skills and his ability to see the glass as half full—Land O' Lakes creameries and Farm Bureau gas stations were cooperatives at least. Benson saw the glass half empty and in need of his refilling activity.[28]

National political changes caused by the New Deal made Benson's zeal more costly to Farmer-Laborism. President Franklin Roosevelt's farm program worked through local committees linked to county agents and the Farm Bureau, thus giving farmers an incentive to join the Farm Bureau. After sinking to about five thousand members in 1933 (roughly equal to the liberal Farmers Union), the Minnesota Farm Bureau increased its membership to nearly 18,000 by 1935 (the Farmers Union dropped under 5,000 by 1938). To make matters worse for the liberal cooperators, Roosevelt's rural electrification agency showed a marked preference for conservative electric cooperatives tied to the Farm Bureau, rather than liberal ones linked to Midland. In 1937-38, Governor Benson sided openly with the Farmers Union and Midland by firing moderate leaders in the state agriculture department and by pushing a bill to sever the Farm Bureau–county agent link (the bill failed). Benson thus helped create a conservative-to-moderate farm group aiding his rival, Hjalmar Petersen, who campaigned in 1938 to unseat Benson.[29]

By 1937-38, New Deal labor laws and policies unintentionally aided one faction in the labor half of the FLP coalition. The Committee for Industrial Organization (CIO) sought to organize one union in each industry, across craft lines. That set it at odds with the craft unions in the American Federation of Labor (AFL). A group organizing the steel industry for the CIO obtained a union contract at Duluth's U.S. Steel plant in March 1937, although Range miners did not win a contract for another six years; a similar group won a contract for lumberjacks with Benson's help. The more conservative AFL fought the CIO bitterly and resented Benson's pro-CIO tendencies. One sign of the split came at the 1937 state AFL convention in Hibbing, when delegates blocked the Range's own Farmer-Labor congressman, John T. Bernard, who worked for the CIO's steelworker group, from addressing the gathering. Going into 1938, the AFL was ready to side with Petersen or most anyone who opposed Benson.[30]

International political changes caused by the rise of fascism in Hitler's Germany and Mussolini's Italy also made Benson's zeal costly. Previously hostile to democratic reformers like Farmer-Laborites, the international Communist movement switched in 1935 to a 'Popular Front' strategy of allying with them against the more dangerous fascists. And, the Farmer-Labor party that had barred Communists from membership in the FLA changed its policy. On October 18, 1935, Olson secretly met with Earl Browder, the national Communist leader, and a deal later emerged whereby Communists could join the FLA and participate in its conventions as long as they did not reveal their Communist allegiance. Communists did join and

Governor Elmer Benson speaks to the Farmer-Labor State Convention at Duluth, 1938. *Courtesy of the Minnesota Historical Society.*

participate, so much so that a Communist leader who came to Minnesota to examine this deal complained of this "policy of recklessly furtive goings and comings through side doors" that was making the Communists "a semisecret society for conniving in other organizations." If the connivers complained, then how much more might the victim organizations object! Voters would also protest once they learned of the deal. Groups like the AFL and Farm Bureau had another reason to oppose Benson, who met privately with Communist leaders, favored the deal, and advanced it while trying to conceal it from the public.[31]

Benson compounded the problem by making national speeches for Popular Front causes. As one of the few radical-to-liberal politicians in high elected office, he was flattered with many requests to appear around the nation, and did not resist what was also a weak national movement's flattery of the one successful state-level farmer-labor coalition. One Farmer-Labor state senator told Benson that voters "say if you discuss state problems and issues, they are for you, but . . . that you have spoken entirely too much upon national subjects, such as the Courts, war, foreign problems, etc."[32]

This Popular Front coalition was exposed to public view and public disapproval. Angered when conservative legislators blocked some of Benson's proposals during the 1937 session, Popular Front leaders like John

Bosch organized a rally in early April that drew over fifteen hundred marchers to the state capitol—a People's Lobby to pressure legislators. Addressing them, Benson stated, "It's all right to be a little rough once in a while." As the day wore on, moderate protesters left and the radicals took over, including Communists such as Harry Mayville, Sam Davis, and Chester Watson. They broke into a locked room where the Senate Tax Committee was meeting. Mayville hurled insults at a conservative senator. The senators beat a hasty retreat. The mob-in-the-making took over the Senate chamber for the night. It took a word from the governor to get them to vacate the chamber. Benson's public statement was not widely seen as clear condemnation. Public opinion and the legislators were outraged. An unruly crowd treated the state's governmental headquarters and its duly elected lawmakers as if the former were an aristocratic mansion inhabited by plundering nobles (the latter)—when their own political party controlled much of this government and legislature.[33]

Farmer-Laborism was undone by a lack of moral self-discipline when tempted: by joblessness to turn state government into a party job fair; by the seeming collapse of capitalism to turn to a radical form of cooperation or to communism; by an international anti-fascist crusade to admit Communists as members, then hide that from voters. The Ordinances used one-room schools and local churches to teach moral self-discipline. Progressives turned to science, expertise, higher education, and a faith in democracy as a process. Farmer-Laborites shared the postwar disillusionment with moralistic Progressive rhetoric and tried to replace it with a moralistic ideology of the virtuous people against immoral Big Business. Yet that ideology did not give the people tools for disciplining themselves when tempted by state jobs in return for party loyalty or when tempted to use state government for narrow partisan ends.

Harold Stassen's Insider Revolution Overthrows the Outlier Regime

Farmer-Laborism's collapse was not inevitable. Petersen led a drive to reform the party from within when he ran against Benson for the FLP nomination for governor in the June 1938 primary. A small-town editor from Askov, Petersen started his newspaper in 1914 and shared the Progressive, good-government views of that era's editors. His drive aimed to return to that pre-MCPS era. He called for a civil service system to end the

FLA political machine, for an end to the deal with the Communists, and for a return to the old weak-party independence symbolized by his primary challenge to his party's governor. His was not a purely internal Farmer-Labor crusade. Republicans aided him or crossed over to vote for him—thinking their party could not defeat Benson. Nor was it, morally self-disciplined. Some of his supporters used anti-Semitism, pointing to the coincidence that some Communists and Benson advisers were Jewish. The strong party FLA and its state employees worked hard and beat Petersen by a narrow margin of 51 percent to 49 percent.[34]

That result indicated voter dissatisfaction with the FLP. If it would not reform itself at its conventions, or be reformed by voters in its primary, then it might be beaten by the rival Republicans. In early 1938, that did not seem likely, for GOP Old Guard leaders were set to run either Martin Nelson, who had lost to Olson and Benson, or the mayor of Minneapolis, George Leach. Republicans had to show voters that they had changed since the failed

Harold Stassen (center) campaigns for governor at Sauerkraut Days in Henderson, Minnesota, 1937. *Courtesy of the Minnesota Historical Society.*

policies of Herbert Hoover, and neither Nelson nor Leach could do so.[35] Surprisingly, a 31-year-old county attorney won the GOP nomination on the primary day when Petersen lost. Raised on a truck farm in West St. Paul (Dakota County), Harold Stassen climbed the insider's job ladder: a college education at the University of Minnesota, where he led the Gray Friars who ran campus politics; University law degree; election as county attorney; head of the Young Republicans. A hard worker, he accomplished this at an amazingly young age without offending his peers but succeeding in enlisting young men like Elmer Andersen in his cause. Stassen's ties to South St. Paul, site of the state's largest stockyards, created a tie to the rural districts. Campaigning in 1938, Stassen recruited a Hook 'Em Cow Club of horseback-riding young men from South St. Paul who rode into small towns ahead of the candidate to make Stassen appear rural. Old Guard dislike of the young Stassen helped him by highlighting his new views. He endorsed much of the New Deal, spoke at the AFL state convention, sounded the old Progressive notes, and called on voters to throw the FLP rascals out and reinstate good government.[36]

Petersen gave Stassen the basic critique of Benson and the key issues of patronage, corruption, communism, and a political machine. Roosevelt's New Deal programs meant that Minnesota voters no longer looked to state government for jobs, relief funds, and economic hope—so they were more willing to entrust it to a member of Herbert Hoover's party, especially one who renounced Hooverism.

Stassen crushed Benson in the November election, winning 59 percent of the vote to Benson's 34 percent. The Democrat received only 6 percent. Benson won only six counties. Five of them were the most outlying counties of the outlier section: Koochiching, Lake of the Woods, Roseau, Pennington, Clearwater. St. Louis County had a strong CIO presence on its Iron Range and in Duluth's docks and steel plant. Apart from those six, Minnesota had been turned outside in. By voting Republican, the state also rejoined the national two-party consensus and repudiated its unique Farmer-Labor identity of the past eight years.[37]

Minnesota returned to its older identity as a Progressive Republican state rather than launching on some totally new course. Historian John Earl Haynes interprets Stassen Republicans as "young, honest, sincere, middle-class, professional or business people who . . . had no truck with either 'standpat' conservatism or with . . . demagogic New Deal liberalism." Here was the renewed "religious moralism of progressivism." Their campaign literature often featured a photo of a Lutheran church. Here was "a sort of secularized Scandinavian Lutheranism: earnest, moralistic, well meaning, and moderate." Of course, many Farmer-Laborites like Petersen and Benson had been Scandinavian Lutherans too. The Stassen revolution resulted in a change of opinion in the state's core Scandinavian-Lutheran electorate over which political version of "religious moralism" or secularized Lutheran social reform to embrace. Ultimately, that electorate could not support the patronage-driven, corruption-tolerating, Communist-accepting Benson faction within Farmer-Laborism. The state would have to see whether the Stassen version was capable of restoring the moral self-discipline needed for effective self-government.[38]

1. "new Farmer-Labor party's," Gieske, *Minnesota Farmer-Laborism*, 73-80; Stuhler, *Gentle Warriors*, 121, 155, 204-05; White, et al., comps., *Minnesota Votes*, 36-37.

2. "drop in farm prices," Richard M. Valelly, *Radicalism in the States: The Minnesota Farmer-Labor Party and the American Political Economy* (Chicago: University of Chicago Press, 1989), 72-73; Keillor, *Cooperative Commonwealth*, 290-96, 300-03.

3. "led to outlaws," Conzen, *Germans in Minnesota*, 72-74.

4. "were disappointed," Stuhler, *Gentle Warriors*, 187-205.

5. "lack of electricity," Keillor, *Cooperative Commonwealth*, 321-22; David L. Nass, "The Rural Experience," in Clark, ed., *Century of Change*, 137.

6. "New York Mills," Wasastjerna, ed., *Finns in Minnesota*, 144-63.

7. "urban insider section," David A. Lanegran and Ernest R. Sandeen, *The Lake District of Minneapolis: A History of the Calhoun-Isles Community* (Minneapolis: University of Minnesota Press, 2004), 22-25, 41-47, 52-54, 60-64.

8. "Jewish residents," Hyman Berman, "The Jews," in Holmquist, ed., *They Chose Minnesota*, 500-01; W. Gunther Plaut, *The Jews in Minnesota: The First Seventy-Five Years* (New York: American Jewish Historical Society), 266-79; Wingerd, *Claiming the City*, 37-38.

9. "St. Paul was in the insider section," Wingerd, *Claiming the City*, 49-50, 112-13, 252-56, 260-61; Paul Maccabee, *John Dillinger Slept Here: A Crooks' Tour of Crime and Corruption in St. Paul, 1920–1936* (St.Paul: MHS Press, 1995), 64-65, 134-35.

10. "Twenties' images," Michael E. Parrish, *Anxious Decades: America in Prosperity and Depression, 1920-41* (New York: W. W. Norton, 1992); Clark, ed., *Century of Change*, 233-36, 300-05.

11. "former Minnesotan," Parrish, *Anxious Decades*, 178-82; Joyce Milton, *Loss of Eden: A Biography of Charles and Anne Morrow Lindbergh* (New York: HarperCollins, 1993), 132, 144.

12. "Twenties' youth culture," Keillor, "Premodern, Modern, Postmodern," 124; Harrison E. Salisbury, *A Journey for Our Times: A Memoir* (New York: Harper & Row, 1983), 85; Carl Warmington, "Reminiscences," 28, Carl Warmington Papers, MHS.

13. "Concordia College," Carroll Engelhardt, *On Firm Foundation Grounded: The First Century of Concordia College* (1891–1991) (Moorhead: Concordia College, 1991), 56, 62-65, 83-86, 93.

14. "Republicans restored," Gieske, *Minnesota Farmer-Laborism*, 90, 105, 120; Daniel J. Elazar, *A Model of Moralism in Government*, Clark, ed., *Century of Change*, 344-45; Blegen, *Minnesota: A History*, 478-79.

15. "local high-stakes speculator," Wingerd, *Claiming the City*, 256-57; George H. Mayer, *The*

Political Career of Floyd B. Olson, reprint ed. (St. Paul: Minnesota Historical Society Press, 1987), 69 note.

16. "suffered the effects," Clark, ed., *Century of Change*, 144, 158 (quoted), 184, 238, 263; D. Jerome Tweton, *The New Deal at the Grass Roots: Programs for the People in Otter Tail County, Minnesota* (St. Paul: Minnesota Historical Society Press, 1988), 24-27. Richard Hudelson and Carl Ross, *By the Ore Docks: A Working People's History of Duluth* (Minneapolis: University of Minnesota Press, 2006), 162 (quoted).

17. "the life of Elmer Andersen," Elmer L. Andersen, *A Man's Reach* (Minneapolis: University of Minnesota Press, 2000), 31-46, 59, 110-11.

18. "Floyd B. Olson," Mayer, *Floyd B. Olson*, 5-6; Warmington, "Reminiscences," 43-48.

19. "Personable Olson," Andersen, *A Man's Reach*, 43.

20. "looked to Governor Olson," Mayer, *Floyd B. Olson*, 62 (quoted), 67-68; Gieske, *Minnesota Farmer-Laborism*, 148; Valelly, *Radicalism in the States*, 59-60, 63-64.

21. "achieved successes," Gieske, *Minnesota Farmer-Laborism*, 147-48, 173-77; Keillor, *Hjalmar Petersen*, 94-95; Mayer, *Floyd B. Olson*, 66, 68-70, 122-23, 132-42.

22. "use state government jobs," Valelly, *Radicalism in the States*, 58-62; Gieske, *Minnesota Farmer-Laborism*, 177-78.

23. "Membership," Valelly, *Radicalism in the States*, 62.

24 "a political machine," Valelly, *Radicalism in the States*, 59; Keillor, *Hjalmar Petersen*, 118-22; Gieske, *Minnesota Farmer-Laborism*, 182-83.

25. "this Farmer-Labor machine," Gieske, *Minnesota Farmer-Laborism*, 186-93, 199-200; Keillor, *Hjalmar Petersen*, 104-08; Keillor, *Cooperative Commonwealth*, 315-17, 335-36.

26. "Vince Day," quoted in Keillor, *Cooperative Commonwealth*, 312.

27. "radical consumers' cooperation," Keillor, *Cooperative Commonwealth*, 308-21.

28. "Olson had kept," Keillor, *Cooperative Commonwealth*, 310, 318-19, 330, 335; Mayer, *Floyd B. Olson*, 290-91, 300-01; Valelly, *Radicalism in the States*, 101, 119, 139; Gieske, *Minnesota Farmer-Laborism*, 233-34.

29. "costly to Farmer-Laborism," Valelly, *Radicalism in the States*, 97-102; Keillor, *Cooperative Commonwealth*, 321-31, 335.

30. "the labor half of the FLP coalition," Valelly, *Radicalism in the States*, 120-27; Clark, ed., *Century of Change*, 184-85, 211-12; Hudelson and Ross, *Ore Docks*, 184-87.

31. "changed its policy," John Earl Haynes, *Dubious Alliance: The Making of Minnesota's DFL Party* (Minneapolis: University of Minnesota Press, 1984), 12-22; Valelly, *Radicalism in the States*, 128, 140-41; Hudelson and Ross, *Ore Docks*, 199-202; Keillor, *Hjalmar Petersen*, 150-53.

32. "state senator told Benson," Keillor, *Hjalmar Petersen*, 165.

33. "organized a rally," Gieske, *Minnesota Farmer-Laborism*, 241-42; Valelly, *Radicalism in the States*, 141-42.

34. "Petersen led a drive," Keillor, *Hjalmar Petersen*, 143-61; Gieske, *Minnesota Farmer-Laborism*, 265.

35. "GOP Old Guard leaders," Gieske, *Minnesota Farmer-Laborism*, 200, 230, 262, 265.

36. "Harold Stassen," Gieske, *Minnesota Farmer-Laborism*, 262, 265, 270; Barbara Stuhler, *Ten Men of Minnesota and American Foreign Policy 1898–1968* (St. Paul: Minnesota Historical Society Press, 1973), 145-47; Valelly, *Radicalism in the States*, 149-52; Andersen, *A Man's Reach*, 111.

37. "crushed Benson," Gieske, *Minnesota Farmer-Laborism*, 272-73; Hudelson and Ross, *Ore Docks*, 221-222.

38. "Historian John Earl Haynes," John E Haynes, *Reformers, Radicals, Conservatives*, Clark, ed., *Century of Change*, 380-81.

9 The Greatest Generation Looks to the Nation

In 1938, Harold Stassen defeated the twenty-year Farmer-Labor coalition of MCPS victims. They sought to reverse the Republicans' drive in 1917–18 to make Minnesota more like the nation—to 'nationalize' the state, so to speak. Nationalizing an industry means government ownership of private firms. Nationalizing a state means the nation or its government reduces a state's autonomy and unique identity, or the state's people minimize them to become more like the rest of the nation. The Farmer-Labor outlier's revolt against the nation's dominant economy and culture was effectively ended by Stassen's win. By restoring major party control of state government, Stassen returned Minnesota politics to the national norm. His presidential ambitions led him to make reforms seen as relevant to the nation's problems, not just to those of a unique outlier state. His movement of young Republicans attempted a new 'nationalization' of the state, one that learned from the mistakes of 1917–18.

Stassen's ambitions meant the nation heard much about Minnesota and him. He went to Washington in December 1938 to meet with New Deal officials, other Republican governors, and the press corps. He gave his first national radio talk in January 1939. He then returned to Washington in May 1939 to answer a question a few were asking: was he old enough to run for president? The answer was: not yet. He also announced that he was running for governor in 1940, a statement normally made in Minnesota. He went to the New York World's Fair to speak at Minnesota Day, although the state did not have a building there. "It is because we are so absorbed in the Minnesota and the America of the Nineteen Forties, the Fifties, and the Sixties that we find here at this Fair an articulation of our own sustaining philosophy," he said. His front-page article, "Democracy in the Land of Lakes," for the magazine section of *The Christian Science Monitor* in March 1940 featured a map of Minnesota on the cover.[1]

In his first legislative session, Stassen scored victories that gave momentum to his presidential hopes and his drive to return the state to the national two-party norm. He got a law passed requiring applicants for state government jobs to take competitive civil service tests. He had until August 1, 1939, to fire Farmer-Labor jobholders and replace them with non-tested Republicans. Over 2,000 state employees were fired and replacements hired under this temporary exemption. Yet Stassen had kept his campaign promise of civil service reform. He redid the state government's organizational chart, replacing the Rube Goldberg contraption of dependent bureaus and independent agencies and semi-independent commissions with corporate-style departments whose heads reported to the governor. He won legislative approval of a labor-management conciliation bill to avoid the bitter strikes that hit Minnesota in the 1930s. Publicized investigations of Farmer-Labor official wrongdoing strengthened his good-government image.[2]

Setting up scaffolding and repairing the structure of state government did not impact Minnesotans as much as the New Deal programs run out of Washington did. As a progressive Republican, Stassen refused to oppose the New Deal, unlike the GOP Old Guard. The nation's major impact on Minnesota came from foreign affairs, but that aided Stassen's 'nationalization' drive in the long run, as events unfolded.

Debate over a New War in Europe Renews an Old Split in Minnesota

On September 1, 1939, Germany's invasion of Poland upset the 'nationalizing' unity Stassen promoted. It repeated the old split over U.S. entry into European wars and the old face off between outlier and insider sections. After Germany invaded Denmark and Norway in April 1940, the British retreated from Dunkirk, and France surrendered (June 22, 1940), business, civic, and academic leaders in Minneapolis formed a chapter of the Committee to Defend America by Aiding the Allies (CDAAA). With its carefully worded title, the CDAAA rallied Minnesotans to aid Britain and, ultimately, to enter the war as Britain's ally. Like the interventionists of 1915–17, the CDAAA was an insiders' group led by bankers such as Edgar M. Jaeger of Northwestern National Bank, financed by flour-milling families like the Pillsburys and Christians, headquartered in the Foshay Tower, and aided by Twin Cities newspapers—by John Cowles, owner of the

Minneapolis Star-Journal and *Minneapolis Tribune*, and by *Star-Journal* editor Gideon Seymour. By March 1941, over 130 University of Minnesota faculty belonged to it.[3]

A loose outlier coalition opposed the steps leading to U.S. entry into the war: first, weapons and ships sold to Britain, then sold on credit, then "leased"; then U.S. bases being set up in the Atlantic region; then U.S. naval ships escorting supply ships headed to Britain. Rural, Scandinavian-American, small-town opinion often perceived Hitler's aggressions and Roosevelt's gradual steps to meet it in terms of the First World War. Exaggerated Allied propaganda of 1914–17 was to blame; false reports of atrocities by the Kaiser's army led to deep mistrust about stories of Nazi SS soldiers' atrocities, which were true.

A Norwegian-American lawyer in Fergus Falls, Henry Nycklemoe saw the new war in light of the old. Twenty-two years old in 1914, Nycklemoe heard atrocity stories, enlisted, and grew 'disillusioned' about the war. In the early 1920s, a history professor at St. Olaf College taught him the revisionist view that U.S. entry into the war only led to a tragically flawed Versailles Treaty. A Farmer-Laborite, Nycklemoe went to Europe in 1939, toured Germany for weeks, found ordinary Germans to be angry at Versailles and supportive of Hitler, and admired the clean, orderly externals of German society. Nazi repression escaped his notice. Back in the United States, his call for U.S. neutrality got him into a pointed correspondence with Francis Flint, a printer in St. Peter. Flint felt Nycklemoe's do-nothing stance on "the slaughter of human beings" in Europe was "insipid" and "gutless." Nycklemoe told Flint to go to Canada and enlist. Flint returned to the atrocities of "the German-Nazi war party," which America could not ignore. Nycklemoe described at length his visit to Germany, assuming personal experience and first-hand observation trumped Flint's hearsay.[4]

Nycklemoe was a rare Minnesotan in having spent weeks in Nazi Germany but a common one in his desire for U.S. neutrality. In the summer of 1941, a Gallup poll found 85 percent of Minnesotans were in favor of keeping the nation out of World War II. As in 1914–16, the state's senators and congressmen wanted that same thing. The CDAAA's rally at the Minneapolis Auditorium in late January 1941, drew 4,000 people. The neutralist America First Committee attracted 12,000 to that venue in May to hear celebrity aviator and native son Charles Lindbergh give the keynote speech. Almost every phrase of Lindbergh's call to stay out of war "was interrupted by applause and cheering." Lindbergh cited his father's courageous stand against the financiers and politicians whom he had felt were leading the United States into World War I, and the son noted in his journal that his "greatest satisfaction" in any of his neutralist speeches was the Minneapolis audience's applause at mention of his father. When he concluded, "thousands broke for the platform in an effort to shake his hand." Senator Henrik Shipstead, Hjalmar Petersen, and other leaders were on the platform with him to display Minnesota's pro-neutral consensus.[5]

Minnesotans shrank from the loss of young lives and war's other sacrifices. They doubted that World War I had been worth the sacrifice. Sincerely or to rationalize their reluctance, they used arguments to offset interventionists' alarm at Nazi brutality: this was only the most recent in Europe's long history of wars; it grew out of the last war and the vengeful Versailles Treaty; Germans justifiably tried to undo that treaty; France and Britain had imperial ambitions too; the United States could never end this cycle of warfare.[6] They were largely right on this history, but the present reality was that U.S. troops in 1918 had helped create the Versailles world order, Germans looked to a militaristic party to undo it, that party turned to a war of aggression, and Americans would have to help maintain that world order.

National Unity in World War II
Facilitates a 'Nationalizing' of the State

Walter Benjamin, son of a Pipestone physician, saw Nazi and Fascist aggressions as "lightning strikes coming closer." In "the hot summer of 1939," he had trouble sleeping on his family's front porch. "The grave voices of William Shirer in Berlin and Edward R. Murrow in London floated from the living room radio to the porch as they spoke of mobilization and ultimatums." CBS Radio news bulletins battled "the singing crickets and cooing mourning doves." On December 7, 1941, "table devotions, breakfast, Sunday School, church, and a dinner of roast chicken" indicated normalcy. A photographer come to take their picture asked, "Have you heard what has happened in Hawaii?" On Monday, Walter's school met to hear Roosevelt's response to Pearl Harbor – a request for a declaration of war against Japan.[7] Three days later, Hitler declared war on the United States, ending neutralists' attempts to keep out of Europe's war.

Minnesotans in the army and navy were struck by the lightning of war. A naval reserve unit on the USS *Ward* fired at a Japanese submarine approaching Pearl Harbor. Returning to "Pearl" on the USS *Chester*, signalman Maurice Crowley of Minneapolis saw "great billows of smoke" rising from burning ships. The USS *Nevada* was "listing to starboard and submerged to the main deck." A National Guard company from Brainerd, stationed at Fort Stotsenburg in the Philippines, came under aerial bombardment "within hours of the Pearl Harbor attack." Captured after the U.S. surrender at Bataan on April 9, 1942, these 62 men endured the Bataan Death March to prisoner of war camps, and only 32 men returned alive.8

Being attacked by Japan and forced into a European war by Germany created more wartime unity than all the World War I propaganda posters. Pearl Harbor gave a clear cause for war, a clearly aggressive enemy whose goals were global, and a clear consensus in the state. Minnesota's entry into World War II began promisingly for this effort at 'nationalizing' the state, unlike the disunity of 1917–18. The MCPS mistake was not repeated. State government set up war agencies—a Defense Council, War Finance Committee, and State Postwar Council—but all under the control of executive, legislative, and judicial branches. Reinvigorated in the past twenty years at a rebuilt Camp Ripley, the 8,000-man National Guard was called into federal service ten months before Pearl Harbor. Units like the Brainerd tank battalion retained their Minnesota identity.9

Thousands of draftees or enlisted men and women entered military life at Fort Snelling, thus starting with a Minnesota identity at the old post. Unlike the Civil War or World War I, most did not train there but were inducted into the army or navy, tested, and classified so they could be sent to training camps. By bus or train, hundreds arrived daily to wait in line to complete forms, have their teeth and bodies checked, take intelligence and aptitude tests, be interviewed, get their inoculation shots, sign up for insurance, and get uniforms. Over 250,000 men passed through Fort Snelling's lines. Being Minnesotan was not a qualification for any one branch of service or military job. Tests and interviews classified men based on other characteristics. Minnesotans were dispersed to dozens of training camps and hundreds of units. Being thrown into units with Americans from distant states contributed to the 'nationalizing' effect the war had on them.10

One exception proved the rule. The Army's 99th Battalion of Norwegian-speaking soldiers trained for an invasion of German-occupied Norway. Organized in the summer of 1942 at Camp Ripley, the 99th had Norwegian Americans and Norwegian citizens. Despite protests that this set a dangerous precedent and violated the goal of assimilation, the nation used an ethnic enclave and its loyalty to a foreign language. In the 99th Battalion were Minnesotans like Marvin Skogrand of Montevideo. When recruited for the 99th and asked if he could speak any foreign language, Skogrand recalled, "I said no, because I never considered Norwegian a foreign language. But then I thought about it and said, well, I can speak Norwegian." That qualified him for the 99th, which trained at Fort Snelling to improve its Norwegian and its skiing skills. After D-Day, it served in France with other American units who thought its Norwegian speech sounded German and demanded answers to questions about baseball teams in order to prove its identity and loyalty.[11]

Before Pearl Harbor, loud complaints had sounded over very un-Minnesota-like conditions at some army training camps, particularly Camp Claiborne in Louisiana. "We are used to the climate of the north and not this extreme heat of the South," one private wrote to Stassen, asking him to arrange a transfer "to some camp in Minnesota." "Also, we can't get the rest we do when we are in Minnesota." A Lutheran pastor interceded for trainees plagued by "Louisiana chiggers," poison ivy, a "water shortage," and swamps. After Pearl Harbor, Minnesotans patriotically adapted to such conditions.[12]

A Great Migration Reduces Regional Loyalty & Increases National Identity

There could be no question of the state's duty when the nation was attacked. Out of patriotism, anger, a desire for revenge, racial bitterness toward the Japanese, a desire to prove one's manhood, and social pressure, Minnesotans enlisted. Many waited to be drafted. In ten months, 125,000 Minnesota men were in the service; by war's end, 304,000 had served. About 22,000 women served in women's units: the WACS (Women's Army Corps), WASPS (Women Airforce Service Pilots), or the Navy's WAVES (Women Accepted for Volunteer Emergency Service).[13]

Civilians at home eagerly enlisted too. Benjamin recalls the impact on Pipestone. Two newspapers ran war photos and articles, addresses of soldiers, and lists of draftees. A Lutheran pastor chaired the draft board. A scrap metal drive drew the headline "LET'S JOLT THE JAPS WITH JUNK FROM PIPESTONE!" Coffee rationing cut intake to a cup per day; sugar, gasoline, and tires were rationed. War bond drives netted $400,000 one year. High school boys had a rifle club. A Ford dealer got a defense contract. And seven acres of Victory Gardens were plowed. Community pressure enforced rules and duties in "a form of therapeutic tough love," as "well-justified gossip

[was] directed at miscreants." Benjamin noted, "I lived . . . within the arms of family, neighborhood, school, church, and flag. . . . I accepted the moral canon, 'Do good and you will do well,' as a law of the universe." Moral effort nationalized a town.[14]

Thousands of civilians moved. Some rural counties lost 18 to 24 percent of their residents from out-migration in the 1940s, much of it from 1940 to 1945. Farm labor was needed to bring in vital wartime harvests, but rural economies stagnated as rationing of consumer goods left businesses with less to sell. Thousands of rural people moved to work in Twin Cities defense plants—Northern Pump (Fridley), Twin Cities Ordinance Plant (TCOP, in Arden Hills), and Gopher Ordinance Works (GOW, in Rosemount). Federal aid to this migration came in the form of mortgage insurance and subsidies for construction of 1,100 homes, offered first to defense workers, some of whom had moved in from rural areas.[15]

Defense work was an intense team effort unifying Minnesotans. Boasting "I'm the only man who can defend America," tough-talking Texas-born John B. Hawley Jr. engineered Northern Pump into the nation's model naval ordinance plant, featured in the *Saturday Evening Post* and *Life*. Hawley ran his machinists and his two miles of production lines fast, long, hard, and far ahead of schedule. Men could work eighty hours a week. Workers seemed close to the front lines. "Remember Pearl Harbor" signs hung from ceilings. Rail cars carrying the naval gun mounts away had morale-boosting caricatures of Axis leaders like Hitler. Columnist Cedric Adams took a five-hour tour, "an amazing experience . . . you see a Victory purpose in the complete co-ordination of the personnel." Young women delivered meals and snacks to work stations in stainless steel wagons. "Everybody in the plant is fed in eight minutes." By May 1942, 6,000 people worked there. Hawley gave every worker a U.S. flag.[16] Workers were not laboring for Northern Pump or Hawley or themselves, but for the nation.

The TCOP night shift saw a national symbol when President Roosevelt toured that 8,000-worker small arms ammunition facility for an hour on September 19, 1942. A hole cut in the back wall allowed FDR to enter in a car, with Stassen and the plant's boss in the back seat. Workers applauded and gawked. The visit was "the greatest morale builder the workers have had since Pearl Harbor," said a company executive. FDR's visit, and Stassen's back-seat position, symbolized how World War II involved Minnesota in an intense national enterprise that eclipsed the state's narrower identity. Those working for firms temporarily engaged in war production (Cargill's shipyard at

Savage, Honeywell's manufacture of automatic pilots, etc.) were caught up in a patriotic project far beyond one firm's bottom line.[17]

The "Gopher Gossip" in *The Powder Keg*, the GOW employee magazine, showed how the personal mobility of war mobilization eclipsed Minnesotans' sense of state residence. Workers transferred to and from this plant until they seemed to lack any rootedness. "Fred Conner . . . has again been transferred to Sioux City. . . . Harold Kline . . . [is] now with Uncle Sam in the army at Camp Polk. . . . 'California here I come,' says Agnes Modahl. . . . Agnes has disposed of all personal belongings in 'good old Minnesota' and will be traveling light, but far. . . . Dale Levitt [is] now with the Seabees at Davisville, Rhode Island. . . . Happiness and fervid anticipation of the wonders to come in California shone in Mary Ashley's eyes" at her going-away party. "Art Erickson . . . has arrived safely in Hawaii. . . . He says the country is beautiful and the weather quite different from our Minnesota weather." They resided in 'a state of war'—distant army camps, naval bases, and Kaiser Shipyards were linked more closely together than Minnesota towns.[18]

Thousands of Minnesotans moved to the West Coast to work at Kaiser Shipyards in Richmond, California, and the Seattle area or at the Boeing airplane factories in Seattle. Richmond's population increased six-fold in three years; Seattle's nearly doubled, as Boeing had 50,000 workers and Kaiser's shipyards had up to 100,000. Poor housing caused workers to quit jobs—turnover rates were high. Francis Olson of Minneapolis saw Boeing's newspaper ad and took the train for Seattle with a girlfriend. Boeing provided them a three-room "patio home" and trained Olson to operate a rivet gun on the B-29 assembly line six days a week. Boeing gave them a raise to keep the homesick young women, but some "got lonesome, and it was time to go home." Well-paying defense jobs existed back home, and Olson got one at Twin Cities Ordinance Plant. Betty Sarner and a girlfriend went to Kaiser's Richmond shipyard, where Sarner did office work before returning home and signing up with the WAVES. Some Minnesotans never returned.[19]

Those Minnesotans who went overseas and into combat experienced the most intense, most unfamiliar scenes. Many were like Manuel Aguirre of St. Paul's West Side who recalled, "I was never out of the state of Minnesota, other than Iowa," before serving on the USS *Ozark* for the landings on Iwo Jima and Okinawa. Onboard the USS *Chester*, Signalman Crowley witnessed the Battle of the Coral Sea in May 1942.[20]

A Near-Miss in the Pacific Ocean

"I counted five torpedoes discharged toward the *Yorktown*. How they all missed, I'll never know. . . . As one of the enemy planes banked away from the carrier [*Lexington*], I put a glass to it and saw a 'Rising Sun' for the first time . . . three torpedo planes had approached the *Chester* from the starboard. . . . I watched the other [plane] and waited for it to hit us. My fingers were digging into the steel shield. The miracle that it missed can be accredited to the Jap pilot. Scared by our AA fire, he . . . launched the projectile too soon."

Maurice M. Crowley, "A View From the Bridge"

A mother reading a letter from her soldier son fighting in World War II, 1943.
Courtesy of the Minnesota Historical Society.

Gerald Heaney of Goodhue, a graduate of the University of Minnesota Law School, enlisted in the Army and served with the 2nd Ranger Battalion that went ashore on D-Day on Omaha Beach, where things went wrong. Allied bombers hit a mile away from their beach targets; a protecting mortar barrage did not materialize; and the Rangers were dropped off in the water, not on shore. "We all hit the ground at the seawall . . . and the Germans had us zeroed in with mortars. *Boom! Boom! Boom!* We knew we couldn't stay there." They climbed and took Pointe du Hoc and suffered 60 percent casualties by Heaney's reckoning. "You just realized how lucky you were. To have survived."[21]

D-Day was a turning point in Europe. In the Pacific, the Allies slowly made their island-hopping advance toward Japan. Minnesotans followed the fighting in their local newspapers and gained a second-hand geographical lesson through maps and photos. The papers printed excerpts from soldiers' letters home—the *Tyler Journal-Herald*, in a section called "Bits." In January 1945, a Tyler soldier in North Africa described Arab customs, an army field hospital worker compared Italy and France, and a corporal told how he won an argument with a sergeant who gave in after being struck by lightning. February 1945 brought news from the Pacific theater. First-person accounts of foreign lands written by local women and men increased Minnesotans' interest in the rest of the world.[22]

Some Minnesotans Return Home, Minnesota Does Not Revert to Pre-War Status

Victory over Germany (May 1945) and Japan (August 1945) did not end this great migration, for many Minnesotans did not return. Tragically, around 6,300 of them died in the war—nearly twice as many as in World War I—and thousands more were wounded. Late in the war, from 1944 to 1945, the governor's office received weekly lists of Minnesota's dead and wounded, along with the addresses of their parents or spouses or other close relatives—a roll call of the state's regions, cities, and ethnic enclaves.[23]

Some veterans lived elsewhere once they were back in 'the States.' The Danish-American town of Tyler lost some: an army air corps veteran went to work at a Montana airport; a navy pilot became a naval air instructor in North Carolina; a worker at a California defense plant remained in that state; a medically-discharged army veteran married a Minneapolis woman and resided in that city. War-trained pilots did not want to be grounded once they were back in their hometowns. So small towns and cities built airports. By May 1946, the state had twice as many airports and five times as many certified pilots as before the war. Tyler planned three airstrips. State government paid half of the construction costs.[24]

Those who returned found many things unchanged—like Scandinavian reserve. When John Granath returned from the harrowing Battle of the Bulge to Swedish-American Dassel, his close relatives "welcomed [him] with a lengthy handshake, as warmly as their Swedish reserve would permit. . . . The farm dog Pal, however, showed no such restraint. He just kept running in ever-widening circles, wagging his tail as fast as he could wag it."[25]

Other aspects of life did change. There was no returning to the days when Minnesota had been mainly a rural, farm state. By 1950, 53.9 percent of its people lived in urban areas (with populations of 2,500 or more). The number of rural residents declined in the 1940s. The number of farms dropped by 9 percent; farmers' sons and daughters left; mechanized, tractor-powered farms required fewer workers; crossroads communities slowly disappeared. One result was a realization that rural kids must have a high school education to prepare them for urban occupations. In 1940, Minnesota ranked 47th out of the 48 states in the percentage of white farm boys, ages 16 and 17, still in school. The state improved that ranking by 1950, as one-room country schools were closed and rural students went to consolidated schools where education more closely paralleled urban standards. Reducing the language difficulty in rural schools, the percent of foreign-born residents and their school-age children dropped significantly, making the state more like the nation. Rural electrification lessened the rural-urban divide, as did the radios and TVs that electricity powered. The prewar outlier section became more like the Twin Cities and the national norm.[26]

Postwar Minnesota United by Three Moral Visions of Politics & Government

This 'nationalizing' unity did not create a seamless web of political harmony but did conform the state to the nation's two-party contest. Wartime unity in a 'good war' against fascist dictators brought a postwar burst of moral energy very unlike the collapse of moral fervor, cynicism about a futile war, and flouting of Prohibition after World War I. The second war vindicated moral causes. Three leaders personified three moral visions: Governor Luther W. Youngdahl represented a Lutheran one; Mayor and Senator Hubert H.

Humphrey, an academic one from political science; and Congressman Eugene McCarthy, a Catholic one. These visions largely coincided to produce a consensus. These three men also represented three strands of higher education in Minnesota: McCarthy, the Catholic one of St. John's University; Humphrey, the secular one of the University of Minnesota; and Youngdahl, the Protestant and Lutheran one of Gustavus Adolphus College.

Humphrey's moral vision came first and was vital in completing 'nationalization.' Experienced Farmer-Labor leaders from the 1930s, like Elmer Benson, saw wartime unity as a brief interlude after which the battle of the haves against the have-nots and Minnesota's unique role as the home of the strongest have-not party would both resume. Humphrey, and others, believed that Democratic and Farmer-Labor liberals must merge if anyone was to compete with Stassen's Republicans. The creation of the Democratic-Farmer-Labor party in 1944 was a second step in nationalizing state politics, arising out of the first step, Stassen's defeat of Farmer-Laborism. Humphrey played a key role.

Born in 1911 in South Dakota to a pious Norwegian-American mother and a political, Democratic father, Humphrey was trained to take over the family drug store so his father could advance in politics, but he escaped to the University of Minnesota to study political science. In 1937-39, his professors rejected Populists' politics of class conflict, Progressives' experts prescribing the one fair and efficient solution to each problem, and Republicans' confidence that free markets fairly picked the most efficient winners. Instead, they stressed that American society was an interdependent mixture of groups and interests, with democratic governments alone able to balance and harmonize competing interests, as the two political parties combined a multitude of interests into only two viable options for voters to choose from. The New Deal was American politics at its best, these political scientists believed, negotiating policies to deal with the Depression while remaining flexible and pragmatic. During the 1939-40 academic year that he spent at Louisiana State University, Humphrey wrote a master's thesis lauding the New Deal.[27]

Returning to Minneapolis to support his young family, a Democrat in a state where they finished last, Humphrey could hardly reconcile the state's politics with his professors' ideas or with national norms all at once. He had to start small by running (1943, 1945) for the nonpartisan office of mayor of Minneapolis. That meant confronting the messy, moral issues of a city corrupted by crime networks (Kid Cann's Syndicate and Tommy Banks'

Combination) that "ran gambling, prostitution, and liquor in a wide-open town." Mill City police were bribed to overlook gambling dens. Humphrey appealed to church-attending Protestants with his Sunday school teaching, his sermon-like talks in church basements, and his anti-vice theme. Stressing an honest government enforcing the law made Humphrey's wider moral vision credible. Labor union support aided his June 1945 victory. Humphrey kept his promise to clean up the police department so it could clean up Minneapolis. It took courage—he was offered a bribe and was shot at once. City government's integrity was at stake. He told business leaders, "[O]ne is not worthy of respect and confidence of the community if he becomes a pawn or stooge for . . . some outside influences."[28]

He helped negotiate the Democratic-Farmer-Labor (DFL) merger, a bizarre, Byzantine poker game of secrecy, complicated by both sides' efforts to use each other, orders from Moscow to Communists in the FLP, and a mentally-disturbed woman claiming to link Communists to the White House. Serious moral issues were involved. In a 1944 article, Humphrey's professors, Evron Kirkpatrick and Herbert McClosky, argued that Nazis and Communists were similar: one-party rule, no free elections, secret police . . . what came to be called totalitarianism. Their comparison seemed to justify a moral crusade against Communist Russia like the one against Nazi Germany. For Benson's Farmer-Laborites, that was a bogus comparison. They saw Russia as a workers' democracy and those who critiqued it as fascists. The wartime alliance with Russia was a window of opportunity for merging two sides that disagreed on what words meant. Benson and Democratic leader Elmer Kelm personified the mismatch. "Benson regarded Kelm as a patronage politician" and disliked Kelm's Catholicism. "Kelm detested the Communist influence in the Benson camp." Humphrey mediated between the two and the merger was made in April 1944.[29]

Humphrey complacently felt that the professors and he were the advanced thinkers, that thirties' Farmer-Labor factionalism was history, that Benson's faction was just another interest group. Then Benson's faction used the 1946 precinct caucuses, their skill at conventions, and their followers' willingness to stay late at party meetings in order to seize control of the DFL in 1946. Minnesota's Farmer-Labor heritage would not wither away on its own. Humphrey and his allies had to work to end it. They had to make public charges against Communists as Petersen and Stassen did in 1938. The events of 1946 and 1947—Communist regimes in Eastern Europe, Churchill's Iron Curtain speech, the Truman Doctrine of aid to nations fighting Communism, and the call for a Marshall Plan to aid Western Europe—distanced Benson's pro-Moscow views from the views of most Americans and most Minnesotans. How could this new party succeed if it was tied to Russian foreign policy?[30]

It would be easy to confuse this 1946-48 Minnesota debate with the later (1950-54) national debate over McCarthyism. Wisconsin Senator Joseph McCarthy made wild, unsubstantiated charges of Communism in key American institutions. Legislation denied Communists the right to speak freely, to organize as a party, and to teach in the schools. Although he later participated in drafting this legislation, Humphrey in 1947-48 worked within the DFL to defeat (by the party's ordinary procedures) a Benson faction that denied Communists influenced the DFL when evidence showed that they did. The issue was not Communists' right to have their own party but their 'right' to secretly meddle in another party, while that party's leaders deceived voters by denying Communists did so.[31]

The showdown came on Friday night, April 30, 1948, at over 2,000 DFL precinct caucuses.[32] The precinct caucus became Minnesota's symbol of grassroots politics. Ironically, Republicans seeking to end the NPL's tactic of winning the GOP primary had obtained a law in 1922 that gave precinct caucuses the right to endorse candidates. Minnesota's caucuses never garnered the national attention of the New Hampshire primary or the Iowa caucuses. They rarely impacted the presidential race. They remained a state affair, the bottom of the pyramid of election-year politics, the night when neighbors met to select delegates to a city or county convention. Conventions were the pyramid's next level toward the top, where a party's candidates were chosen. Minnesota law did not require voters to register as Republicans or Democrats, but a caucus was not an election run by election judges. A caucus was run by a party that tried to exclude those not in sympathy with it and its candidates. Parties used caucuses to create legitimacy for candidates and to set up a grassroots organization of door-knockers and envelope-stuffers to aid them. A caucus seemed like decision-making from the bottom up, but party factions often organized it from the top down. It was too vital to be left to spontaneous local whims.[33]

Humphrey's anti-Communist faction was organized and led by Marine veteran Orville Freeman (the DFL state secretary), Arthur Naftalin, Macalester student Walter Mondale, Rev. John Simmons, Eugenie Anderson of Red Wing, Dr. William Kubicek, Eugene McCarthy of St. Paul, and many others. A pro-Humphrey man recalled caucus night: "I took my eighty-year-

Senator Hubert H. Humphrey and Governor Orville Freeman watch a football game at Memorial Stadium, University of Minnesota, Minneapolis, 1955.
Courtesy of the Minnesota Historical Society.

old father, my brother, his girlfriend, my sister, her boyfriend and several neighbors. When we walked in, we had a three-to-one majority and I had my sister nominate me as precinct chairman." Victory was not so easy everywhere, but the Benson faction was weakened by its support of third-party presidential candidate Henry Wallace. Humphrey's group tried to exclude Wallace supporters from the caucuses as members of another party. When the elections and meetings reached the pyramid's top level, the DFL state convention at Brainerd in mid-June, Benson was beaten and Humphrey was chosen as the DFL candidate for U.S. Senate, a seat he won in November.[34]

Effectively ended was the Benson faction's attempt to reverse 'nationalization' and to return to the state's 1930s politics of an outlier third party at odds with the nation. The Wallace and Benson supporters left the DFL—or were kicked out—and many did not return for another twenty years. Unique Farmer-Labor politics never returned.

Also elected that November 1948 was a new congressman for St. Paul, Eugene McCarthy, a sociology professor at the College of St. Thomas who had lived in that city for two years. McCarthy appeared to belong to Humphrey's urban, academic group but did so only in part. He came from the Stearns County German Catholic enclave, and his anti-Communism came from a fervent Catholicism. He had a rather different moral vision, but as one of over four hundred congressmen, he had little chance to enact it into law. Yet, in him, that enclave's communal emphasis found an influential voice.

Born and raised in Watkins in Meeker County, the son of an Irish father and German mother, McCarthy attended St. John's University in Collegeville. "[A]n outstanding student," he read widely but embraced most deeply the Benedictine views of St. John's monks, who taught him European Catholic thinking in this European immigrant, Catholic enclave. Their thinking was cosmopolitan, not derived from this provincial corner of the state, but consistent with its family-centered, traditional, church-led, communal life. They criticized American individualism and free-market capitalism for fragmenting society, destroying community, hindering the God-given roles of family and church, and leaving people tempted by the false community of Communism. The answer was a return to rural life, to church-centered community, to a holistic union of worship and work that would reverse fragmentation. McCarthy and his wife Abigail tried to start "a cooperative community" at their St. Anne's farm, near Watkins, but the attempt failed.[35] The area's German Catholic dairy farmers who kept their sons on the land and obeyed the priests rather than rebelling like individualists, had not failed at this task. Broadly, McCarthy's vision was theirs. Yet the anti-Catholic sentiments of some of the state's Scandinavians, the anti-liquor views of Protestants and Progressives, and the anti-German feelings sparked by the two world wars meant that the state's voters would not enact a Stearns County vision into law.

And yet, the state's ethnic enclaves and their politics had changed gradually over seventy years. Language preservation became a matter of convenience for old-timers more than a passionate cause. School consolidation and increasing college attendance made local school boards less able to keep the young from becoming Americanized. Perhaps McCarthy's moral vision was the best way for the college-educated professional to maintain the best of the ancestral heritage while adapting it to a greatly changed world.

More politically successful was the Scandinavian Lutheran vision of three-term Governor Luther Youngdahl. Raised in a pious Swedish-American home, he graduated from Swedish Lutheran Gustavus Adolphus College and then studied for a law degree. Over six feet tall and 200 pounds, "with a ruddy complexion and blue eyes," he looked every bit the Big Swede of Minnesota folklore. Service from 1930 to 1946 as a municipal, district, and state supreme court judge made his moral vision a judicial one too. He felt laws on the books ought to be enforced. As a judge, he was not active in a political party; that independence lingered after he was elected governor as a Republican in 1946. A judge must be an honest broker between two sides, as he tried to be between labor and management. He defined politics as "the machinery by which society makes its moral decisions." Youngdahl quoted the Chinese proverb, "If there is harmony in the home, there is order in the nation," and felt it worked in reverse too. Disorder in state or nation entered the home. Scandinavian Lutheran churches had remained fairly conservative theologically but avoided the fundamentalist-modernist split in the Old Stock Protestant churches. The fairly evangelical Youngdahl appealed to liberal (the *Christian Century* praised him) and conservative Protestants (he invited Billy Graham to speak at a "Crusade for Freedom") and gained support from Catholics also.[36]

A Song Sung by Darrell Fischer and His Log Jammer at Breezy Point Lodge, Pelican Lake[38]

I feel so sorry for Daisy, the dice maid,
Down at the corner saloon;
She'd shake with anybody
Who came in the door;
She'd shake them on the table
Or throw them on the floor.
Then Youngdahl got elected
And it sure played hob,
For now our Daisy is out of a job.

His first fight was to enforce the state law banning gambling. Despite the law, some 8,500 slot machines annually earned $7 or $8 million. He saw this illegal gambling while hiking with his sons near the family cabin on

Gull Lake. Passing Bar Harbor resort, he recalled, "Drunken drivers were tearing up and down the road in their automobiles. . . . My sons and I had to leap into a ditch several times to get out of their way. . . . An orchestra was blaring inside, and we could see great crowds at the bar. Hundreds were in line to get at the slot machines." He vowed to end this scofflaw scene. Bar Harbor and other night spots were left over from the outlaw twenties. The bar was now legal but not the slots. In his first legislative session (1947), he asked for a law to cancel the license of any business with slot machines. A terrific row ensued as opponents claimed that resorts, county fairs, and American Legion clubs would be hurt by loss of gambling revenue. Churches rallied to Youngdahl's support, and their members wrote letters to legislators. The bill passed both houses and became law. The ex-judge insisted it be enforced, even after county sheriffs pointed out to him that that meant going after church raffles.[37]

Youngdahl's stand for full law enforcement established the integrity of his moral vision that he then applied to other issues, despite pressure from the interest groups, taunts of "Sunday school governor," Republicans' doubts about this issue, and risks to his reelection. He expressed this vision not in religious but in professional terms like "youth conservation" and "the conservation of human resources." They sounded secular, avoided denominationalism, and gained him support from Catholics, Jews, and Protestants—the religious triad invoked in the postwar years.[39] He campaigned for programs for juvenile delinquents and for teens in danger of taking that path, for humane treatment of inmates at the state's hospitals for the insane (he helped to throw straight-jackets and manacles onto a Halloween bonfire at Anoka State Hospital in 1949), for an end to hiring discrimination, and for a conference of states to examine American Indian problems. In 1948-49, he enlisted church groups and others to sponsor displaced persons from the war who were living at temporary camps in Europe. Around 7,000 displaced persons came to Minnesota.[40]

Independent-minded, he did not use these programs and policies to build up the GOP. It benefited little from his popularity among voters. "There is something in the Minnesota character that rises above all party lines to back programs that involve human values," he told citizens in his farewell speech. "I know that many of our fine programs would have been scuttled by certain self-interest groups were it not for your help." One GOP state chairman complained that "Youngdahl appealed directly to the people," which meant "over the heads of party leaders," and "[h]e failed to understand the . . . vital role of the party in American politics." He "succeeded wonderfully in dramatizing state politics," but "he did not draw new blood into the GOP." The chair may have compared him to Humphrey, who did draw new blood into the DFL.[41]

As a political scientist Humphrey understood the role of parties and did not place the pejorative prefix "self" in front of interest groups. He pursued similar human-rights programs, especially the fight against discrimination. As mayor, he started the Mayor's Council on Human Relations, fought to get hiring discrimination outlawed in the city, and secured a Fair Employment Practices Committee to lead this effort. From the nonpartisan post of mayor, he could not openly use this program of human and civil rights for the DFL, but he did not intend to remain mayor. As his 1948 campaign for the Senate neared, he "built his national reputation as a liberal Democrat on his interest in 'human relations.' " Sincere about civil rights issues, he also used it to change the Democratic party's image in Minnesota from that of a self-interested group of federal job seekers to that of a movement of idealists. Labor unions or other interest groups could be seen as 'self-interest groups,' but activists whose interest was in the rights of *others* could not. Humphrey's drive culminated in his stirring civil rights speech to the Democratic National Convention on July 14, 1948. The party adopted a civil rights platform and Southerners exited the convention. The mayor became a national figure and a U.S. senator that year.[42]

The DFL gained its first win and lost the burdens of the past: Bensonism's Communist ties and the anti-Semitic nastiness linked to prior anti-Communist attacks on it; the idea that Democrats were only Irish Catholics, would-be postmasters, and segregationists; and the view that idealist liberals must form a third party due to Democrats' deficiencies. Humphrey's group made their interest-group politics idealistic. They advanced political scientists' stress on two responsible parties collecting the demands of interest groups, balancing these demands once in power, and making democracy function. Humphrey combined old-fashioned retail politics with the new political-scientific approach. He ran on the issues but offered patronage rewards. He made ethnic appeals—going to ethnic picnics, citing his Norwegian ancestry—but joined in a national debate of ideas. He removed a possible 1954 foe when he persuaded Truman to make Youngdahl a federal court judge. The way was open for a DFL governor.[43]

The way was closed for a return to the thirties when a third party ruled Minnesota. The state's dissent from national norms was ended. The "Greatest Generation" conformed to the national norm. (In his 1998 book by that name, Tom Brokaw coined the term "Greatest Generation" to describe the generation that came of age during the Depression and fought World War II.) The national government delivered the state from the Depression and could alone deliver it from the Communist threat. New Deal programs could enable that generation to settle down to home ownership, family formation, and the personal security they craved. Thirty years later, political scientist Daniel Elazar would identify Minnesota as having a "moralistic" style and culture of politics—that is, clean campaigns fought on the issues and not on personalities or patronage, and a faith that government could and ought to pass and enforce laws encouraging moral and punishing immoral behavior.[44] Some observers attributed this to a Yankee and Scandinavian heritage, but Yankee-and-Scandinavian Minneapolis had seen corrupt city government. No, it took reform efforts like Humphrey's and Youngdahl's and moral visions like theirs and McCarthy's to make Minnesota moralistic.

1.   "went to Washington," *St. Paul Pioneer Press*, 18 December 1938, 1; *New York Herald Tribune*, 13 January 1939, 7; *St. Paul Pioneer Press*, 3 May 1939, 1; *Minneapolis Star*, 3 May 1939, 13; *New York Times*, 4 May (5), 27 June (1, 3), and 1 July (9), all 1939; *Christian Science Monitor*, 23 March 1940, Magazine Section, 1, 2, 15. For quotes from the Monitor article, see Robert Esbjornson, *A Christian in Politics, Luther Youngdahl: A Story of a Christian's Faith at Work in a Modern World* (Minneapolis: T. S. Denison, 1955), 128-29.

2.   "Stassen scored," Keillor, *Hjalmar Petersen*, 172-73; Gieske, *Minnesota Farmer-Laborism*, 282; Clark, ed., *Minnesota in a Century of Change*, 381.

3.   "formed a chapter," George W. Garlid, "Minneapolis Unit of the Committee to Defend America By Aiding the Allies," *Minnesota History*, Vol. 41 (Summer 1969), 267-83; "An Outline of Inception, Growth and Activities of The Committee to Defend America, Minneapolis Unit," 30 September 1941, and "Financial Reports," Box 4, CDAAA Papers, MHS; Keillor, *Hjalmar Petersen*, 180-81

4.   "Norwegian-American lawyer," Terry L. Shoptaugh, "Henry Nycklemoe's Crusade for Neutrality," *Minnesota History*, Vol. 53, No. 4 (Winter 1992), 145-55. For the general Farmer-Laborite view on World War I as a mistake, see George W. Garlid, "The Antiwar Dilemma of the Farmer-Labor Party," *Minnesota History*, Vol. 40, No. 8 (Winter 1967), 365-74.

5.   "desire for U.S. neutrality," Shoptaugh, "Henry Nycklemoe's Crusade," 146; *Minneapolis Sunday Tribune*, 11 May 1941, 1, 2; Charles A. Lindbergh, *The Wartime Journals of Charles A. Lindbergh* (New York: Harcourt Brace Jovanovich, 1970), 485-86.

6.   "they used arguments," Wayne S. Cole, *Charles A. Lindbergh and the Battle Against American Intervention in World War II* (New York: Harcourt Brace Jovanovich, 1974), 78-80. See also Hjalmar Petersen's editorials in *Askov American*, 7 and 14 and 28 September 1939, 12 October

1939, and 21 December 1939 (all 4).

7. "Walter Benjamin," Walter W. Benjamin, *The Magical Years: A Boyhood Remembrance* (Edina, Minn.: Beaver's Pond Press, 1999), 340-44, 347-48.

8. "lightning of war," Blegen, *Minnesota: A History*, 542; Maurice M. Crowley, "A View from the Bridge," 44-45, typed manuscript, 17 March 1954, MHS; Dave Kenney, *Minnesota Goes to War: The Home Front during World War II* (St. Paul: Minnesota Historical Society Press, 2005), 9-13, 65-67, 223-24.

9. "State government set up," Blegen, *Minnesota: A History*, 541-44.

10. "at Fort Snelling," Kenney, *Minnesota Goes to War*, 27-32.

11. "Army's 99th Battalion," Gerd Nyquist, *The 99th Battalion* (Decorah, Iowa: Anundsen Publishing Co., 1981), 21-23, 41-43, 45-46, 54-55, 100, 143; Kenney, *Minnesota Goes to War*, 31, 33.

12. "loud complaints," Private Matt Prebonich to Harold Stassen, 7 July 1941, and Pastor P. J. Seltz to Stassen, 26 June 1941, both in Governor Harold Stassen Records, Box 110.E.10.10F, State Archives, MHS.

13. "Minnesotans enlisted," Blegen, *Minnesota: A History*, 542, 543; Kenney, *Minnesota Goes to War*, 18, 21; Anne Bosanko Green, *One Woman's War: Letters Home from the Women's Army Corps 1944–1946* (St. Paul: Minnesota Historical Society Press, 1989), x-xi; Anne Kaplan, "Fifty Years Ago: Exploring World War II at the Minnesota Historical Society," *Minnesota History*, Vol. 54, No. 7 (Fall 1995), 317. Taking Kaplan's figure of 326,000 men and women and subtracting 304,000 men leaves 22,000 women.

14. "Benjamin recalls," Benjamin, *Magical Years*, 350-65.

15. "civilians moved," Keillor, *Hjalmar Petersen*, 228; Kenney, *Minnesota Goes to War*, 48-57, 69-70, 109-10; clippings, 20 March 1942, in "News Stories of Northern Pump Company," bound volume, MHS.

16. "Northern Pump," *Saturday Evening Post*, 20 February 1943, 20-21, 98; *Life*, 12 January 1942; "News Stories of Northern Pump," 96, 97, 148, 149-50; Kenney, *Minnesota Goes to War*, 111-15.

17. "President Roosevelt toured," Kenney, *Minnesota Goes to War*, 119-21, 127-30, 144-46; Kirk Jeffrey, *The Major Manufacturers: From Food and Forest Products to High Technology*, Clark, ed., *Minnesota in a Century of Change*, 239-42.

18. "personal mobility," *The Powder Keg*, February 1943, 10-11, MHS.

19. "to the West Coast," Gerald D. Nash, *The American West Transformed: The Impact of the Second World War* (Bloomington, Ind.: Indiana University Press, 1985), 58, 69-73, 76, 79-81; Thomas Saylor, *Remembering the Good War: Minnesota's Greatest Generation* (St. Paul: Minnesota Historical Society Press, 2005), 74-77.

20. "witnessed," here and below, Crowley, "A View from the Bridge," 73-74.

21. "Gerald Heaney," Saylor, *Remembering the Good War*, 125-28.

22. "soldiers' letters home," *Tyler Journal-Herald*, 4 January 1945 (3), 11 January 1945 (3), 25 January 1945 (2), 8 February 1945 (1, 8).

23. "did not return," Blegen, *Minnesota: A History*, 474, 543; Navy and Army Casualties, 27 December 1944 to 6 January 1945, Box 110.E.13.9(B), Governor Edward J. Thye Papers, State Archives, MHS.

24. "lived elsewhere," Keillor, *Hjalmar Petersen*, 220; *Tyler Journal-Herald*, 18 January 1945 (1), 25 January 1945 (1), 3 January 1946 (1), 14 March 1946 (7), 2 May 1946 (8), and 3 October 1946 (1).

25. "John Granath returned," John Granath, *Growing up and going to war* (Dassel, MN: Dassel Area Historical Society, 2006), 63.

26. "Other aspects of life," Lowry Nelson, Charles E. Ramsey, and Jacob Toews, "A Century of

Population Growth in Minnesota," *Agricultural Extension Station Bulletin* No. 423 (February 1954), 5, 10; Charles E. Ramsey, et al., "Migration in Minnesota, 1940–1950," *Agricultural Extension Station Bulletin*, No. 422 (January 1954), 9-10; Lowry Nelson and George Donahue, "Social Change in Goodhue County 1940-65," *Agricultural Extension Station Bulletin* No. 482 (1966), 9-11, 40-41; John E. Dobbin, Ruth E. Eckert, and T. J. Berning, "Trends and Problems in Minnesota's Public Schools," in *Higher Education in Minnesota* (Minneapolis: University of Minnesota Press, 1950), 40-41.

27.   "Born in 1911," Hubert H. Humphrey, *The Education of a Public Man: My Life and Politics* (Garden City, NY: Doubleday, 1976), 19-27, 56-57, 59, 62-63; Jennifer A. Dalton, *Making Minnesota Liberal: Civil Rights and the Transformation of the Democratic Party* (Minneapolis: University of Minnesota Press, 2002), 19-37.

28.   "start small," Humphrey, *Education*, 77-79, 90-91, 94; Carl Solberg, *Hubert Humphrey: A Biography* (New York: W. W. Norton, 1984), 90-91, 99-102.

29.   "merger," Haynes, *Dubious Alliance*, 107-31 (quote from 114), 179.

30.   "Humphrey complacently felt," Haynes, *Dubious Alliance*, 125-40.

31.   "easy to confuse," Haynes, *Dubious Alliance*, 212-15. This interpretation is largely my own, however.

32.   "over 2,000," Haynes, *Dubious Alliance*, 179.

33.   "The precinct caucus," For a good description of the precinct caucus, see G. Theodore Mitau, *Politics in Minnesota* (Minneapolis: University of Minnesota Press, 1960), 44-46; and Citizens League, "The Party Caucus: An Inquiry," Report dated 5 April 1991, 3-4. The interpretation here is mine.

34.   "faction was organized," Haynes, *Dubious Alliance*, 179-94; Dominic Sandbrook, *Eugene McCarthy: The Rise and Fall of Postwar American Liberalism* (New York: Alfred A. Knopf, 2004), 46; Solberg, *Humphrey*, 119-22.

35.   "McCarthy attended," Sandbrook, *Eugene McCarthy*, 3-29.

36.   "politically successful," Esbjornson, *Luther W. Youngdahl*, 67, 70-75, 80-81, 87-90, 94, 116, 119-20, 134-35, 158-64, 202-03, 210-12, 219, 225; "God's Word is Law in Minnesota," *Magazine Digest*, 115-20, clipping at MHS; Alton M. Motter, "Crusading Governor," *Christian Century*, 18 February 1948, 204-06.

37.   "first fight," Esbjornson, *Luther W. Youngdahl*, 141-49; Rufus Jarman, "The Governor and the Gamblers," *Saturday Evening Post*, 13 December 1947, 22-23, 56, 59, 62. For a photo of Bar Harbor, see Kathryn Strand Koutsky and Linda Koutsky, *Minnesota Vacation Days: An Illustrated History* (St. Paul: Minnesota Historical Society Press, 2006), 200.

38.   "Song Sung," Esbjornson, *Luther W. Youngdahl*, 149.

39.   "Youngdahl's stand," Esbjornson, *Luther W. Youngdahl*, 139-40, 169-70, 171; "God's Word is Law in Minnesota," 118.

40.   "Youngdahl campaigned," Esbjornson, *Luther W. Youngdahl*, 169-89; Holmquist, ed., *They Chose Minnesota*, 3.

41.   "Independent-minded," Esbjornson, *Luther W. Youngdahl*, 211-12, 225.

42.   "As a political scientist," Dalton, *Making Minnesota Liberal*, 99-105, 119 (quoted), 134, 149-50.

43.   "Humphrey's group," Dalton, *Making Minnesota Liberal*, 153-69.

44.   "Daniel Elazar," Daniel Elazar, *American Federalism: A View from the States* (New York: Crowell, 1972), summarized in Elazar, "Model of Moral Government," in Clark, ed., *Minnesota in a Century of Change*, 354-56.

10   The Family Fifties & Early Sixties

Ordinary Minnesotans of whatever class, race, gender, or ethnicity had a simple moral vision for their postwar years: to raise a family. Depression and war had delayed that pursuit for many, but the war finally ended, and it ended the Depression, so that they could form families after 1945. True, the nation had the new goal of defeating Communism, but the Cold War might be a poker game of bluff—terrifying, but if the nation acquired superior military cards, the Soviets might not force it to use them. Acquiring nuclear weapons and new naval and air capabilities prolonged the war's defense-spending prosperity. Such prosperity enabled Minnesotans to form families and buy new houses for their new families.

It launched an upward mobility in careers, housing, and recreation. Returning to the state after the war need not involve a return to the farm or hamlet or cramped urban apartment of the prewar years—the Minnesota that appeared backward and provincial compared to other parts of the nation. New industries and new housing developments created a new suburban region of Minnesota that shared the high status of the nation's booming sectors. Raising a family was now trendy, and everyone was doing it. You could raise a family in Minnesota in style and status if you had the right job and right residence.

Minnesotans followed a national, generational trend: the Greatest begat the Baby Boomer generation. The federal government helped them secure good housing, which had been a barrier due to private lenders' restrictive rules and a wartime scarcity of building materials. New Deal legislation and its Federal Housing Administration (FHA) and Federal National Mortgage Association (Fannie Mae) loosened up mortgage terms. Home buyers need make only a small down payment, with no balloon payment at the end, and twenty years to repay instead of ten, plus lower interest rates. After the war, the Veterans' Administration (VA) offered similarly favorable terms to veterans, who had until 1957 to take advantage of them.[1]

The federal government did not loan dollars. It created a business landscape in which banker or builder faced little risk in multiplying new mortgages and new houses to meet the pent-up demand for housing. Millions of new home buyers were back from the war. The government guaranteed a veteran's mortgage so banks could not lose and set construction standards so home buyers would have a sturdy house they could resell after a few years, if need be. The VA and FHA's looser terms meant lower monthly payments that most home buyers could afford. And, Fannie Mae, FHA, and VA favored lower-priced, smaller homes, so that as many families as possible could benefit from these programs. The federal government virtually wrote the business plan for hundreds of home builders who geared up to meet this demand. The flat prairie landscape adjacent to the Twin Cities proved ideal for new construction.[2]

In the late 1940s, hundreds of two-bedroom $7,000 "GI houses" in the Cape Cod style sprouted on rectangular-grid streets in suburbs like Richfield, Crystal, Robbinsdale, Falcon Heights, and Roseville. Most were built by small family firms that had a few homes or a few blocks, not large ones like the Levitt brothers of Levittown, New York. Tom Willmus of Roseville recalled that veterans "came back from the war and needed a place to live. Built a house, and pretty soon someone wanted to buy that house, so they built another home, and that's how they became builders." Some platted lots on the family's "old truck farm" of "20 to 30 acres" and "built 4-5 houses a year." Big investors were unsure if this zeal to form families would last or if a Cape Cod would earn a profit.[3]

By the mid-1950s, investors saw that they would. The baby boom began in the mid-1940s with older couples getting a delayed start on a family. It was prolonged by younger couples who saw postwar prosperity would last and give their children a future, so they married earlier and had children earlier and at shorter intervals. With housing demand strong, lenders like the Eberhardt Company financed builders like Orrin Thompson for large-scale construction. In 1958, Orrin Thompson built 1,000 homes. To get in on the boom, Eberhardt began residential construction and hired a builder, Clayton Miller, to do the work; however, Miller found he could make more money on his own. Few businesses were more risk-free than building single-family suburban houses. Greater profits per house came from building larger, more luxurious houses; however, federal policy and consumer demand dictated the focus on the small family-formation rambler or Cape Cod.[4]

Family Life in the New Twin Cities' Suburbs of the Fifties

At first no one called this new residential growth north on Snelling into Roseville or south on Portland into Richfield by the ten-dollar word 'suburbanization.' Willmus recalls migrants from St. Paul's 40-foot lots thinking Roseville's 80-foot, one-third-of-an-acre lots would support "livestock. . . . So they would have a pony, and they wanted to have a cow." So "developers put in restrictions that you were not allowed to raise horses or cattle or chickens on your newly acquired lot in Roseville." You could raise a family.[5]

Richfield was a typical 1940s–50s suburb. People moved to an area next to their city neighborhood—from the Roosevelt High School area in south Minneapolis due south to Richfield, a flat landscape easy for small builders to develop a few blocks at a time. This working-class and middle-class suburb was built before freeways. People commuted to their old jobs by their old routes. Young couples just needed a house, not an apartment, as children arrived. It needn't be a large house. On South Murray Lane, lots were 75-feet wide and ramblers had "three bedrooms, a bathroom, a living room, and a fairly large kitchen," but no dining room or garage. Each house had its well and septic tank. Richfield had no municipal water or sewer in 1950. After the husband, a returning veteran, found a job with Northwest Airlines, a couple bought a house and "raised six children in their little three-bedroom rambler." It was also just the right size for their retirement.[6]

The second-tier suburb (one suburb lay between it and the central city) Bloomington typified a later, more complex stage. Its flat central and eastern part was developed early like Richfield. Its hillier western section awaited the 1960s–70s trend of larger lots and more expensive houses. Its commercial and industrial growth relied on the freeways built then: east-west I-494 and north-south I-35W. Its upper-class bluffs gave a grand view of the Minnesota River Valley. From his house there, author Frederick Manfred protested in 1955 against its suburban, boosterish name and called for a return to the old-fashioned rural name of Oxboro. His idea went nowhere, while one writer to the *Bloomington Sun* asked, "Have you ever seen a village burst into bloom more rapidly than ours?" Bloomington Township had fewer than 4,000 people in 1940; the city of Bloomington had 50,498 in 1960.[7]

Manfred typified the cultural elite who deplored the fifties' family-focused suburbs. Few critically-acclaimed novels were written about or in a two-bedroom rambler on a 75-foot lot, but many families were raised in one. The new suburb tried to create genuine community. A week before Manfred's proposal, the Community Youth Council held a Family Community Night, "a family evening where parents may bring their children to enjoy the music" of the high school band and church choirs and the Civic Chorus, "meet some of the village and school officials," and learn of "the opportunities for group work." A square dance club, the Neighborhood Good News club, a Civic Theater troupe, and the Jaycees were groups featured on the program. By 1960 the Bloomington Athletic Association ran a sizeable Little League baseball program for young Baby Boomers.[8]

In a new society under construction, as in pioneer years, government, school, and church cooperated with families. Home ownership and a rough equality for the majority were the foundations, as with the pioneer 160-acre farm. Home owners were less likely to move and more likely to build a community with schools and churches that could educate future citizens and create a moral society that could govern itself. As more homes and families with school-aged children came, Bloomington's voters approved ten bond issues from 1949 to 1960. Even so, the school board had to run some classes on a split shift for fourteen years. Fledgling congregations met in schools until they could build a church. Bloomington's Free Lutherans met in Cedarcrest school in September 1951, sixteen families formed Emmaus Lutheran Church in December, and they dedicated their church building in June 1955. They used construction materials taken from Minneapolis schools they "bought and dismantled." Minneapolis lost population as the suburbs gained it.[9]

F. Wilson Pond, grandson of missionary Gideon Pond, personified the pioneer Ordinance tradition: for forty years he farmed, served on the school board, taught Sunday School, was an elder in Oak Grove church, and led the Hennepin County Farm Bureau. In 1955, a pioneer-era issue arose, a proposal to grant liquor licenses in the dry village. The dry Pond joined with a young DFLer, Gordon Midlethun, the mayoral candidate of young homeowners opposed to liquor sales—perhaps, due to the 'not-in-my-backyard' syndrome, for they could easily drive to bars elsewhere. Proponents wanted revenue from liquor licensing to pay some government expenses and, thus, lower their taxes.[10] The drys' ad in the *Sun* featured Baby Boomers "Tommy and Mary" writing to their parents to put family first (this ad reflected what good fifties parents were supposed to think).

Tommy and Mary to Mom and Dad

"First, most of you have given us good homes, schools and church training . . . don't undo the good work by exposing us to saloons in our town! . . . Yet, what have we been hearing . . . vote for liquor so that we can build a new school, pave our streets . . . . Really, we're confused. . . . And when you mark your ballot, don't see 'Dollar Signs,' but see *us*, your *children*!"[11]

Pond's anti-liquor drive won, as did Midlethun. The stress on forming families meant that many parents did give the Boomers good homes, schools, and church training.

In Roseville, the consolidation of seven rural school districts into one independent school district came in 1947, about the time Roseville and Falcon Heights incorporated. The district's new high school, named after Alexander Ramsey, opened in September 1953. Three elementary schools and three junior high schools were built from 1956 to 1967, as enrollment more than tripled. Roseville's population increased 422 percent in the 1950s. In most suburbs, home owners disliked the rising real estate tax bill resulting from bond issues and levy increases. The typical response was not a tax revolt but a demand that the suburb try to attract industrial and commercial firms to help pay the taxes.[12]

For Jeanne Drange, the mother of two sons and two daughters, parenting occurred in the school building as well as the home. Raised on a 2½-acre "mini farm" with two cows and "an alfalfa field" just east of the present Har Mar Mall, she and her husband 'built a small house' several blocks south of her parents' home after the war. She did much of the washing by hand before they moved to a house that 'had hot water heat.' "I was involved in PTA and I was a den mother for cub scouts for a long time." The PTA handled the hot lunch program, but "it was a lot more sociability" for suburbanites in the fifties than later. Her "boys were always in Little League, high school and grade school football."[13]

Suburban as Anti-Urban:
The Struggle for Local Autonomy & Low Taxes

Minneapolis and St. Paul had a low housing density compared to Eastern cities, but suburban migrants sought one even lower. Rose Township incorporated as Roseville in 1948 after residents heard that St. Paul was about to annex the township. Richfield residents "distrusted and were determined to have nothing to do with the residents and officials of the 'big city' next door—Minneapolis," recalled city manager Leroy Harlow. Townships and smaller areas incorporated at a furious rate to escape big city officials' voracious tax-raising appetites. In 1950, the metropolitan area had 68 incorporated places; by 1958, it had 104.[14] First-time homeowners saw rising taxes to fund new schools, roads, and services as a threat to their ability to pay their mortgages. They felt they could control a small suburb, whose officials would not start grandiose projects.

To multiply municipalities was to step away from Progressive-era expertise and efficiency that had produced the Twin Cities Sanitary District for sewage control in 1933, for example. Suburban autonomy meant each house had its own septic system and well; each suburb, its school district, police, and fire department. This was a step toward the Ordinances' stress on local control—new suburban cities like Bloomington, Minnetonka, and Eden Prairie were the old townships now incorporated. Suburbanites engaged in civic affairs lest their city be absorbed by outside forces—either the 'big city' or a metro-area agency under 'big city' control. Richfield city council meetings were "attended by so many citizens it was necessary to drive the fire trucks out of the fire station onto the driveway apron and set up for the council meeting in the fire hall," Harlow recalled.[15]

What doomed this attempt at low-tax self-sufficiency was contamination of well water. Even a lot 80 feet wide and 150 feet deep was too small for water and sewer self-sufficiency. By 1959, nearly half of the home wells were contaminated from septic tanks. "The Federal Housing Administration threatened to stop insuring mortgages for homes that were not tied into a central sewer system," thus endangering the economic basis of working-class and middle-class home ownership in those suburbs that refused to hook into another city's system or build their own. That fall Governor Orville Freeman spoke to his advisory committee on suburban problems about this issue. So controversial was it that Freeman called for more study, "for the *short term measures* essential to safe water and sewage"—namely, a water and sewer system in each suburb—while he cautiously skirted the long-term problem by asking if anyone "had any objections to the idea of a common sewage system for the metropolitan district." He did not call for such a system.[16]

The DFL governor did take some initiative. His chief aide George Farr was on the Bloomington planning commission for a time. Mayor Midlethun worked with Freeman's advisory committee, and Bloomington civic leader

Kingsley Holman chaired it. The DFL party made early gains in the new suburbs, whose new homeowners were not so distanced from their working-class origins. In 1956, the party experimented successfully with "suburban coffee parties for women," similar to Tupperware parties. It pioneered intensive use of election-eve television broadcasts in its campaigns and mass distribution of DFL "sample ballots" that linked the entire DFL ticket together. Old forms of campaigning like political rallies simply did not work in the new suburbs.[17] By contrast, the rural county-seat leaders and downtown business elites still dominated the GOP and often failed to connect to suburbanites. The Conservative-dominated but nonpartisan legislature had not reapportioned itself in forty years; its rural leaders did not focus on metropolitan issues.

One New Industry Supporting Suburban Families: The Computer Industry

Second-tier suburbs like Bloomington could not rely on their residents commuting to old jobs in Minneapolis or St. Paul forever. They needed new industries not dependent on waterpower from St. Anthony Falls, rail service, or proximity to downtown clients and customers. One was the computer industry. In the 1950s and 1960s, Twin Cities' suburbs became an early center, like California's Silicon Valley in the 1990s. For engineers designing and building computers, this industry offered financial and occupational upward mobility that matched the residential upward mobility of suburban housing. This industry also exemplified the evolution of Minnesota's economy from producer-focused to consumer-focused.

World War II defense contracts jump-started computer design and production in the Twin Cities. The key innovator was Engineering Research Associates (ERA), which used Northwestern Aeronautical's old glider plant on St. Paul's Minnehaha Avenue and its ties to the Navy to land a contract to design computers for the Navy. The nation's Cold War need for high technology gave ERA a single, secure customer. Its engineers were Midwestern farm boys or working-class sons who had attended state universities, "Moo Us" like the University of Minnesota, and resented the Ivy League snobbery of business-computer giant IBM and its slick salesmen. With guaranteed government sales, ERA engineers could sit in Sheetrock cubicles in the two-block-long, government-gray plant, with sparrows flying above and rat poison on the floor, and design scientific computers for other engineers without worrying about image or consumers. They could start a family and "buy one of the neat little postwar homes that were sprouting up around the Twin Cities."[18] University alumni William Norris and Seymour Cray were among them.

The early computer industry was an ERA spin-off. Sperry-Rand acquired ERA's engineers to improve the Univac computer, but Norris, Cray, and others felt Sperry-Rand stifled innovation. In the summer of 1957, they left to form Control Data with offices in Minneapolis on the Mississippi's West Bank; engineers leaving Univac to "swim the river" to Control Data were called "wetbacks." Control Data was the first start-up company in the industry "to be publicly financed." Its initial public offering of 600,000 shares at $1 per share was modest by later standards. A stock craze hit engineers, who drove to Edina to hear a sales pitch and buy Control Data shares. "Other engineers organized investment clubs . . . and purchased mostly local stocks," often high-tech start-ups. To land the best engineers, start-ups offered stock options that could make them millionaires. Medtronic pioneered a similar burst of energy in the new medical-technology industry.[19]

High-tech start-ups sought cheap suburban land for research labs and assembly plants. In 1960, Control Data bought 130 acres of cornfields in east Bloomington, near the airport. In 1962, two buildings were ready. Headquarters had "a large open atrium" three stories high, and one new hire fresh from "Moo U" eagerly exclaimed, "Sure would hold a lot of hay!" Sperry-Rand moved its Univac operations to Roseville. Control Data built an assembly plant in Arden Hills as it grew from 325 employees (1959) to 1,500 (1961) to 3,500 (1963) to 5,500 (1965). Suburbs housing young, upwardly-mobile couples suited young, upwardly-mobile companies. Engineers from farm and land-grant university could own a large lot and raise a family as they adjusted to urban life. Suburban freedom from 'big city' control matched a freedom from Ivy League management types at work.[20]

Many founders of start-ups were workaholics, but their employees had time to spend with their families at the suburban home. In most industries in the 1950s, companies offered sick leave, forty-hour work weeks with weekends off, and paid vacations to their white-collar workers, and these were the workers most likely to live in the suburbs.[21] Suburbanites often used this leisure time for the family and local community—coaching or watching Little League games, participating in community groups, taking the annual family vacation, or maintaining the suburban house, lawn, and garden, or shopping.

America's First Mall, Southdale,
Helps Make Consumerism Part of Americanism

The proud producer identity of 'geek' engineer oblivious to image gave way to image-conscious consumer identity. Minnesota led the nation. Southdale, the nation's first enclosed, two-level shopping mall, opened in October 1956. It foreshadowed the coming consumer kingdom. The Dayton department-store family built it in the upper-class, trend-setting suburb of Edina. Middle-class families from Richfield, Bloomington, and other suburbs could drive there to see which dresses or shoes were fashionable—and to learn that consuming store goods was fashionable and the key to personal identity, not one's job as a producer. Minnesota's frigid winters caused noted architect Victor Gruen to design an enclosed mall, whose Garden Court was the center of an inward-looking set of over sixty stores and two department stores (Dayton's and Donaldson's). Critical of suburbia's "avenues of horror" cluttered with "billboards, motels, gas stations, shanties, car lots," Gruen intended it to be "an antidote to suburban sprawl." It was to be a central, planned civic square with pedestrians, concerts, plays, and meetings of community groups. However, shopping trumped debates, motions, and resolutions.[22] A family could safely bring small children, for the interior excluded dangerous automobiles.

Leading magazines covered the opening. One reporter christened Southdale "part of the American Way." The *Architectural Record* noted that "[o]ther shopping centers . . . seem provincial in contrast with the real thing—the city downtown. But in Minneapolis, it is the downtown that seems pokey and provincial in contrast with Southdale's metropolitan character." With Southdale, suburbs competed against the 'big city' at its strongest point, its retail district. Real estate taxes paid by middle-class homeowners in Richfield and Bloomington did not pay for Southdale. The federal government subsidized shopping malls by offering accelerated depreciation. Developers made money on their tax returns if not on their rental income. Southdale turned shopping into recreation and entertainment and turned citizens into consumers increasingly indifferent to politics.[23]

At first, Southdale's consumerism could be regarded as gender-limited, and the producer-husband could imagine himself free from it; however, over the long term, even the design and marketing of producer-focused products like the engineers' computers would have to conform to this new consumer-oriented economy and society.

Political Issues Arising From
Population Change, Suburbs & Expanded Families

Governor Freeman had an electronics advisory committee too, and his DFL party sought the suburban vote by contrasting its forward-looking program with the old rural-dominated Conservative legislature. The rural-versus-urban battle had several sides, some trivial and some vital. One issue was Daylight Savings Time (DST). Pushing the clock an hour ahead would give suburban parents an extra hour in the evening to attend that Little League game, mow the lawn, or enjoy family recreation. Farmers opposed it. DST would delay their field work in the morning, as the dew would still be on the grass at the new 10 a.m., while stores in town would close at 5 p.m.—the old 4 p.m.—and limit farmers' chances to buy a new part or a new supply of feed. Nevertheless, the legislature passed DST in 1957.[24]

Rural areas fought against state government's push for school consolidation and against political scientists' and journalists' call for an end to township governments. Local control was at stake. Conservatives had more success in opposing the latter call.[25]

Reapportionment of the legislature was a key issue. The 1950 census showed 54 percent of Minnesotans living in urban areas. Yet rural areas had a majority in the legislature. Ramsey and Hennepin counties had 34 percent of all Minnesotans but 22 percent of the legislators. The legislature had last redrawn legislative district lines in 1913 in a minor way. By the early 1950s, about 34 percent of the state's voters elected a majority of the legislature. Rural legislators were reluctant to vote themselves out of office. They persisted in a loyalty to the county. They equated a county's role in the state to a state's role in the nation. Each state was entitled to two U.S. senators, so each county should have at least one state senator. One county's interests were thought to differ from its neighbor's. Wabasha County's senator represented 17,000 people in 1952; a senator from suburban Hennepin County (including Richfield and Bloomington) had over 150,000 constituents.[26]

Rural legislators were irked when a Minneapolis newspaper caricatured and captured this injustice by placing a proportionately shrunken photograph of a suburban couple on its front page next to a greatly enlarged picture of a Wabasha County couple.

This disparity violated the state constitution. Article IV required representation to be "apportioned equally throughout the different sections of the State, in proportion to the population thereof" and gave the legislature authority "to apportion anew" after a census. Like rural-run legislatures in other states, it had failed to apportion anew or equally. One Twin Cities' resident jokingly suggested a rule of "one vote per acre" rather than per person, to spare voters "the nuisance of going to the polls after we move to the cities."[27]

Sen. Elmer Andersen from Rural Ramsey County

"Anytime there was any issue of city versus country, the farm bloc would . . . decide the matter in the country's favor. Yet I had a slight advantage . . . because I was counted as part of the so-called farm bloc. . . . I still represented a dwindling number of hog farmers. . . . [Anderson's bill to exempt Ramsey County's cars from the gas tax] was overwhelmingly defeated. My farm bloc friends had all opposed it. Senator Almen, who sat behind me, tapped me on the shoulder and said, 'Senator, I hope you didn't take your membership in the farm bloc too seriously.' "[28]

Here too, the state resembled the nation. Southern senators who were predictably reelected for decades used the seniority system to chair committees and run the U.S. Senate. Conservative rural legislators like Gordon Rosenmeier of Little Falls, who were predictably reelected, chaired key committees because they had served longest in the legislature. They ran things in St. Paul. Mere governors came and went. Legislators could wait until the present one went. Their ways never changed. Conservative representatives roomed at the Ryan Hotel; Conservative senators lodged at the more expensive St. Paul Hotel. They ate and drank together. Lobbyists often picked up the tab. Urban liberals like Donald Fraser of Minneapolis, a Humphrey protégé, had to take a back seat. Governor Freeman fought with Senate Conservatives over taxes—he favored income tax withholding; they sought a sales tax. The nonpartisan legislators caucused as Liberals or Conservatives, but Conservatives tended to be Republicans and Liberals, DFLers—with the latter more open about it. Nonpartisan confusion persisted. GOP candidates for governor pledged to oppose a sales tax while GOP-leaning Conservative legislators fought for a sales tax.[29]

Suburban growth requiring new schools was a key reason why state government needed added revenues, from the income tax or from a new sales

Henry J. Bukowski is shown painting the Minnesota State Seal for a Works Progress Administration exhibit at the Minnesota State Fair, 1938.
Courtesy of the Minnesota Historical Society.

tax. Traditionally, state government used income tax revenues to aid local school districts, and the DFL party favored this progressive, 'scientific' tax and its use for school aid, so that homeowners' property taxes could be kept low. The state income tax was a tax on producers; however, the state's economy was centering more on the citizen's role as a consumer. Upwardly-mobile suburban families spent more on luxuries and less on necessities like food, clothing, and housing. DFL dislike of a sales tax because it taxed those items became outdated. Far more revenue could be garnered from taxing the sales at Southdale than from taxing sales clerks' incomes. GOP opposition to pay-as-you-go withholding from each paycheck—in hopes taxpayers would revolt if they had to pay the entire balance due in the spring—was also outmoded in rejecting this modern, efficient system.

Rural rule led to one oddity: a law restricting sales of margarine in Minnesota. Dairy farmers fought against it as 'faux' butter. Lawmakers passed a law banning sales of yellow margarine. Consumers protested, so legislators relented. A new law "allowed the sale of a bead of food coloring in white margarine. The consumer would have to open a little capsule of coloring and knead it into the margarine to make it yellow." This deliberate nuisance for consumers represented producers going against the fifties' tide. Some consumers drove to Iowa and returned with colored margarine by the carload.[30]

Minnesota celebrated its statehood centennial on May 9-11, 1958. On Friday the 9th came the Scandinavians—a Norwegian princess, Swedish prince, and the prime ministers of Denmark, Finland, and Norway—to call on Freeman at the capitol. They visited ethnic enclaves or colleges: Danish Tyler, a Finnish area near Duluth, Norwegian Northfield (St. Olaf), and Swedish St. Peter (Gustavus Adolphus). Saturday's parade in St. Paul drew 200,000 onlookers and featured "blaring bands, rainbow-hued floats and precise drill units," with floats "ranging from ox carts and covered wagons to moon-bound rocket ships." The governor and other dignitaries reviewed it at the State Fair grandstand. Marchers' "costumes ran from the crinolines of early days to flouncy modern formals and sleek swim suits, and the dances from Indian and folk types to a touch of rock-and-roll shuffle." On Sunday the 11th, Scandinavian guests attended their ethnic churches: the Norwegian Lutheran *Mindekirken*, Danish St. Peder's Lutheran, and Swedish Ebenezer Lutheran, in Minneapolis. In the afternoon, 18,000 people at the University's Memorial Stadium heard Judy Garland sing and Secretary of State John Foster Dulles speak.[31]

In that year's election, Eugene McCarthy became the state's first Catholic U.S. senator and the first from the German-Catholic enclave. Freeman won his third term as governor. In 1959, legislators reapportioned and partially gave suburban areas equal representation. Politics was not the source of entertainment and sociability that it was for Minnesotans in 1858. New sources replaced it. The excitement of the state's first presidential campaign in 1860 with torchlight parades and Wide Awakes would be impossible to recreate.

Weekend Cabin at the Lake: Family Entertainment & Escape from Politics

Some new entertainments Minnesotans enjoyed were the ones other Americans relished: TV shows like *I Love Lucy* and *The Honeymooners*; Hollywood films like *Rebel Without a Cause*; songs by Bing Crosby and Frank Sinatra. Minnesota contributed little to this mass entertainment, with one exception: Max Shulman's TV series *Dobie Gillis* was based on his books about student life at the University of Minnesota. The state's cities or rural areas, its ethnic enclaves and mines, were not among the standard settings: Brooklyn apartments, California ranch homes, Western cow towns, the Southern backwoods. To the degree that these stories seeped into Minnesotans' consciousness, they lost a bit of their distinctiveness as they hummed country-western songs, imitated California surfers, or accepted New Yorkers' opinions as the rule for life and leisure.

This land of 15,000 lakes offered one distinctly Minnesotan recreation: the lake cabin. fifties' prosperity enabled a middle-class family to afford a seasonal lake home on a small lot, which only the wealthy could afford earlier. The low-cost suburban answer to year-round housing enabled a family to consider a weekend place. The forty-hour work week, paid holidays, and paid vacation gave families time to spend at the lake. Upward mobility in careers and housing occurred in recreation too. The spread of lake-cabin ownership to the middle and working classes was a long, slow process unlike postwar suburbanization. No one built a thousand lake homes per year, nor did the federal government guarantee loans to purchase them. Lake development had advanced by spurts over eighty years.

Pioneers saw lakes strewn across the landscape as obstacles to farming, railroad-building, logging, and mining. Although they were plentiful sources of fish, lakes had been eclipsed as tourist spots by the Mississippi and its grand steamboats. Early resorts like Israel Garrard's St. Hubert Lodge at Frontenac were on the Mississippi. In the 1860s and 1870s, the scenic beauty of Lake Minnetonka twenty miles from downtown Minneapolis converted wealthy Minnesotans and tourists from rivers to lakes. Minnetonka became the pioneering model for recreational use of Minnesota's lakes. Roughing it by tenting on the shore came first, followed by Minneapolis business leaders building small cottages, still primitive housing in deliberate contrast to their fancy city homes. Then flour millers and lumber barons upgraded by building beach front mansions, and fine hotels—the St. Louis, Lake Park, and Lafayette—enabled the upper class to summer near the millionaires. Seasonal socializing was written up in Twin Cities newspapers for the middle class to envy.[32]

As St. Paul preceded Minneapolis, so its White Bear Lake preceded Minnetonka, only to fall behind its western counterpart. White Bear was more accessible by rail from the city. Cottages and hotels sprang up in the 1870s. Manitou Island was its most exclusive site; the less wealthy settled for nearby Bald Eagle Lake, whose $500 to $2,000 cottages, "hidden from each other in the woods," later proved to "typify thousands of the cottages on lakes of the future far" from the Cities. Easy rail access also typified the next stage of lake development, as the Milwaukee Road, St. Paul & Sioux City, Soo Line, Minneapolis & St. Louis, the Northern Pacific, and the Great Northern promoted lakes along their routes such as Big Stone Lake, Lake Elmo, Lake Shetek, and Lake Tetonka.[33]

After World War I, the automobile let the middle class reach lakes remote from railroads. Developers like Minnesota Park Region Land Company bought lakeshore acreage, platted it into lots, and sold them to Midwesterners. Breezy Point Lodge publicized the relaxed life on Brainerd lakes in the 1920s and 1930s and encouraged Minnesotans with extra income to buy a lake lot. In 1933, Governor Olson built his two-story cabin on Gull Lake. Youngdahl followed later that decade, on Gull Lake. By 1960, "the Gull Lake Recreational Area . . . embraced ten thousand summer inhabitants." By then, nearly all Minnesotans owned a car that gave them access each summer weekend to their lake cabin, if they had one.[34]

Prosperity expanded the market for lake lots. Earlier stages had created pockets of developed lakeshore near Brainerd, on Mille Lacs, in Otter Tail County, and on Lake Minnetonka and White Bear Lake. Now new areas

Ice fishing contest on White Bear Lake during the St. Paul Winter Carnival, 1948.
Courtesy of the Minnesota Historical Society.

could be platted, sold, and built upon. A 1970 study found a great concentration: "two-thirds of the lake homes occupy only 13 percent of the shoreline . . . lakeshore residences on developed lakes often reach urban densities." Lakes in Becker County averaged thirty homes per mile of shore.[35] High density and individual septic systems brought pollution like that on suburban lots except now entire lakes were polluted. Lake home owners formed lake associations to enforce rules and seek funds for treatment. Associations dealt with other issues like fluctuating lake levels. Weekenders faced politics after all, the politics of lake associations.

Minnesotans' love affair with walleyes and lake cabins continued. The year's calendar centered on the cabin: go to the fishing opener in mid-May; open up the cabin in May or June; go north every other weekend, plus for the two-week vacation; attend the local water carnival, fishing contest, or Fourth of July parade; watch out-of-staters leave in mid-August; pull in the dock and winterize the cabin in October, return next May.[36] A weekly traffic calendar marked the summers: Friday night traffic jams northbound to the lake; Sunday evening southbound ones returning to the Cities and to work.

A cultural elite might deplore weekend escapism as they did the suburban escape from the 'big city,' but the lake cabin aided in family formation. A summer resident of Star Island in Cass Lake noted, "This is a place where most of the people who come deliberately plan major family reunions every summer . . . people are gathering their family around and enjoying their family in a relaxed environment that just doesn't exist in the world they are leaving behind.[37] The middle and working classes used the occasional summer weekend at a lake closer to the Cities for the same family 'gathering' as these academics and retirees did on Star Island two hundred miles north of the Cities.

Professional Sports Teams
Promote a State Identity to the Nation

Family-centered fishing, canoeing, and hunting shaped the state's identity in tourists' minds but did not attract publicity on TV or radio or in the nation's newspapers like college and professional sports did. At the University, Bernie Bierman's Gopher football team did so by winning five national championships (1934-36, 1940-41). After the war, the rapid growth of professional leagues upped the ante. To be respected, a city or state must have a team in the big leagues. The Twin Cities had minor league teams in 1945: in baseball, the Minneapolis Millers played at Nicollet Park at Nicollet

Tailgating grew to be a favorite pre-game activity. Here, fans chow down before a Minnesota Vikings football game at Metropolitan Stadium in Bloomington, 1974. *Courtesy of the Minnesota Historical Society.*

Avenue and Lake Street; the St. Paul Saints were at Lexington Park, near Lexington and University avenues. A few pro teams had struggled in hockey, basketball, and football. But as the major leagues became established after the war, Minnesota had a team in none of them.[38]

Sports reporters had a strong interest in having pro teams come to Minnesota. No conflict-of-interest principles barred them from promoting and recruiting such teams. Minneapolis sportswriter Sid Hartman led the maneuvers resulting in the Minneapolis Lakers starting their first NBA season in 1947 with blue-and-yellow Swedish colors and 'Swede' Carlson plus other ex-Gophers on the team. With six-foot-ten George Mikan at center and Hamline grad Vern Mikkelsen at power forward, the Lakers went on to win six NBA championships, a fantastic return on an initial investment of $15,000. After losing money and failing to obtain their own arena, the Lakers moved to Los Angeles in 1960, but their successes encouraged Twin Cities leaders to woo professional teams in other sports.[39]

Baseball was the most popular fifties' spectator sport and the one the Twin Cities most eagerly pursued. The Saints-Millers rivalry made it hard to agree on one bid until they chose a neutral stadium site in Bloomington, as close to Minneapolis as it was to St. Paul. The Washington Senators moved there in 1961 and took the name of Minnesota Twins to unite the two cities' fans behind one team. Gopher great Paul Giel played for the Twins briefly, but they were never a team of native Minnesotans, as the early Lakers were. Nor did they enjoy the Lakers' success. They won the American League title in 1965 but lost the World Series to the Los Angeles Dodgers. With day games, youth promotions, and a site in a family-friendly suburb, the Twins were the most family-focused pro sports team in town.[40]

The Duluth Eskimos competed in the small NFL in the mid-1920s, but Minnesota had no NFL team after they folded. By the late 1950s, the 41,000-seat Met Stadium was available, and former Lakers' owner Max Winter led a recruiting drive, aided by rivalry between the NFL and the new AFL. Minneapolis leaders used this competition to secure an NFL franchise. The Minnesota Vikings began play at the Met in September 1961. Few ex-Gophers or Minnesota natives starred for the team, but cold winter games at the outdoor Met gave them a home-field advantage and a Minnesota identity.[41]

Minnesota's winters were even more instrumental in its identity as a hockey state. A University team played ice hockey as early as 1895; high school, amateur club, and town teams took up the sport also. Minnesota stars like Moose Goheen, Ching Johnson, Cooney Weiland, John Mayasich, and John Mariucci played for U.S. Olympic teams or pro teams—some, after stellar careers at the University—but Minnesota had no pro hockey team. In 1966, a group of Twin Cities business leaders obtained an NHL franchise as the NHL expanded, and chose neutral Bloomington as the site for an arena, right next to Met Stadium. The North Stars played their home opener in late October 1967. The state was now represented in three of the four major professional leagues.[42]

Boundary Waters Canoe Area: Away from the Masses, the Cabins, the Stadiums

Besides its national reputation as the Land of Ten Thousand Lakes, Minnesota gained fame among wilderness enthusiasts for its border lakes area, saved from the dam-building paper-making ambitions of Edward Backus in the 1920s and early 1930s. About a thousand lakes and numerous streams covered this area on the U.S.-Canadian border, whose beauty was enhanced by granite outcroppings, pine forests, and small islands. Its remoteness protected it from all but the lumbermen. The U.S. Forest Service, the Izaak Walton League, the Quetico-Superior Council, and other groups worked to prolong that protection from new intrusions—cars, airplanes, motorboats, and snowmobiles. Opposing this were local people who wanted more intensive use of the area's resources so they could share the nation's prosperity and its normal forms of family-based recreation.[43]

The locals had a case for roads, resorts, lake cabins, seaplane bases, and motors—except for the area's undeniable uniqueness and the availability of these amenities elsewhere. Early conservationists were outsiders—Ernest Oberholtzer from Davenport, Iowa, and Harvard; Twin Cities leaders like David Winton. Oberholtzer advocated multiple use and not total wilderness, but his intense love of the area, his prodigious 3,000-mile canoe trip through it, and his celebration of its wildness as "its value to the public," all created a cult of wilderness later advanced by his successor, Sigurd Olson of Ely. Fathers took their sons canoeing there, but true appreciation of the BWCA became a mark of a worldview superior to—and contrasted to—the liking for the family's weekend lake cabin. Locals were annoyed as outsiders looked down on them. Here was the NIMBY phenomenon: wilderness is fine, perhaps, but not in their backyard.[44]

Here was a unique Minnesota identity distinct from the national norm *and* from Minnesota masses who did not join it due to disinterest, love of comfort, age, physical disability, or lack of money and time. It was a lifestyle not a political identity. For most canoeists, it was very short-term—a week of roughing it to escape civilization. For some, it became a protest or a dream. Few things were further from eating a TV dinner in a Bloomington rambler after a day's work at Control Data and before an evening Twins game—than eating dried beef by a campfire at a portage to the next lake in a week-long wilderness canoe trip. Some men dreamed of doing it full time. The few that did became models. Dean of Ely Junior College, a confirmed trekker with a habit of weekend trips, Sigurd Olson quit his job in 1947 to write, canoe, guide, and work on conservation.[45] His example became more popular in the later, individualist reaction to the family fifties.

Some Minnesotans did not rebel and leave suburban life—racial prejudice and low incomes meant they rarely participated in fifties' ramblers, lake cabins, Southdale shopping, or the reaction against this identity. The state had long been home to African Americans, although not in large numbers. There were only 759 blacks in the state in 1870 and almost all were in the urban areas. With some exceptions, African Americans never knew the Ordinance-designed rural life of family farming (Southern sharecropping was very different). They migrated from the South to the Twin Cities without the money from selling a farm that a white family might have brought with it to aid its adjustment. In St. Paul, they resided in the Rondo area along University Avenue west of the capitol. In the Mill City, they moved north of downtown, near present Olson Highway and Lyndale Avenue, and also south, to the area between Lyndale and Chicago avenues.

Historian David Vassar Taylor portrays their pre-1960s communities as confined but therefore cohesive ones, with churches giving leadership, professional men providing services and political clout, settlement houses working with families, and little crime or illiteracy. They voted Republican until Franklin Roosevelt. They benefited from effective newspapers in the *Western Appeal* (1880s to 1920s) and the *Minneapolis Spokesman* (begun in 1934). The Twin Cities mostly missed the great migration of blacks from South to North during and after World War I, and it bypassed (until 1967) the racial riots that occurred in some Northern cities. Humphrey and Youngdahl's anti-discrimination work helped, as did the efforts of black community leaders to defuse tensions. Appearances of a quiet stable community proved deceptive, as the construction of I-94 in the mid-1960s through the heart of Rondo displaced families and the Civil Rights revolution helped to launch a revolt against the status quo that would be felt in the Twin Cities too.[46]

In the 1960s, racial minorities and non-English-speaking groups were still a small part of the population. Over 9,000 Ojibwe and nearly 4,000 Dakota lived in the state in 1960. That same year, there were about 3,500 Mexicans, nearly 1,900 Chinese, and over 1,700 Japanese living in Minnesota. In 1970, even after the sixties in-migration, there were only 35,000 African Americans.[47] These groups were concentrated in the Twin Cities, in older sections of Minneapolis and St. Paul, and were most visible to churches, school officials, teachers, and others who had daily dealings with them in those cities. For many rural and suburban whites, they seemed largely invisible—although, again, the Civil Rights revolution of the sixties would change that semblance.

Backlash 1966:
State Resists Being Pushed Into the Future

Sometimes politics becomes an arena of battle for cultural and social forces more than competing policy options. That was true of the 1966 race for governor. The stage was set in 1962 by Lieutenant Governor Karl Rolvaag's miniscule 91-vote victory over incumbent Governor Elmer L. Andersen after a long recount. DFL campaigners made last-minute, erroneous charges of poor-quality construction work on Interstate 35 near Hinckley—perhaps motivated by Senator Humphrey's need to have a DFL governor to appoint a successor should he run for Vice President in 1964. Impossible to verify in the campaign's last week, the charges gave Rolvaag his victory, but Rolvaag's perceived shortcomings and poor image ended up costing Humphrey much grief.[48] Andersen went on to a productive career as University regent, newspaper publisher, and elder statesman.

By the mid-1960s, at least to the young, Rolvaag represented an older Minnesota of the Greatest Generation. A son of famed Norwegian-American novelist Ole Rolvaag, Karl dropped out of St. Olaf College due to lack of funds after his father's death in 1931. He worked as a Depression-era laborer in the West "logging, feeding stock, doing odd chores," until he had enough cash to reenter St. Olaf. He graduated in 1941, went to war, was wounded in France, earned promotion to captain, and won a hero's honors. A returning veteran, he entered DFL politics, paid his dues by twice running unsuccessfully for Congress in a heavily Republican district, served four years as DFL state chair and four terms as lieutenant governor. In 1962, the party felt he deserved its endorsement for governor, and he won, but his staff's poor performance and his own blunders caused the party pros to turn against him and toward the new lieutenant governor.[49]

Lieutenant Governor A. M. "Sandy" Keith represented the young, professional, suburban Minnesota of the future. The son of a Mayo Clinic doctor, a graduate of Yale Law School, Keith had worked as a Mayo lawyer and still lived in Rochester, a city of professional, scientific, and managerial sophistication. With a lock of hair falling over his forehead and a handsome, high-energy style, the 37-year-old Keith looked and acted Kennedy-esque. The visual contrast with Rolvaag, eighteen years his senior, was striking.[50]

Fittingly, DFL leaders secretly gathered in July 1965 at a ski resort near Grand Rapids complete with golf course, lodge, swimming pool, and a cabin called "The Meetin' House" to air their grievances about the out-of-fashion Rolvaag, who also had a drinking problem that threatened to become public. The week before, Rolvaag added to his image problems while hosting the National Governor's Conference: screaming on camera after his driver slammed a door on his finger, sporting a bandage for the conference, and wearing "slacks and an untucked sports shirt" while standing next to New York Governor Nelson Rockefeller for a widely-circulated photo. Sensitive to East Coast opinion, Minnesotans felt embarrassed by that contrast. At Sugar Hills the next weekend, DFL leaders erupted in a mighty consensus that

Rolvaag should not run in 1966. That fall, the press reported the secret meeting and Rolvaag's pride was wounded, thus ending the chance of a tactful, private resolution of the DFL problem.[51]

The DFL luminaries in national office in Washington failed to resolve the growing Keith-Rolvaag feud in the next year. When the DFL state convention met in Minneapolis in mid-June 1966, the delegates were so evenly divided and so stubborn that it took twenty ballots before Keith won. Keith's young delegates beat Rolvaag's older ones. The next day Humphrey appeared with Keith to say that Rolvaag was "an honorable man," but "you can't live forever on the older generation." Yet many Minnesotans reacted with an outpouring of sympathy for the older man. To them, "Keith was a ruthless, brash, ambitious young man, a dime-a-dozen Kennedy-aping politician who had gone after his boss' job." Rolvaag challenged Keith in the September primary with the slogan, "Let the People Decide." Using the underdog Truman of 1948 as his model, Rolvaag planned an old-style campaign in his "old Chevy station wagon . . . stumping the state. . . . I plan to make county fairs, farmers' picnics, and community celebrations."[52]

Keith tried the DFL tactics of sample ballots and suburban coffee parties but lacked the funds for a TV broadcast at the end. It wouldn't have made a difference, for the past trumped the future and Rolvaag beat Keith by a landslide. The Republican Harold LeVander defeated the divided Democrats in the fall, but the Keith-Rolvaag donnybrook showed the tensions within Minnesota society between old and new, Greatest and Boomer generations, rural and suburban. These tensions would soon explode over a very different set of issues.

1.   "federal government enabled," Kennedy, *Freedom from Fear*, 368-70; Rebecca Lou Smith, "Postwar housing in national and local perspective: a Twin Cities case study" (Minneapolis: Center for Urban and Regional Affairs, 1978), 4-5.
2.   "created a business landscape," Smith, "Postwar housing," 5, 8.
3.   "late 1940s," Smith, "Postwar housing," 6, 8-9, 21-23; Interview with Tom Willmus, 22 October 1998, conducted by Mary Bakeman, Remembering Roseville Oral History Project (RROHP), MHS.
4.   "investors saw," James T. Patterson, *Grand Expectations: The United States, 1945–1974* (New York: Oxford University Press, 1996), 76-80; Tom Gilsenan, "The Eberhardt Company and the Postwar Building Boom," *Hennepin County History*, v. 48 (1989): 28-31.
5.   "Willmus recalls," Interview with Tom Willmus, 22 October 1998, RROHP.
6.   "Richfield," Connie Murray, "Richfield: A Classic 50's Suburb," M.A. Thesis (University of Minnesota, December 1992), 1-2, 5-7, 26-28, 37-38, copy at MHS.
7.   "Bloomington typified," Scott Donaldson, *The making of a suburb: an intellectual history* of

Bloomington, Minnesota (Bloomington: Bloomington Historical Society, 1964), 41-43, 45-46; *Bloomington Sun*, 9 June 1955 (1, 19) and 16 June 1955 (4).

8. "new suburb tried," *Bloomington Sun*, 2 June 1955, 1; Donaldson, *The making of a suburb*, 50.
9. "new society," Donaldson, *The making of a suburb*, 42, 50; *Bloomington Sun*, 9 June 1955, 13.
10. "Wilson Pond," Donaldson, *The making of a suburb*, 46, 47-49.
11. "Tommy and Mary," Donaldson, *The making of a suburb*, 48.
12. "In Roseville," *Roseville, Minnesota: The Story of Its Growth, 1843–1988* (Roseville: Roseville Historical Society, 1988), 40, 42, 47, 78; *Rose Tribune*, 10 September 1953, 1.
13. "Jeanne Drange," Interview with Jeanne Drange, 30 March 1998, conducted by Mary Bakeman, RROHP.
14. "suburban migrants," Interview with Tom Willmus, 22 October 1998, RROHP; Murray, "Classic 50's Suburb," 39-40; LeRoy F. Harlow, *Without fear or favor: odyssey of a city manager* (Provo, Utah: Brigham Young University Press, 1977), 210, 214-22; Twin Cities Metropolitan Planning Commission, *The Challenge of Metropolitan Growth* (St. Paul: TCMPC, 1958), 18.
15. "step away from," Arthur Naftalin, *Making One Community Out of Many: Perspectives on the Metropolitan Council of the Twin Cities Area* (St. Paul: Metropolitan Council, 1986), 11-13; Harlow, *Without fear or favor*, 211.
16. "contamination of well water," Naftalin, *Making One Community*, 14-15; Murray, "Classic 50's Suburb," 39-40; Minutes of Special Meeting on Water Pollution, 25 September 1959, Governor's Advisory Committee on Suburban Problems folder, George A. Farr files, Records of Governor Orville Freeman, State Archives, Box 115.E.16.8F, MHS.
17. "DFL governor," Donaldson, *The making of a suburb*, 49; *Bloomington Sun*, 2 June 1955, 1; Rodney E. Leonard, *Freeman: The Governor Years 1955–1960* (Minneapolis: Hubert H. Humphrey Institute of Public Affairs, 2003), 19-21, 34, 54-55.
18. "key innovator," Kennedy, *Minnesota Goes to War*, 154-59; David E. Lundstrom, *A few good men from Univac* (Cambridge, Mass.: Massachusetts Institute of Technology, 1987), 1-3, 22-23; Charles J. Murray, *The Supermen: The Story of Seymour Cray* (1997), 21-23, 28, 45.
19. "early computer industry," James C. Worthy, *William C. Norris: Portrait of a Maverick* (Cambridge, Mass.: Ballinger, 1987), 33, 35-38, 47; Lundstrom, *A few good men*, 36-37, 53, 69-71; Kirk Jeffrey, "Major Manufacturers," in Clark, ed., *Minnesota in a Century of Change*, 242-45.
20. "High-tech startups," Murray, *Supermen*, 103; Worthy, *Portrait of a Maverick*, 55-57; Lundstrom, *A few good men*, 69, 71, 72, 110-11
21. "companies offered," Patterson, *Grand Expectations*, 321.
22. "Southdale," William Severius Kowinski, *The Malling of America: An Inside Look at the Great Consumer Paradise* (New York: William Morrow, 1985), 116-23; Malcolm Gladwell, "The Terrazzo Jungle," *The New Yorker*, 15 March 2004, 20-27; *Bloomington Sun*, 11 October 1956, 14.
23. "covered the opening," Gladwell, "Terrazzo Jungle," 21, 25.
24. "Daylight Savings Time," Keillor, *Hjalmar Petersen*, 229; Andersen, *A Man's Reach*, 153-55.
25. "fought against," Keillor, *Hjalmar Petersen*, 229-30.
26. "Reapportionment," Keillor, *Hjalmar Petersen*, 230-32.
27. "jokingly suggested," Keillor, *Hjalmar Petersen*, 231; Patterson, *Grand Expectations*, 565.
28. "Sen. Elmer Andersen," Andersen, *A Man's Reach*, 143.
29. "rural legislators," Andersen, *A Man's Reach*, 139-43, 155-56; Royce Hanson, *Tribune of the People: The Minnesota Legislature and Its Leadership* (Minneapolis: University of Minnesota Press, 1989), 61, 68-69, 102-04; Leonard, *Freeman*, 126-41; G. Theodore Mitau, *Politics in Minnesota* (Minneapolis: University of Minnesota Press, 1960), 66-71, 74.

30. "one oddity," Andersen, *A Man's Reach*, 159-60.
31. "celebrated its centennial," *St. Paul Pioneer Press*, 9 May, 10 May, 11 May, and 12 May, all 1, all 1958.
32. "the lake cabin," here and above, Paul Clifford Larson, *A Place At The Lake* (Afton, Minn.: Afton Historical Society Press, 1998), 11-69.
33. "White Bear Lake," Larson, *Place at the Lake*, 71-93 (quotes from 93), 95-120.
34. "the automobile," Larson, *Place at the Lake*, 126-33.
35. "A 1970 study," John R. Borchert, *Minnesota's Lakeshore: Summary Report of the Minnesota Lakeshore Development Study* (Minneapolis: University of Minnesota, 1979), Vol. 1, 12-13.
36. "love affair," William Albert Allard, *Time at the Lake: A Minnesota Album* (Duluth: Pfeifer-Hamilton, 1998), 20-23; Carol Ryan, *Star Island: A Minnesota Summer Community* (St. Paul: Pogo Press, 2000),17-18, 133, 161-62.
37. "summer resident," Ryan, *Star Island*, 182.
38. "college and professional sports," Ross Bernstein, *Pigskin Pride: Celebrating a Century of Minnesota Football* (Minneapolis: Nodin Press, 2000), 81-90; Ross Bernstein, *Batter-Up!: Celebrating a Century of Minnesota Baseball* (Minneapolis: Nodin Press, 2002), 15, 18, 23, 25.
39. "Sports reporters," Ross Bernstein, *Hardwood Heroes: Celebrating a Century of Minnesota Basketball* (Minneapolis: Nodin Press, 2001), 14-37.
40. "Baseball," Bernstein, *Batter-Up!*, 19-21, 28-37.
41. "Duluth Eskimos," Bernstein, *Pigskin Pride*, 13-16, 22-25.
42. "hockey state," Ross Bernstein, *Frozen Memories: Celebrating a Century of Minnesota Hockey* (Minneapolis: Nodin Press, 1999), 12-17, 37, 39, 42-43, 44-49.
43. "its border lakes area," R. Newell Searle, *Saving Quetico-Superior: A Land Set Apart* (St. Paul: Minnesota Historical Society Press, 1977).
44. "The locals," in general, see Searle, *Quetico-Superior*; Joe Paddock, *Keeper of the Wild: The Life of Ernest Oberholtzer* (St. Paul: Minnesota Historical Society Press, 2001); and David Backes, *A Wilderness Within: The Life of Sigurd F. Olson* (Minneapolis: University of Minnesota Press, 1997). The interpretation is my own, not that of these authors.
45. "a unique Minnesota identity," Backes, *Wilderness Within*, 37-42, 43-45, 133-37, 181-82, 187-90.
46. "Historian David Vassar Taylor," these two paragraphs, here and above, are based on his *African Americans in Minnesota* (St. Paul: Minnesota Historical Society, 2002), 1-39.
47. "racial minorities," Holmquist, ed., *They Chose Minnesota*, 23, 27, 74, 94, 531, 558.
48. "91-vote victory," Andersen, *A Man's Reach*, 241-45, 254; Finlay Lewis, *Mondale: Portrait of an American Politician* (New York: Harper & Row, 1980), 118-19.
49. "Rolvaag represented," David Lebedoff, *The 21st Ballot: A Political Party Struggle in Minnesota* (Minneapolis: University of Minnesota Press, 1969), 16-20, 27-31, 35-37, 44-46, 49-52.
50. "Keith represented," Lebedoff, *21st Ballot*, 36-37, 79, 145.
51. "DFL leaders," Lebedoff, *21st Ballot*, 1-15, 55-61. For Rolvaag's drinking problem, see, e.g., Lewis, *Mondale*, 119-21.
52. "DFL luminaries," Lebedoff, *21st Ballot*, 72-73, 98-102, 123-35, 137, 139 (quoted), 149.

Divided Nation, Divided State

To some extent, leaders like Mondale and Humphrey failed to head off the Keith-Rolvaag battle because they focused on events in the nation's capital. Six months before the ski resort coup, Lyndon Johnson's inauguration showed Minnesota's prominence. "Parade Honor Spot for Minnesota—Right Behind Texas" and "State Proudly Shares Day With Texas" read the headlines. In keeping with Vice President Humphrey's rank, Minnesota's units came second, ahead of other states. The University of Minnesota's marching band played the Minnesota Rouser; the National Guard's 47th ("Viking") Division band marched; and the float "Accent on Brainpower" had "eight rotating . . . photomurals depicting Minnesota's record" in science, technology, and medicine. The *Minneapolis Star* lamented the brainpower float's "grammatical error—using the contraction of 'it is' " in a sign boasting, "Minnesota Proudly Gives the Nation It's Vice President Hubert H. Humphrey." That error, it feared, "brought many a snicker along the parade route."[1]

The previous summer Johnson had considered both Minnesota senators for the vice-presidency. He toyed with Senator Eugene McCarthy. Feeling used, McCarthy took himself out of the picture. Johnson had closer ties to Humphrey. In the 1950s, he was the Senate majority leader needing northern liberals' support; Humphrey, the civil rights firebrand, needed a Southern friend as he faced segregationist Southern senators' anger. Johnson convinced Humphrey that he was no threat to Humphrey's presidential hopes—no Southerner could be elected president. Kennedy's assassination made him one. He relied on Humphrey to lead the fight for the Civil Rights bill in 1964. Sensitive to slights from Ivy League, upper-class East Coast liberals, Johnson liked the prairie druggist's son and his DFLers, feeling that they were allies closer to Johnson's rural Texas upbringing. That Minnesotans could be seen as valued allies showed that Humphrey's 'nationalization' of Minnesota politics had born fruit.[2]

In late June 1964, after Humphrey defeated a Southern filibuster against the Civil Rights bill and just before its final passage, President Johnson came to the Twin Cities and praised Humphrey's DFLers at their state convention, "Your national capital is afire with the principles and programs you stand for." That evening, at the Minneapolis Auditorium, he addressed the state, "You have seen your principles and beliefs shape the course of an entire nation." Partly, this was flattery, the famed Johnson Treatment pressed on an entire state. "Minnesota believes in human rights. We are about to pass the strongest and best civil rights bill in this century. . . . Minnesota also believes in peace. In the last four years we have moved toward peace." Then he added, "Minnesota has always believed in the future. And that future contains battles to be fought, enemies to be faced, victories to be won"—and, it turned out, he was not being merely metaphorical.[3]

Winning forty-four states in November 1964, the Johnson-Humphrey ticket seemed set to shape the nation's course with Minnesota's approval. Three days after the inaugural, Humphrey basked in Minnesotans' pride as grand marshal of the St. Paul Winter Carnival parade. In the next three weeks decisive changes occurred: the Viet Cong killed U.S. advisers at Pleiku in South Vietnam; Johnson ordered bombing raids against North Vietnam; Humphrey sent him a memo questioning if such escalation was "politically understandable to the American public," warning that "political opposition [to it] will steadily mount," thus landing himself in LBJ's doghouse, excluded from shaping LBJ's course. The "FL" in Humphrey's DFL stemmed from some Minnesotans' protest against President Wilson's war. Minnesotans in the 1960s were unlikely all to 'stand by the president' (the World War I slogan) in an unpopular war straining a Texas-Minnesota alliance and threatening Humphrey's 'nationalization' of state politics.[4]

Minnesotans Fighting in the Vietnam War: The "Minnesota Twins Platoon"

Thousands of Minnesotans served in the military during the Vietnam War and spent time 'in country' battling Viet Cong guerrillas and North Vietnamese Army (NVA) units. Not typical, but symbolic of the state's contribution to the nation's war effort was the "Minnesota Twins Platoon," more than "one hundred young men, as well as four young women" inducted into the Marine Corps at a Twins baseball game on June 28, 1967. Before the game, a Marine Corps color guard led the young men from the stands to the first base line and third base line. After the national anthem, they swore the Marine oath and watched six innings before being bused to the airport and flown to San Diego. They were dispersed to many Marine units and never fought as one Minnesota unit.5

They were recruits, not draftees. Some enlisted in the Marines because their fathers had fought as Marines in World War II. One was Kenny Goodman of Stewart, Minnesota, whose father Virgil fought on Iwo Jima. Timothy Sather of Minneapolis had a grandfather, Iver, in World War I, and a father, Allen, in World War II.[6]

After boot camp, Goodman had a few days' leave before shipping out to Vietnam. Back home in Stewart (a dozen miles southwest of Hutchinson), he proposed to his girlfriend and became engaged. He landed at Da Nang in early December 1967 and was deployed to Khe Sanh shortly after Christmas. The U.S. commander in South Vietnam, General William Westmoreland, was determined to defend Khe Sanh against an expected NVA attack, as was the President. LBJ "followed events there closely" and had "a sand-table scale model of Khe Sanh built in the White House basement." Press reports also focused on Khe Sanh, so the Goodman family knew their son was in extreme danger. On January 21, 1968, two NVA battalions stormed Hill 861, where Kenny Goodman manned an M60 machine gun to help repel them. Trained as a medical histologist, he also assisted the corpsmen in caring for the wounded. But three days later, during a quiet phase, he was hit by shrapnel from a mortar round and died within hours. Sunday morning, January 28, the Goodmans heard the tragic news just after mass at their Catholic church.[7]

In 1966, Goodman had written to Johnson. His small-town paper printed the letter two weeks after he died. "Dear Mr. President: I have to do something to help my country, which I dearly love. I feel in this day and age people, citizens of the United States, are dead, unpatriotic." He cited the antiwar protests, "We see men burn draft cards; demonstrators, strikes, sit-ins, flag burnings, etc." Goodman was angry and determined, "I am patriotic, because I love my country so much that I'll even die for her."[8]

Larry Rademacher was a short, stocky graduate of Shakopee High School, where he was on the wrestling team and played in the band. He enlisted in the Twins Platoon and arrived at Da Nang three weeks after Goodman but was assigned to patrol a river on an armed amphibious tractor, or "amtrac." He was given an antitank weapon to use against Viet Cong bunkers. Around the time of the Khe Sanh battle, his convoy of amtracs ran into Viet Cong mines and rocket propelled grenades. He saw a Marine next to him "standing headless" after an RPG hit. When the Marines realized the incoming fire was coming from a Buddhist pagoda, Rademacher aimed his "rocket launcher" and scored a direct hit, detonating an ammunition cache inside the pagoda. Rademacher survived the war.[9]

Many in the Twins Platoon who survived were dismayed at the antiwar feelings they encountered back home. Home on medical leave, one took a girlfriend (she had been at the Twins game to see him off) to a restaurant. She told him, "In case someone hasn't told you, the war in Vietnam is wrong! I've been protesting against it for some time." They agreed to disagree and eventually married, but not all such exchanges ended so happily. One veteran fought a loud war critic at a bar on University Avenue. Others grew depressed that their patriotic sacrifices were contemptuously seen as warmongering. Some felt guilty for having served rather than running off to Canada or getting a college deferment. What began with 11,000 Twins fans' applause ended with a quiet thud.[10]

Antiwar Protest Gathers Strength & an Increasingly Countercultural Agenda

Humphrey's prediction of antiwar protest came true. University of Minnesota students and faculty led the way. The Students for a Democratic Society (SDS) chapter formed in 1964 brought thirty-one University students to the SDS Easter (1965) weekend antiwar rally in Washington. An all-night teach-in on Vietnam on May 24-25, 1965, drew over 4,000 to the main session at Northrop Auditorium, and nearly 2,000 were at Coffman Union for the midnight-to-4 a.m. breakout sessions. The academic, balanced, and factual May event gave credibility to antiwar critics, who organized a more passionate October 1965 teach-in, with SDS playing a greater role. The University's Twin Cities campus, the state's largest, teemed with Baby Boomers, as enrollment more than doubled from 21,000 (1950) to over 46,000 (1967). The 'U' had the critical mass of students so that antiwar leaders, groups, and views won enough followers to sustain them and gain visibility in the state's society. Students at small colleges joined the antiwar drive. A 'region' of college students was created. It opposed the war and any party supporting the war. Its male members were subject to the draft if they left school and lost their student deferments, so the number of graduate students prolonging their education increased, as did the sense of an age enclave banding together to resist outside dangers.[11]

The brightest college students used specific facts of America's war in Vietnam to generalize about society. That LBJ was an unusually manipulative, deceptive politician, and Vietnam a place unusually ill-suited to fighting Communism—these specifics were too limited for a radical antiwar movement. SDSer Todd Gitlin noted, "The bureaucrats and generals and fathers had rested their legitimacy on a single 'American way,' so that when the rationales of the Pentagon and the University of California" were made to look absurd, all authority "seemed to unravel." Illogically, radicals unraveled a family-focused culture along with Pentagon and University authority.[12] In Minnesota, antiwar protest morphed into a New Left critique of society and creation of an age-and-lifestyle enclave.

This protest differed from the 1917–18 antiwar sentiment. Apart from those who broke draft or drug laws, 1960s protesters were not often persecuted by the government or vigilantes. Liberal Democrats were in power in Washington and in many university administrations, and they did not normally harass protesters. Conservatives' accusations in 1917–18 that antiwar groups had radical, Bolshevik, free love, anti-family views were mostly incorrect, but they would prove on target fifty years later.

This antiwar movement did not start out that way. At the University of Minnesota, Old Left professors who had questioned the Cold War and supported Henry Wallace in 1948 took the initial steps.[13] Their fight against the Vice President who loyally backed Johnson's war was Round Two of a fight begun in 1948 to control the DFL. Humphrey used Cold War anti-Communist arguments to win then. An unpopular anti-Communist war hurt him now. For faculty with homes and families, being against the war did not mean joining the counterculture. Students' lifestyles were not fixed but open to alternatives to conventional values, alternatives that set them apart from the norms of state society.

Changes swept the University from 1964 to 1968: a debate between Prof. Mulford Q. Sibley of the political science department and St. Paul civic leader Milton Rosen over academic freedom; the new SDS chapter; growing dissent over Vietnam; antiwar rallies; a loosening of sexual restraints in dress, language, and behavior; an opposite-sex closed-door visitation policy in the dorms; the *Daily's* call for legalized abortion; a San Francisco-style countercultural district on the West Bank; a Free University; a West Bank underground press (*Raisin Bread*, *HAIR*, and, later, *Hundred Flowers*) promoting drug use and sexual freedom. The University did not promote this district, but its students or ex-students patronized it and made it possible. The district's papers, drugs, and views were soon exported beyond the campus.[14] A smaller district, Dinkytown on the East Bank, became more countercultural as this tidal wave of new views swept the campus.

The People Occupy Dinkytown

"Warm winds and blue skies yesterday made a party of the rally which is supporting the people who have occupied the Dinkytown buildings which Red Barn plans to replace with a restaurant. About 400 people turned out to stand in front of the five vacated stores which the occupation has turned into peoples' services. . . . As people gathered, a mock contingent of soldiers marched up to the tune of a kazoo and began to pelt them with marshmallows."[15]

Some students and ex-students exported these to Georgeville, Stearns County, a hamlet twenty-five miles west of McCarthy's Watkins and a dozen miles south of Meire Grove. In January 1968, dropouts from the University, Carleton, and St. Olaf started a rural commune here. The "early settlers" acquired a two-story brick bank building, two frame structures, and two acres. They made pottery to sell at a 'trading post' in one corner of the bank's first floor, tended a sizeable garden, smoked marijuana, and used organic 'speed.' A dormitory, library, study and sewing lounge, and kitchen filled the rest of the first floor. A "hodge podge" of objects adorned the rooms: crocks and pots "very reminiscent of a grandmother's kitchen about 1900–1920," for there was no refrigerator and only a wood stove, and in the lounge, "a photo of Karl Marx" below a Russian poster picturing and praising the "Red plowman." About twenty people lived a life not typical of Stearns, students, antiwar McCarthyites, or Minnesota—but symbolic of cultural changes impacting thousands of Minnesotans.[16]

This tidal wave hit the DFL precinct caucuses on March 5, 1968, due to Eugene McCarthy's campaign. Urged by antiwar liberals to mount a presidential bid to force Johnson to change course, Senator McCarthy agreed to do so after Robert Kennedy and other senators refused. McCarthy had many motives: opposition to the war, solidarity with fellow antiwar Catholics, dismay at the President's disregard for the Senate's foreign-policy role, a wish to repay LBJ for toying with his vice-presidential hopes in 1964, a rivalry with Humphrey who was the only Minnesota DFLer to run for president thus far (in 1960), and dissatisfaction with the Senate routine. He did not seek to spark a countercultural revolt when he announced his candidacy on November 30, 1967. His backers were old allies of Adlai Stevenson like economist John Kenneth Galbraith. White, suburban professionals liked his reasoned, understated, academic speeches.[17]

McCarthy's main campaign was in New Hampshire that March, but antiwar DFLers, "Concerned Democrats," organized intensively. Many were middle class and suburban, but the most visible were West Bank students who canvassed neighborhoods, tabulated data on an IBM computer, phoned likely caucus attendees, packed meetings, and rejuvenated that old Minnesota institution, the precinct caucus. They battled DFL leaders, one of whom wrote that "the generation gap was more like a canyon." A thousand people jammed into a Minneapolis hotel ballroom for one ward convention. Tension was high, as McCarthyites, some of them former SDS members, ousted incumbents. Both sides were angry. Students used harsh epithets: "fascists, warmongers, immoral."[18]

McCarthyites did not only seek to change Johnson's Vietnam policy but to take over the party, to seize posts like ward chair unrelated to foreign policy, to deny minor offices to their foes. So a factional war erupted at the June state convention. By then, Johnson had withdrawn and Humphrey entered the race, so that two Minnesotans ran against each other. Humphrey won the Democratic nomination at a violence-marred national convention in Chicago that August but lost the election to Richard Nixon, after McCarthy's late support for Humphrey failed to end DFLers' split.[19]

The Vietnam War ended by 1975, but the students' cultural issues persisted for decades. As historian John Haynes noted, "Every DFL convention saw clashes between 'regular' liberals and the new 'movement' liberals and their radical allies, who supported, variously, gay rights, amnesty for draft resisters and evaders, the legalization of marijuana, . . . a variety of environmental causes, militant feminism, and a 'pro-choice' stand favoring legalized abortion." The 'regulars' opposed these ideas in the 1970s. In one district near campus, movement liberals dumped an incumbent DFL legislator and nominated a University professor who called for the legalization of marijuana, abortion, and "all sexual acts between consenting adults."[20] This agenda would come up at precinct caucuses and state conventions for the next forty years.

The movement's moral vision argued that the war was immoral. It reasoned that a society supporting war, Southern segregation, Northern racial prejudice, and corporate control of the economy must also be immoral. Therefore, activists who opposed this status quo must be moral, and their causes also moral. The enemies of immorality must be the friends of morality. The causes that Haynes lists came into Minnesota politics under the umbrella of antiwar protest. Most of them would have been unthinkable a mere four years earlier. And, to non-movement Minnesotans, many were still unthinkable.

State Government Issues Still Reflect Pre-Vietnam War Debates, 1967–1973

Change took time. State politics not dealing with foreign policy still followed the old tracks. Governor Harold LeVander personified several Minnesota traditions: a nineteenth-century-style orator, son of a Swedish-American Lutheran pastor, a lay preacher who spoke at hundreds of churches, a lawyer who represented rural electric cooperatives and livestock commission firms at the South St. Paul stockyards. A "citizen politician," LeVander relied on a network of friends in churches and cooperatives to win. Like Youngdahl, he was a "very moralistic person," advancing the state's interests, and not skilled in advancing the GOP party. GOP-leaning Conservative legislators also advocated a part-time citizen legislature and claimed to be free of political-party interests.[21]

LeVander copied his former law partner, Stassen, in being a government-friendly Republican. He did not advance his party by defining it as anti-government and anti-taxes in contrast to the DFL. He added key new state agencies: a Human Rights Department to fight discrimination, the Pollution Control Agency, a Department of Labor and Industry, and the Department of Economic Development—plus the Metropolitan Council, an appointed body that reviewed cities' plans and grant applications and, thus, tried to shape the metro area's future. A 1969 act allowed rural areas to set up regional development commissions to review plans, approve grant applications, and shape their area's future in ways similar to the Met Council. Copying Stassen, LeVander reorganized government so department heads functioned as the governor's cabinet. He seemed unconcerned that DFL successors might utilize new agencies to increase the role of government further.[22]

Aiding LeVander were his able chief of staff, David Durenberger, and younger Conservative legislators from the metro area seeking accomplishments for themselves and the GOP in order to compete successfully with the DFL in the growing suburbs. They raised state aid to K-12 schools greatly but needed more revenue to pay for it. Aiding LeVander *and* his DFL successor was the Citizens League, a largely Twin Cities group that exemplified Minnesota's spirit of citizen participation in government.[23]

The thorniest issue was the sales tax. DFLers opposed it by arguing that low-income citizens' shares would be higher in proportion to their incomes, for they spent a larger percent of their incomes. Higher-income citizens saved more, spent less (compared to their incomes), and would be taxed less. When campaigning in 1966, LeVander promised to veto any sales tax bill that did not call for a voter referendum on the issue. He kept his promise, but the legislature overrode his veto after a compromise on a 3 percent sales tax exempting purchases of medicine, food, and clothing convinced some DFL (Liberal) legislators to support it.[24]

Believing in the "citizen politician" who sees public office as an "honorable but temporary privilege," LeVander announced that he would not run for reelection. A DFL state senator from St. Paul, former Olympic and Gopher hockey player, and Swedish American, Wendell R. Anderson won in 1970. In 1971, he sparked a showdown with Conservative legislators by submitting an ambitious plan to increase the state share of K-12 education expenses from 43 percent to 70 percent, to fund that increase from income tax and sales tax revenues, and to equalize the amounts wealthier and poorer school districts spent on education. After the regular January-May session failed to pass his proposal, Anderson's battle of wills and public opinion with legislators led to three special sessions. Not until October 30 did the legislature finally adjourn after passing Anderson's plan.[25]

Heralded as the "Minnesota Miracle," the plan won national acclaim, and its state popularity propelled DFLers to victory in the 1972 legislative elections, after a very divisive June 1972 DFL convention had seemed to sink their chances. The Humphrey regulars and the movement DFLers spent "two days of bickering and haggling" over the convention rules and over gay marriage, amnesty, marijuana, and abortion, so that "a breakup of the convention appeared possible." One Humphrey leader charged that many delegates elected at local caucuses "were unrepresentative of their areas." Ordinary citizens disliked going to precinct caucuses where activists argued non-compromisable positions. They disliked arguing with neighbors in lengthy sessions. In this representative democracy, that arguing function was assigned to legislators; a precinct caucus was a direct democracy that was often not for the faint of heart. DFL candidates and leaders like Governor Anderson "disavowed" the convention's more controversial planks. They then gained control of the state house of representatives and state senate in the fall election.[26]

Movement liberals pushed their issues (and 'regular' ones) in the 1973 and 1974 sessions. A Conservative dam burst, and liberal change overflowed. In two breakthrough sessions, legislators passed "an income tax checkoff for public financing of campaigns and tax credits for political contributions . . . a state energy agency . . . no-fault automobile insurance . . . the proposed Equal Rights Amendment to the U.S. Constitution, . . . the first state minimum-wage law, . . . laws protecting tenant rights and human rights, and legislation making it illegal to discriminate against homosexuals," public employees' right to bargain and strike, a partisan legislature, and an open-meeting law.[27]

The mid-1970s were a heyday for state and local governments. Inflation drove taxpayers into higher income tax brackets ('bracket creep'), producing de facto tax hikes and higher revenue. With budget surpluses, state government hired new employees—the number of state employees doubled from 35,000 in 1961 to 72,000 in 1981—expanded existing agencies, and added new ones. Anderson's "Minnesota Miracle" redistributed income by collecting the lion's share of income and sales taxes in wealthy suburban districts and the downtown Twin Cities, then giving it as aid to schools and small cities in rural Minnesota.[28] School districts and cities hiked annual budgets without making local property taxpayers feel the pain. High-income suburban Republicans who did feel the tax pain were so politically weakened by Nixon's Watergate scandal that they could do little about it.

This "Minnesota Miracle" became a "Minnesota Mess," argues political scientist Royce Hanson, by weakening a key check on local government and school district spending—taxpayers' complaints over higher property taxes. Local entities saw state aid as a given, an entitlement. Formulas committed the state to pay the aid, even when its tax revenues declined. The legislature partly lost control. By 1975, over half the state budget was promised to recipients (cities and schools) powerful in each legislator's district; less than 40 percent went to state agencies, whose bureaucrats were not influential with voters. "Thus, instead of working on the budget of an agency that works for it, the Legislature increasingly found itself working on the budgets of those for whom it works" (local governments and school districts).[29]

Yet these were long-range consequences. Wendell Anderson and the state reaped short-term benefits. On August 13, 1973, *Time* featured Anderson on its cover and in an 11-page article, "Minnesota: A State That Works." A positive, almost sentimental, Norman Rockwell portrait in words, the article said nothing about movement issues that had almost created a convention and a party that didn't work. It highlighted the computer industry, the skilled professional workforce, family life in the suburbs with easy access to a lake cabin, and citizen-CEO participation in civic affairs. The article was "a publicity coup planted and cultivated" by David Lebedoff, a close adviser to Anderson. The governor's aides housed the *Time* staff "at the governor's mansion, led them around the state and spoon-fed them sources," many of whom were DFL loyalists. *Time* praised Anderson highly and speculated on his future as a vice presidential candidate in 1976.[30]

The Abortion Issue Has Close Ties to Minnesota & Far-Reaching Consequences

However, abortion became a contentious issue threatening Anderson's hopes and DFL unity. It was the first movement proposal to achieve legalization. On January 22, 1973, the U.S. Supreme Court's *Roe v. Wade* decision legalized abortion. Minnesota was closely involved, for the decision was written by Justice Harry Blackmun, who had served as legal counsel at the Mayo Clinic in Rochester in the 1950s. He was assigned to write it by Chief Justice Warren Burger, his childhood friend. They both grew up in the Dayton's Bluff area of St. Paul. Blackmun served as best man at Burger's wedding. After Burger was appointed Chief Justice in May 1969, he undoubtedly suggested Blackmun's name for a future vacancy. President Nixon named Blackmun to the court in April 1970. In jest or disparagingly, Court watchers called them the 'Minnesota Twins.' Having lost the presidency in 1968, Minnesota seemed to get the judiciary as a consolation prize.[31]

The divisive abortion issue made it a prize giving little consolation. The sixties' sexual revolution and civil rights drive revived the women's movement. Blacks' success in securing equal rights provided an example, and the need came as more women obtained college degrees, professional careers, and jobs outside the home. A demand for legalization of abortion arose due to those trends—and to a loosening of sexual restraints, a rise in cohabitation outside of marriage, and a rise in out-of-wedlock pregnancies. In Minnesota, out-of-wedlock births made up 2.9 percent of all births in 1960, but 8.9

U.S. Chief Justice Warren Burger, speaking during the visit of King Carl XVI Gustav of Sweden, April 8, 1976. Governor Wendell Anderson is seated at left.
Courtesy of the Minnesota Historical Society.

percent in 1972.[32] The reproductive consequences of a very sexualized society fell disproportionately on women, many of whom began to demand the option of a legal abortion.

Legal cases on abortion ascended the judicial ladder toward the Supreme Court. A Minnesota case seemed likely to be the one that would force the 'Minnesota Twins' to decide the issue. In April 1970, Dr. Jane Hodgson of St. Paul broke the 1873 Minnesota law against abortion by performing one on a married woman whose pregnancy was threatened by rubella. For *The Mayo Alumnus*, she wrote an article defending her action. "[A]n ever-increasing emphasis on sexuality" led to higher "illegitimacy rates and sexual promiscuity . . . [and] illegitimate births." Forced marriages or unwanted children were not solutions, she claimed, but the "competent physician—not a legislator—is in the best position to decide" what a woman should do. A woman could "choose another" option, and abortion should be one. Hodgson felt "religious opposition to abortion reform is also crumbling."

After Hodgson was prosecuted, proponents of legalized abortion raised funds to take her case to the Supreme Court, but *Roe v. Wade* made her case moot.[33]

Opponents of legalized abortion also organized to defend Minnesota's law against legislative bills revoking or amending it. Minnesota Citizens Concerned for Life (MCCL) became the strongest such group. MCCL pioneered many anti-abortion tactics and helped to organize national pro-life organizations. Its membership grew to about 8,000 families by July 1972. One tactic was to display pictures of the fetus. In November 1972, MCCL president Marjory Mecklenburg showed pictures on a PBS show. A pro-choice leader called it "the most damaging national TV coverage in our history." On the other side, the Abortion Rights Council of Minnesota, Planned Parenthood, and other groups mobilized to change Minnesota's law. Blackmun and Burger knew the issue was very divisive.[34]

Blackmun knew the medical profession from his experience at the Mayo Clinic—and perhaps Burger felt he could influence his friend—so Burger assigned the *Roe* opinion to Blackmun, who wrote to a Mayo Clinic librarian for information. The case was delayed a year. He went to Rochester on July 23, 1972, for two weeks of research at the Mayo library. To avoid undue curiosity from his old hometown friends and newspaper, he gave the *Rochester Post-Bulletin* a nostalgic interview about his years in Rochester and announced he was coming for "his annual checkup at the Clinic" and to visit friends. His opinion stressed doctors' right to practice medicine freely (plus a woman's "right to privacy"). In the hot debate to follow, a pro-choice stress on women's right to abortion and a pro-life stress on a fetus' right to life swamped Blackmun and Hodgson's attempt to frame the issue in dispassionate professional terms.[35]

Blackmun shared Progressives' moral vision of scientific experts like doctors and lawyers deciding moral issues. The secular sixties saw religion as a relic unqualified to decide. Yet pregnancy was no disease or abnormality clearly in the doctor's professional realm but rather a natural process. Its problematic aspects were not medical and legal but social and moral—e.g., the unfairness of placing the burdens of a society's sexual promiscuity on women only and the serious moral claim of the fetus to life. Solutions must be social and moral—involving family, school, church, and government that formed this society in Ordinance days but had lost influence over its sexual practices. Films, TV broadcasts, magazines, radio, and LP records flooded local spaces with a tide of sexual images. Local forces could not stop the tide, but sexual activity still often had the localized consequence of pregnancy.

A narrowly judicial or medical answer was inadequate. Blackmun and Hodgson denied that legalizing abortions done for the mother's health meant "abortion on demand" as critics charged.[36] Doctors would control access to abortion, they argued. However, the courts defined "health" very broadly, and specialized abortion clinics arose to insure that the supply of abortions would meet the growing demand for them. The problem could not be fit into a legal brief. Despite narrowly-professional medical and legal reasoning, the push for legal abortion was part of a broad social trend— Boomers rebelling against fifties' family formation, wanting sex without marriage and pregnancies without births. *Roe v. Wade* would spark decades of conflict between pro-choice and pro-life forces in the DFL and GOP. It would help to end the friendship of the 'Minnesota Twins,' for Burger came to believe that it went too far.[37] It would help religion make a comeback in the 1970s. It would de-legitimize government in the eyes of thousands of Minnesotans, for whom government's defense of human life was the main reason for its existence.

A Seventies' Religious Revival Hits Minnesota & Opposes 'Movement' Causes

Various religious faiths experienced a revival, a renewed interest from members and from seekers, and a rethinking of their approach to society and social issues. It began in the sixties. The Vatican Council II (1962-65) dropped obligatory use of Latin in the mass and made other changes adapting Catholicism to modern times. Israel's capture of the West Bank and Jerusalem in the Six-Day War (June 1967) rekindled Jewish pride and a sense of Zionist mission and, thus, a Jewish fundamentalism of the Orthodox and the Hasidim. Evangelical Protestantism, especially its campus ministries, faced the daunting task of evangelizing countercultural, secular campuses and sought innovative approaches. Partly, the Sixties' Boomers revolted against the circular reasoning of fifties' family values. What was the family *for*? Just to produce more families of children and grandchildren, so they could form families? Religious faiths sharpened their answers to basic questions.

Minneapolis was the headquarters of the Billy Graham Evangelistic Association. The Baptist evangelist launched his career in Minnesota. In September 1969, he hosted the first U.S. Congress on Evangelism; 5,000 delegates came to the Minneapolis Auditorium for six days of inspiration and innovation. Graham had recently "been donning old clothes, sauntering along Sunset Strip in Los Angeles and talking with California hippies." They sought love, that's what churches offered, and churches must learn to communicate that message to a new generation. "God is not tied to 17th-century English, 18th-century hymns, 19th-century architecture, and 20th-century clichés," Rev. Leighton Ford announced. The flexible Graham included Lutherans (vital in Minnesota), marketing techniques, social action, perhaps politics, and Pat Boone's music in his wide-ranging conference. This was not your grandfather's Oldsmobile, but a sharp, sporty model of religious faith in action.[38]

There were other signs of a religious stirring in Minnesota. Lutherans and Catholics joined in a charismatic movement featuring speaking-in-tongues, prayers for healing, and contemporary styles of music and worship to guitar chords not organ chords. A local variant of the hippie Jesus people, Jesus People Church, drew hundreds to its services.[39] The less-pentecostal Campus Church drew a thousand to its Sunday morning services near the University—its TV broadcasts appeared on stations around the state. Charismatic Lutherans began to turn St. Paul's North Heights Lutheran Church into a popular mega-church. Park Avenue Methodist enjoyed success among South Minneapolis' African Americans. These stirrings occurred among young people who felt they had found answers to sixties' questionings, higher goals than family formation for its own sake, and a spiritual movement opposing 'movement' goals, especially legalized abortion. 'Movement' liberals met a different foe than they expected. A cultural battle began. It would mar the state's politics and precinct caucuses for decades.

Other Sixties Issues not as Divisive, Influential, or Long-lived in Minnesota

In the late 1960s and early 1970s, Minnesota did witness the other national issues that made this an unsettled period. Earlier migrations of Southern blacks to the North during the two world wars had largely bypassed Minnesota, but the Twin Cities saw a 400 percent increase in its African-American population from 1950 to 1970. Most of that immigration came in the sixties, due to blacks' "[b]elief in Minnesota's liberal racial climate, expanded employment opportunities, more generous public assistance, and progressive legislation," historian David Taylor suggests. The Civil Rights movement raised blacks' expectations of progress and an end to racial discrimination. The long-established leaders and institutions in the black community were less able to absorb these new migrants and to acculturate them to that community's fairly traditionalist approach.[40]

In July 1967, civil disorder hit North Minneapolis' Plymouth Avenue shopping district. National Guard troops were dispatched to restore order. On first weekend of September 1968, similar disturbances occurred in Minneapolis and St. Paul.[41] These two incidents were small compared to the riots in Watts (1965), Chicago (1966), Newark (June 1967), and Detroit (July 1967). Political leaders from both parties tried to meet the legitimate concerns of blacks, whose numbers in the Twin Cities were much lower than in these other cities. Even after the 1960s migration, blacks made up less than 4 percent of the Minneapolis-St. Paul population. This minority's economic and sociological problems were not easily resolved, but a consensus on orderly change was fairly easily reached.

Migration also occurred among the state's American Indians, from the rural areas and reservations to the Twin Cities. The numbers of American Indians in Minneapolis and St. Paul increased ten-fold from 1950 to 1970. State and city governments could not credibly claim that these American Indians remained solely the responsibility of the federal Bureau of Indian Affairs, as they were when they remained on the reservations. Yet their problems of poverty and discrimination were severe, and they made up only 1 percent of the population, so their political clout was minimal. In 1968, activists such as Dennis Banks and Clyde Bellecourt formed the American Indian Movement. Encouraged by blacks' civil rights organizations and tactics, they used confrontational tactics to press for national attention to Indian issues. Their most dramatic protest occurred at Wounded Knee, South Dakota.[42] They did not have a dramatic, long-term, broad impact on Minnesota's politics despite occasional moments of tension.

The abortion issue had such an impact. It potentially affected all families, of all races or creeds. Legalized abortion proved quite controversial in rural ethnic enclaves—especially Catholic ones like Stearns County. Compromise between pro-life and pro-choice positions proved impossible. Public opinion was closely divided between the two sides. The fact that the Supreme Court ruled abortion legal meant the issue was nearly permanent, for such rulings proved very hard—or perhaps impossible—to overturn.

Divisions Lead to the 1978 "Minnesota Massacre"

When *Time*'s salute to Minnesota and Anderson appeared, the DFL had nearly a monopoly of the state's key political offices and solid control of its legislature. Anderson won reelection in 1974 by a more than 2-to-1 margin. In 1970, McCarthy did not run for reelection, and Humphrey regained a seat in the U.S. Senate that year; in 1976, he won by a nearly 3-to-1 margin over his Republican foe. In the 1977 Minnesota legislature, DFL legislators outnumbered Republicans 3-to-1 in the House and over 2-to-1 in the senate. Mondale was sworn in that January as the second vice president from Minnesota. The state's Republicans were reeling from Watergate and Nixon's resignation. In 1975 they changed their name to the Independent Republicans (IRs) in order to broaden their base.[43]

This mid-1970s DFL Minnesota created a long-lived perception that the state was, almost by definition, a liberal one.[44] In the long term, those who wished it was so helped maintain that misperception by portraying later Republican victories as abnormalities. In the short term, this misperception led to DFL overconfidence and DFL mistakes.

Walter Mondale (left) and Hubert H. Humphrey (right) in the chamber of the Minnesota House of Representatives on Inauguration Day, 1975.
Courtesy of the Minnesota Historical Society.

By winning the vice-presidency, Mondale had to vacate his U.S. Senate seat. Governor Anderson was advised to name a short-term senator and then run for the seat in 1978. Instead he resigned, Lieutenant Governor Rudy Perpich became governor in late December 1976, and Perpich appointed Anderson to the Senate seat. DFL overconfidence contributed to what voters resented as Anderson's "self-appointment."[45]

A further blow to the DFL occurred in January 1978, when Senator Humphrey died after a long battle with cancer. Extremely popular with voters, many of whom he knew by name, Humphrey had been a reliable go-between whose reputation reassured voters that the DFL party was still sound, even if they disliked its platform.

The new leader, Rudy Perpich, later filled a similar role; he communicated well with ordinary citizens, urban and rural, in small groups. A Catholic pro-lifer and Iron Ranger, he softened the DFL image as a party of Twin Cities secular professors and liberal professionals. Yet in 1977 the state's voters were still getting to know him. He personified the formation of a stable society on the Range over the preceding sixty years. Born in Carson Lake, the son of Croatian parents determined to see their four sons get a good education, Rudy earned a DDS degree, practiced dentistry in Hibbing, won a seat on the school board that ran the luxurious Hibbing High School (paid for by mining companies' taxes), and won a state senate seat in 1962. His brothers, Tony and George Perpich, were also dentists and state senators. The immigrants' children had made it.[46]

If the DFL's main problems had been Anderson's "self-appointment" and the death of Humphrey, it could have solved them by advancing new leaders like Perpich. Yet the main problem was that the 'movement' liberals supported causes that most Minnesotans, most DFLers even, did not support. The popular Humphrey and Anderson had shielded the party from voters' dissatisfaction but were no longer able to do so. In 1978, a trio of causes came together to maximize dissatisfaction: congressional efforts to ban motorboats from much of the Boundary Waters Canoe Area (BWCA), the abortion issue, and gun control (plus the "self-appointment"). The DFL near-monopoly meant warring sides fought first in that party, where the political power was believed to reside.

Making the crisis worse, the other new leader did not distance himself from 'movement' causes, as Anderson and Humphrey had. Minneapolis Congressman Donald Fraser, the son of a University law school dean and an early ally of Humphrey in 1948, became the first DFL supporter of 'movement' causes to run for a key statewide office—Humphrey's Senate seat.[47] He became a lightning rod drawing rural pro-life, northern-Minnesota discontent with these causes to himself. A perfect storm was on its way.

Storm clouds formed at the precinct caucuses, as pro-life and pro-choice factions got their supporters to turn out to elect delegates to the June state convention. There, pro-life state senator Doug Johnson of Cook, in the north's 8th congressional district, ran as a protest candidate against Fraser. Fraser was pushing a bill in Congress to end almost all use of motorboats in the BWCA. Twelve hundred opponents of Fraser's bill came to the convention hall, picketed it, sat in the audience section of the hall, and booed so long and loud when Fraser tried to speak that 8th district Congressman James Oberstar had to quiet them before Fraser could proceed. Fraser was endorsed as the DFL candidate, but "Dump Fraser" bumper stickers appeared on pickup trucks in the northwoods and elsewhere.[48]

A culture war seemed to pit rural against urban Minnesota. The two sides did not divide that neatly by geography, but rural voters tended to oppose the pro-choice, pro-gun-control, and pro-wilderness causes they associated with Fraser. Urban professional and educated classes tended to see Fraser as a hero for making his stand for these causes despite their unpopularity. This split is captured in the term 'outstate' that was then used to refer to Minnesota outside the Twin Cities area, whose people often felt they were effectively out of the state—at least, out of its ruling area. In turn, they viewed Twin Citians as outsiders trying to take away their guns, motorboats, and access to the border lakes.

Things were not that simple. A seventies' back-to-the-land return to traditional life, organic gardening and farming, handicrafts, and sustainable energy brought many 'movement' supporters to parts of rural Minnesota. They flocked to precinct caucuses, sometimes outvoted the long-time residents, and represented their rural counties at DFL conventions. On the other side, an Edina millionaire and hotel owner, Bob Short, was the candidate whom 'outstaters' supported against Fraser in the DFL primary. Short spent nearly one million dollars of his own money on advertising against Fraser. He courted Republicans' votes (they could vote in the DFL primary) by attacking big government and promising a $100 billion tax cut in the form of $250-per-person tax rebates.[49]

Humphrey on the Outstate—In-town Split

"Hubert Humphrey was fond of saying the Twin Cities is nothing but a group of people who moved to town. It was a line he used to remind us of our rural heritage and the need to be 'sensitive' about issues affecting rural folks who have not moved to the Twin Cities and never intend to. He used his special 'politics of joy' to make peace with urban and rural—a balance that made him a successful politician."[50]

The day of the primary (September 12), northern Minnesota saw "winds gusting up to 49 miles per hour." The Fraser-Short fight turned into an all-night cliffhanger that added suspense to the cultural symbolism. Fittingly, the last ballots to be counted and sent in from the remotest 'canoe precincts' (or, more likely, motorboat precincts) in northern Minnesota finally gave Short a 3,400-vote victory. Short had ten-to-one margins in the Ely area, and he flew there in his private plane the next day to thank his supporters. At the Ely airport, a crowd gathered and one man held a sign saying, "Winners Bob Short and the Little People." A small-town effort finally defeated the Big City, or so it seemed.[51]

Actually, Republican crossover votes saved Short and allowed Northern precincts to claim the last-minute rescue. And, Short's pro-life, anti-government, tax-cut message foreshadowed real Republican victories to come, based on that same message. Short was defeated that November by Republican David Durenberger, LeVander's former aide.[52] The pro-life, anti-'movement' faction led in 1978 by Bob Short proved unable in the long run to defeat 'movement' liberals within the DFL party. Those activists who badly wanted to defeat them tended to migrate to the Republican party over time. Catholic pro-life Democrats who liked Short often became 'Reagan Democrats' and then Republicans.

No popular unifier like Humphrey was there to save Short from liberals' anger at his destruction of Fraser, or Wendell Anderson from voters' anger at his "self-appointment," or Perpich from being identified with Anderson's action. Republicans ran strong campaigns against all three DFLers. In November, Durenberger beat Short; Plywood Minnesota owner Rudy Boschwitz defeated Anderson; and Congressman Al Quie defeated Perpich.

A GOP party on the ropes two years earlier seized the state's three top political positions. From holding only one-third of the state House, they had now advanced to a tie with the DFL. Some called this the "Minnesota Massacre," in contrast to the "Minnesota Miracle." Boschwitz merely indicated, "We're going to return the two-party system to Minnesota." And that did happen.[53]

Despite the unpopularity of the Vietnam War, there was no return to any unique state identity—although 'movement' liberals did form a Farmer-Labor Association. The state in 1978 proved to be remarkably in tune with the nation's turn to the right, which was about to unseat President Carter and Vice President Mondale. The 'nationalization' of state politics accomplished by Stassen in 1938 and continued by Humphrey in 1948, was a bipartisan nationalization so aligned with modern forces of linkage between states—TV, interstate highways, WATS lines, etc.—that it could not be undone.

1. "focused on events," *Minneapolis Star*, 20 January (1B), 21 January (1C), and 22 January (8A, "Minnesota Hat's Off to Thee?"), all 1965; *St. Paul Pioneer Press*, 21 January 1965, 1

2. "previous summer," Solberg, *Humphrey*, 221-27; 239-43; Robert A. Caro, *The Years of Lyndon Johnson: Master of the Senate* (New York: Alfred A. Knopf, 2002), 439-62; Robert Dallek, *Flawed Giant: Lyndon Johnson and His Times 1961–1973* (New York: Oxford University Press, 1998), 113-20. I am indebted to John Haynes for the idea of "nationalization" of politics; Haynes, "Reformers, Radicals, Conservatives," in Clark, ed., *Century of Change*, 387.

3. "President Johnson came," *Minneapolis Tribune*, 28 June 1964, 1A, 5A, 14A.

4. "Humphrey basked," *St. Paul Pioneer Press*, 24 January 1965, 1, 2; Dallek, *Flawed Giant*, 247-53; Solberg, *Humphrey*, 270-73.

5. "symbolic of the state's contribution," Christy W. Sauro, Jr., *The Twins Platoon: An Epic Story of Young Marines at War in Vietnam* (St. Paul: Zenith Press, 2006), 9, 16, 24-26.

6. "Some enlisted," Sauro, *Twins Platoon*, 20, 22-23.

7. "Goodman had," Sauro, *Twins Platoon*, 82-83, 94-110.

8. "Goodman had written," Sauro, *Twins Platoon*, 113-14, 287.

9. "Larry Rademacher," Sauro, *Twins Platoon*, 83, 86-92.

10. "dismayed at," Sauro, *Twins Platoon*, 221-24, 251-59.

11. "came true," *Minnesota Daily*, 28 September 1964 (9), 20 April 1965 (1), 25 May 1965 (1, 4, 12, 26 May 1965 (1), and 19 October 1965 (4, 5); Stanford Lehmberg and Ann M. Pflaum, *The University of Minnesota1945-2000* (Minneapolis: University of Minnesota Press 2001), 325.

12. "Todd Gitlin," Keillor, "Premodern, Modern, Postmodern," 178.

13. "Old Left professors," Alpha Smaby, *Political Upheaval: Minnesota and the Vietnam Anti-War Protest* (Minneapolis: Dillon Press, 1987), 2-37, 78-79, 125-26.

14. "the University," Keillor, "Premodern, Modern, Postmodern," 185-88, 197-99, 206-09, 211-13.

15. "Dinkytown," *Minnesota Daily*, 8 April 1970, 13.

16. "Georgeville, a hamlet," Alex G. Stach, "Hippie Communes U.S.A.: Five Case Studies, 1970" (Ph.D. diss.: University of Minnesota, 1971), 202-05, 211, 214 (quoted), 215, 218 (quoted).

17. "McCarthy's campaign," Sandbrook, *Eugene McCarthy*, 143-51, 155-56, 160-62, 164-74.

18. "antiwar DFLers," David Lebedoff, *Ward Number Six* (New York: Charles Scribner's, 1972), 3-6, 7 (quoted), 8-28, 30-32, 34-50, 58 (quoted), 69; *Minnesota Daily*, 6 March 1968, 12, 14. Alpha Smaby's book is a McCarthyite's attempt to construct a different interpretation than Lebedoff's, for he was in the Humphrey camp; however, her multiple interviews with participants do not seem to disprove his points.

19. "take over the party," Lebedoff, *Ward Number Six*, 34-35, 58, 62, 74-77.

20. "cultural issues," Haynes, "Reformers, Radicals, Conservatives," in Clark, ed., *Century of Change*, 389; *Minnesota Daily*, 9 April 1968, 2; Lebedoff, *Ward Number Six*, 112-13, 119. Haynes was a DFL participant in 1968 who organized 'regular' college students for HHH.

21. "Harold LeVander," Arthur Naftalin, Minnesota Governors videotapes, "Harold LeVander" (19 December 1980), MHS; Bruce L. Larson, "Scandinavian and Scandinavian-American Governors of Minnesota and Education" in Dag Blanck, et al. eds., *Scandinavian Immigrants and Education in North America* (Chicago: Swedish-American Historical Society, 1995), 172-83.

22. "LeVander copied," "Harold LeVander" videotape, MHS; Larson, "Governors of Minnesota and Education," 178-79; GOP State Central Committee, "A Look at the Record…The First Three Years of the LeVander Administration" (1969), 1-2, 5, MHS; William C. Johnson and John J. Harrigan, "Innovation by Increments: The Twin Cities as a Case Study in Metropolitan Reform," in *Western Political Quarterly*, 209, 211-12, clipping at MHS.

23. "Aiding LeVander," Daniel J. Elazar, Virginia Gray, Wyman Spano, *Minnesota Politics and Government* (Lincoln, Nebraska: University of Nebraska Press), 121-23, 124.

24. "thorniest issue," Lass, *Minnesota: A History*, 289.

25. "he sparked a showdown," Betty Wilson, *Rudy! The People's Governor* (Minneapolis: Nodin Press, 2005), 50-51; Elazar, et al., *Minnesota Politics*, 123-24, 175.

26. "Heralded," *Minneapolis Tribune*, 10 June (5B), 12 June (1A), 13 June (1A, 4A), 15 June (2B), and 30 July (6A), all 1972.

27. "Movement liberals," Haynes, "Reformers, Radicals, Conservatives," in Clark, ed., *Century of Change*, 389; Wilson, *Rudy!*, 56-58 (quotes from 57); Elazar, et al., *Minnesota Politics*, 124.

28. "hired new employees," Elazar, et al., *Minnesota Politics*, 116, 124.

29. "'Minnesota Mess'," Royce Hanson, *Tribune of the People: The Minnesota Legislature and Its Leadership* (Minneapolis: University of Minnesota Press, 1989), 198-201.

30. "*Time* featured," *Time*, 13 August 1973, 24-35; Wilson, *Rudy!*, 63; *St. Paul Pioneer Press*, 13 August 1993, 8A (quoted). I am indebted to Wilson for this reference.

31. "movement proposal," Linda Greenhouse, *Becoming Justice Blackmun: Harry Blackmun's Supreme Court Journey* (New York: Henry Holt, 2005), 6, 8-11, 15, 18-19, 20-23, 41, 42-46, 49-52, 63, 100-01.

32. "In Minnesota," Institute for Population Research and Analysis, "Out-of-Wedlock Births to Minnesota Residents," *Data Display*, Vol. 3, No. 1 (February 1983), 1.

33. "Minnesota case," Jane E. Hodgson, "Abortion: The Law and the Reality 1970," *The Mayo Alumnus*, October 1970, 1-4; David J. Garrow, *Liberty and Sexuality: The Right to Privacy and the Making of Roe v. Wade* (New York: MacMillan, 1994), 428-31, 474; *St. Paul Pioneer Press*, 17 April 1970, 1, 2. Fundraising and court-challenge plans are detailed in Jane Hodgson Legal Defense Fund Papers, MHS.

34. "organizing," *St. Paul Dispatch*, 18 July 1972, 14; Garrow, *Liberty and Sexuality*, 429-30, 579; Marjorie Bingham, "Keeping at It: Minnesota's Women," in Clark, ed., *Century of Change*, 456. For a pro-life analysis countering Garrow's, see Joseph W. Delapenna, *Dispelling the Myths of Abortion History* (Durham, N.C.: Carolina Academic Press, 2006).

35. "Blackmun knew," Greenhouse, *Becoming Justice Blackmun*, 74, 76-77, 82-83, 87, 88, 90-91, 99-100; Garrow, *Liberty and Sexuality*, 532-34, 548, 553-55, 557-59, 587-95; Teresa

Opheim, "Justice Harry A. Blackmun," *The Mayo Alumnus*, Summer 1990, 3-6; *Rochester Post-Bulletin*, 21 July 1972, Second Section, 13, 16.

36. "Blackmun and Hodgson," Hodgson, "Law and Reality," 3; Greenhouse, *Becoming Justice Blackmun*, 90-100; Garrow, *Liberty and Sexuality*, 607.

37. "ending the friendship," Greenhouse, *Becoming Justice Blackmun*, 127, 145, 183-84, 185-88.

38. "September 1969," *Minneapolis Tribune*, 8 September (44), 9 September (13), 10 September (44), 11 September (13), 12 September (21), 13 September (11), and 14 September (1A, 14A), all 1969.

39. "charismatic movement," See Richard Quebedeaux, *The New Charismatics: The Origins, Development, and Significance of Neo-Pentecostalism* (Garden City, NY: Doubleday, 1976); and Quebedeaux, *The New Charismatics II: How a Christian Renewal Movement Became Part of the American Religious Mainstream* (San Francisco: Harper & Row, 1983).

40. "migrations of Southern blacks," Taylor, *African Americans*, 51-52; Lass, *Minnesota: A History*, 290; Holmquist, ed., *They Chose Minnesota*, 74.

41. "civil disorder," Taylor, *African Americans*, 54-55.

42. "Native Americans," Holmquist, ed., *They Chose Minnesota*, 28-29; David Beaulieu, "A Place Among Nations: Experiences of Indian People," in Clark, ed., *Century of Change*, 423-24.

43. "nearly a monopoly," White, et al., comps. *Minnesota Votes*, 59, 63, 218; Hanson, *Tribune of the People*, 39; Lass, *Minnesota: A History*, 277-80, 295.

44. "long-lived perception," For an analysis of this misperception, see Elazar, et al., Minnesota Politics, 49-51.

45. "U.S. Senate seat," The best account of this event is in Wilson, *Rudy!*, 63-71.

46. "Rudy Perpich," Wilson, *Rudy!*, 3-6, 9-11, 13-14, 17-20, 23, 25-27, 28-30, 45.

47. "Donald Fraser," Haynes, *Dubious Alliance*, 7, 153. For a description of Fraser, see Iric Nathanson, "Toppling the Establishment, Revisited," *Hennepin County History*, Vol. 58, No. 4 (1999), 6-7. See also Wilson's chapter on "The Minnesota Massacre" in *Rudy!*, 95-108.

48. "Storm clouds," Christopher Anglim, "Loaves and fishes: a history of pro-life activism in the Democratic-Farmer-Labor party of Minnesota's Fifth Congressional District (1968-81)," 50-52, 87-91, typed ms. (1981), MHS; Wilson, *Rudy!*, 98-99, 100-01; James N. Gladden, *The Boundary Waters Canoe Area: Wilderness Values and Motorized Recreation* (Ames, Iowa: Iowa State University Press, 1990), 56-57, 70, 72; Nathanson, "Toppling," 9-10; *Minneapolis Tribune*, 3 June 1978, 1A, 8A.

49. "the other side," Nathanson, "Toppling," 8-9, 10; Wilson, *Rudy!*, 102; *Minneapolis Tribune*, 13 September (1A, 8A) and 14 September (1A, 11A), both 1978.

50. "Split," *St. Paul Pioneer Press*, 14 September 1978, 2.

51. "the primary," *Minneapolis Tribune*, 13 September (1A, 8A) and 14 September (1A, 11A), both 1978.

52. "saved Short," Nathanson, "Toppling," 13-14 and note 17, 15.

53. "No popular unifier," Lass, *Minnesota: A History*, 295-97; Wilson, *Rudy!*, 105-06; *Minneapolis Tribune*, 8 and 9 November 1978, both 1A; *St. Paul Pioneer Press*, 8 November 1978, 1, 2.

Marketplace Minnesota

By running Al Quie for governor in 1978, Republicans returned to their rural Scandinavian Lutheran base. The 200-pound, six-foot-two-inch Quie seemed another Youngdahl. Raised on a dairy farm in a Norwegian enclave south of Northfield, he graduated from St. Olaf College. He ran his parents' farm, but ten terms in Congress (1958-78) forced him to get a renter. A devout Lutheran lay leader, Quie joined the congressional prayer-group movement. He had a small role in the seventies' religious revival by facilitating the conversion of Watergate felon, and later evangelical leader, Chuck Colson.[1] Republicans faced criticism for using religion. An evangelical anti-prostitution activist mailed 20,000 letters endorsing Quie days before the election. The Sunday before the vote, Quie forces placed 250,000 pro-life handouts on cars in church parking lots. Both Perpich and Quie ran as pro-life candidates, but some anti-*Roe* groups felt pro-life Republicans were more reliable than pro-life DFLers whose personal stance conflicted with their party's. At the national level, the GOP passed pro-life resolutions while Jimmy Carter, an evangelical Democrat, avoided the issue.[2]

Quie seemed a potential three-term governor like Youngdahl (a governor's term was now four years, not two). As a Lutheran, he was a go-between to unite evangelical voters and Catholic voters, many of whom left the DFL over the abortion issue. In 1978, the GOP ticket had a religious, ethnic, and geographical balance—a German Catholic, Durenberger, from Stearns County where his father was athletic director at St. John's; Boschwitz, a Twin Cities Jewish entrepreneur; and the Protestant Quie from southern Minnesota. On his specialty issue, public education, Quie was a Stassen-type Republican willing to spend tax dollars like a GOP moderate.[3] On cultural issues arousing Catholics and evangelicals, he shared their views. He united both wings of Minnesota's GOP.

Minnesota was 'nationalized.' Its political parties must have the same platforms—not just the same names—as national ones. Conservative supporters of Ronald Reagan controlled the Republican party. They shared Quie's moral values. They boosted Reagan to victory in 1980. Yet Reagan and his advisers used market forces more than moral forces to turn back the liberal tide. Getting the Supreme Court to overturn *Roe*, the school prayer decision, and other rulings proved very difficult. First Amendment rights prevented censorship of the free-wheeling media. Conservatives turned to markets to discipline a society refusing to be disciplined by calls for patriotism, old-time religion, or upper-class good manners. Pot smokers, sexual libertines, and utopian dreamers must face bankruptcy, unemployment, and hunger until they learned self-discipline.

In the process, public morality was narrowed to an economic size and shape. It was thinned out, in a process mainly unintended by conservatives, who did not intend that Quie be politically destroyed in the process. There was another ironic, unexpected result of using markets as moral discipline: the main victims in the eighties' markets proved to be farmers, whose jobs were seen as moral foundations for the Ordinance-based society. They turned out to be useful protest symbols for those who opposed this market focus.

National Economic Climate Shifts in the Eighties & Minnesota Must Adjust

Fueled by the oil embargo of 1973-74, inflation took off in the 1970s. Americans expected prices to keep on rising in the future, so they bought now, on credit, and their purchases added to inflation. Workers and senior citizens won COLAs (cost-of-living adjustments) that increased wages and social security benefits to keep pace with inflation. Minnesota's government relied on 'bracket creep,' as taxpayers earning higher wages were pushed into higher tax brackets that yielded more tax revenue. Their land values skyrocketing, farmers used land as security to borrow large sums in order to expand production and purchase new buildings and machinery. By October 1979, the inflation rate had risen to 12 percent. Inflation was seen as a fact of life, like frost in February.[4]

To wean state government off what they saw as its unfair inflation-based revenue gains, Quie's Republicans passed income-tax indexing in the 1979 session. Brackets changed with inflation, so that taxpayers did not pay at a higher tax rate unless the increase in their income exceeded inflation.[5] Their timing proved to be bad. (Also, state government's expenses rose with inflation, but it now had less revenue in real dollars.)

That October, the Federal Reserve Board decided to fight inflation by reducing the money supply, keeping interest rates high, forcing recession, and squeezing inflation expectations out of the economy like water out of a sponge. By April 1980, the prime interest rate was at 18.5 percent and a recession was underway. In the short term (for Quie there would be no long term), Reagan's tax and budget policies added to the problem. Due to the recession, his 23 percent federal tax cut produced large budget deficits that helped keep interest rates high and extend the recession into 1982.[6]

Quie had the fiscal rug pulled out from under him. To aid taxpayers, he had cut tax revenue by about $4.5 billion. Now the recession threw many of them out of work and cut revenues even more. The Minnesota Miracle required state government to aid local governments and schools, which saw such aid as an entitlement. The deep recession required more state aid to the jobless. In 1981-82, Quie had to call six special legislative sessions to patch up the fraying state budget. He did not run for reelection. [7]

The Reagan Revolution did not intend to hurt the Republican Quie. Nor did it intend to help Rudy Perpich, one of 1978's massacred DFLers. Perpich adjusted to the new market focus after serving as a Control Data representative in Europe for three years. Once anti-business, he now admired corporations, knew the global economy, and saw how exports created jobs at home. In April 1982 he returned to run for governor with the slogan "Jobs, Jobs, Jobs." A DFLer could narrow government's goals to economic ones. He did it to defeat the DFL-endorsed candidate in the 1982 primary with the aid of pro-life and anti-gun-control voters just as Short did in 1978—but with the positive message of "Jobs" too.[8]

Republicans' stress on markets represented the views of entrepreneurs who could use free markets. Perpich's stress on "Jobs" put a DFL spin on economic growth and represented the views of workers who could use jobs and who guessed that DFLer Perpich meant good-paying union jobs with benefits. "Jobs" had a moral aspect. A worker must have self-discipline, a work ethic, sobriety at work, a long-term commitment to the job, and basic honesty and reliability. Yet it was a 'thinner' vision than the fifties' stress on family formation. A jobholder need not be married, moral on weekends, a member of a church that could instruct his or her children, or a good parent sacrificing personal desires to provide for the next generation. This 'thinner' vision was easier to sell to a Minnesota public now divided over the specific family vision of the fifties.

The slogan *could* have a family meaning. It did in northeastern Minnesota, where 10,000 jobs were lost due to the recession, and the jobless rate hit 17 percent. There and elsewhere in depressed regions, a job meant a family's survival and a home's rescue from foreclosure.[9] But to single yuppies (eighties' young, upwardly mobile professionals) living by the lakes in southwest Minneapolis, "Jobs" need not mean family—and Perpich's focus on global trade was just as likely to bring added jobs to this group. Like many political slogans, "Jobs" had various meanings in the eyes of various beholders.

Other moral visions beyond the economic ones were possible. Conservatives like Representative Glen Sherwood of Pine River advocated the vision arising from the 1970s religious revival. A biologist, devout Christian, and lay minister, Sherwood also ran for governor in 1982. A former DFLer who left that party due to its 'movement' causes, he "helped organize a 'Pro Family, Pro Decency, Pro Life,' caucus, a bipartisan group of legislators who held weekly prayer breakfasts and championed antiabortion, anti-pornography and 'family' legislation," writes reporter Betty Wilson. This more specific agenda proved controversial. Its meaning was not up to the beholder. Many Minnesotans disagreed with it and called it intolerant, yet all moral visions are intolerant of what they define as immoral. Sherwood was not endorsed by the GOP, which often chose a thin economic agenda in the next two decades. In November 1982, its candidate was Wayzata millionaire Wheelock Whitney, who used narrow budget issues but lost to Perpich.[10]

Perpich & the Intense Workplace-Marketplace Minnesota of the Eighties

In the intensely competitive eighties, a state must compete too. Doing traditional duties of state government—governing, policing, educating, taxing—was not enough. A state must compete against other states to attract businesses by offering the low taxes, efficient services, and skilled workforce they demanded of a 'business climate.' The former Control Data salesman in Vienna understood that new reality once he was back in the governor's office in St. Paul in January 1983. After a temporary income tax hike to balance the budget in 1983-84, Perpich and the legislature put through a $920 million tax cut in 1985 that improved the state's business-climate ranking by lowering it to the fifth highest state in per capita income taxes on individuals. They lowered the top income tax rate from 16 percent to just under 10 percent.

The state's chief salesman now had better terms to offer. Perpich traveled often to Europe and the East Coast. In the summer of 1983, his trade mission to Europe lasted twenty-six days. In 1985, his travels included: 1) nine days in January, first to San Francisco to try to win the Super Bowl for Minnesota, then to Copenhagen to finalize a deal for a cheese plant in Little Falls, to Vienna to see if an Austrian company would run a casino in the state, and to Zurich to talk to other companies; 2) trips to Detroit in February and March to offer General Motors a $1.2 billion package of tax breaks and other incentives to build a Saturn plant in the state; 3) to New York in February "to discuss a wild rice cookbook McGraw Hill intends to publish"; 4) a visit to Salt Lake City in March in hopes of bringing the Utah Jazz team to the Twin Cities; 5) May trips to New York and Washington, D.C.; 6) a July trip to Winnipeg to meet the Ghermezian brothers, who owned a mall in Edmonton and wanted to build one in Bloomington; 7) ten days in France and Austria in September "on a trade mission to promote sales of Minnesota products and investments in Minnesota"; 8) four October days in New York "to meet with paper and printing companies regarding expansion in Minnesota"; and 9) a week-long trip to Austria over Halloween to inspect an Austrian castle for possible use as a University of Minnesota study center.[11]

Republicans complained of the price of hotel rooms and meals and the purpose of the castle trip. Perpich shot back. "Let me tell you what I like the best when I go to New York," he said. "I like a reuben sandwich better than anything else." A DFL politician joked, "Only in Minnesota can a governor be criticized for staying in a first-class hotel with his wife." (Lola Perpich often went with her husband.) His travels did bring firms to the state and cause others to expand operations here, adding new jobs as he promised.[12] A more serious complaint was that a state's traditional functions like policing and taxing rested on moral foundations—that it had a moral right to maintain order and charge citizens for doing so—which were weakened in the long term if it offered tax breaks to attract businesses or dropped its prohibition of gambling to lure others. Both political parties joined in this narrowing of government to mainly economic goals.

That government might be seduced or threatened or influenced was symbolized when the Ghermezian brothers paid for eighty-eight legislators plus nearly sixty other Minnesotans in July 1985 to fly to Edmonton to see their megamall. They sought to cajole legislators into aiding their planned megamall in Bloomington. Nothing improper was done in a narrow sense—and a few legislators paid for their own plane tickets—but, in effect, a state was wined and dined like a corporate customer. (The legislature did turn down the demand for a state subsidy.)[13] Yet a corporation did not have to use force to evict a farmer behind on his mortgage payments or arrest demonstrators blocking a sheriff's sale of his farm. A state had to do such tasks and look morally justified in doing them.

The Legislature is Adjourned—to Edmonton!

The Ghermezians "spent $25,000 to fly 146 Minnesotans— legislators, lobbyists, Bloomington and state officials, reporters, and photographers—to Edmonton. . . . The trio included such lavish touches as a champagne breakfast and steak dinner aboard the plane and a seafood buffet with fresh lobster, shrimp, crab and oysters in Edmonton. . . . During a three-hour walking tour of their mall, the Ghermezians ordered the compliant legislators around like schoolchildren. Some legislators took exception to the treatment."[14]

The 1980s Farm Crisis
Hits Rural Minnesota & Provokes Moral Protest

1985 also saw the worst of the farm crisis in Minnesota. A month before flying to Edmonton, legislators passed a law giving farmers time to catch up on their payments before lenders could seize their farms, but it fell short of farmers' hopes for a moratorium such as Floyd B. Olson had secured in the 1930s. From June 1984 to July 1985, 5,000 Minnesota farms went out of business, more than in any other state. By September 1985, the "Minnesota farm-price index, a composite measure of prices paid for all of the state's [agricultural] commodities, hit a seven-year low." The Federal Reserve's high interest rates to slow the economy and inflation hit farmers hard, as did Reagan's tax cuts and deficits to shrink government and halt liberals' social programs.[15]

Partly, the crisis was path-dependent: farmers' adjustment to the seventies left them vulnerable to the eighties. The seventies gave farmers high agricultural exports, high crop prices, and the inflation that led many to buy more land or tractors on credit before the price went higher. The skyrocketing value of their land was security for their loans. This inflationary bubble burst in the early eighties. What was smart to do before now became foolish. With falling crop prices, they could not afford to pay 18 percent interest on these loans. Farmers depend on credit and are vulnerable to interest rates. As land values declined, bankers grew worried and demanded farmers pay back loans. Many could not. Banks and insurance companies seized farms to reduce their losses from bad loans.[16]

For those who saw a farm merely as another business, these failures were no different than those of stores caught with too much inventory or factories out-competed by Japanese factories. In national and state history, however, farming had taken on a moral, symbolic meaning—the individual family working hard to produce goods that people unquestionably needed and teaching its kids and forming communities as it did so. Republican free-market conservatives did not intend their economic revolution to hit farmers hard, but when it did, their foes were given a symbolic moral case against them. It wasn't the inefficient farmers but the young, expanding ones who were hit hardest.[17]

Around 10,000 farmers and rural people, "many of them wearing snowmobile suits and stocking caps to protect them from the frigid wind," came to the capitol on January 21, 1985. That day Reagan was sworn in for his second term (in the nation's capital) after he handily defeated Walter Mondale in the 1984 election. (Mondale carried his home state by only 3,761 votes). A new group, Groundswell, organized this rally to demand that the legislature force a delay in farm foreclosures. Governor Perpich spoke to them before heading off to Copenhagen to finalize the cheese-plant deal.[18]

Groundswell did not wait for legislative action. It made a test case of the February 1st sheriff's sale of the 480-acre dairy farm of Jim and Gloria Langman near Starbuck. Jim Langman was a recent president of the Minnesota unit of another farm-protest group, the American Agricultural Movement. The Langmans had low-interest government loans until 1979 "when their barn burned and 36 milk cows were destroyed." Then they could only get high-interest loans of $320,000 from Travelers Insurance. The eighties' drop in crop prices meant they could not make payments. They owed $22,000 in interest. At the sale, Travelers could get the farm and cut its losses. Groundswell threatened to "initiate a people's moratorium and physically try to stop the foreclosures."[19]

A thousand people came to Glenwood (the county seat of Pope County, in which the Langmans' farm was located) on February 1st to prevent the sale, although Travelers had asked for a postponement due to the protest. At the March 18th attempted sale, the crowd of five hundred shouted "no sale, no sale" for over an hour. The sheriff could not conduct the oral bidding and called it off. Twenty-three protestors were arrested for obstructing his movements. On Monday, April 1, three thousand were in Glenwood—plus civil rights leader and 1984 presidential hopeful Rev. Jesse Jackson. Travelers requested another delay. Ten farmers had committed suicide in this west-central area, and families faced tragedies. The crowd heard speeches by Jackson and Paul Wellstone, Carleton College political science professor and radical organizer for various groups. A fiery DFL orator, Wellstone ran for state auditor in 1982 (but lost) and was a Groundswell leader.[20]

A Shout Against Narrow Economics

Wellstone "urged people not to bear silent witness to the destruction of farms and communities. 'Why does the administration spend billions for star wars technology in space, but not to feed the hungry in the world? This is an administration that says it is pro-family, but it has abandoned family farms, school children who are hungry and the poor of America."[21]

From Glenwood, a 65-car caravan went to St. Paul to demand that a farm-foreclosure moratorium bill be passed. "They packed the gallery of the House chambers." Speaker Dave Jennings "threatened to clear the gallery" if they didn't quiet down. The Republican Jennings accused the DFL of using Groundswell for its political purposes and called Wellstone "a professional political hack." Actually, Wellstone was a former champion wrestler, who saw the farm crisis as his Republican opponents' vulnerable point—useful for a reversal and possible pin. Perpich tried to sidestep the moratorium issue. He favored market solutions such as using corn-derived ethanol to raise corn prices. The state used ethanol in its vehicles and gave a loan guarantee for an ethanol production plant. Despite these steps, the mid-1980s saw two different economies—a depressed rural one and a booming urban one that shared in the nation's recovery from the recession.[22]

Minnesota Women's Movement Features
Group Cooperation, Not One Leader

Perpich was also noted for his supportive attitude toward women in politics and public office. In 1982, he chose St. Paul businesswoman Marlene Johnson to run with him as a candidate for lieutenant governor. Since then, both successful and unsuccessful candidates for governor have chosen women as their running mates. No woman has as yet received a major-party nomination to run for governor. With her marketing knowledge from owning an ad agency, Lt. Governor Johnson went on trade missions to advance Perpich's marketing of Minnesota. In his first term, Perpich appointed law professor Rosalie Wahl as the state's first woman on its supreme court. When he left the governor's office in 1991, a majority of supreme court justices were women.[23]

Women had won relatively few major political offices by the early 1990s. In an immigrants' state where ethnicity, religious faith, culture, and family were intertwined, many Minnesotans had more conservative views on women's role than their openness to liberal economic views might suggest. Eugenie Anderson had lost out to Eugene McCarthy in 1958 for a Senate seat. The state's first female congresswoman, Coya Knutson, was defeated that year when running for a third term. Elected in 1974, Secretary of State Joan Growe performed commendably in that office but lost by a large margin when she ran against Boschwitz in 1984. Women's share in the legislature rose to 15.4 percent of the seats in 1987, as a network of feminist activists in both parties encouraged and supported female candidates.[24]

Like its men, Minnesota's women were divided by religion, social class, ethnicity, geography, and political party. Some lower- and middle-class women felt the women's movement enabled professional women to climb the career ladder while endangering the culture of family and marriage that aided most women. They divided on abortion. Some, like the governor's sister-in-law Connie Perpich, worked for pro-choice groups like Planned Parenthood. Others led pro-life groups like MCCL. They tended to be steady cooperators and networkers; none became a national feminist celebrity. Historian Marjorie Bingham notes, "If Minnesota goes into history without many *great* women, it is perhaps because it has so many good ones, active and involved."[25]

Pay equity for women fit Perpich's "Jobs" vision and Minnesotans' work ethic and sense of fairness. The state led the nation in mandating a 'comparable worth' pay scale for state and local government jobs, which were ranked according to education required, supervisory duties, and responsibility—for job categories in which women and men predominated. Jobs of equal 'worth' were compensated equally. A history of wage discrimination by gender was ended. Perpich supported this program, initiated in 1984-85. He did not apply it to the private sector, where labor markets set wages.[26]

Perpich brought competition to education. Educating had always been one of the state's chief duties—delegated to local districts but supervised and later funded largely from St. Paul. Debates had raged among religious and ethnic groups about what to teach students, and they now raged among movement liberals, seventies religious believers, and a group with mainly career goals for its kids. Catholic parochial schools revived, new evangelical Christian schools began, and more parents 'home schooled' their kids. A national commission diagnosed "a rising tide of mediocrity" in education in 1983.[27]

With such disunity, market-like 'choice' was one option, and Perpich took it. The media-driven youth culture that undermined education by suggesting smart was not cool—well, a governor could not change that. Perpich won an "open enrollment" law letting juniors and seniors attend a high school outside their district and a "post-secondary" law letting them take college courses with state-paid tuition. The state later authorized charter schools. Minnesota gained a national reputation as a leader in school choice.[28] Perpich also won a high school for the arts, but school choice combined with an eighties' stress on money and careers to prioritize education for success rather than the traditional civic, liberal arts, and social service goals. A divided society could not agree on what the latter goals should include, so students and parents focused on the former ones.

A Casino or Lottery is a Marketplace Too: Legalized Gambling in Minnesota

As Republicans narrowed their message to markets, taxes, and business climate, and Perpich narrowed the DFL message to "Jobs," state government lost the moral authority to prohibit certain private behaviors, like gambling. Movement liberals never persuaded legislators to legalize marijuana and drugs—these affected work performance among other things—but gambling was seen as an economic transaction between consenting adults.

The state's anti-gambling tradition meant that steps to legalize it had to come one at a time and benefit some good purpose like charity, added state revenue, or new jobs. A 1978 law allowed charitable gambling using raffles and other devices, and in 1981, pull-tabs could be sold "as a stand-alone game" by charities; a 1983 law allowed pari-mutuel betting on horse races at Canterbury Downs race track. In 1986 Perpich began promoting a state lottery whose proceeds would go to fund job programs in urban areas and a Greater Minnesota Fund for rural economic development. Legislators put a constitutional amendment authorizing a lottery on the 1988 ballot. Voters approved it. By 1989, the state had a Gaming Department to oversee the industry and run the lottery. Charitable gambling proceeds increased ten-fold, from $100 million (1985) to $1 billion (1989).[29]

The state, the charities, and the track did not foresee how legalizing gambling plus the state's history of largely ignoring its Indian reservations would add up to a pair of aces for its two American Indian tribes. The key new factor was the U.S. Supreme Court ruling in the *Cabazon* case (1987): a state could prohibit gambling outright and everywhere, but if it legalized *some* games like bingo and horse races, then semi-sovereign Indian nations could operate *any* games, even casino ones like roulette or blackjack or slot machines. Minnesota had legalized some, and its American Indian bands were now free to offer all. Congress in 1988 passed the Indian Gaming Regulatory Act that called for states to negotiate deals or "compacts" with the tribes, and Minnesota was the first state to do so. Perpich negotiated deals with eleven bands that let them open seventeen casinos.[30]

By 1995, Minnesotans were gambling about $3.5 billion each year at these casinos. The casinos' percentage 'take' from this revenue stream did greatly improve the economy on those reservations near the Twin Cities or otherwise easily accessible to those who wished to gamble. Thus, past economic injustices committed against American Indians were reversed, to a degree. It could also be argued that the casinos earned this income by providing entertainment, restaurant meals, celebrity concerts, etc., to their clientele. More morally problematic was the gigantic redistribution of billions of dollars from one group of players to another merely because one guessed '6' and another, '7.' An unknown number of Minnesotans became addicted to gambling; one study showed that 60 percent of such "pathological gamblers" committed crimes in order to keep playing.

Once legalized—with charities, the state budget, tourism, and American Indian economies partly reliant on gambling proceeds—the gambling revolution in Minnesota was all but impossible to stop.

Gorbachev at Control Data:
Seeing the Economic Past That Had Worked

One of Perpich's successes was in getting Soviet President Mikhail Gorbachev to visit Minnesota in early June 1990. Gorbachev was leading the Soviet Union away from Communism's government-owned economy and toward free-market capitalism. He saw his meeting at a hotel with 145 business executives as his main purpose; like Perpich flying to Austria, he was on an economic-development mission to recruit U.S. investment in his country. He was to visit a dairy farm south of Rosemount, but that was of lesser priority, cancelled on arrival on June 3. He made it to the Bloomington headquarters of Control Data, which was selling six mainframe computers to the USSR. Control Data had had business dealings with the Soviets for twenty-two years. A key adviser and speechwriter for its founder William Norris originated the idea to invite Gorbachev to Minnesota.[31]

Al Eisele, the adviser, suggested that Gorbachev would leave thinking "that he [had] seen the future in Minnesota and it work[ed]." Actually, at Control Data he saw the past that had worked. A Soviet leader transitioning from public to private ownership would want to see Control Data, which pursued the public-private economic partnerships that DFL leaders (like its former employee Perpich) favored. After the 1967 riot in North Minneapolis, Control Data opened an assembly plant there to create jobs. That success led to a St. Paul plant and to a City Venture program selling "management and consulting services" at business and technology centers to aid new businesses in inner-city areas. Control Data also founded Rural Ventures, which offered small farmers computer-based farm-management software and ran pilot projects in Pine City and Princeton to train farmers. Norris' theme was that a business could make a profit by meeting a social need. It could, in the old seventies' business climate.[32]

That was not Wall Street's theme in the eighties. The Reagan revolution changed the business climate. Now, the new ideas were to cut taxes, shrink government, open up chances for small businesses to innovate new products on their own—with no partnership with government. Wall Street investors fixated on the bottom line (earnings per share) in the last quarter, not the long term. Wall Street looked with special skepticism at Norris and Control Data, which suffered "disastrous reversals" from 1982 to 1985. The company recovered from a half-billion dollar loss in 1985, but its corporate philosophy, popular in Minnesota's socially-concerned corporate culture, never proved popular in the 1980s.[33]

In June 1987, Minnesota's DFL leaders were eager to protect this state corporate culture against Wall Street's corporate raiders. Hours after the head of Dayton's warned Perpich that Dart Group of Maryland was attempting a hostile takeover and asked for protective legislation, the governor called for a special legislative session. In what the *St. Paul Pioneer Press* called "a boggling show of clout," Dayton's lobbied for and got "some of the nation's toughest [legal] barricades against hostile takeovers" in a one-day session. Corporate directors facing a decision to accept or reject a takeover bid could "consider the interests of the corporation's employees, customers, suppliers and creditors, the economy of the state and the nation, community and societal considerations, and the long-term as well as short-term interests of the corporation and its shareholders." Wall Street focused almost exclusively on shareholders' short-term interests.[34]

These barricades worked temporarily for Dayton's, but two years after Gorbachev left its Bloomington headquarters, Control Data was split into two companies—and its focus on mainframes sold to governments and businesses was not the wave of the future.[35] Innovative 'geeks' creating personal computers and software in Silicon Valley and Seattle for the eighties' consumer proved better able to thrive in the new business climate than the generation of World War II engineers that Norris represented. Minnesota served as a great environment for the latter but much less so for the former. Gorbachev's visit had little lasting impact, for both he and Perpich were soon out of office.

Ultimately, two different moral visions of the economy competed. The eighties' market vision was that free markets would punish and even destroy the lazy, inefficient, spendthrift, consumer-ignoring corporation—a moral justice. Minnesota CEOs and DFL leaders felt that the corporation donating 5 percent of its profits to community non-profits and to charity and building its business on serving society's needs would be rewarded in the economy and by a state government that rewarded the virtuous—a moral justice too. A national vision necessarily dominated a state one, but the latter might survive locally.

Populist Wellstone Creates
an Anti-Markets Morality Play on a Green Bus

A national vision narrowing morality to free markets got its comeuppance in 1990—but only a temporary rebuke in one state. It was vulnerable to an underdog campaign that spotlighted the markets' innocent victims who were not lazy spendthrifts—even if markets decided justly in 95 percent of cases, spotlighting the 5 percent might convince the public of their injustice. The wrestler Wellstone seized this vision and its defender—Senator Rudy Boschwitz, whose Plywood Minnesota business had won in the markets—at their point of vulnerability. He ran for Boschwitz's Senate seat in 1990.

Central casting would never have picked Paul Wellstone for senator. A short, muscular man at 5' 6" with his hair looking uncontrolled and frizzy, a sixties' movement guy from the University of North Carolina who still got angry and shouted and pounded the podium, Wellstone looked like the very last guy that quiet, reserved Minnesota voters would pick for senator. He was the stereotypical radical professor in jeans and T-shirt whom many students loved but Carleton College's trustees deeply distrusted. He fit the stereotype of the DFL as the party of the professors. A movement liberal, he wrote his Ph.D. dissertation on the black ghetto of Durham, North Carolina; he used the tactics of the civil rights movement—personalizing an issue in terms of victims and victimizers, making demands, and forcing authorities into a corner by public protests and civil disobedience.[36]

Central casting would never even have picked Wellstone to play a Minnesotan. He was far too intense for that. Two reporters who covered his campaign wrote, "On first hearing a Wellstone speech, many Minnesotans, famous for their emotional reserve, were literally frightened by the emotion and sheer, screaming volume, if not the content."[37]

Wellstone was a local organizer fighting local battles of west-central farmers against a power line construction project, the Groundswell cause in Glenwood, the P-9 strikers against Hormel in Austin.[38] He used local battles to protest the nation's capitalist and corporate economy, while largely bypassing state government, whose mediating role in U.S. politics was to manage that economy's negative local effects so it could proceed without protest. Wellstone wanted to dramatize negative local impacts, not end them.[39]

His local organizing won him the DFL nomination in 1990. The regular state DFL leaders opposed him and feared he would drag the party down to defeat. The precinct caucuses were crucial. Only about 2 percent of voters attended them. A few activists who could get a few thousand people to attend the February 27th caucus could control the DFL state convention in June. Wellstone's three DFL rivals had more clout in the legislature and state government, but he was better at local organizing. In their suits and ties, they were more typical Minnesota politicians, but he was more passionate and interesting.

Wellstone shared Fraser's views but learned from Fraser's 1978 primary loss: a Twin Cities liberal should not get out of touch with any large group of voters. He would never be out-maneuvered so that a millionaire like Short could fly into Ely to the cheers of its "little people." He was for the "little fellas," not the Rockefellers, as he put it. He stressed economic issues closest to workers and farmers, not what could be portrayed as elitist issues—BWCA, gun control, Metro light rail, etc.—or movement issues like the legalization of marijuana (he avoided that issue). He campaigned so often on the Range, the site of Fraser's main problems, that he almost lived there. He beat his pro-life foe in the DFL primary by a four-to-one margin there. Wellstone was a "little fella." He lived in outstate Northfield, not the Twin Cities, but he received support from metro liberals. As the battle narrowed to Wellstone vs. Boschwitz, his small size and small campaign bank account became part of the David vs. Goliath morality play being staged. Another part was a 1968 Chevrolet school bus the campaign bought for $3,500, painted green and white, and used to drive him around the state as a symbol of his plucky underdog status.[40]

Rudy Boschwitz was an intriguing figure, not a faceless lawyer in a three-piece suit. His "folksy campaign style" often had him in a plaid shirt. His home-improvement chain, Plywood Minnesota, made money by meeting suburbanites' social need to add a porch or deck or finished basement to their fifties' tract house. He gave his constituents excellent service and did very well at raising campaign funds from small donors. He was more personable than his fellow millionaire, Bob Short. Yet he had been in Washington for eleven years, and its morally-questionable practices of raising money from lobbyists and groups demanding special treatment from Congress had begun to tarnish his reputation.[41]

For the play to work, David had to be morally pure as well as small, and Goliath had to be morally corrupt by comparison. Wellstone raised the normal liberal issues of health care, jobs, union rights, and the fight against poverty. Yet money in politics was the issue dramatized and personified when Boschwitz, with $1.5 million in his campaign bank account in the summer of 1990, faced Wellstone, who could not come up with $10,000 for a Washington dinner.[42] The issue of money in politics was not a technicality, for it morally symbolized the eighties' stress on free markets—in this case, that the free market of influence-purchasing lobbyist 'consumers' picked out the best officeholders.

That oversimplified charge against Boschwitz had enough credibility to persuade voters. With the bus, door-to-door campaigning, and funny ads, Wellstone got underneath Boschwiz—closer to the grassroots—and used the moral power of that position to flip and pin him. Republican conservatives' narrowing of morality to markets hurt them. Boschwitz pointed to the high costs and higher taxes that Wellstone's programs would cost, but voters knew Wellstone was very unlikely to get the Senate to pass his proposals. They elected him for his outspoken sincerity and intriguing, entertaining differentness from the quiet, professional lawyers and managers who usually sought their vote.[43]

After he beat Boschwitz in November 1990, Wellstone took the green bus to the nation's capital for his swearing-in as senator in early January 1991. He soon proved he was no typical Minnesotan by thrusting an antiwar audiotape at Vice President Dan Quayle, staging an antiwar press conference at the Vietnam Veterans Memorial Wall, and confronting President George H. W. Bush over the impending Gulf War at a White House reception—all violations of Washington protocol and good manners. He wasn't representing a state, which had something to lose from Washington's annoyance, but a protest movement, which didn't. He won some victories, but the tide of his Democratic Party was against his populism, as centrist New Democrats like Bill Clinton took control. Like most plays, Wellstone's 1990 upset victory changed very little in the real world. Two years later, Minnesota voters elected a very conservative man, former TV news anchor and first-term Congressman Rod Grams, to join Wellstone in the U.S. Senate.[44]

The Nineties' Marketing Focus Symbolized by Minnesota's Mall of America

Wellstone hoped the nineties would be "more of a public-interest decade than a private-interest decade," but that did not happen, even in Minnesota.[45] Minnesotans were too divided over what the public interest was to sacrifice their more certain private interests for it. Wellstone's hope that moral anger and protest would reestablish people's control over markets was not realized. Most Minnesotans found their multiplying options as consumers so attractive that anger at occasional injustices was forgotten. Republicans' hope that markets would morally discipline people and reward them was disappointed. The Democrat Clinton reaped the political rewards of the nation's economic boom of the 1990s. Opening in August 1992, the Mall of America symbolized all of this.

Constructed where the old Met Stadium used to sit and several miles from where Wilson Pond's still older farm used to be, the Mall was a bit smaller than the Ghermezian brothers first proposed, and they were now minority shareholders. The mall-developing brothers Mel and Herb Simon of Indianapolis took the lead in planning and building it. The largest mall, the largest retail marketplace in the United States, its statistics were impressive: its three levels had floor space equal to 88 football fields or 35 city blocks; its ramps had more parking spaces than Minnesota had lakes; 150,000 people came on opening day, about 50,000 "at any one time, below its 67,000 maximum capacity, but still a load"; 13,000 people worked in 520 stores; to walk past each one meant walking 4.2 miles; a 7-acre Camp Snoopy amusement park gave 20,000 rides in four hours.[46]

St. Olaf Professor at Mall of America Opening

"[W]e wandered back to the main stage for the fireworks scheduled for 10:30. When they went off, Riki turned to me and said, 'Wow, are they real fireworks?' My first impulse was to treat this as a silly question, but it triggered questions of my own: Was that the real Ray Charles? Were we really singing along with him? . . . After the fireworks we drifted around, occasionally bumping into look-alikes: Elvis, John Wayne, Mae West, Ernestine, Indiana Jones."[47]

To some outsiders, it didn't seem to really be in Minnesota. A writer for the *Los Angeles Times* commented, "That America's Mall was built in Minnesota seems ironic to some. Home to dour Scandinavians with conservative life style and liberal politics, the state has always had an unextravagant sort of bent." That was an inaccurate stereotype, but even conservative Germans or radical Finns, also part of the state's identity, would find the Mall a bizarre bazaar. Inside, Minnesotans bored with the state's dour image could escape it and non-Minnesotans would hardly know they were there. "The Mall has its own geography" and its streets suggested different locales. Walking along East Broadway, you are in New York City. "Along West Market there is a mellow California glitz." "[L]andscaped with tall palms," North Garden street looked "Mediterranean."[48]

The Mall had family, school, church, and government. Couples married at the Chapel of Love Wedding Chapel. Camp Snoopy was family-friendly and kid-centered. Next to Bloomingdale's, the Leila Anderson Learning Center housed a high school program of "Mall classes and internships" at the stores that students could choose—especially ones who were bored with normal classrooms. Indirectly, this was part of Perpich's school-choice legacy. Church services were held on Sunday mornings. The Mall's managers were its governors. Their security guards broke up fights, confiscated weapons, and enforced rules over the years as the Mall became a teen hangout.[49]

These four elements of an Ordinance-ordered society were subject to markets here—not surprisingly, for a mall is a marketplace. In bars like Gators and America's Original Sports Bar, mates were selected and dropped according to the present criteria for a trophy wife or Mr. Right.[50] In the learning center, students found the Mall's choice-rich streets very different from rules-based classrooms. The church service was an odd interloper one morning a week. It had to compete for attention, and the Mall's atmosphere may have affected its message more than the reverse.[51] State government insisted its laws be enforced there, but it competed with other states to get the Mall. The Ghermezians had threatened to go elsewhere. Neither the GOP nor DFL got what it wanted: this market encouraged immorality at Hooters or Gators, and it was run by retailing Rockefellers while the "little fellas" had non-union "Jobs" at minimum wage and without benefits.

1. "Al Quie," Wilfred Bockelman, *Politics with Integrity: Al Quie of Minnesota* (Minneapolis: Eye of the Needle, 1978), 13-16, 18-19, 22-25, 30, 91-92, 95-97, 115.

2. "faced criticism," *Minneapolis Tribune*, 4 November 1978, 1A, 4A, 11A; Wilson, *Rudy!*, 105, 107; David T. Courtwright, "Which Sides Are You On?: Religion, Sexuality, and Culture-War Politics," in Mark C. Carnes, ed., *The Columbia History of Post-World War II America* (New York: Columbia University Press, 2007), 325-26.

3. "Stassen-type Republican," Haynes, "Reformers, Radicals, Conservatives," in Clark, ed., *Century of Change*, 391.

4. "inflation took off," Michael Barone, *Our Country: The Shaping of America from Roosevelt to Reagan* (New York: Free Press, 1990), 587; Neil E. Harl, *Farm Debt Crises* (Ames, Iowa: Iowa State University Press, 1990), 5, 7, 13-15, 37-39; James T. Patterson, *Restless Giant: The United States from Watergate to Bush v. Gore* (New York: Oxford University Press, 2005), 148.

5. "Quie's Republicans," Hanson, *Tribune of the People*, 199-201.

6. "fight inflation," Patterson, *Restless Giant*, 148, 157; Harl, *Farm Debt Crisis*, 3, 5, 7.

7. "the fiscal rug," Hanson, *Tribune of the People*, 199-201; Elazar, et al., *Minnesota Politics*, 125-27.

8. "Perpich adjusted," Wilson, *Rudy!*, 109, 111-12, 117-18, 121-26.

9. "northeastern Minnesota," Clark, ed., *Century of Change*, 189 (the job loss was measured in

1984); Wilson, *Rudy!*, 151.

10. "Other moral visions," Wilson, *Rudy!*, 126-30 (quote from 127-28).

11. "traveled often," Wilson, *Rudy!*, 145, 175-76; *St. Paul Pioneer Press Dispatch*, 9 February 1986, 1A, 8A, 9A (I am indebted to Wilson for this reference).

12. "Republicans complained," Wilson, Rudy!, 176-77; St. Paul Pioneer Press Dispatch, 9 February 1986, 9A.

13. "Ghermezian brothers paid," *St. Paul Pioneer Press Dispatch*, 27 July 1985, 1A, 4A; *Minneapolis Star Tribune*, 27 July 1985, 1A, 2A, 11A; Wilson, *Rudy!*, 160-64.

14. "Adjourned – to Edmonton!," *St. Paul Pioneer Press Dispatch*, 27 July 1985, 1A, 2A.

15. "the farm crisis," *Minneapolis Star Tribune*, 28 December 1985, 1A, 2B, 3B; Wilson, *Rudy!*, 167.

16. "the crisis," Harl, *Farm Debt Crisis*, 5, 7, 11, 13-15, 38-39.

17. "inefficient farmers," Harl, *Farm Debt Crisis*, 20, 21, 24-25.

18. "10,000 farmers," *St. Paul Pioneer Press Dispatch*, 22 January 1985, 1A, 14A; Wilson, *Rudy!*, 149, 151.

19. "made a test case," *Pope County Tribune*, 31 January (1A) and 7 February (1A, 2A, 7A), both 1985.

20. "thousand people," *Pope County Tribune*, 7 February (1A, 2A, 7A), 21 March (1A), and 4 April (1A, 2A), all 1985; *St. Paul Pioneer Press Dispatch*, 2 April 1985, 1A, 4A.

21. "Shout Against," *Pope County Tribune*, 4 April 1985, 2A.

22. "From Glenwood," *St. Paul Pioneer Press Dispatch*, 2 April (1A, 4A) and 3 April (1A, 4A), both 1985; Wilson, *Rudy!*, 147-48, 151, 167.

23. "supportive attitude," Wilson, *Rudy!*, 89-92, 144; Lass, *Minnesota: A History*, 298-99.

24. "slow to win," Lass, *Minnesota: A History*, 285-87; Wilson, *Rudy!*, 119; Clark, ed., *Century of Change*, 453, 458, 459.

25. "Minnesota's women," Bingham, "Keeping at it," in Clark, ed., *Century of Change*, 459, 461, 463 (quoted); Wilson, *Rudy!*, 137. The one book about Joan Growe's campaign illustrates this emphasis on the group, not the individual. It is not so much about Growe as it is about the committee of women who aided her campaign; Barbara Stuhler, *No Regrets: Minnesota Women and the Joan Growe Senatorial Campaign* (St. Paul: Braemar Press, 1986).

26. "Pay equity," Clark, ed., *Century of Change*, 460; Wilson, *Rudy!*, 142.

27. "national commission," Clark, ed., *Century of Change*, 501.

28. "Perpich took it," Wilson, *Rudy!*, 156-57, 222.

29. "steps to legalize it," Wilson, *Rudy!*, 171, 210-11; Richard Hoffer, *Jackpot Nation: Rambling and Gambling Across Our Landscape of Luck* (New York: HarperCollins, 2007), 187.

30. "key new factor," Robert Goodman, *The Luck Business: The Devastating Consequences and Broken Promises of America's Gambling Explosion* (New York: Free Press, 1995), 103-07, 112-14; Lass, *Minnesota: A History*, 300-01; Wilson, *Rudy!*, 211.

31. "Perpich's successes," Wilson, *Rudy!*, 237-38; *St. Paul Pioneer Press Dispatch*, 3 June (1A, 10A) and 4 June 1990 (1A, 4A, 7A, 10A).

32. "Al Eisele," *St. Paul Pioneer Press Dispatch*, 4 June 1990, 10A; James C. Worthy, *William C. Norris: Portrait of a Maverick* (Cambridge, Mass.: Ballinger, 1987), 7, 12-13, 107-17, 120, 125, 151-56; Control Data Corporation, *Responding to the Technological Challenges*, 8-11.

33. "special skepticism," Worthy, *Portrait of a Maverick*, 13.

34. "eager to protect," *St. Paul Pioneer Press Dispatch*, 26 June 1987, 1A, 6A; Wilson, *Rudy!*, 198.

35. "Control Data was split," *St. Paul Pioneer Press Dispatch*, 28 May 1992, 1A, 6A, 1E.

36. "Central casting," Bill Lofy, *Paul Wellstone: The Life of a Passionate Progressive* (Ann Arbor: University of Michigan Press, 2005), 11-55.

37. "play a Minnesotan," Dennis J. McGrath and Dane Smith, *Professor Wellstone Goes to Washington: The Inside Story of a Grassroots U.S. Senate Campaign* (Minneapolis: University of Minnesota Press, 1995), xv.

38. "local organizer," Lofy, *Paul Wellstone*, 31-36, 39-43, 51-52. Wellstone did not totally ignore state government: he briefly served as a special assistant to Perpich, sought a farm-foreclosure moratorium from the state legislature, and ran for state auditor (a job he later admitted being unqualified for).

39. "local organizing," Dennis J. McGrath and Dane Smith, *Wellstone Goes to Washington*, 70-76, 77-78, 90-94, 97-105.

40. "Wellstone shared," Paul Wellstone, *The Conscience of a Liberal: Reclaiming the Compassionate Agenda* (New York: Random House, 2001), 13, 17-18, 24; McGrath and Smith, *Wellstone Goes to Washington*, xvii-xviii, 17-21, 36-38, 65, 84, 136-37, 158.

41. "Rudy Boschwitz," McGrath and Smith, *Wellstone Goes to Washington*, xiv-xv, 88-89, 106-08, 163-65, 182-84.

42. "money in politics," McGrath and Smith, *Wellstone Goes to Washington*, 164, 187, 191-92.

43. "Boschwitz pointed," McGrath and Smith, *Wellstone Goes to Washington*, 227. They have a different analysis of why Wellstone won. See their *Wellstone*, 274-82.

44. "After he beat Boschwitz," *St. Paul Pioneer Press Dispatch*, 1 January (6A), 2 January (1A, 6A), and 4 January (1A, 5A); Lofy, *Paul Wellstone*, 2-3, 66-68; McGrath and Smith, *Wellstone Goes to Washington*, 284-92. All 1991.

45. "Wellstone hoped," McGrath and Smith, *Wellstone Goes to Washington*, 290 (quoting Wellstone).

46. "Constructed," *Minneapolis Star Tribune*, 12 August 1992, 20A-22A; *St. Paul Pioneer Press Dispatch*, 26 April (1A, 8A) and 9 August (8H), both 1992; Eric Nelson, *Mall of America: Reflections of a Virtual Community* (Lakeville, MN: Galde Press, 1998), 1-2, 3-4, 26-27, 57; Wilson, *Rudy!*, 164.

47. "St. Olaf Prof," Nelson, *Mall of America*, 9.

48. "really be in Minnesota," Nelson, *Mall of America*, 2-3, 14-15.

49. "Mall had family," Nelson, *Mall of America*, 8-9, 91-93, 147-67, 245.

50. "bars like Gators," Nelson, *Mall of America*, 105-12.

51. "church service," Nelson, *Mall of America*, 245-47.

13 A Physical State in a Virtual World

When the Mall of America opened in August 1992, Arne Carlson was governor. Blessed with an ideal Scandinavian name for Minnesota politics, Carlson was the son of lower-class Swedish immigrants in the Bronx. He came to the University for graduate studies and stayed to work at Control Data. He became a Republican, won a seat on the Minneapolis City Council, then served in the legislature until being elected state auditor in the 1978 Massacre. He faced a social-issues 'ceiling' barring him from rising further: he was pro-choice on abortion and at odds with most Republican convention delegates.[1]

A weird, bitter last-minute election scandal in late October 1990 made Carlson the governor, but practically a politically friendless one. Tired of losing with men whose cautious ways matched their social conservatism, GOP delegates chose Jon Grunseth, a handsome corporate vice-president (Ecolab) who spoke "with a booming voice," looked like a governor, and had pizzazz. Carlson ran against Grunseth in the primary and lost by a large margin. Conservatives did not know Grunseth had so much charm that he had long been a womanizer. In a series of secretive maneuvers, Carlson fed Perpich inside data on Grunseth, Perpich fed the media Grunseth's divorce records, then two young women (aided by a DFL lawyer and Perpich backer) accused Grunseth in a *Star Tribune* story of swimming nude with teenage girls at a pool party in 1981, which Grunseth denied. His campaign was finished by newspaper accounts of a nine-year adulterous affair. He dropped out of the race on October 28th, ten days before the election."[2]

Disgusted, Some Voters Had Their Own Bumper Sticker: "Vote No for Governor"[3]

The state supreme court placed Carlson on the ballot as the Republican candidate. While disgusted with Grunseth, voters also blamed Perpich for these last-minute charges against his foe. Carlson had fed information to

Perpich, but voters saw Carlson as the least-sullied and elected him. He had few allies. DFL politicians disliked him as a GOP partisan. Republican partisans disliked him as too independent and disdainful of them. In a way, he was the last-minute choice of voters disgusted with a precinct caucus system that produced candidates who were too liberal or too conservative.[4] He was None of the Above.

He became Governor No, who vetoed more bills than any prior governor. He could not make new policy proposals and get them accepted. Neither the DFL nor GOP supported him. In his eight years, he vetoed 179 bills; the previous six governors, in their thirty years, had vetoed 105. A vetoing governor was just what the state needed in the early 1990s. He tamed a budget process untamed since the Minnesota Miracle. Several political scientists describe him as seeming "to see his role as the jockey on an untamed horse with the whip as the preferred method of persuasion." When he left office, the state had a rainy-day fund in case of future recession and a $2 billion budget surplus.[5] He also rode the horse of the nineties economic boom, which carried him to popularity on its own. Minnesotans' per capita income increased by 36 percent, and the state rose to 13th in the nation in that category. Its unemployment rate fell to 2 percent.[6] A boom in high technology, especially personal computers and the software designed for them, fueled this prosperity.

Minnesota Rides the Wave of the Past Again: World Wide Web Replaces "Gopher"

Minnesota was not a key innovator of technology. Its main computer plant was IBM Rochester, which designed and built midrange computers for businesses, not supercomputers for governments and universities, nor the personal computers leading the nineties boom. The IBM PC was developed at Boca Raton, Florida. Nicknamed "Fortress Rochester" for its employees' fierce loyalty, IBM Rochester won the Malcolm Baldridge Award in 1990 for its AS/400 computer. Dropping IBM's corporate secrecy and its engineers' zeal to design computers for other engineers, it involved its customers by asking what they wanted. Yet its size (8,100 employees in 1990-91), its hierarchical chain-of-command and employees' tolerance of hierarchy inhibited the rebellious creativity, the throw-away-the-rule-book innovativeness that enabled Silicon Valley's geeks to win the computer revolution.[7]

Creative rebellion existed among the University of Minnesota's programmers, but not the entrepreneurial zeal for marketing. In 1990, the University sought "a campus-wide online information systems network." To design one, it appointed a committee run by administrators of campus mainframes. Seeing the inefficiencies, several programmers who favored PCs over mainframes designed a simpler one, which searched the full text of files in the University's computer system for any term(s) the user chose. They digitized a cookbook; the user typed in 'eggplant,' for example, and located all recipes with that word. They built a hierarchical menu of files and folders and text-searching choices. The University installed their system on campus. They called it "Gopher" after the school's mascot and distributed it free on the Internet in April 1991. By 1992, several hundred Gopher servers appeared around the globe, for it could do text searches on the entire Internet if the user had access to a Gopher server. By 1994, 8,000 Gopher servers existed. Gopher "made the Internet into a neat and orderly place, like a library."[8]

Libraries are not for-profit firms. The team never patented their system. The University charged no access fee for setting up Gopher servers. It held annual GopherCON seminars for hundreds of techies eager to learn the hot Internet innovation. "The university loved the publicity, trotting out Goldie Gopher as a goodwill ambassador to greet guests from around the world." Libraries are too hierarchical, orderly, and text-based for those people who seek a free-wheeling system open to an individual's complex mental associations not just a librarian's ideas of what he *should* associate with what. In 1993, Marc Andreessen and others at the University of Illinois invented the Mosaic browser that enabled the World Wide Web, designed by Tim Berners-Lee, to overtake and supplant Gopher in 1994. The Web handled graphics and sound, which Gopher did not do. It was rapidly commercialized, to the disgust of Mark McCahill, a key Gopher designer. "I think I'm in the library business, not the billboard and ad business," said McCahill. The Web soon was in the billboards and ads business.[9]

In 1995, the University's software developers tried to compete. Using the state's egalitarian ethos shared by its land-grant university, they designed Minuet, a program that gave poorer students and citizens with obsolete PCs "equal access" to the Internet and its more advanced software. Minuet was free shareware anyone could download. They also upgraded Gopher with a TurboGopherVR [virtual reality] system that McCahill hoped would form "virtual libraries. . . . Visitors would browse through rows and rows of information—including text, graphics and video—arranged by category."[10]

TurboGopherVR Tries 3-D Virtual Reality

"Using TurboGopherVR . . . the familiar Gopher hierarchies of files and folders become clusters of objects on a plain. Using a mouse or keyboard, Power Mac users are able to examine a file or folder from any direction. They can circle around it like a car driving around a building, or take gigantic leaps across a Gopher landscape, or become airborne to view objects from above. When they spot something of interest, they can click on it as they would in two-dimensional gopherspace."[11]

These updates went nowhere.[12] Rapid improvements in personal computers made sophisticated PCs affordable to more people and largely solved the equal access problem. Markets lowered prices quicker than the University could empower lower-class users. Users chose a chaotic Web over a library-like Gopher. Gopher ran on a minimal technical capability so that older computers could use it; a revolution in miniaturizing silicon chips made technical capability no longer an issue.[13] Gopher piggybacked on the PC revolution but could not lead a new one. Minnesotans and their institutions proved too non-profit-minded, too engineer-focused, too rule-bound and logical to lead an Internet revolution. Their tradition of cooperatives and ethnic sharing made the early Internet ethic of free sharing of new programs congenial to them, but that was not where the Web was headed.

Nor did Minnesota have a large share of the spin-off, start-up firms of the dot-com boom. The Web was said to make geography irrelevant as it shared information across distant spaces and boundaries, but the venture capitalists who funded these enormously risky new businesses had "strong local orientations." It is easier to assess risk up close, when one knows the inventors, their competitors, and the rival technologies. Thus, high-tech innovation clustered in Silicon Valley, Boston's suburbs, the Seattle area, and not in the Twin Cities, despite state government's efforts to lure it there. In the late 1990s, the Twin Cities were the 14th-ranked metropolitan area in terms of venture capital invested, and they were not in the top 15 areas in the number of Internet domain names.[14]

The Twin Cities had an educated, skilled work force and inventors. It pioneered in the medical-technology industry. Medtronic spawned "baby

Medtronics" like Cardiac Pacemakers, St. Jude Medical, and Cardio-Pace Medical. The doctor was the consumer who chose the pacemaker. Firms did not have to consider patients' style preferences. One professional (a medical engineer) communicated with another (a doctor).[15] In Internet-related services, the user-consumer's preferences were vital. Minnesota had never been a trend-setting design site. Its investors and inventors always had to worry that an East Coast or West Coast firm would beat them just on style, advertising, and consumer tastes.

Decentralizing New Technologies & New Sprawl Weaken Elites' Power

Tens of thousands of Minnesota consumers purchased personal computers in the 1980s and acquired dial-up or cable connections to the Internet in the 1990s. New media technologies like videocassettes, cable TV, and satellite-dish TV fragmented and decentralized the culture. People no longer depended on three TV networks, their city's daily newspaper, or a few Hollywood film companies for their news and entertainment. Film and network TV were never controlled from the Twin Cities, but the slow decline of the Twin Cities' daily newspapers did affect culture and politics. A related trend was the accelerating urban sprawl in the 1980s and 1990s that also fragmented and decentralized the metro area and left outlying residents feeling no longer connected to the core cities.

In the 1930s, Minneapolis had three dailies—the *Star*, the *Journal*, and the *Tribune*—while St. Paul had two—the *Pioneer Press* and the *Dispatch*. By the mid-1980s each city had one: the *Star Tribune*, which dropped the "Minneapolis" to cover the entire metro area, and the *Pioneer Press Dispatch*. These two dailies' editorial pages and news coverage tried to shape public debate in the state but had to compete with other news and editorial sources: news-oriented Web pages, locally-delivered national papers like *The New York Times* and *Wall Street Journal*, a network of Minnesota Public Radio stations, the PBS-affiliated TV stations, Cable News Network (CNN), and numerous others. With the explosion of entertainment options on cable, Web, radio, etc., Minnesotans tired of news could escape it altogether and lose all contact with the state's public debates.[16]

Some counter-trends strengthened the core cities after the suburbanization of the 1950s and 1960s. Young professionals moved to neighborhoods like Summit Hill and Kenwood that were gentrified as property values skyrocketed, run-down houses were rehabilitated, and new businesses arose to serve affluent new residents.[17] Minneapolis' dailies and downtown leaders reversed their 1950s loss of pro sports to Bloomington by building the Metrodome as the new site for the Vikings and Twins. As opponents lost fly balls in the light colored roof and were confused by the noise, the Twins won the World Series there in 1987 and 1991, thus partly lessening fans' dislike of indoor baseball. A new NBA team, the Minnesota Timberwolves, came to Minneapolis' new Target Center, and St. Paul secured an NHL franchise, the Minnesota Wild, to play in its Xcel Energy Center, replacing the North Stars who had left for Texas. The dailies' coverage of pro sports teams retained some lower- and middle-class male readers who did not agree with, or even read, their editorials.

Yet strong factors kept pushing new home construction out to second- and third-tier suburbs, to rural townships sixty miles from the outer belt of interstates (I-494 and I-694) finished by the early 1980s. Over half of metro area jobs were in office buildings, warehouses, stores, and factories located by freeways. Interstates 35 and 94, and other highways, provided easy commutes to these job sites from all four directions. Seventy miles northwest of the Twin Cities, St. Cloud was a fast-growing nucleus for further sprawl, as was Rochester, ninety miles to the southeast. High-density development along lakeshores north of Brainerd became a nucleus for rapid population growth; cabin owners upgraded to year-round homes and retired or worked from their homes; businesses arose to serve the newcomers. PCs and the Web allowed people to telecommute. The amenities of lake living meant they wanted to work from Brainerd, not Brooklyn Center.[18]

One factor causing sprawl was migration from rural areas losing population due to the 1980s farm crisis and its aftermath. Areas such as southwestern Minnesota that lacked lakeshore amenities and interstates connecting them to the Twin Cities lost population as people moved away. During the 1980s, at least 10 percent of the population moved away from nearly all counties in an L-shaped area from Breckenridge south to Luverne, then east to Blue Earth, and back northwest through New Ulm, Redwood Falls, and Morris. Earlier out-migrations had occurred in the 1940s, and young people had always moved away, but this movement took young couples and middle-aged leaders of communities too and left an increasingly elderly population. Towns withered away. Main Streets all but closed.[19]

Some migrants moved to the Twin Cities' rurban frontier, the low-density fringe of townships and newly-incorporated suburbs on the outskirts, to own a few acres of independence within commuting distance of its thriving job market. Many Minnesotans viewed urban life skeptically and would not be converted by elites. Generations on the farm, weekends at the cabin up north, and visits to relatives in rural areas maintained their rural ties and made a retirement move to the Brainerd area or a couple's starter home on a rurban three-acre lot conceivable. They were not locked in to urban living.

Not rural, they had left the face-to-face, personal relationships of towns where their families had been for generations. Many lived anonymous lives among strangers. They did not adopt urban ways. Their septic systems, private wells, gravel driveways, and double-wide mobile homes gave some independence from local governments. Young parents joined neighbors, for the kids' sake, in youth hockey and baseball associations, new church plants with Sunday schools and vacation Bible schools, and parents' groups at local schools. All was voluntary. A bewildering variety of lifestyles sprouted on this frontier: trailer parks for single male construction workers, 20-acre horse farms, isolated home businesses like beauty parlors and auto repair shops, and upper-class mansions.

Rurban living was not necessarily for family formation, unlike fifties' suburban living. There was no return to a consensus to buy the same kind of rambler in order to raise the same kind of family sharing the same values and watching the same TV shows. The nineties continued the sixties' rebellion of the individual, whose right to choose was still nearly the highest value. The rurban area could have starter families and PBS, but it might also have strip joints and bars near the single males' trailers, or a motorcycle club rather than a youth hockey association. Rurban isolation made it easier to argue that one's actions were not harming others—or to keep those actions out of sight.

These cultural trends hit older, higher-density suburbs, core cities, and rural areas also. But the rurban districts symbolized wide-open individualism, for rurban residents were less accountable to local government's zoning rules and service fees, traditional churches, a small town's moral supervision, or close neighbors' complaints.

Rural Areas Change in a Virtual World

"Online connection blurs the importance of location. It tends to make every place seem like every other place. However, connectivity does not imply community. . . . It is easy enough to imagine a countryside with only a handful of convenience stores, in which communications provided by both traditional phone lines and cell phones, faxes, e-mail, the world wide web, satellite and cable, remain to serve people's immediate needs and provide threads of electronic connectivity to distant communities."[20]

The Twin Cities metropolitan area became one of the lowest-density, fragmented, and decentralized in the nation. In 1950, its population per square mile of urbanized area was over 4,000; the fifties' suburbanization cut that in half to 2,000 per square mile; the succeeding decades left the figure at around 2,000. Of the major metro areas, only Kansas City had a lower density. By 1990, the Twin Cities area had over 1,000 square miles of urbanized land, broadly defined. Only 22 percent of the population lived in the core cities of St. Paul and Minneapolis. It had 344 local governments. Depending on what measure was used, it was second or fourth in the nation in terms of governmental fragmentation. That could be seen as a problem, especially by elites seeking centralized control, but many suburban and rurban residents saw this ranking as an index of their freedom. Their voice spoke louder at the small city or township hall, and government's voice was softer.[21]

Rurban sprawl became a hot political issue. Environmental problems resulted: runoff from parking lots and streets into creeks, rivers, and lakes; old problems of sewage disposal and clean drinking water. Urban advocates pointed to racism—'white flight' from contact with African Americans in the inner cities—as some rurban exiles' motive. The Metropolitan Council tried to halt sprawl by limiting lot sizes in outlying areas and by setting the borders of an urban services area, beyond which water, sewer, and other services would not be extended. Advocates of high-density cities fought for more dollars for urban transit—buses and a light-rail system. Suburban and rurban residents insisted freeways be widened to six or eight lanes, and that more be built. Anti-sprawl battlers tried to restrict highway construction.[22] Both sides had valid concerns, but the battle was also about political power. Sprawl threatened urban elites' power by dispersing citizens so far from downtown as to be uninfluenced by it. Rurban exiles saw sprawl as freedom.

State senator Myron Orfield of Minneapolis became a national expert on suburbs and sprawl. As a policy wonk, he typified elites' viewpoint, which focused on the social-scientific data that governments and policy makers thought was crucial: state aids, tax capacity, tax-based sharing, regional government, etc.[23] For rurban residents, sprawl was about their rights to ride ATVs, to skip the helmet when driving a motorcycle, to enjoy the lowest possible taxes, to hunt, to do target practice, and to minimize government.

One man who symbolized the freedom-loving, elites-defying rurbanite was Jesse Ventura, the mayor of Brooklyn Park from 1991 to 1995. A second-tier suburb, but a large one with large sections of undeveloped land, Brooklyn Park was agitated in the early 1990s by citizens' alarm over crime, problems in the schools, the decline of nearby Brookdale Mall, and an influx of blacks and other minorities into next-door Brooklyn Center. "[A] citizens' group calling itself 'the Legion of Doom' made a highly public push to limit affordable housing in Brooklyn Park."[24]

Jesse Ventura Finds the Seams in the Zone Defense of Public Morality

A former pro wrestler and movie actor, Ventura became a candidate for governor in 1998. By then, he had moved to his 32-acre horse ranch in Maple Grove, a third-tier suburb. He appealed to working-class rurban males who were fed up with politics as usual and who were attuned to a working-class culture imported into Minnesota: the demolition derby, stock car racing, country western music, tabloids, soap operas, talk shows, and B-movies. A former Navy SEAL, the burly 6-foot-4 inch, 245 pound Jesse "The Body" Ventura spoke in a deep, often menacing voice on his talk show on KFAN radio. He ran for governor that year as the candidate of the new Reform Party.[25]

The national Reform Party was created for Ross Perot's 1992 presidential race, and Perot received nearly 24 percent of Minnesota's votes that year. Dean Barkley ran as the Reform candidate for U.S. Senate in 1994 and 1996, and won at least 5 percent of the votes both times—thus qualifying the state Reform Party as a major party eligible to receive public financing for its 1998 campaign. Barkley convinced Ventura to run in 1998.[26]

At first Ventura was not taken seriously—perhaps he ran to raise his talk-show ratings. The serious DFL candidates were Mark Dayton, of the Dayton department-store family, and 'My Three Sons'—Mike Freeman, son of ex-Governor Orville Freeman; Ted Mondale, son of Vice President Walter Mondale; and "Skip" Humphrey, son of Vice President Hubert Humphrey. They were heirs of the state's storied DFL past, but that ridiculing nickname showed they could be dismissed as has-beens—has-been-a-politician's-son. His father having been the most famous, Skip Humphrey won the primary. Winning the GOP primary was Norm Coleman, mayor of St. Paul and former aide to Attorney General Humphrey. Ventura could run against two lawyers. Running as the pro-life social conservative (in contrast to Humphrey), Coleman's Brooklyn accent, big-city style, reputation as a wheeler-dealer with corporate investors, and ignorance of farming failed to connect with rural voters, a key group of pro-life conservatives.[27]

Precinct caucuses often did not pick up rurban or centrist sounds. Pro-life conservatives ruled GOP caucuses. Pro-choice liberals ran DFL ones. Other people often stayed away. The system was vulnerable to a Ventura. A shuttle bus driver at the Twin Cities airport favored Ventura: "he's going to tell all those Bible-thumpers on the right and the tree-huggers on the left to vote for their own, and he'll unite all the disaffected voters in the middle in a new party."[28] The two sides caricatured each other as thumpers and huggers, but that oversimplified the reality. Each took part of the Judeo-Christian moral tradition—protecting the unborn, aiding the poor—but that left it divided against itself. Seizing on the split, Ventura argued government should exercise moral supervision over neither culture (as conservatives wished) nor economics (as liberals wished).

To make matters worse, the two sides' candidates, Humphrey and Coleman, came off looking like two 'suits,' two well-financed, scripted, policy-wonk politicians. Wellstone had shown that a populist close to the people could upend such elitists. A Coleman hobby was playing squash; Skip favored herbal tea over coffee—elitist tastes.[29]

He had a $500,000 house and a ranch, but the wealthy Ventura played the role of an ordinary Joe close to the people. One person noted, "He talks like he's in a bar." Asked his solution to a current strike against Northwest Airlines, Ventura said he'd lock up labor and management in one room, station the National Guard outside, and feed them C-rations until they reached a deal. At the State Fair, he sold thousands of his "Retaliate in '98" T-shirts, talked pro wrestling and movies with fairgoers, and gave them his political views—which mostly favored getting government off their backs by cutting taxes, letting them ride motorcycles without a helmet and carry concealed handguns in public without a sheriff's permission, keeping DFLers who liked to tax and regulate business out of "the boardroom" and Republicans who sought to outlaw abortion and prevent gay marriage out of "the bedroom." Jesse was a libertarian.[30]

In six televised debates, Humphrey and Coleman attacked each other and not Ventura, for both hoped to gain votes from his supporters once they realized a vote for him would be 'wasted.' On October 21, Ventura gave his foes ammunition when he brought up the idea of legalizing prostitution. They attacked him for his comment, but the Twin Cities' dailies did not investigate Ventura's ideas or his background. The comment proved to be an indicator of what a governor Ventura would be like, but Humphrey and Coleman lacked the moral authority to pounce on it, and columnist Nick Coleman (no relation) praised Ventura's blunt honesty. The press gave Ventura nearly a free ride.[31]

A key factor reducing the moral legitimacy of state government and validating Ventura's anti-government views was the budget surplus. The state was simply taxing the people far more than it needed to do in order to fund the government's activities. The state could earn interest on surplus funds that taxpayers should have been able to invest. The surplus hit $2.1 billion as of February 1998; that was the sixth straight year the state enjoyed a surplus. Ventura claimed that it was this surplus that angered him and made him run in 1998. He went to the steps of the state capitol to demand, "Give it back."[32]

Ventura and his backers cleverly seized on all these factors. Under Minnesota's generous public funding of campaigns, Ventura was eligible for $326,000 in public money—after the election, to make sure he received the necessary 5 percent of the vote. His backers secured a bank loan, hired Wellstone's former advertising man, and ran some quirky action-figure commercials in the final days on Vikings broadcasts, FOX sports, and other shows watched by Ventura's target audience—working-class males from 25 to 54 years old. The last four days before the election, Ventura and company took a "Drive to Victory" in three RVs, mainly around the outer suburbs. The Internet was a key tool. On their Web site, they put photos taken at the thirty-four stops so people could see themselves. The TV coverage and local radio interviews built an accurate impression of momentum.

A State Campaign Live on the World Wide Web

"Ventura's campaign Web site is already wildly popular. . . . [T]he site was getting 50,000 hits a week; a week before the election, Barkley says, the number jumped to 121,000 hits. . . . 'And already the Internet community worldwide is beginning to take an interest in the *Jesse Ventura Show* that's going to be occurring on this "Drive to Victory" tour over the weekend.' . . . 'During the tour the Jesse Ventura Web site, www.jesseventura.org, is going to be live, highly interactive, twenty-four hours a day,' according to [Phil] Madsen. 'We're going to have ongoing discussion sites going on so people can interact with the tour.' "[33]

The RV tour benefited from a law letting people register to vote on election day. In most states, it would have been far too late for people excited by the tour to register. In Minnesota over 332,000 voters registered on election day; one statistical analysis indicates that 70 percent voted for Ventura. They gave him his margin of victory. So did the rurban area. Ventura received more votes than his rivals combined in many outer suburbs and rurban areas: across the north from Ramsey to Andover, Ham Lake, and Bethel to Blaine, Lino Lakes, and Hugo—in the northwestern district of Champlin, Brooklyn Park, Annandale, and Buffalo—in Isanti and Chisago Counties—in the western area of Howard Lake and Waverly. Ventura won a donut-shaped ring; Humphrey took the core cities; Coleman, the wealthy suburbs as well as the genuinely rural areas of southern and western Minnesota.[34]

To the shock of most Minnesotans and most national observers, Ventura won with 37 percent of the vote, to Norm Coleman's 34 percent and Skip Humphrey's 28 percent.[35] To Republicans' dismay, a talk-radio anti-government shout elected a pro-choice libertarian; to DFLers' dismay, Wellstone's populist tactics worked for an anti-tax, anti-government millionaire not so different from Bob Short. To the astonishment of secularizing elites, religion had been removed from politics—not by a professor, but by a pro wrestler!

Ventura Mocks Ordinance's "Religion, Morality & Knowledge Being Necessary . . . "

The eyes of the nation, even the world, were now on Minnesota to see what kind of state this was and what kind of governor Ventura would be. At least for those with little direct knowledge of the state, its reputation was in Ventura's hands for four years. The Northwest Ordinance decreed public support of education because "Religion, morality and knowledge [were] necessary to good government and the happiness of mankind." He did a decent job in November and December 1998 in picking a cabinet and preparing to govern, but his inaugural bash at Target Center on January 16, 1999, showed he would try to separate "happiness" from "religion [and] morality." His "People's Celebration" was "one of the most raucous gubernatorial inaugural parties in our nation's history," writes KSTP-TV reporter Tom Hauser. It was "political Woodstock." Ventura wore "earrings, a leather-fringed jacket, a Jimi Hendrix T-shirt, and a handkerchief wrapped on his head," as he sang "Werewolves of London" with Warren Zevon.[36]

As governor, Ventura's raucous behavior would mainly try to separate "religion [and] morality" from "good government." His first legislative session had the easy task of deciding how to rebate the surplus to voters and how to cut taxes to prevent more surpluses. Not much moral self-sacrifice by citizens was needed, so the governor need not call for any. After much wrangling between Ventura, a DFL-controlled senate, and a GOP-controlled legislature, a deal was finally struck for $1.6 billion in income tax and property tax cuts and a $1.3 billion sales-tax rebate to be mailed to taxpayers by August. The popularity of state checks in people's mailboxes kept Ventura's popularity high.[37]

While he pursued good government, he marketed himself nationwide in an amoral and anti-religious manner. He had signed a six-figure book deal, and his agent was set to take movie offers (NBC made an unauthorized one). Ventura action figures were on sale at the Mall of America and elsewhere— with proceeds going to charity and his campaign committee. As the session ended, his publisher released *I Ain't Got Time to Bleed* (a Ventura line in the film *Predator*) to maximize publicity and sales. "The remarkable contrast between Ventura as 'statesman' and Ventura as 'brothel-frolicking Navy SEAL' is too good to pass up," Hauser notes, for the publisher had to cover "as much as a $500,000 advance" to him. The book boasted of drug use, heavy drinking, and steroid use during his pro wrestling career. He prepared for a national book tour after the session.[38]

Legislators reacted. "Governor, your bragging is sending very mixed messages to the young people of this state," state senator Jane Ranum complained. "Governor, the young people of this state are looking to you as their role model."[39] Well, the message wasn't 'very mixed' and 'role model' was a term for sports stars and celebrities. A governor headed a law-making and law-enforcing machine that must arrest and imprison drug users, drunk drivers, prostitutes, and their clients—and look morally justified in doing so. How could the governor profit from his book mentioning past law breaking and then have his state troopers punish it without looking morally inconsistent?

On his way to the governor's fishing opener (an annual media event promoting the start of Minnesota's fishing season), Ventura visited Grand Rapids High School to students' cheers. When he asked them, "Should I apologize [to the] bunch of hypocrites down there [in St. Paul]," they roared, "No! No! No!" Ventura defended the book as "honesty," but when he unapologetically defended drinking, drugs, and dives to local youth he broke the state's compact with parents, churches, schools, and local communities. They instilled law-abiding morality partly for its benefit; it should not undercut them.[40] Honesty without an apology undercut the moral standards or laws that had been violated—while silence or hypocrisy could be the tribute that vice pays to virtue, as the saying goes.

After the session, Ventura's book tour took him to California (*the Tonight Show*), New York City (Barnes & Noble, *the Today Show*, and *Live with Regis and Kathie Lee*), and Washington, D.C. (*Larry King Live*, etc.). The *Jesse Ventura Story* appeared on NBC. Reporters covering Ventura were his most consistent critics and questioners. They accepted a separation of religious morality from politics, so they focused on minor matters like the state paying for troopers who were Ventura's security detail on his book tours. He countered that newspapers and TV stations marketed their product and obsessed about ratings.[41]

In August 1999, he refereed the World Wrestling Federation (WWF) Summer Slam at Target Center—for over $1 million. "This is a whole new level of raunchiness that I don't think is appropriate for the governor to be involved with," observed House majority leader Tim Pawlenty. The pay-per-view event did "feature sex, violence, and raunchiness." Ventura made $2 million in nine months—plus his state salary. Five weeks later, *Playboy* published an interview in which Ventura called "organized religion . . . a sham and a crutch for weak-minded people," minimized a sexual harassment case, ridiculed "fat people," favored legalizing prostitution, and dismissed "[t]he religious right" for "tell[ing] people how to live." The outcry was long and loud. Senate majority leader Roger Moe accused him of "tarnishing our national image." The Taxpayers League's head noted, "We are becoming a laughingstock all around the country."[42]

Some criticisms remained technicalities. The citizens' group Common Cause protested that a state employee's deal with the WWF was a "conflict of interest"; Ventura exploited his office to obtain the estimated $1.5 million fee. That argument had merit (a judge dismissed it) but missed the larger point. In a professionalized, specialized society, issues were divided and subdivided into smaller pieces so one specialist could decide them by using one law or rule. That method often worked, but Ventura defied piecemeal critics. He had the votes, book sales, and popularity that counted for much in a celebrity-centered society. The state's congressmen "marvel[ed] at Ventura's ability to draw a crowd" in Washington. Like his wrestling "bad guy" image, he was a bully, a Goliath who scoffed at the critics, none of whom was a pure enough David to upend him.[43]

In 2000, another huge surplus of $1.6 billion helped him regain his popularity after *Playboy*. After more wrangling with the DFL senate and GOP House, the three sides split the future surplus three ways—Ventura cut license-tab fees, the DFL raised education spending, and the GOP cut income taxes—and mailed rebate checks totaling $640 million, the surplus already collected from taxpayers. "The check is in the mail" had a new, positive spin in the Ventura years. Yet his mixing good government with bad entertainment continued, as an announcer for the WWF's new football league, the XFL, in its February-April 2001 season—during a legislative session. Critics pounced by charging improper use of his office to shill for the raunchy XFL. He retaliated mainly against the press, calling them "jackals" and issuing "Official Jackal" press badges.[44]

On May 8-9, 2001, the Dalai Lama came to Minnesota to speak to Tibetans and others at the University and to address the legislature. One legislator boycotted his talk and called Buddhism a cult incompatible with Judeo-Christian ideas "that he believes formed the 'public religious ethic' of the United States." Ventura asked the Dalai Lama "if he'd ever seen *Caddyshack*," a comedy in which Bill Murray's character claims to have caddied for a Dalai Lama "who would say 'Gunga galunga' as he blasted drives into Himalayan crevasses." The real Dalai Lama told Ventura he had not seen the film.[45]

The legislator could consistently have boycotted Ventura's speeches to the legislature, for popular culture was Ventura's public ethic, more than Judeo-Christian ideas. Yet he had a point. This state society and its laws had been built on the foundation of Judeo-Christian "religion, morality, and knowledge," even if it was maintained by the strong preservatives of inertia, legal precedent, and tradition in 2001. Ventura's shocking election and job performance showed such preservatives were not guaranteed to work. If they didn't work with white rurban residents, could they work with the new immigrants?

New Immigrant Groups Bring
New Benefits & Challenges for a State Society

By 2006, Minnesota had more Tibetans than any other state except New York. St. Paul had more Hmong residents than any other U.S. city. In 2005, Minnesota received more refugees than any other state except California. That role dated to the late 1940s when churches resettled DPs (displaced persons) from World War II and continued in the 1970s when they welcomed Vietnamese boat people fleeing the end of the Vietnam War. Government agencies joined in to assist the churches financially, and non-religious organizations participated. By 2006, the state was home to 60,000 Hmong, at least 25,000 Somalis, another 25,000 Vietnamese, and thousands of Cambodians, Russians, and Ethiopians—all refugees from wars, political or religious persecution, or failed states.[46]

Quite different in place of origin, in culture, and in means of migration were the state's 175,000 Hispanic residents. In the 1980s, when agricultural processing plants moved to small towns and outstate cities that offered lower costs and low-wage, non-union labor, these Hispanic Minnesotans increasingly became permanent residents. The old pattern of seasonal labor in the fields was replaced by year-round work in the plants. As the farm crisis caused some rural Anglos to move to rurban areas, Hispanics bought properties and Main Street businesses. By 2006, some small towns in southwestern Minnesota were 20 percent Hispanic—divided, of course, between legal migrants, citizens, and a group of undocumented workers who had no legal status in this country.[47]

Resettled refugees and immigrants brought many benefits to the state. The well-educated ones became professionals, teachers, community leaders, legislators, and law-enforcement personnel. The less-educated took minimum-wage jobs in turkey processing plants, for example, that other Minnesotans refused to consider. All of them formed families, ethnic or religious societies, and sometimes published newspapers or journals.[48]

On the negative side, racial prejudice and ignorance cut them off from many whites and from each other. In Marshall, the turkey processor Heartland Foods arrived in 1988, employed several hundred workers, and paid wages of $6 per hour. The first year's turnover was 255 percent - up to 15 percent of workers quit on a single day. The racial composition of the workforce fluctuated: Asians flocked to the plant, then left; Somalis did likewise; the percent of Hispanics rose steadily. The Immigration and

Naturalization Service raided the plant in 1993 and found eighty-one illegals. Crime rose in Marshall and neighboring towns. Racial antagonism rose. Yet all of this proved to be manageable over time.[49]

Education, conciliation meetings, and growing familiarity with each other might ease racial prejudice and ignorance over time. Yet, the very nature of some of these new immigrants' cultures brought challenges—apart from the challenge of misunderstanding.

The practice of polygamy by 270 to 450 Hmong males in St. Paul threatened Hmong families, risked prosecution by the Ramsey County attorney, and aroused public opposition from younger Hmong who fought against the practice. Secular non-Hmong saw the practice as violating women's rights, but it was the Judeo-Christian prohibition of polygamy that lay behind the state's prohibition of it—which remained the law even if no Hmong woman asserted her rights in rejecting it. One Hmong editor argued, "Polygamy is wrong and it destroys families here in America," and this state society was built upon the family. More anti-polygamy, younger Hmong were more susceptible to the new problems coming from U.S. society—prostitution, drugs, and gangs. The Hmong had brought some new problems to the state society, but that society had brought new ones to the Hmong people.[50]

Physical Refugees' Virtual Link to Home

"Abbas Mehdi was a professor at St. Cloud State University and founder of an exile dissident group devoted to democracy in Iraq. . . . Refugee life was different than it used to be in the American Midwest, he said. It was still sort of a no-man's-land for some people, especially for those who yearned for home. But it was a no-man's-land with cell phones and the Internet, the communication tools that made all the difference. 'If it weren't for technology, I probably wouldn't be living in Minnesota,' he said."[51]

Other cultural differences posed difficulties. Somalis' clan-based society—the Hmong and others had strong clan loyalties—conflicted with Americans' individualistic society. If it encouraged clan retaliation for crimes and discouraged one clan member from reporting another to the police, then it would hinder the state's law enforcement. Somali distrust of government meant that "to many immigrants taxation was nothing more than 'institutional robbery,'" reporter Gregg Aamot discovered. To them, cheating on tax returns was just a case of turnabout being fair play. That attitude had to change.[52]

Some new immigrants' cultural attitudes had to be altered if they were to fit in with this state society. A secular rationale for change seemed superficial. "Many immigrants," Aamot noted, "felt that America's most marketable ideas—respect for free speech and religion, economic opportunity, a fondness for individual achievement, its celebration of cultures—seemed somehow watered down."[53] Economic individualism seemed thin gruel compared to their communal religiosity. Popular culture could have a stronger appeal to the young. Historically, it had united ethnic groups who would not accept each other's religious, high-brow, or folk cultures, but who would accept a Disney cartoon they all liked. In the Internet age, popular culture was split into many parts and could not unify people in the same way.

Linguistic, cultural, and religious differences were greater now. Hindu, Muslim, Buddhist. Asian, African, European. Urban and rural heritages. All were mixed together now. The old state society, its government, and its laws imposed external order on Minnesota; however, they also rested on the cultural and religious attitudes of individuals that made them less likely to challenge or disrupt that order and more likely to cooperate voluntarily with each other to solve local problems—making it unnecessary for the state to do so. Trust in the moral character of neighbors is essential to such cooperation. The idea of a family retaliating for a crime against one of its members rather than relying on the state was distant from their thoughts. Near to them was the idea that God was no respecter of persons or family ties, nor should the state be. God was omniscient, so the individual's thoughts (not just actions) were subject to His judgments, and consequences lasted beyond this life into eternity. Secularization had occurred, but these ideas were still part of the molecular structure of state society. They made possible a relatively weak state that had few police per thousand Minnesotans to enforce the laws and one that left many problems to local communities, churches, voluntary associations, and families to solve.

Conservatives were likely mistaken to think that excluding immigrants would preserve the state society's Judeo-Christian basis. Powerful forces in the media and the Internet undercut it among the majority—Ventura was no newcomer. Liberals were likely wrong to think that just welcoming immigrants, learning about them, tolerating their new ways, and teaching them "watered down" "marketable ideas" would integrate them into the state society. Deeper, more powerful forces were at work in forming a state society. How would new cultures and religions affect citizens' respect for the state and its laws? Most likely, new immigrants would adjust as individuals to the state's economic, educational, and political life but keep their traditional communal and religious life. The result might be external order in neighborhoods of strangers, who each had a chosen community sharing interests or ages or hobbies or politics or language—across the globe, on the Internet—but did not interact with people down the block or across the highway.[54]

Minnesota Society Enters the Twenty-First Century With Its Specific Identity Still Contested

Jesse Ventura chose not to run again in 2002. In a race between DFLer Roger Moe, the Reform party's Tim Penny, and Republican Tim Pawlenty, voters chose Pawlenty—Ventura's opposite in many ways. An evangelical Christian, Pawlenty was the most conservative governor the state had had in perhaps fifty years. That October, Paul Wellstone was killed in a plane crash near the Eveleth airport while campaigning for his third term in the Senate. After an emotional, partisan memorial service at Williams Arena, voters picked Norm Coleman over Wellstone's last-minute replacement, Walter Mondale. After the end of the dot-com stock market boom and the September 11th attacks, a national recession put the state budget back in the red. Yet Pawlenty was reelected in 2006. Minnesotans perhaps still had some 'buyer's remorse' after Ventura's wild years. In the war on terrorism, the National Guard fought in Afghanistan and Iraq. The state had the same military and political roles—just in very changed circumstances. Yet it had less power to shape its own identity than the state that entered the Union in 1858. Through twenty-first-century technologies, its citizens could largely ignore their physical state and interact with a virtual world. The long-term effects of technological revolutions upon a state's identity, and on what exactly statehood still meant, were yet to be determined.

---

1. "Arne Carlson," Wilson, *Rudy!*, 244-45; Andersen, *A Man's Reach*, 379-80; Elazar, et al., *Minnesota Politics*, 130.

2. "election scandal," The best account of this is in Wilson, *Rudy!*, 245-52. Two Grunseth campaign leaders have written a book that makes serious charges against some politicians and

against the media; however, it is impossible for me to ascertain the degree of truth in these charges. See Dave Hoium and Leon Oistad, *There is No November* (Inver Grove Heights, Minn.: Jeric Publications, 1991).

3. "bumper sticker," Wilson, *Rudy!*, 248.

4. "placed Carlson," Wilson, *Rudy!*, 245, 249-55; Elazar, et al., *Minnesota Politics*, 130-31.

5. "Governor No," Elazar, et al., *Minnesota Politics*, 114, 130-32; Jacob Lentz, *Electing Jesse Ventura: A Third-Party Success Story* (Boulder, Colorado: Lynne Rienner, 2002), 93. I am not knowingly borrowing this term for Carlson from someone, but it seems so obvious a one that it may have been used before.

6. "economic boom," Lentz, *Electing Jesse Ventura*, 79.

7. "main computer plant," Arthur L. Norberg and Jeffery L. Yost, *IBM Rochester: A Half Century of Innovation* (IBM Rochester, 2006).

8. "programmers," *St. Paul Pioneer Press*, 4 March 1996, 1F, 2F; *Minneapolis Star Tribune*, 5 November 2001, D1, D5; Philip L. Frana, "Before the Web There Was Gopher," *IEEE Annals of the History of Computing* (January-March 2004), 20-21.

9. "never patented," *St. Paul Pioneer Press*, 4 March 1996, 1F, 2F; *Minneapolis Star Tribune*, 5 November 2001, D1, D5; Tim Berners-Lee, *Weaving the Web: The Original Design and Ultimate Destiny of the WORLD WIDE WEB by Its Inventor* (New York: Harper Collins, 1999), 40-41; Kevin Hillstrom, *Defining Moments: The Internet Revolution* (Detroit: Omnigraphics, 2005), 23, 26, 28-29; Frana, "Before the Web," 25.

10. "tried to compete," *St. Paul Pioneer Press*, 7 June 1995, 3C.

11. "TurboGopherVR," *St. Paul Pioneer Press*, 7 June 1995, 3C.

12. "updates went nowhere," *St. Paul Pioneer Press*, 4 March 1996, 1F, 2F.

13. "Gopher ran," Frana, "Before the Web," 22, 25.

14. "was said to make," Matthew A. Zook, *The Geography of the Internet Industry: Venture Capital, Dot-coms, and Local Knowledge* (Malden, Mass.: Blackwell, 2005), 3 (quoted), 4-7, 30-31, 57.

15. "medical-technology industry," Kirk, "Major Manufacturers," in Clark, ed., *Century of Change*, 245-46.

16. "three dailies," George S. Hage, "Evolution and Revolution in the Media: Print and Broadcast Journalism," in Clark, ed., *Century of Change*, 306-07, 316, 320-21.

17. "counter-trends," John R. Borchert, "The Network of Urban Centers," in Clark, ed., *Century of Change*, 89.

18. "strong factors," Borchert, "Network of Urban Centers," in Clark, ed., *Century of Change*, 88, 91-93.

19. "migration from rural areas," Joseph Amato and John W. Meyer, *The Decline of Rural Minnesota* (Marshall, Minn.: Crossings Press, 1993), 28-29, 40-41, 46-47. I do not fully agree with their analysis.

20. "Rural Areas," Joseph A. Amato and John Radzilowski, *Community of Strangers: Change, Turnover, Turbulence & the Transformation of a Midwestern Country Town* (Marshall, Minn.: Crossings Press, 1999), 45, 46.

21. "metropolitan area," Robert Bruegmann, *Sprawl: a compact history* (Chicago: University of Chicago Press, 2005), 62-63, 97, 145-46; Myron Orfield, *American Metropolitics: The New Suburban Reality* (Washington, D.C.: Brookings Institution Press, 2002), 62, 132, 134.

22. "hot political issue," Bruegmann, *Sprawl*, 96-98, 274 note 29; Orfield, *American Metropolitics*, 49-50, 116 note 10.

23. "national expert," Orfield, *American Metropolitics*, v-ix, xii, xiii; Bruegmann, *Sprawl*, 279.

24. "man who symbolized," Orfield, *American Metropolitics*, 15. He does not indicate exactly what position Ventura took on these issues.

25. "former pro wrestler," Tom Hauser, *Inside the Ropes with Jesse Ventura* (Minneapolis: University

of Minnesota Press, 2002), 1-3, 7, 38, 39, 47.

26. "Reform Party," Hauser, *Inside the Ropes*, 173; Lentz, *Electing Jesse Ventura*, 22-23, 82-84.
27. "not taken seriously," Hauser, *Inside the Ropes*, 1, 8, 173; Lentz, *Electing Jesse Ventura*, 16-19, 21-22, 27-28, 31-32, 35, 37.
28. "Precinct caucuses," Lentz, *Electing Jesse Ventura*, 15-16; Kevin Glynn, *Tabloid Culture: Trash Taste, Popular Power, and the Transformation of American Television* (Durham, N.C.: Duke University Press, 2000), 242 (quoting the driver).
29. "looking like," Lentz, *Electing Jesse Ventura*, 37.
30. "wealthy Ventura," Lentz, *Electing Jesse Ventura*, 28-30, 69, 72; Hauser, *Inside the Ropes*, 6-8, 39.
31. "six televised debates," Lentz, Electing Jesse Ventura, 38-40, 42-43, 46-47, 49-50; Hauser, *Inside the Ropes*, 11-16, 17-18.
32. "budget surplus," Lentz, *Electing Jesse Ventura*, 25-26, 39, 93; Hauser, *Inside the Ropes*, 68, 173.
33. "State Campaign Live," Hauser, *Inside the Ropes*, 21-22 (quoting Barkley and Madsen); Lentz, *Electing Jesse Ventura*, 53.
34. "took advantage," here and above, Lentz, *Electing Jesse Ventura*, 53-54, 66, 73; Orfield, *American Metropolitics*, Map 8-7 following 160, and 161; *Politics in Minnesota: The Directory, 1999–2000* (St. Paul: Minnesota Political Press, 1999) gives each candidate's percent of the vote on the page introducing each senate district. It calculates percentages by legislative district, and district lines do not exactly follow city or county boundaries.
35. "Ventura won," Hauser, *Inside the Ropes*, 40.
36. "eyes of the nation," Hauser, *Inside the Ropes*, 87-89.
37. "easy task," Hauser, *Inside the Ropes*, 86, 95, 98, 139-40, 166.
38. "marketed himself," Hauser, *Inside the Ropes*, 69-70, 74-75, 137-39, 148-49, 157-59.
39. "Ranum complained," Hauser, *Inside the Ropes*, 157-58.
40. "Ventura visited," Hauser, *Inside the Ropes*, 161-63.
41. "book tour," Hauser, *Inside the Ropes*, 167-71, 177-84.
42. "he refereed," Hauser, *Inside the Ropes*, 195-204, 211-14, 220-27, 237-41, 244-46.
43. "technicalities," Hauser, *Inside the Ropes*, 190, 216-20.
44. "huge surplus," Hauser, *Inside the Ropes*, 281, 308-09, 322-24, 326-28, 330-32, 336-38, 341-44, 347-50.
45. "Dalai Lama," *St. Paul Pioneer Press*, 9 May (1A, 14A) and 10 May (14A), both 2001; Hauser, *Inside the Ropes*, 354-55; Gregg Aamot, *The New Minnesotans: Stories of Immigrants and Refugees* (Minneapolis: Syren Book Company, 2006), 114.
46. "Minnesota had," Aamot, *New Minnesotans*, x, 11-13, 32, 61, 112.
47. "Hispanic residents," Aamot, *New Minnesotans*, 13, 18-20, 126-29.
48. "many benefits," examples of these are found throughout Aamot, *New Minnesotans*.
49. "In Marshall," Joseph A. Amato, *To Call It Home: The New Immigrants of Southwestern Minnesota* (Marshall, Minn.: Crossings Press, 1996), 56-60.
50. "polygamy," Aamot, *New Minnesotans*, 26-32, 35-39.
51. "Virtual Link," Aamot, *New Minnesotans*, 80.
52. "The Somalis'," Aamot, *New Minnesotans*, 26-28, 55-56, 59, 95-98.
53. "seemed superficial," Aamot, *New Minnesotans*, 64.
54. "result," this phrase is taken from Amato and Radzilowski, *Community of Strangers*.

Index